THE ISLAMIC SYNCRETISTIC TRADITION IN BENGAL

ASIM ROY

The Islamic Syncretistic Tradition in Bengal

Princeton University Press
Princeton, New Jersey

Published by Princeton University Press, 41 William Street,
Princeton, New Jersey 08540
In the United Kingdom: Princeton University Press,
Guildford, Surrey

Library of Congress Cataloging in Publication Data will
be found on the last printed page of this book

ISBN 0-691-05387-1

Publication of this book has been aided by a grant from the
Paul Mellon Fund of Princeton University Press

This book has been composed in Linotron Caslon type

Clothbound editions of Princeton University Press books are
printed on acid-free paper, and binding materials are chosen for
strength and durability. Paperbacks, although satisfactory for personal
collections, are not usually suitable for library rebinding.

Printed in the United States of America by Princeton
University Press, Princeton, New Jersey

In Loving Memory
of my Grandfather
and Father

Contents

Preface

1

It is conventional to recognize this study as an outgrowth of my doctoral dissertation, but I should rather like to trace its beginning much farther back to those few years before the partition of 1947 when, as a boy, I found myself at pains to understand, far less to accept, that my Muslim friends in a small suburban town in east Bengal[1] (present Bangladesh) were so different as to make it impossible for all of us even to "live together separately" as we always did in a society divided by castes and creeds. As I grew up I sought to understand this, if I could.

Not long after I began my excursions into this area of study I became increasingly aware of a very significant beginning of a qualitative and quantitative change of self-perceptions among Bengal Muslims through the 19th century. The essence of this change was not so much a vital concern about the retardation of Muslim life in Bengal, for such concerns were often expressed before, as we shall see later.[2] It consisted more in an unprecedented denunciation and condemnation of what came over the years to represent the dominant notions and meanings of Bengalis being Muslims. The new ideology primarily inculcated by the resurgent Muslim reformists and

[1] Bengal, in this study, basically comprises what recent history would recognize as the State of West Bengal in India and the new country of Bangladesh. To avoid confusion between the former and a geographical reference to the western part of undivided Bengal, lower capital as in "west Bengal" has been used to denote the geographical area.

[2] See *infra*, pp. 69-72.

revivalists demanded purificatory purges of non-Islamic accretions and excrescences from Bengal Muslim life,[3] and laid bare, in the process, the roots of cleavage and dualism in Bengal Muslim's cultural position, caught between the opposite pulls of Bengal localism and the Islamic extra-territoriality. As the success of the Pakistan mission in Bengal in 1947 clearly subordinated the Bengali identity to the Islamic, I found myself ineluctably drawn towards ascertaining the nature and development of the Muslim tradition that came under the fire of the Muslim reformists, purists, and political separatists. A clear understanding of its nature seemed seminal to any interpretive study of the Bengal Muslim mind in the 19th and 20th centuries. The diversion proved a complete preoccupation in itself. It took me into areas and introduced me to literatures which warranted far greater commitments in interest, time, and overall importance than I had originally anticipated. My concern stretched itself fully to uncover what it was that changed rather than the what, why, and how of the change itself.

2

The inquiries into Islamic tradition in Bengal presented a few interesting problems, academic and otherwise. It did not take me very long to find out that the standard literary sources for the history of Islam in Bengal—consisting of some meager information in a few Persian chronicles on the Muslim rule in India, even fewer chronicles focusing primarily on the political affairs of the Muslim rulers in Bengal in the 18th century, some much-used *sufi* hagiological literature of either general or particular nature for Bengal, some *sufi* cor-

[3] The Islamic revitalizing and purificatory movements in Bengal in the 19th and 20th centuries, such as the *Farāizi*, *Tariqa-i Muhammadiyah*, *Ahl-i hadith*, and *Taayuni*, which largely derived their inspirations from sources outside the region, launched a massive campaign against what they regarded "innovations," "accretions," and "deviations" in the regional Islam.

respondence (*maktubāt*) and sayings (*malfuzāt*) with bearings on Bengal, and some sundry travel reports and observations—were totally inadequate for the types of questions I sought to raise and answer about the religiosity of the bulk of Muslim believers in Bengal.

Then came the unexpected and the greatest single moment of my academic explorations: I almost stumbled on what eventually turned out to be a mine of gold for my research investigations, namely, Munshi A. Karim's Collection of Bengali manuscripts of Muslim authorship which are held by the Manuscript Section of the Dacca University Library, Dacca, Bangladesh.[4] The collection contains Muslim writings in Bengali spread over a few centuries, including the earliest known among them. As an added attraction they largely relate to the subject of Islamic tradition in Bengal. My elation seemed short-lived, when in 1966-1967 the government of Pakistan refused me permission to visit Dacca to consult these manuscripts. For the same reason I became a little more conscious of the extra-academic implications of this study. I must place on record my deep gratitude to Professor A. L. Basham, whose wide contacts and influence helped to procure microfilms of a large number of these manuscripts. The emergence of Bangladesh, subsequently, gave me the opportunity of a personal visit to examine the originals in Dacca.

3

The seminal issues in this study concern an analytical evaluation of the dominant tradition of syncretistic Islam clearly emerging from this literature, and also an assessment of its historical significance. A rather common failure in avoiding individual or collective value judgments about the meaning and significance of religious expressions in the lives and practices of believers often tends to attribute to religious and cul-

[4] See Introduction, note 7.

tural development labelled "syncreticism" or "syncretism" such pejorative connotations as to reduce these terms almost to "dirty words." A less aggressive but no less simplistic compromise seeks to resolve the issue by simply dumping all "innovations" and "deviations" into the bottomless pit of what is conveniently called "folk" or "popular" religion.

It is my finding and contention that the Islamic syncretistic tradition, emanating from this literature, is a descriptive and analytical label for the religious tradition that the Muslim "cultural mediators" in Bengal reconstructed rather consciously, urged by a deep sense of obligation towards the masses of the believers, with their specific needs and demands in the social and cultural milieus of Bengal.[5] It only adds a human touch to the supreme courage which they brought to bear on their historic mission that most of them revealed some psychological discomforts—a feeling that they clearly shared in common with other "cultural mediators" in history.[6]

Undoubtedly the syncretistic tradition could not have been the sole Muslin tradition in Bengal. In fact, the circumstances of the construction of the syncretistic model[7] clearly point to the existence of an exogenous Islamic tradition based on Perso-Arabic literatures that obviously failed to interact with the world of the exclusively Bengali-speaking Muslims,[8] and was consequently set aside for them in favor of a locally

[5] See Chapter 2, especially pp. 69-72.

[6] For the role of the "cultural mediators," see *infra*, pp. 71ff. For the mediators' dilemma, see *infra*, pp. 76-78. Arnold Toynbee mentions the ambivalent position of "intelligentsia" as mediators "being" in "but not" of "two societies and not merely one." See "The Disintegrations of Civilizations" in his *A Study of History* (New York, 1962), vol. V, pp. 154-58; E. Shils, *The Intellectual Between Tradition and Modernity: The Indian Situation* (The Hague, 1961), pp. 60-61; also for David Kopf's reference to intelligentsia as "the marginal man," see his *British Orientalism and the Bengal Renaissance. The Dynamics of Indian Modernization, 1773-1835* (Berkeley and Los Angeles, 1969), p. 1.

[7] *Infra*, Chapter 2.

[8] As late as 1969 the Pakistan Year Book records that 98.42 percent of the population in East Pakistan spoke Bengali, while 0.61 percent spoke Urdu.

more familiar and meaningful syncretistic Islamic tradition. The latter, with its primary preoccupations with mystic discipline, cosmogony, eschatology, religious mythology, and so on, all embodied within a very extensive and rich literature, some reaching to the height of excellence attained by the contemporary Bengali literature, cannot be brushed aside as a motley assortment of amorphous "folk" beliefs and practices.

I have, on the other hand, identified a rather different type of Muslim Bengali composition in the form of ballads on the imaginary exploits of a *pir*, fictitious, legendary, or historical.[9] In their pragmatic and mundane concerns, as well as in their total lack of literary sophistication, the tradition contained in this literature belongs to the world of "little tradition" of Islam in Bengal, the indigenous syncretistic tradition having, for all practical purposes, assumed the role of Islamic great tradition for the bulk of Bengal Muslims.

4

The "mediators" achieved their mission, and the syncretistic tradition remained the dominant form of Islamic acculturation in Bengal for several centuries until the 19th century witnessed the introduction of a new phase of Islamization of Bengal as part of far wider global movements of Islamic revitalization. These new movements, combined with the changed social and political circumstances of Bengal under the British domination, sharpened the focus, as never before, on the "Islamic" identity of the Bengali believers, with the result that a massive and organized assault on the syncretistic tradition and on the cultural values and norms, necessary to sustain it, followed.

The Islamic revitalization movements and their impact on Bengal is a very significant area of study that remains beyond the scope of the present work. There is no dearth of general

[9] *Infra*, Chapter 6.

studies on the Islamic revitalization movements in India.[10] But the first serious attempt to explore this area in the context of Bengal was made by M. A. Khan. Khan's contributions to this area are spread over a number of publications,[11] but his studies have been rather limited by his effective non-utilization of a vital source of information, namely, a significant volume of Muslim *puthi* (*punthi*)-*sāhitya* or *punthi* literature.[12] Directly reflecting the viewpoints of either the reformists or their traditionalist opponents, and occasionally depicting actual situations of debates, confrontations, and hostilities between the reformists and the traditionalists or between groups of reformists themselves, this literature is a very valuable source indeed. The gap left by Khan has been very successfully covered in a most recent study on Bengal Muslims by R. Ahmed.[13] Although Ahmed, like others before him, reveals no better perception of the nature and the appropriate historical background and significance of Bengal's syncretistic reformulations of what he labels "orthodox traditions" than

[10] See Q. Ahmad, *The Wahabi Movement in India* (Calcutta, 1966); also two recent publications by S.A.A. Rizvi, *Shāh Wali Allāh and His Times. A Study of Eighteenth Century Islam: Politics and Society in India* (Canberra, 1980) and *Shāh Abd al-Aziz. Puritanism, Sectarian Polemics, and Jihād* (Canberra, 1982).

[11] *Selection From Bengal Government Records on Wahhābi Trials, 1863-70* (Dacca, 1961); "Research in the Islamic revivalism of the nineteenth century and its effect on the Muslim community of Bengal," in P. Bessaignet (ed.), *Social Research in East Pakistan* (Dacca, 2nd rev. edn., 1964), pp. 38-65; "Taayyuni opposition to the Farāidi movement," *Journal of the Pakistan Historical Society* (Karachi, April 1964), pp. 150-54; *History of the Farāidi Movement* (Karachi, 1965).

[12] The term *punthi* has the original meaning of a handwritten manuscript in Bengali, and in this sense all Bengali mss. used in this work, especially Munshi A. Karim's Collections, are part of the *punthi* literature. With the advent of printing, the meaning of the word was extended to include all Bengali printed works in verse. From the 19th century the terms *Ecchlāmi Bānglā* (Islamic Bengali) came to be applied to the growing volume of a new type of Muslim *punthi* literature written in a highly stylized form of mixed Urdu-Bengali dictions.

[13] *The Bengal Muslims 1871-1906. A Quest for Identity* (Delhi, 1981).

the omnibus categorization of "folk" Islam,[14] he has accomplished a valuable task by critically assessing, with the support of the *punthi* literature, the impact of the 19th-century Islamic revitalization movements on Bengal. Of particular interest to me has been his detailed exposition of the difficulties and limitations in the achievement of the reform movements, as foreshadowed in my earlier studies.[15] The fact that the militant fundamentalist reform movements led by the *Tariqa-i Muhammadiyah* and the *Farāizi* were gradually taken over by the traditionalist-inspired revitalizing movement of the *Taaiyuni* under the leadership of Mawlānā Karāmat Ali; that the successors of the early zealous reformers emerged considerably more moderate, including one who received from the British government the honorific title of "Khān Bahādur"; that many so-called "reformed" Muslims were reported to be indulging in a life-style inconsistent with the reformistic ideals; that the reformers encountered a fierce and protracted polemical as well as active opposition from the *sabiqis* (traditionalists); and, finally, that the traditional way of life and its values survived, in some instances at least, despite the decades of reformistic campaigns—all clearly underline the strength and vitality of the pre-reformist traditions.[16]

[14] *Ibid.*, p. 55; M. R. Tarafdar, *Husain Shāhi Bengal, 1494-1538. A Socio-Political Study* (Dacca, 1965), pp. 163-64; M. A. Rahim, *Social and Cultural History of Bengal*, 2 vols. (Karachi, 1963-1967), vol. I, pp. 335-36; A. Karim, *Social History of the Muslims in Bengal (down to A.D. 1538)*, (Dacca, 1959), pp. 158-59; also pp. 143-44 and 162ff.

[15] "Islam in the Environment of Medieval Bengal," Ph.D. thesis (Canberra, Australian National University, 1970), p. 489; also "The Social Factors in the Making of Bengali Islam," *South Asia*, III (August 1973), p. 35.

[16] For the hostility between the reformists and the traditionalists, several *punthis* in "Islamic Bengali" constitute the most illuminating sources, namely: *Saif al-Mumenin* of unknown authorship (Calcutta, 1875); Muhammad Mallik, *Akhbār al-Marifa* (Calcutta, 1283 B.S./1876); Muhammad Abd al-Karim, *Irshād-i Khaliqiyah* (Calcutta, 1903); Muhammad Naim al-Din, *Adillā-i Hanafiyah, Radd-i Lāmazhabiyah* (Karatia, 1904); Shāh Muhammad Kavirāj, *Del Śikṣā* (Calcutta, 1914); Muhammad Khair Allāh, *Sirājganjer Bahās* (Khulna, 1926); Muhammad Basr Biśwās, *Lakṣmipur Hanafi o Muhammadider Bahās*

And yet the significance of the reformers' mission cannot be underrated. They introduced new elements in the Muslim religious life, the cumulative result of which was to create a chasm between Muslim's "Islamic" and "Bengali" identities. The syncretistic tradition had blended both these identities well. All through the period when the syncretistic tradition remained dominant, the exogenous Islam and its adherents remained aloof and indifferent from, though disapproving of, the syncretistic development. A Bengali Muslim was, therefore, not confronted with a problem of identity. In contrast, the reformers and the revivalists unleashed a vicious and vituperative attack. The persistent and vigorous insistence on a revitalized Islamic consciousness and identity, with

---

(Calcutta, 1921); Muhammad Kobad Ali, *Nabābpure Hanafi-Muhammadidiger Bahās* (Calcutta, 1923); Muhammad Maqsud Ali, *Narendrapurer Bahāse Bi-dati Dalan* (Narendrapur, 1924); Muhammad Ruh al-Amin, *Dafāyel-i Mufasdin* (Calcutta, 1925); Hābil al-Din, *Radd-i Hanafi o Mazhab-darpan* (Calcutta, 1925). See also R. Ahmed, *Bengal Muslims*, Chapter 2, especially pp. 50ff.; M. A. Khan, "Taayyuni Opposition," pp. 150-64; his *Bengal Government Records*, pp. 287, 294-95; his "Research on Islamic Revivalism," pp. 59-63; and, finally, his *History of Farāidi Movement*, Introduction.

For the persistence of traditional life-styles and values among Bengal Muslims in the 19th and 20th centuries, a variety of sources may, with laborious and patient sifting, yield valuable results. Of them, many official and non-official reports, surveys, and observations (several included in the Bibliography), census reports, particularly the notes compiled at the district level, the district gazetteers, local and regional histories in both English and Bengali, and the Christian missionary sources, are all of considerable value. The most informative and reliable source in this area as well is provided by the *punthi* literature in "Islamic Bengali," especially those which formed the reformists' exposés of the traditionalists' aberrations. Some important ones among them are: Abd al-Qādir, *Akhbār-i Pir-i Najdi* (Calcutta, 1874); Abd al-Aziz, *Tariqa-i Muhammadiyah* (Calcutta, 1283 B.S./1876); Munshi Basir al-Din, *Zalālat al-Fuqrah* (Calcutta, 1878); Abd al-Jabbār, *Islām Dharma Parichay* (Calcutta, 1906); also his *Islām-chitra o Samāj-chitra* (Gaffargaon, 2nd edn., 1914); Muhammad Haidār Chaudhuri, *Ahwāl-i Zamāna* (Sylhet, 1907); Sakhi al-Din Ahmad, *Islām-pradip* (Calcutta, 1907); Yusuf Ali, *Fatwā Radd-i Bida* (Calcutta, 1916); Muhammad Tāj al-Islām, *Tāj al-Mumenin* (Rangpur, 1916); and written in a different style and form, but kindred in spirit, is Muhammad Imdād Ali, *Ku-riti Varjan* (Barisal, 1922).

its corresponding denigration of Islam's local roots and associations in Bengal, sapped the very basis of the syncretistic tradition and of the Bengali identity in general. A ceaseless and relentless anti-syncretistic propaganda forced in the community a growing awareness of what they believed and practiced as Muslims, individually and collectively. The first few decades of the present century saw the emergence of a number of Muslim journals in Bengali under the control of the Muslim theologians (*ulamā*), which largely opposed fundamentalism, but called forth Muslims to refurbish their faith and Islamize their lives.[17] In 1919, a Muslim complained that "almost a quarter" of the traditionalist "Hanafis" in Bengal "did not care for the prayers (*namāz*)," and contrasted them with the "Muhammadis" or the followers of the reformist sect of *Tariqa-i Muhammadiyah*.[18] About a quarter of a century later, two distinguished Bengali Muslim compilers of an anthology of Bengali poems attributed the "gradual waning" of "popular" Islam to the purgatory "decrees" (*fatwā*) of the reformist "missionaries of Islam" and to the new Muslim *punthi* writers who urged "to crack the heads" of the traditionalist mendicants. These writers concluded: "The peace and quiet of a Bengal village was disturbed by the acrimonies of the Wahābis and the Hanifis. The Muslim masses felt lost in this whirlpool and their finer sentiments became almost dried up."[19] [My translation.]

[17] *Al-Islām* (monthly), ed. M. A. Khān, first published (Calcutta, 1915); *Islām-darśan* (monthly), ed. S. A. Rahim, first published (Calcutta, 1916); also *Islām-darśan* (monthly), ed. M. A. Hakim & N. Ahmad, first published (Calcutta, 1920); *Sharia* (monthly), ed. A. A. Ināyatpuri, first published (Calcutta, 1924); also *Shariate Islām/Shara-i Islām*, ed. A. A. Ināyatpuri, first published (Calcutta, 1926); *Raoshan Hedāya* (monthly), ed. M. Ibrāhim, first published (Calcutta, 1924); *Hanafi* (weekly), ed. M. R. Amin, first published (Calcutta, 1926); and *Māsik Muhammadi* (monthly), ed. M. A. Khān, published regularly from 1927 (Dacca) after a long break in continuity.

[18] Manir al-Jamān Islāmābādi, "Anjumān-i ulamā o samāj samskār," *Al-Islām*, V, no. 3 (1326 B.S./1919).

[19] A. Qādir & R. Karim, *Kāvya-mālancha* (Calcutta, 1945), p. 32.

As a syncretistic Muslim's total life-style lay naked before the puritan's scanning eyes it covered him with a sense of "shame" and "guilt." The former did not quite emerge as "reformed" or "fundamentalist," as observed earlier, but as a Muslim he became more conscious of himself than ever before. The purists seemed to achieve their objectives almost despite themselves. Slowly but steadily the continuous flow of at least the syncretistic literary tradition maintained through several centuries suffered a progressive contraction both in quantity and quality. A new variety of Islamic *punthi* literature of mixed Urdu-Bengali dictions, as noted above, proliferated to replace the old, while the more literate Bengalis increasingly turned towards an altogether new form of Islamic literature of historical, biographical, and polemical nature, written not in traditional verse but in modern prose. The syncretistic performer seemed to have lost both his stage and audience.

5

The far-reaching political consequences of the gradual demise of the syncretistic tradition are more easily understood than its cultural implications. To most observers this entire process is perhaps no more than an infusion of "Islamic" spirit into a docile flock of Bengal Muslims "without a shepherd" and steeped in "superstitious rites of the Hindus."[20] The resultant deepening of Muslim consciousness has, quite appropriately, been identified as an important contributory factor in Muslim political separatism.[21]

At least some among Bengal Muslims have perceived its significance in non-political terms and also in its wider cul-

[20] J. Wise, *Notes on the Races, Castes and Trades of Eastern Bengal* (London, 1883), p. 21. (The book is not published, and only 12 copies were printed for private circulation. The author consulted the copy held at the British Library, London.) We have already noted how widely this idea of "folk" Islam permeated the thinking of observers and scholars.

[21] R. Ahmed, *Bengal Muslims*, *passim*.

tural contexts than what is conveyed by the idea of mere puritanical purges of "popular" or "folk" Islam. One of them is Kazi A. Wadud, one of the most brilliant products of the Renaissance movement in Bengal, and himself a leading figure of a pioneering band of Bengal Muslims who became directly involved in a courageous but abortive attempt to launch a "movement for the emancipation of intellect" (*buddhi-mukti āndolan*) in Islam and in the Muslim society. Wadud considered "the total change in Muslim perceptions" resulting from the revivalist movements a "greater reason" for distinguishing between Bengal Muslims' old and new ages than the political and economic changes.[22] To him, the pre-revivalistic culture represented "an accord between Hindu and Muslim thoughts," a truth which, as he pointed out with a touch of sarcasm, is "generally distressing to educated Muslims today," since "they look upon it as a measure of their self-liquidation." A logical consequence of the acceptance of this "Wahabi-inspired view" was, for him, a denigration of "the time-honoured *sufi* tradition" as "a nuisance," a position which "the Muslim society generally and many Muslim thinkers in particular refuse to hold till now."[23] The Muslim mystics called *marfati-panthis* by Wadud formed a vital part of his notions of the syncretistic tradition, and his bold defense of the vitality of the mystical quest and of its creative response to its social and cultural milieus drew from him some sharp comments directed at the apologists of canonical Islam. In his address to the annual session of the Muslim Students Association of Faridpur (August 14, 1927) he declared:

The *mawlānās* of Bengal cannot provide a clue as to how Islam is to fulfil itself in the lives of the Bengalis as much as the *marfati-panthis* are able to do. This is so, because the latter, despite their shortcomings, do represent a living religion, the throes of a crea-

[22] K. A. Wadud, *Ājkār Kathā* (Calcutta, 1941), pp. 8-9.

[23] K. A. Wadud, "Bānglār Musalmāner kathā," in his *Śāśvata Banga* (Calcutta, 1951), p. 98.

tive process, and an organic response to its environment. The *mawlānā* is a mere imitator, a keeper of unused books—and rootless and lifeless.

The community of our *ālims* [*ulamā*] have, as you know, applied their might against the *marfati-panthis*. . . . The most important reason for speaking out against this deployment of the *ālim's* power is that they do not choose to conquer one achievement by another of their own. Instead, they resort to sticks to suppress those who are even weaker to them.[24]

Wadud was not alone in his positive appreciation of the syncretistic Muslim mystical tradition in Bengal. M. A. Qādir adopted a more conciliatory tone and chose to appeal to the Islamic religious establishment in Bengal:

Men cannot live deprived of happiness; how long could religious dogmatism and strict discipline go on dominating life? This has led Islam as popularized in Bengal to change itself in response to the needs of happiness and grace in life. For the same reason we find people from both Hindu and Muslim communities come in tens of thousands to accept the spiritual discipleship of the so-called *faqirs* and *shāhs*. . . . There cannot be much doubt in the inference that the Islamic notion of the unity of godhead, sufism, and universal love as popularized by these so-called *faqirs* might have eventually engulfed the whole of Bengal within a short time. I, therefore, urge the promoters of the *sharia* [Islamic religious laws] to try to realize themselves the truth and beauty in the lives of Muslim *bāuls* [a mystical order of syncretistic import]. It is no use issuing decrees providing for the destruction of *bāuls*. What we really need today is to adapt the ideals of *bāuls* and *faqirs*, as far as possible, to make them acceptable to our needs for both diversities and happiness in life.[25]

In the light of subsequent history the concerns of Wadud and Qādir would seem to have remained ignored by more of their Bengali believers than less. But history cannot be called upon to offer a simple answer in absolute terms, be it positive or

[24] K. A. Wadud, "Abhibhāṣan," in his *Nava Paryāy*. 2 vols. (Calcutta, 1926-1929), vol. II, pp. 37-38.

[25] M. A. Qādir, "Bānglār lok-sangit," *Śikhā* (Dacca), I, 1333 B.S./1926, pp. 46-47.

negative. In any case an answer to this question falls beyond the ambit of this study.

6

No man is an island, and no work of scholarship is autonomous and self-sustaining. Spread over many years of study and reflections, the work has taken me to various places and people. Though drawn heavily on material used in my doctoral dissertation, the present study may rightfully claim itself as substantially different. On some substantive issues my perceptions have either been subjected to a process of further distillation or undergone significant modifications. In these two separate phases of academic excursions I have benefited from many quarters. I do not wish to list so many names that I overlook any one of them. My appreciation of all help and advice has always been acknowledged and communicated individually. I feel obliged, however, to make particular mention of Professor A. L. Basham for his sustained interest in my research work and moral, as well as material, support to it; late Professor Nihar Ranjan Ray, Professors Sib Narayan Ray, Tapan K. Raychaudhury, A. F. Salahuddin Ahmed, Edward C. Dimock, Jr., and David Kopf for their inspiring comments on my study, and the last-named especially for recommending the Princeton University Press and introducing me to Dr. Margaret Case, the highly efficient, understanding, and informed Editor for South Asia and the Middle East area of the Press; Dr. Richard P. Davis and Dr. Kit S. Liew, my colleagues in the History Department, for being constant sources of intellectual stimulation, especially the former for his immeasurable assistance with the manuscript of the present study; James J. Wise, my former student and one-time colleague, for his keen interest and ungrudging help; the staff of the Dacca University Library and Bangla Academy in Dacca; the National Library of India, Asiatic Society of Bengal and Bangiya Sahitya-Parisat in Calcutta; the British

Library and the India Office Library in London for their ready and courteous cooperation; and Mrs. Patricia Dovadola and Mrs. Kati Thomson for prompt and generous assistance in preparing the final typescript. To Sabita, my wife, I owe an enormous debt for her patient deciphering of my scribbles to present a readable typed version of the completed draft. The other areas of her contributions to the successful completion of this study are matters of rather personal appreciation than of public proclamation. Also, I should love to mention Konya, our first-born and one of my greatest admirers whose first few words included "thesis." She may not know a great deal about my research, but she does not need to be told about the dedication and hard work that are necessary components of it; she may even be seeing in its completion much greater meanings than perhaps I do. Finally, I acknowledge most gratefully the full financial support and other assistance that I received, at various stages in this study, from the Australian National University, and the Australian Research Grant Committee, Canberra, and also the University of Tasmania, Hobart, Australia.

ASIM ROY

Abbreviations

ADG	*Assam District Gazetteer*
BDG	*Bengal District Gazetteer*
BS/B.S.	Bānglā Sāl (Bengali Calendar)
BSI	*Bānglā Sāhityer Itihās* by S. Sen
DCBM	*A Descriptive Catalogue of Bengali Manuscripts in Munshi Abdul Karim's Collection* by Munshi Abdul Karim and Ahmad Sharif, Eng. edn. with an Introduction by Syed Sajjad Husain
DGEBA	*District Gazetteer of Eastern Bengal and Assam*
HB I & *HB II*	*History of Bengal* (Dacca University), vol. I, ed. by R. C. Majumdar and vol. II ed. by J. N. Sarkar
DMS	Bengali manuscripts in the Dacca University Library (see *DCBM* above)
HBL	*History of Bengali Literature* by S. Sen
HBLL	*History of Bengali Language and Literature* by D. C. Sen
JASB	*Journal of the Asiatic Society of Bengal*, Calcutta
JASP	*Journal of the Asiatic Society of Pakistan*, Dacca
JRAS	*Journal of the Royal Asiatic Society*, London
JMS	Jaynagar Manuscript (see under Bibliography)
mc	Refers to the unpaginated folio no. of a manuscript cited according to the sequence in its microfilm copy.
MBS	*Muslim Bānglā Sāhitya* by M. E. Haq
sl	Refers to the serial no. of DMS (see above) as given in *DCBM* (see above)

Transliterations

For understandable reasons, non-English names and terms abound in this work. Drawing on material in several languages, Eastern and Western, and confronted with the problems of substantial variations between the traditional and later renderings of the same word as well as between its standard grammatical and adapted regional and local forms, I found consistency in matters of transliteration and transcription a despair. The Bengali, Sanskrit, Persian, and Arabic words are transliterated according to systems generally familiar to Indologists and Islamists. To facilitate and expedite copy editing, diacritic marks are drastically reduced, only to denote the long vowel "ā" as well as to differentiate among the three different "s" in Sanskrit-Bengali alphabet such as "ś," "ṣ," and "s," the first two being generally pronounced as English "sh" in "shine," and the last as in "sign."

The authors of non-English "primary sources," in manuscript and print, are cited with their full names and also listed in the Bibliography alphabetically, by their first names, the only exception being the authors of regional and local accounts in Bengali, whose full names do not appear in the footnotes and who are listed in the Bibliography by their surnames.

THE ISLAMIC SYNCRETISTIC TRADITION IN BENGAL

Introduction

SECTION I: THE ISSUES

Islamic contact with Bengal is as old as the role of the religion is significant in the historical development of this region. It is rather paradoxical that the phenomenon of Islamization in Bengal has drawn far less academic attention than what would seem warranted by its historical significance. Its importance does not simply consist in the fact that the undivided Bengal saw the largest concentration of Muslims (about 34 million) in the Indian subcontinent, and that their present aggregate in divided Bengal (the Indian state of West Bengal and Bangladesh) makes them the second largest Muslim population in the world (over 100 million), after Indonesia (over 140 million). Bengal's numerical importance has, in recent times, assumed greater meaning in the dramatic and tragic developments of the partition of the land in 1947 and the subsequent birth of Bangladesh in blood in 1971. Beneath these traumatic experiences in relatively quick succession, one is vaguely aware of an undercurrent of tension and conflict involving the self-perception and identity of Bengali Muslims. Like other seminal historical developments, the roots of the problem of Bengali Muslims' self-image go deeper into their historical past. This, in its turn, underlines the importance of the syncretistic tradition of Islam in Bengal, which remains almost totally unrecognized and unappreciated because of the lack of adequate knowledge and much systematic study.

Indian Islam has, in general, been noted by scholars for its "exclusiveness" and "unadaptability."[1] Islam in traditional Bengal was, in contrast, marked by its tendency towards convergence with and assimilation to the local cultural milieu. A late-nineteenth-century observer of the phenomenon remarks: "It would . . . be impossible for the Arab to connect the *corrupt Hinduized rites* [italics mine] he witnesses in Bengal with those celebrated at Mecca. . . ."[2] A recent study relating to the early sixteenth century Bengal notes: "Islam, in its simple and austere aspect, does not appear to have characterized the life of the people [of Bengal] . . . a careful study of the literature of the time shows that there prevailed *a sort of folk Islam* [italics mine] having hardly any connexion with the dogmas of religion."[3] The locally acculturated form of Islam in Bengal was, no doubt, noted by sundry observers, but it was perceived as a form of "corrupt" "folk" or "popular" Islam. This raises a very fundamental question about our approach and perspective bearing on the study of Islamization as a social and cultural process operating in Bengal, where Islam is not a primary but a secondary culture, that is, exogenous and not endogenous to the particular region, and also where Islam is not a single or the only great tradition since it entered a land which was not culturally virgin, and confronted the long-established endogenous Hindu great tradition. These factors, *inter alia*, are significant considerations in a study of Islamic contact and communication with Bengal.

[1] Cf. "The divisive forces have proved much more dynamic than the cohesive ones . . . Islam in India continued to retain throughout the centuries, despite secondary Indian environmental and ethnic influences, its original foreign character." A. Ahmad, *Studies in Islamic Culture in the Indian Environment* (London, 1964), pp. 73-74. See also P. Spear, *India, Pakistan, and the West* (London, 1958), p. 88; J. N. Sarkar, *History of Aurangzeb* (Calcutta, 1912-1925), vol. V, pp. 487-88; A. L. Basham, *The Indian Sub-continent in Historical Perspective* (London, 1958), p. 14.

[2] J. Wise, *Notes on the Races*, p. 6.

[3] M. R. Tarafdar, *Husain Shāhi Bengal*, pp. 163-64.

An adequate appreciation and explanation of the cultural dynamism of this interaction involves a crucial problem of perspective.

In the absence of much significant empirical research on Islam in South Asia, its study has been largely dominated by the normative or macro vision of the early Orientalists and Islamists, giving currency to a form of rather idealized and limited conceptualization of the protean and creative process of Islamization in the area. This idealized normative approach helped to foster an universal notion of an Islamic monolith and a world-Islam, defined essentially in terms of orthodox *sunni* ideals of Islam. The simplicity of Islamic dogmas, its rigid monotheism, egalitarian principles, well-defined scriptures, traditions, and decisions of jurists all help, on one hand, to create a monolithic facade, and to conceal, on the other, significant inner social and cultural differences of both an inter- and intra-regional nature. The most serious limitation of this idealized view of religious and cultural interaction lies in its tendency to evaluate an Islamic phenomenon and a believer in terms of the degree of conformity to the ideals or orthodox norms. In a study of religious change this deductive approach suffers from a self-imposed limitation by beginning with a definition of Islam and accepting or rejecting everything to the extent that it measures up to this standard. Such an approach fails to interpret the religion in terms meaningful to one who calls himself its believer and claims the religion as his own. If the purpose of studying a religion is not to define but to find it,[4] this normative inquiry, trying to sift "good" from "bad" Muslims, is very likely to be directed to a wrong channel. Failure of this nature has given rise, as in the case of Bengal, to presumptive theories and fallacious assumptions rather than analysis. On one hand it fostered a naively idealistic notion of uniformity in Islamic

[4] C. Geertz, *Islam Observed: Religious Development in Morocco and Indonesia* (New Haven and London, 1968), p. 1.

developments; on the other, an obvious awareness of a disjunction between the ideal and the actual often prompted two equally presumptive and self-contradictory explanations. One is the theory of "incomplete" or "nominal" conversion, and the other is that of "corruption" and "degeneration." A modern Bengali Muslim scholar regards incomplete conversion a "channel through which un-Islamic practices passed into Indian Islam . . . long years of association with a non-Muslim people who far outnumbered them, cut off from the original home of Islam and living with *half-converts* [italics mine] from Hinduism, the Muslims had greatly deviated from the original faith and had become Indianized."[5] These arguments are contradictory since degeneration does not follow from a situation of incomplete conversion. On the other hand, to call a Muslim something less than a Muslim is a value judgment and not a description or analysis of the condition of being a Muslim from the believer's own point of view. Above all, the common argument of degeneration in the Bengal context is patently unhistorical. For sheer lack of knowledge and study of the nature of Islamization in traditional Bengal, the Islamic revivalists and reformers[6] and other observers since the nineteenth century found it easier to make those assumptions and use them as a rather convenient rationale for change to their liking. One has to search in vain for any historical evidence to maintain that the so-called degenerate and Hinduized Islam in Bengal in the nineteenth century was anything other than what it had been there in the past. On the contrary, we gather from the earliest extant Muslim Bengali literary sources, dating largely from the sixteenth century

[5] A. R. Mallick, *British Policy and the Muslims in Bengal, 1757-1856* (Dacca, 1961), pp. 7, 26. See also M. Mujeeb, *The Indian Muslims* (London, 1967), p. 22; Jafar Sharif, *Qānun-i Islām*, English tr. by G. Herklot, ed. by W. Crooke (London, 1921), Introduction.

[6] *Supra*, Preface, note 3 and *passim*.

A.D.,[7] that the masses of Bengali Muslims, denied direct access to Islamic tradition embodied in Arabic and Persian literatures, remained steeped in local non-Muslim tradition. The authors of the early Muslim Bengali literature were themselves instrumental in casting Islamic tradition in syncretistic moulds.[8] The Islamic revivalists and other observers were faced with a situation that resulted, not from the later decadence or corruption of local Islam, but from original conditions of culture-contact in the region, which gradually blossomed into a syncretistic and an acculturated tradition. The so-called degenerate and de-vitalized Islam in later Bengal was nothing but an embodiment of an earlier perception and formulation by Bengali Muslims of their religion in a syncretistic frame of reference.

The early Muslim Bengali literature raises, therefore, two vital issues that concern an adequate understanding of the process of Islamization in Bengal. First, it demands a social and cultural explanation of the paradoxical situation that there existed a mass of Muslim believers in Bengal debarred by a linguistic and cultural barrier from an alien Islamic tradition and hence immersed in the pre-existing non-Muslim local tradition. Secondly, it also calls for a careful analysis of the nature of syncretistic tradition emerging from the corpus of this religious and semi-religious literature, together with the

[7] The reference here is to the vast corpus of Muslim Bengali writings in manuscript which constitute the primary sources for this study. These were collected by the unflagging zeal and untiring efforts of Munshi A. Karim, and now held as a collection in his name by the Manuscript Section of the Dacca University Library. These holdings are catalogued, largely on the basis of brief descriptive notes of the collector himself, by his nephew and a scholar of Bengali literature, Ahmad Sharif. This is published as A. Sharif (ed.), *Puthi-parichiti* (Dacca, 1958) and its later English edition, S. S. Husain (ed.), *A Descriptive Catalogue of Bengali Manuscripts* [*DCBM*] (Dacca, 1960). All references to the Dacca Manuscripts [DMS] in our study, quoting the manuscript number followed by the serial [sl] number, are as given in *DCBM* or as otherwise indicated.

[8] *Infra*, Chapters 2-5.

role of this pioneering band of Muslim Bengali writers as cultural mediators for Bengali Muslims. In the two separate parts of the present work both these vital issues underlying the emergence of the Islamic syncretistic tradition in Bengal have been considered in depth.

SECTION II: THE SOURCES

The present study has used the earliest available Muslim Bengali writings in manuscripts as the primary source. Anyone with even a little experience of grappling with relatively old manuscripts should be well aware of the hazards and challenges inherent in the task. In our particular instance it is rendered more difficult by a combination of factors.

No manuscripts in a clearly identifiable original form have been left for us. The later copies, mostly using papers of a very inferior quality in a fiercely destructive tropical climate, are in a rather brittle condition, which has been further aggravated by the utterly neglected state of their preservation by their indigent private owners until recovered by the sole pioneering efforts of Munshi A. Karim. The battered pages of the manuscripts are occasionally found either unpaginated or pagination is faded out of recognition and hence disarranged.

Besides, the language of the literature belonging to the middle Bengali period[9] is archaic enough. But the extensive use of Bengali words of only sub-regional local usage depending on the particular writer's territorial affiliation, along with a profusion of Perso-Arabic words, make them very difficult reading indeed. The effect of archaism in this literature, especially of the esoterical type, is heightened by the

[9] Bengali literature is generally divided into three periods: the old (from the eleventh to the fifteenth centuries A.D.), the middle (from the sixteenth to the eighteenth centuries), and modern (from the nineteenth century onwards). See J. C. Ghosh, *Bengali Literature* (London, reprint, 1976), p. 11.

degree of literary sophistication of the writers, who had, in the absence of a prose style in contemporaneous Bengali literature, no choice but to suffer the additional strain of a versicle composition. And we have little hesitation to add that, judged by performance, not many of our writers were born poets.

Moreover, the scribe's role was often to make this confusion worse confounded. Apart from omitting pagination occasionally leading to disarrangement of the folios, as already mentioned, the illegibility of some scribes' handwriting has been a strong deterrent to a precise interpretation of some of these writings. Where legibility is not in question, the scribe's ignorance of the subject-matter, particularly when it is abstruse and esoteric, came in the way. It is important in this context as well as interesting from the standpoint of the Islamic syncretistic tradition in Bengal that a popular scribe of this literature was a Hindu, Kālidās Nandi.[10] Occasionally, a scribe also suffered from an indomitable impulse to seek poetic glory by interpolating a few couplets or stanzas of his own into the work he was copying. Although the interpolation is often acknowledged, and if not, the scribe is often betrayed by his poetic accomplishment, a careless reader is likely to overlook this little symbol of poetic aspiration of a scribe, and take it as a part of the original. In some rare instances of rather insignificant or obscure works, unscrupulous scribes went to the extent of claiming the authorship for themselves and accordingly making substantial textual alterations.[11]

But the most serious problem concerning the early Muslim Bengali literature lies in a massive confusion and uncertainty regarding its clear identity and history. The supreme importance of these materials for a linear reconstruction of the story of Bengali Muslims cannot be exaggerated, while, strangely

[10] *DCBM*, Introduction, xxii.
[11] *Ibid.*, xxiii.

and regrettably enough, this literature as a whole found very little recognition among those who are concerned with the history of Islamization in Bengal and of Bengali Muslims. Apart from a limited and sporadic use of some of these materials in works of historical import,[12] the literary importance of these writings found no better recognition than that a relatively very small part of this literature has been separately edited and published.[13] The most badly felt need about this literature is a comprehensive and interpretive history. M. E. Haq's *Muslim Bānglā Sāhitya* in Bengali [*MBS*] with its English version, *Muslim Bengali Literature* (Karachi, 1957), is the first and essentially the only attempt in this direction. But as an analytical study of the early Muslim Bengali literature, his effort falls far short of the requirements. His sketchy description of this literature follows very closely the brief descriptive notes prepared by the collector of most of these

[12] Tarafdar, *Husain Shāhi Bengal*; M. A. Rahim's *Social and Cultural History of Bengal* merely used some extracts of this literature appearing in the *Sāhitya-Pariṣat Patrikā* (Calcutta); A. Sharif, *Saiyid Sultān-Tār Granthāvali o Tār Yug* (Dacca, 1972).

[13] Shaikh Zāhid, *Ādya-parichay*, ed. M. M. Chaudhuri (Rajshahi, 1964); Ali Rajā, *Jnān-sāgar*, ed. Munshi A. Karim (Calcutta, 1324 B.S./A.D. 1917); Shaikh Faiz Allāh, *Gorakṣa-vijay*, ed. Munshi A. Karim (Calcutta, 1324 B.S./A.D. 1917); Saiyid Sultān, *Wafāt-i Rasul*, ed. A. Ahmad (Noakhali, 1356 B.S./A.D. 1949); Daulat Qāzi, *Sati Maynā o Lor-Chandrāni*, ed. S. N. Ghosal in *Sāhitya Prakāśikā* (Viśva-bhārati), pt. 1, 1362 B.S./A.D. 1955; Daulat Wazir Bahrām Khān, *Laili-Majnu*, ed. A. Sharif (Dacca, 2nd ed., 1966); Muzammil, *Niti-śāstra-vārtā*, ed. A. Sharif (Dacca, 1965); Afzal Ali, *Nasihat Nāma*, ed. A. Sharif (Dacca, 1969); Sābirid [Shāh Barid?] Khān, *Vidyā-Sundar*, ed. A. Sharif in *Sāhitya Patrikā* (Dacca), I, no.1 (1957), pp. 96-114; Muhammed Khān, *Satya-Kali Vivād Samvād*, ed. A Sharif in *Sāhitya*, III, no. 1 (1959); Zain al-Din, *Rasul-vijay*, ed. A. Sharif in *Sāhitya*, VII, no. 2 (1963), pp. 115-89; Saiyid Alāwal, *Tuhfa*, ed. A. Sharif in *Sāhitya*, I, no. 2 (1957), pp. 56-196; Saiyid Alāwal, *Padmāvati*, ed. S. A. Ahsān (Dacca, 1968), Saiyid Hamza, *Madhu-mālati*, ed. S. A. Ahsān (Chattagrām, 1380 B.S./A.D. 1973); Mir Faiz Allāh, *Sultān Jamjama*, ed. A. Gafur (Dacca, 1969); Hayāt Mahmud, *Hitajnān-vāni, Ambiyā-vāni, Sarva-bhed-vāni* and *Jang Nāma*, all four ed. in M. Islām, *Kavi Heyāt Māmud*/Hayāt Mahmud (Rajshahi, 1961). A number of mystical works have also been edited by A. Sharif in his *Bānglār Sufi Sāhitya* (Dacca, 1969).

works, Munshi A. Karim,[14] and his work may, in effect, be regarded only as a glorified descriptive note rather than as an interpretive history of the early Muslim Bengali literature. The failure to examine closely the contents of the manuscripts has led to rather gross errors concerning the identity, authorship, and dating of a good many of them. We may take a few examples.

M. E. Haq attributes to Saiyid Nur al-Din four separate works: *Daqāiq* or *Daqāiq al-Haqāiq; Hitopadeś* or *Burhān al-Ārifin; Qiyāmat Nāma* or *Rahat al-Qulub*; and *Musār Suwāl.*[15] The first title, together with Haq's observation that the work is a translation of *Kanz al-Daqāiq* by Imām Hafiz al-Din Abul Barkat Abd Allāh,[16] would seem unwarranted. The manuscript used by us (DMS 387: sl 202) as well as its other copies cited in *DCBM* have all had *Daykāt* for the title, the word being a more plausible Bengali corruption of *diqqat* than of *daqāiq*, let alone *daqāiq al-haqāiq*. The author never mentions *Kanz al-Daqāiq* in his work; instead, he clearly acknowledges *Burhān al-Ārifin* as his source, and hints at *Hita-upa* [*deś*] or *Hitopadeś* as a possible title of the work.[17] The latter points to another serious confusion of Haq, listing *Hitopadeś* or *Burhān al-Ārifin* as a separate work. In our reading of the manuscript we find the extract quoted by Haq,[18] connecting *Hitopadeś* with *Burhān* and claiming it as separate from *Daykāt*, appears in folio 6 of *Daykāt* itself.

Similarly, Haq credits Muzammil with two separate works, *Niti-śāstra-vārtā* and *Saad Nāma*, contrary to the opinion of Munshi A. Karim that they are not different texts.[19] The latter opinion is also upheld by A. Sharif, who subsequently

[14] *Supra*, note 7.
[15] *MBS*, p. 287.
[16] *Ibid.*, p. 288.
[17] DMS 387: sl 202, fol. 6.
[18] *MBS*, p. 289.
[19] Sharif (ed.), *Puthi-parichiti*, p. 267.

edited the text entitled *Niti-śāstra-vārtā*. A comparison of the manuscripts concerned (DMS 214: sl 237 and DMS 195: sl 119) convinces us as well that these two works are identical.

Again, to Ali Rajā are generally attributed two works, *Āgam*[20] and *Jnān-sāgar*.[21] The latter is edited by Munshi A. Karim,[22] while S. Husain, the editor of *DCBM*, has incorrectly named A. Sharif as its editor.[23] Karim and Sharif both regard these titles as merely two parts of a single work,[24] and E. Haq shares this view.[25] On close examination of the manuscript (DMS 146: sl 9), the first seven folios of which, according to Karim, form the first part called *Āgam*, and the rest constituting the second part named *Jnān-sāgar*, we are inclined to reject the view that they are two separate parts of a single work, let alone being two independent works. In folio nos. 139 and 203 of the manuscript, Ali Rajā clearly mentions *Āgam* as the title of the entire work.

The same is perhaps the case with the two other works, *Nabi-vamśa* and *Shab-i Mirāj*, attributed to Saiyid Sultān.[26] This prolific writer had set upon himself the stupendous task of writing a comprehensive history of all prophets, culminating in Muhammad, and he seems to have chosen *Nabi-vamśa* or the "Line of the Prophets" as the title of his project. The manuscript of the so-called *Shab-i Mirāj* (DMS 433: sl 490) does not mention this title in the colophons. Rather, the name of *Nabi-vamśa* appears in the colophon in folio 259. Besides, in another manuscript of *Nabi-vamśa* (DMS 656: sl 222), the scribe claims to have completed the first half of the great work, *Nabi-vamśa*.[27]

[20] DMS 146a: sl 9. Also ed. by A. Sharif in his *Sufi Sāhitya*, pp. 323-62.

[21] DMS 146b: sl 9.

[22] *Supra*, note 13.

[23] *DCBM*, pp. 9, 147. A. Sharif has since edited a part of this work left out by Karim. See A. Sharif, *Sufi Sāhitya*, pp. 365-532.

[24] Sharif (ed.), *Puthi-parichiti*, p. 11; also his *Sufi Sāhitya*, p. 311.

[25] *MBS*, p. 279.

[26] *Ibid.*, pp. 143ff.; *DCBM*, pp. 495-97.

[27] Fol. 374.

From the historical point of view even more serious confusion exists in the chronological arrangement of these manuscripts. Except in some cases clear dating of the individual manuscripts is quite hazardous for at least the early literature. The most glaring illustration of this problem is Shāh Muhammad Saghir's *Yusuf-Zulaikha*, for which E. Haq and, following him, others have claimed the distinction of being the earliest of the Muslim Bengali compositions.[28] On the basis of an excerpt from a manuscript held in his personal possession—an excerpt not found in the manuscript we have used (DMS 125: sl 12)—Haq identifies the poet's patron, introduced as the great ruler (*Mahā narapati*) "Gyechh," with Ghiyāth al-Din Azam Shāh (A.D. 1389-1410). He does so on the ground that there is suggestion, in the particular excerpt, of the ruler's taking forcible possession of "Bangāl" (Vanga or the eastern Bengal) and "Gaudiyā" (Gaud in north Bengal) from his father. Apart from the strange omission of the section from manuscripts other than Haq's, its interpretation itself is not beyond question for various reasons. First, the language of Saghir is no more archaic than many other works of the undoubted sixteenth-century origin, and is, in fact, far less so than Mālādhar-vasu's *Śrikriṣna-vijay*, which is regarded as the earliest work in the whole range of Bengali literature with a fairly determinate date. Mālādhar's work is placed about a hundred years later than the claim made in behalf of Saghir's composition. Secondly, the latter bears, according to D. C. Sen, the doyen of scholars on Bengali language and literature, considerable influence of the Bengali literature of Ārākān in the southeast of Bengal which did not flourish until the seventeenth century.[29] Thirdly, Saghir used Hindi-Urdu words like *bāt* (talk) and Urduised Bengali like *nikalila* (came out)[30]—a literary practice that was not quite in

[28] *MBS*, p. 56.

[29] D. C. Sen, *Prāchin Bānglā Sāhitye Musalmāner Avadān* (Dacca, 1940), p. 69.

[30] DMS 125: sl 12, fol. 38.

vogue in Bengali literature even in the sixteenth century. Finally, his writing is interspersed with couplets in the classical *vaiṣnav* style with rather suggestive reference to the frolics of Zulaikha and her friends in Vrindāvan, the center of amorous sports for Kriṣna, Rādhā, and her companions, celebrated in the *vaiṣnav* lyrics of Bengal. The lyrical *vaiṣnav* literature in Bengali is not known to have emerged until the sixteenth century. On the other hand, if Saiyid Sultān's reference, in the early seventeenth century, to an already existing *punthi* on the theme of Yusuf-Zulaikha was to Saghir's work, his *Yusuf-Zulaikha* cannot be placed at least later than this.

This is enough to indicate the magnitude and complexity of the problems concerning an effective study of the Muslim Bengali literature from either a historical or a literary point of view. In our reference to these manuscripts we have, for convenience, generally used the present catalogue in English, that is, *DCBM*, with all its limitations. We have been impelled to this pragmatic course by the realization that it is far beyond our scope and means here to become involved in a historical reconstruction of this literature, which, in itself, is a far more challenging task. An analytical study of the individual works must precede an attempt to write a good history of them. There is no substitute for a collective effort to get these manuscripts methodically edited and published before competent scholars on Bengali literature may find themselves in a position to offer meaningful interpretations of these works and their authors individually and collectively. A. Sharif deserves our finest admiration for having undertaken the onerous responsibility of editing a good many of these manuscripts. It must, however, be stressed that a professional approach to editing a manuscript involves a great deal more than what is often offered in an edited form of these works. Where more than one copy of a manuscript is known to exist, it is incumbent on the editor to compare all of them. This is seldom the case with the Muslim Bengali edited manuscripts. Besides, by the very nature of the problem, the task, as suggested above, requires teamwork, which may seem particularly suited to the function of Bangla Academy in Dacca, Bangladesh.

Part I: Context

1

Social Origins of Muslims in Bengal

The social composition, the geographical distribution, and the demographic patterns of the Muslims in Bengal were seminal factors in the development of Islam in that region. By the end of the nineteenth century the Muslim population in Bengal was recorded around 26 million, which constituted about one-third of the total population of Bengal and about 40 percent of the total Muslim population of India. Distributed regionally the number was more meaningful. In east and southeast Bengal two-thirds, and in north Bengal three-fifths, of the inhabitants were recorded as Muslims.[1]

The Muslim preponderance in the Bengal population, as revealed in the first census of Bengal in 1872, took the British officials and observers by surprise. Ever since their first contact with the people of Bengal the British regarded the Muslims as an insignificant number in that population.[2] William Adam in his extensive Education Reports on Bengal in the 1830s conceded: "Before visiting Rajshahi, I had been led to

[1] E. A. Gait, *Report* on Bengal, *Census of India, 1901* (Calcutta, 1902), vol. VI, pt. 1, pp. 151, 156. Of individual districts, Bagura with 82 percent had the greatest proportion of Muslim population, followed by Rajshahi (78 percent), Pabna (75 percent), Mymensingh (71 percent), and Chittagong (71 percent). (*Ibid.*, p. 156.) See also *The Imperial Gazetteer of India*, ed. by H. Risley *et al.* (Oxford, rev. ed. 1907-1909), vol. I, p. 474.

[2] A. Hamilton, *A New Account of the East Indies*, ed. by W. Forster (London, 1930), vol. II, p. 25; L. Scrafton in *Asiatic Annual Register* (London, vol. II, 1800), p. 20; Risley, *Imperial Gazetteer*, vol. I, p. 475.

suppose that it was a peculiarly Hindu district. Hamilton on official authority [the estimates of 1801] states the proportion to be that of two Hindus to one Musalman; and in a work published by the Calcutta School Book Society for the use of schools (1827), the proportion is said to be that of ten Hindus to six Musalmans." Adam's own investigations led him to reverse this to seven to three, or the proportion of 1,000 Musalmans to 450 Hindus.[3] The first census of Bengal (1872) found it 1,000 Muslims to 288 Hindus.[4] For the early British observers it was "easy to understand, why Muhammadans should be found in large numbers in the Punjab and Sind, which lie on or near the route by which successive hordes of Afghan and Mughal invaders entered India; but it is not at first sight apparent why they should be even more numerous in Bengal proper."[5]

What was more surprising for them was that the Muslim preponderance was not even found within or about the centers of Muslim power. None of the districts containing a very high proportion of Muslims in the population held any of the important centers of Muslim power in Bengal. In Dacca, which for a long time contained the seat of government for the Muslim rulers, Muslims were very slightly in excess of Hindus. In Maldaha and Murshidabad, centers of the Muslim rule for several centuries, Muslims formed a smaller proportion of the population than they did in the adjacent districts of Dinajpur, Rajshahi, and Nadia. All this clearly underlined the predominantly rural character of the Muslims in Bengal—a phenomenon that stood in significant contrast with the general pattern of Muslim distribution in India and

[3] W. Adam, *Reports on the State of Education in Bengal (1835-1838)*, ed. by A. N. Basu (Calcutta, 1941), "The Second Report (1836)," pp. 135-36.

[4] H. Beverley, *Report on the Census of Bengal, 1872* (Calcutta, 1872), p. 131.

[5] Risley, *Imperial Gazetteer*, vol. I, p. 475.

elsewhere.[6] The Muslims appeared in Bengal to take "less readily to a town life than the Hindus; but elsewhere the reverse is the case, and in the United and Central provinces, in Madras, and in many of the adjoining states the proportion of Muhammadans in towns is double that of Muhammadans in the population at large."[7] The census of Bengal, 1901 mentions "the very large proportion of Musalmans who subsist by agriculture" and "the small number engaged in intellectual pursuits," and adds: ". . . it may be said generally, that the occupations other than those connected with agriculture, in which Muhammadans preponderate, are very few."[8] In a contemporary document of the Government of Pakistan, the erstwhile province of East Pakistan, containing the Muslim majority areas in Bengal, has been depicted as "a huge sprawling village."[9]

The British surprise, undoubtedly shared by many Bengalis, Hindus, and Muslims, stemmed from two serious misconceptions about the origin of the Muslims in Bengal. First, that the Muslim population consisted of the foreign invaders and immigrants, and hence they were not identified in large numbers among the people in Bengal. Secondly, that Islam won its numbers by pressure and force, and hence they were to be expected in and around the centers of power alone. The Bengal phenomenon proved both these presumptive theories of Islamization in that region wrong. Central to the subsequent British approach to the problem was the general acceptance of the fact of local conversion largely from the lower levels of the indigenous society, and the substantial rejection of the "fire and sword" theory of conversion. The *Imperial*

[6] G. E. von Gruenbaum characterizes Islam as "a religion of the townspeople." (*Islam*, London, 2nd edn., 1961, p. 142.) See also M. Mujeeb, *Indian Muslims*, p. 10.

[7] Risley, *Imperial Gazetteer*, vol. I, p. 455.

[8] Gait, *Census Report (1901)*, p. 484.

[9] Govt. of Pakistan, *East Pakistan: Land and People* (Karachi, 1955), p. 23.

Gazetteer drew its conclusion to the effect that "It is difficult to apportion the result between the peaceful persuasion of Musalman missionaries and forcible conversion by fanatical rulers, but probably the former had the greater influence. That conversion at the sword's point was by no means rare is known from history, but . . . its influence alone cannot make very many converts. . . ."[10] Gait in his Census Report of 1901 arrived at a similar position. "Cases of forcible conversion" were "by no means rare," but it seemed "probable that very many of the ancestors of the Bengali Muhammadans voluntarily gave their adhesion to Islam."[11] The author of the first Census Report spoke with somewhat greater conviction: "Persecution has rarely, if ever, succeeded of its own innate force to establish any religion. The times and circumstances of the country must demand the revolution before it can be brought about by persecution alone."[12]

The theory of local conversion and, more so, that of lower-class origin, provoked a sharp reaction from the comfortable classes of Muslims in contemporary Bengal. Khān Bahādur Diwān Fuzli Rubbee (Fazl-i Rabbi) of Murshidabad took upon himself to write a refutation of the local conversion theory in his Urdu work entitled *Haqiqa-i Musalmān-i Ban-galah* (The Truth About the Muslims of Bengal) and its Eng-lish version, *The Origin of the Musalmans of Bengal*. The au-thor claimed unconvincingly that the Bengali Muslim society grew largely on a steady influx of foreign immigrants.[13] Fuzli Rubbee has found in recent years a strong champion in M. A.

[10] Risley, vol. I, p. 475.

[11] Gait, *Census Report (1901)*, p. 171.

[12] Beverley, *Census Report (1872)*, p. 133, also Table ib & vb, xxxii, xccv; Gait, *Census Report (1901)*, pp. 450, 166, also vol. VIa, pt. 2, Table xiii, p. 288.

[13] K.B.D. Fuzli Rubbee, *The Origin of the Musulmans of Bengal* (Calcutta, 1895), pp. 4ff. Others came forward immediately in support of his contentions. See Gait, *Census Report (1901)*, p. 166; *The Moslem Chronicle*, 17 January 1895, p. 20.

Rahim, who suspects a "definite intention of lowering the prestige of the Muslims of Bengal" lurking under the British advocacy of the "low class theory."[14] The rejoinder from the opposite camp was no less sharp: "The dislike which educated Muhammadans have for the theory that most of the local converts in eastern and northern Bengal are of Chandal and Koch origin seems to be due to the influence of Hindu ideas regarding social status, according to which these tribes occupy a very degraded position."[15] Admittedly, these historical polemics throve in conditions of obscurity covering the history of the advent and dissemination of Islam in Bengal, as elsewhere in India. In the absence of adequate historical sources on the subject, inference and imagination substituted for factual analysis.

Sporadic references to cases of local conversion from the upper classes may be gleaned from diverse sources.[16] Besides

[14] *Social and Cultural History*, vol. I, p. 57.

[15] Gait, *Census Report (1901)*, p. 171.

[16] The earliest reference was to the conversion of a Mech chief, Ali by Muhammad bin Bakhtyār Khalji during his march through north Bengal against Tibet in the beginning of the thirteenth century. (Minhāj al-Din al-Sirāj, *Tabaqāt-i Nāsiri, Bibliotheca Indica*, 1864, English tr. by H. G. Raverty, Calcutta, 1881, p. 152.) We are also told about the conversion of a *yogi* named "Bhojar Brāhman." The name, which sounds rather strange, can very well be an Arabic or Persian corruption of Vajra-brahman, a name quite appropriate for a Hindu *yogi* or a Buddhist *tāntrik*. (Tarafdar, *Husain Shāhi Bengal*, p. 16.) For reasons unexplained Rahim takes him for a "Vedantist Brahmin" (*Social and Cultural History*, vol. I, p. 66), who came from Kamrup to Lakhnauti, the capital of Bengal, in the reign of Ali Mardan Khalji (1210-13 A.D.) in search of a Muslim scholar for a polemical discussion. He was thoroughly impressed by Qāzi Rukn al-Din Samarqandi and accepted Islam. (*Journal of the Pakistan Historical Society*, I, 1953, pt. 1, pp. 46-51.)

From the same source we come to know about the conversion of another religious personality of Kāmrup, Ambabhanāth. The most celebrated case of local conversion was that of Jitmal or Yadu, son of a Hindu chief of north Bengal, Rājā Ganeś. Following his conversion he came to ascend the throne of Bengal as Sultān Jalāl al-Din Muhammad. (*HB II*, pp. 117ff., 183-84; also H. Askari, "The Correspondence of Two 14th Century Sufi Saints of Bihar with the Contemporary Sovereigns of Delhi and Bengal," *Journal of the Bihar Research Society*, XLII, no. 2, 1956, pp. 177-95.) During the reign of such scattered references, there had always been a general impression of physical resemblance between the bulk of Bengali Hindus and Muslims. In 1860 Colesworthy Grant observed that "a great number of the rural classes of Muslims" were "so mixed up" with their Hindu neighbors "in social

Islām Shāh Sur (A.D. 1545-1553) a Bāis Rājput immigrant in Bengal named Kālidās Gajdāni, who had been converted to Islam (*HB II*, p. 177), left a long line of illustrious successors, including his son, Isa Khān, and grandson, Musā Khān, two of the leading local chiefs of Bengal. Musā Khān had a great Sanskrit scholar, Mathureś, as his court poet. (S. Sen, *Madhyayuger Bānglā o Bāngāli* [Calcutta, 1962], pp. 20-21.) During the governorship of Islām Khān (A.D. 1608-1613), Raghu-rāy, a Hindu chief of north Bengal, embraced Islam. (Mirzā Nathan, *Bahāristān-i Ghaybi*, English tr. by M. I. Borah [Gauhāti, 1936], vol. I, p. 32.) A number of medieval family histories record *brāhman* and *kāyastha* antecedents of some converted Muslim families. The Pirāli, Śer-khāni, and Śrimanta-khāni *brāhmans* were thrown out of the pale of orthodoxy due to Muslim family antecedents. (N. N. Basu, *Banger Jātiya Itihās-Brāhman Kānda*, pt. 3 [Calcutta, 1331 B.S.], pp. 152-58.) Kamāl al-Din Chaudhuri and Jamāl al-Din Chaudhuri, the *zamindārs* of Singhatiā were known to be *brāhman* converts to Islam. The *rājās* of Kharagpur were originally Khetauris, and became Muslims. The Diwān family of Pargana Sarāil in Tripura was of known Hindu origin. The family of Asad Ali Khān of Baranthān in Chittagong was by origin a branch of the Śrijukta family of Naupārā. Their ancestor, Śyām-rāy-chaudhuri was converted to Islam. (Gait, *Census Report [1901]*, p. 170.) The ancestors of Asad Allāh, the *zamindār* of Birbhum in the time of Murshid Quli Khān, were known to be Hindus. (C. Stewart, *History of Bengal* [London, 1813], p. 371.) The genealogical table of the Miyān family of Śrirāmpur in the sub-division of Patuā-khāli, Bāklā, shows their *brāhman* ancestry. Śivānanada Majumdār was converted to Islam and came to be known as Śibān Khān. The same was known about the *rājās* of Rupsi and the Khāns of Sirjug and Bāklā. (R. K. Sen, *Bāklā*, [Bariśāl, 1915], p. 121.) The Muslim Chaudhuri family of Shāhbāzpur in Sylhet traced its origin to the Hindu Jangdār family of Panchakhanda. Svaruprām, son of Śyāmrāy Jangdār of this Hindu family, was converted to Islam and became known as Shāhbāz Khān. The Muslim Chaudhuri family of Daulatpur in Sylhet was also believed to be a branch of the family of Ānanda-rāy, the noted founder of Ānandapur. (A. C. Chaudhuri, *Śrihatter Itivritta*, pt. 2 [Śilchar, 1324 B.S./1917], pp. 216, 466.)

Medieval Bengali literature also alluded to the fact of local conversion. *Śek (Shaikh)-śubhoday*, one of the earliest literary works of medieval Bengal, doubtfully ascribed to Halāyudha, a court-poet of King Lakṣman-sen, depicted conversion by a Muslim divine. (Ed. and English tr. by S. Sen [Calcutta, 1963], Chs. 3-4.) Vrindāvan-dās mentioned *brāhmans* accepting Islam "on habits and appearances" as to be "half-amalgamated."[17] James Wise considered it "impossible even for the most practised observer" to "distinguish between a Muhammadan and a Hindu peasant" in "a crowd of Bengali villagers" with "one and only one type of features, of complexion, and of physique" prevading them all.[18] In reference to the Indo-Mongoloids of north and east Bengal, S. K. Chatterji held that "the masses" who were "the descendants of the Bodos" were "largely Muhammadan in religion."[19] The affinities of the Muslim masses of east and southeast Bengal were noted generally with local *namaśudra* and *pod*, and those of north Bengal with *rājbamśi* and *koch*.[20] *Nasyā* and *shaikh* Muslims in the Jalpaiguri district of north Bengal, who together comprised, according to the 1901 census, 226,379 of the 228,487 Muslims in the district, "resembled the Hindu Rajbamsis."[21] The observation of this identity was based not only on their striking physical resemblance, but also on the fact that the proportions of Hindus of other castes in these parts of the country had always been very small. *Koches* were generally supposed to have spread in any numbers only as far westward as the Mahānandā, which runs through the Purnia district.

---

their accord." (Vrindāvan-dās, *Chaitanya-bhāgavat*, ed. by S. N. Basu [Calcutta, 1955], 1:16.)

Contemporary foreign travellers testified to the phenomenon of local conversion. Barbosa, who visited Bengal in 1518, noticed that of the "Gentiles" (Hindus) "every day many turn Moors [Muslims] to obtain the favour of the kings and the governors." (Duarte Barbosa, *The Book of Duarte Barbosa*, English tr. by M. L. Dames [London, 1918-1921], vol. II, p. 148.)

[17] C. Grant, *Rural Life in Bengal* (London, 1860), p. 177.

[18] J. Wise, "The Muhammadans of Eastern Bengal," *JASB*, LXIII (1894), pt. 3, no. 1, p. 33.

[19] S. K. Chatterji, "Kirāta-jana-Kṛti. The Indo-Mongoloids: Their Contribution to the History and Culture of India," *ibid.*, Letters, XVI (NS), no. 2, 1950, p. 214.

[20] Gait, *Census Report (1901)*, p. 169; Beverley, *Census Report (1872)*, pp. 132-33; *DGEBA. Bogra*, ed. by J. N. Gupta (Allahabad, 1910), p. 33.

[21] *DGEBA. Jalpaiguri*, ed. by J. F. Gruning (Allahabad, 1911), pp. 35-36.

East of that river, where the bulk of the population was *koch*, no less than two-thirds were Muslims, while to the west of it, where the *koch* element was weak, less than one-third of the population was returned under the religion.[22] On the strength of such general impressions and observations, Beverley contended: "If further proof were wanted of the position that the Musalmans of the Bengal delta owe their origin to conversion rather than to the introduction of foreign blood, it seems to be afforded in the close resemblance between them and their fellow-countrymen. . . . That both were originally of the same race seems sufficiently clear . . . from their possessing identically the same physique. . . ."[23]

The pervasive notion of physical identity was found to correspond with the findings of later anthropometric and blood-group studies of the Bengal population. To Herbert Risley may be attributed the pioneering attempt, though extremely limited and dubious, at deploying anthropometric materials to Bengal studies.[24] On the basis of very meager anthropometric data he concluded that the Muslims of Bengal were primarily local converts from the lower rungs of the Hindu caste ladder.[25] It is undeniable as well as understandable that Risley's pioneering venture was not above serious criticism. But one would be mistaken to think, as both Fuzli Rubbie and M. A. Rahim have done, that Risley made a sweeping generalization about the entire Muslim community in Bengal. He sought to prove what actually emerged from his inadequate findings; that the lower strata of both Muslims and Hindus of Bengal sprang largely from the same ethnic stock.

[22] Gait, *Census Report (1901)*, p. 169.

[23] Beverley, *Census Report (1872)*, p. 134; also H. Beveridge, *The District of Bakarganj; Its History and Statistics* (London, 1876), p. 211.

[24] H. Risley's *The Tribes and Castes of Bengal* (Calcutta, 1891) is a monumental work in two volumes, each volume being further subdivided into two parts. Vol. I contains the "Ethnographic Glossary" and vol. II incorporates detailed tables of "Anthropometric Measurements."

[25] *Ibid.*, vol. I, p. 91.

This explained his reliance on the anthropometric data regarding Muslims collected from some one hundred and eighty-five jailed convicts of inferior social classes. For the same reason the corresponding measurements of the Hindus were obtained along caste lines to show that the measurements of the lower class Muslims corresponded, not with the upper section of the Hindu society, but the lower one. Rahim clearly misconceived Risley's object, complaining that "Risley took the measurement of the nose of very lower [sic] class Muslims, while, on the other hand, he had the nasal examination of the persons of all classes of the Hindus."[26] The real weakness in Risley's position concerned the extreme paucity of data and the lack of adequate scientific method and equipment necessary for such investigations. He had, however, set in motion a process of investigation which was carried on and applied to the Bengal situation by P. C. Mahalanobis, B. S. Guha, and others.[27] The most recent and systematic study of the problem was undertaken through the collaboration of an anthropologist, D. N. Majumdar, and a statistician, C. R. Rao, under the auspices of the Indian Statistical Institute. The results of their findings were computed, analysed and incorporated into a quantitative study entitled *Race Elements in Bengal*. An important feature of this investigation was that they proceeded independently on the basis of common data and arrived at similar conclusions. One of their major concerns was whether Muslim and non-Muslim groups could be said to belong to two different populations and, if not, what was the relative place of Muslim groups vis-à-vis the Hindu castes and tribes. The study revealed that nine groups out of a total of fifteen chosen Muslim groups fell "within a narrow range of mean nasal height (21.80 to 22.20)" and had "al-

[26] Rahim, *Social and Cultural History*, vol. I, p. 56.

[27] P. C. Mahalanobis, "Analysis of Race Mixture in Bengal," *JASB* (N.S.) XXIII (1927), no. 3, pp. 301-33; B. S. Guha, *Racial Elements in the Population of India* (Oxford, 1944).

most identical mean values as the two Namasudra[28] groups" included in the study. Five groups had "lower mean values" and stood "very close to tribal cluster," while only one group designated "Muslim of Dacca" occupied "a position close to the caste groups." The Report concludes: "If we agree as to the competence of nasal height in defining group divergences, I feel that we should look among the tribal and scheduled caste non-Muslim groups of Bengal for a possible origin of Muslim population of Bengal, and not in the high caste groups, a fact which differentiates the Muslims of U.P., who cluster with the higher castes in nasal height from those of their co-religionists in Bengal."[29]

The serological data collected by D. N. Majumdar from practically all the districts of Bengal added up to the same conclusion. The three blood groups A, B, and O are found in nearly all known populations, though they vary in their relative frequency. The frequency variation of the A, B, O groups has a regional complexion for "each continent or major sub-division of a continent has its own general character." It has been found that the Muslims of India as a general rule differ significantly from their co-religionists outside, both with regard to anthropometric and serological type. While the Muslims in the Middle and Near East have high A value and low B and AB value, the Muslims in India have low A and high B + AB value. The serological data obtained from the Muslim population in Bengal point to the dissociation of the Bengal Muslims from those outside India and even from those of Uttar Pradesh. This indicates, to quote the Report, "the local origin of the Muslims, if blood groups evidence has any meaning at all."[30]

[28] A depressed or "scheduled" caste group predominant in east and southeast Bengal. (*Infra*, pp. 44-45.)

[29] D. N. Majumdar and C. R. Rao, *Race Elements in Bengal. A Quantitative Study* (Calcutta, 1960), D. N. Majumdar's "Report," p. 96. It may be noted that D. N. Majumdar and P. C. Mahalanobis in collaboration made an anthropometric survey also of the United Provinces (U.P.) in 1941.

[30] *Ibid.*

The similarity of manners and customs observed among people alike in physical particulars added force to the arguments for local conversion. An early-nineteenth-century British traveller, Mrs. Belnos, who in her own words was "a curious and interested spectator of every object . . . characteristic of native opinions and manners in Bengal," and "an attentive observer" of "the festivals and processions, the ceremonials of religion and the practices of ordinary life," noted: "All Musselman born and bred in the country villages in Bengal, assume the manners, language, and dress of the Bengallies. . . ."[31]

A late-seventeenth-century Muslim observer referred to the Muslims whom he met in Assam as "Assamese in their habits, and Muhammadans in their names." He also felt that they "liked the Assamese better" than the Muslims visitors like himself.[32] A British official observed that the *koch* women of the Rangpur district in north Bengal, Hindus and Muslims alike, wore "the old Kamrup [Assam] dress," which offered "a marked contrast to the common Saree of Bengal," and also attended the markets "to the almost total exclusion of men."[33] In some parts of Bengal, especially in the northeastern areas, peopled chiefly by *koch, mech, bodo*, and *dhimāl*, the great mass of the Muslims in the early years of this century had no designations or surnames of Arabic or Persian origin. In these parts there were few *shaikhs* and *khāns* while the great majority were called by a common but unexplained name of *nasyā*. In addition, Hindu names and titles were very common. Names such as Kāli Shaikh, Kālāchānd Shaikh, Braja Shaikh, or Gopāl Mandal were regularly used.[34] The prevalence of Hindu names among Muslims was also observed in

[31] S. C. Belnos, *Twenty-four Plates Illustrative of Hindoo and European Manners in Bengal* (London, 1832), plate 5.

[32] Shihāb al-Din Tālish, *Fathiya-i Ibriya*, summary English translation by H. Blochmann in *JASB*, XLV, pt. 1, no. 1 (1872), p. 83.

[33] E. G. Glazier, *A Report of the District of Rungpore* (Calcutta, 1873-1876), vol. I, p. 6.

[34] *DGEBA. Bogra*, p. 34; Gait, *Census Report*, p. 172.

Nadia.[35] The district gazetteer records about Noakhali[36] in 1911 that "Muhammedans with surnames of Chanda, Pāl and Datta are to be found . . . to this day," and adds: "Formerly, it is said, the Mohammedans kept too many of their old Hindu customs, but about the middle of last century they came under the influence of a reforming priest, Maulavi Imāmuddin, and are now, almost to a man, Farāizis. They abhor all innovations . . . and the worship of saints. . . ."[37]

The phenomenon of local conversion seems evident enough. But it is no less evident that a considerable number of Muslims of diverse ethnic origin found their way into Bengal at different times. It cannot, however, be reasonably assumed that all those who flocked into this region came to settle down in the land. The proverbial bad climate[38] of Bengal could not but discourage the prospective upper-class Muslim settlers. The climatic hazards earned Bengal a sobriquet among foreign Muslims, a "hell full of boons" (*dozakh pur-i niamat*).[39] Zāhid Beg, when appointed by the Mughal emperor Humāyun as the governor of the Bengal province, expressed his concern: "Your Majesty could not find a better place to kill me than Bengal."[40] The Mughal conqueror of Bengal, Munim Khān (1575-1576), and his entourage were destroyed by the ravages of the monsoon and the pestilence that followed in its wake in northwestern Bengal. The newly appointed Mughal governor of Bengal, Prince Shujā, complained to his

[35] K. N. Mallik, *Nadiyā Kāhini* (Rānāghāt, 2nd edn., 1912), p. 225; also *The Moslem Chronicle*, 25 April 1895, p. 177.

[36] "Noakhali is known throughout East Pakistan for the pervading influence of the priestly class called the Mullahs and 'pure' Islam." (A.K.N. Karim, *Changing Society in India and Pakistan* [Dacca, 1956], p. 133.)

[37] *DGEBA. Noakhali*, ed. by J. E. Webster (Allahabad, 1911), p. 39. For a detailed discussion of the reformist impact on Muslim's Bengali names, see R. Ahmed, *Bengal Muslims*, pp. 112-13, and also Appendix A.

[38] *HB II*, p. 186.

[39] Ibn Battutah, *Rehla*, Eng. tr. by H. A. Gibb (London, 1929), p. 267.

[40] Abul Fazl, *Āin-i Akbari*, Eng. tr. by H. Blochmann & H. J. Jarrett (Calcutta, 1873-1894), vol. I, p. 1757.

father, emperor Shāh Jahān, of his own and his family's deteriorating health due to the inclement climate of Bengal.[41] The settled Mughal administration in Bengal caused, on one hand, an undoubted inflow of Muslims of rank, but on the other "the viceroys and nobles governing Bengal amassed wealth rapidly, and returned to spend it in the luxurious palaces of Delhi and Agra. . . ."[42]

In the absence of any historical information on the relative strength of the immigrant and of the locally converted Muslims in the population of Bengal, any attempt to quantify their proportions in periods earlier than the census surveys in the late nineteenth century may seem rather bizarre and confounding. On nothing more than a conjectural basis M. A. Rahim would have us accept "the total Bengali Muslim population" in 1770 as 10.6 million, of which "3.27 million belonged to the stock of the immigrant Muslims, and 7.33 millions were from the converted Muslims."[43] With a view to giving us "an idea about the increase of the immigrant Muslims," he drew a chart of the original settlers, breaking them down racially, showing actual numbers on their arrival and arriving at their respective positions in 1770 after centuries of growth. Calculating "on the basis of 100 percent increase on account of birth-rate," he writes:

> . . . the stock of the immigrant Muslims and the converted Muslims numbered about 8 lakhs[44] and 9 lakhs, respectively, two centuries before. Thus in 1570 the Bengali Muslim population was 27 lakhs and the Hindus were 41 lakhs, in a total population of 68 lakhs, say 70 lakhs with the Buddhists and others, in Bengal. The Muslims represented 39.5 per cent of the total population of the province. In the growth of this Bengali Muslim people, the foreign element contributed 29.6 per cent and the local converts 70.4 per cent. . . .

[41] *Ibid.*, vol. III, pp. 226-29; *HB II*, pp. 193, 334.
[42] J. Wise, *Notes on the Races*, p. 2.
[43] *Social and Cultural History*, vol. I, p. 64.
[44] One "lakh" is 100,000.

. . . of the 70 per cent converted Muslims, at least half of them came from the upper strata of the Hindu and the Buddhist communities and the rest was recruited from the lower class. Thus the Bengali Muslim population was formed of about 30 per cent converts from the upper class non-Muslims and 35 per cent converts from the lower strata of the Hindu society. This explodes the theory that the Bengali Muslims were converts mostly from the low caste people of the Hindus. No society of the sub-continent could claim to represent a larger percentage of the immigrant Muslims and converts from the upper class Hindus as well as the Buddhists.[45]

Such conjectural assertions rather than rational historical analysis claim no serious consideration. For any reasonable idea of the immigrant Muslims in Bengal one is left with the census reports in the late nineteenth century, which grouped Muslims under their respective social categories of *saiyid*, *mughal*, *pathān*, and *shaikh*, indicating their foreign origin. The census figures too cannot be accepted without considerable reservations inasmuch as there has been among the indigenous Muslim aspirants to social advancement a pronounced tendency towards forging foreign lineages in a society which attached exaggerated importance to the Middle Eastern origin.[46] Of the four groups, *shaikh* appeared the most suspect, for an overwhelming majority of the Bengali Muslim agriculturists assumed this particular social designation. With general recognition of the fact that no exact estimate is possible for reasons stated above, we find that the census of 1901 records:

. . . it may be said generally that almost the whole of the functional groups, such as Jolaha and Dhunia, throughout the province, the great majority, probably nine-tenths, of the Shekhs in Bengal proper . . . are of Indian origin. The foreign element must be looked for chiefly in the ranks of the Saids, Pathans, and Mughals. Even here there are many who are descended from Hindus, and . . . high

[45] Rahim, *Social and Cultural History*, vol. I, pp. 64, 68.

[46] For a fuller discussion of the question, *infra*, pp. 58-65.

caste converts are often allowed to assume these titles, and, in some cases, to intermarry with those who are really of foreign descent, their number, however, is possibly only a small proportion of the total, and may be neglected. If the above estimates be taken as a basis, it would appear that the strength of the foreign element amongst the Muhammadans of Bengal cannot, at the most, exceed four millions, or say, one-sixth of the total number of persons who profess the faith of Islam.[47]

The recognition of the triple facts of local conversion, non-militant approach, and lower-class origin of the multitude of the converts did not end all controversies on the subject of Muslim origin in Bengal. Doubts and polemics continued unabated regarding the possible explanations for mass conversions. The social character of the bulk of the converts seemed to have set the pattern of historical speculation. A general consensus among observers was that the social and religious underdogs and malcontents had swelled the ranks of Muslim converts in Bengal.

Islam was thought to have come "as a great deliverance to the persecuted Buddhists of Bengal," as "the Brahmins were persecuting the Buddhists in a worst [sic] form."[48] "Bad blood" between Hindus and Buddhists in Bengal "might conceivably have favoured conversion to Islam."[49] Some British officials regarded Bengal Buddhists as "already lukewarm" and "easily attracted from their old form of belief" to the "creed of Muhammad."[50]

The brahmanical persecution of Buddhists in the period of the latter's decline has been noted at all-India level. Bengal herself provided a few instances of this kind. Jāta-varman of the Varman dynasty was said to have burnt a portion of the

[47] Gait, *Census Report (1901)*, p. 169.

[48] Rahim, *Social and Cultural History*, vol. I, p. 70.

[49] R. C. Mitra, *The Decline of Buddhism in India* (Viśva-bhārati, 1954), p. 82.

[50] Gait, *Census Report (1901)*, p. 171.

Buddhist *vihār* at Sumpur.[51] In the concluding portion of the *Dāna-sāgara*, generally attributed to Vallāl-sen of the Sen dynasty in pre-Muslim Bengal, the king was represented as rising to uproot the *nāstiks* (atheists, implying the Buddhists) in the *kali* age. Buddhists were contemptuously mentioned as *pāṣandi* in middle Bengali literature. The height of hatred was reached in the *Chaitanya-bhāgavat*, where Nityānanda, a *vaiṣnav* disciple of Chaitanya, was portrayed as kicking Buddhists on the head.[52] In the *Śunya-purān* and in the *Dharma-pujā-vidhān*, the followers of Dharma were found to welcome the Muslim advance and later to rejoice at their oppression and humiliation of Hindus at Jājpur in Maldaha and other places.[53] Tārānāth, the noted Tibetan traveller, accused Buddhists of acting as agents and intermediaries of the Turkish invaders of Magadh.[54]

Despite a few sporadic references here and there to Hindu-Buddhist antipathy, the history of Bengal provides countless instances of a contrary nature, creating a general impression of harmony and understanding between them. The general corpus of Hindu and Buddhist literary, epigraphic, and archaeological sources of pre- and post-Islamic Bengal are redolent of a spirit of profound interaction and mutual reverence.[55] Buddhists had undoubtedly provided their share of the converted Muslim populace of Bengal, but an hypothesis of a total Buddhist estrangement as a backdrop to large-scale conversion from Buddhism is likely to remain highly dubious at the present stage of our knowledge.

[51] N. Rāy, *Bāngālir Itihās*. Ādi parva (Calcutta, reprint, 1949), p. 524.

[52] Vrindāvan-dās, *Chaitanya*, 1:6.

[53] Rāmāi Pandit, *Śunya-purān*, ed. by N. N. Basu (Calcutta, 1314 B.S./1907), p. 140.

[54] R. C. Mitra, *Decline of Buddhism*, p. 81.

[55] *Ibid.*, pp. 53-57, 61; *HB I*, pp. 200, 426; *BSI*, vol. I, pt. 1, p. 58; N. K. Bhattashali, *Iconography of Buddhists and Brahmanical Sculptures in the Dacca Museum* (Dacca, 1929), pp. 28, 206; N. Dāsgupta, *Bānglāy Bauddha-dharma* (Calcutta, 1948), p. 89; M. R. Chakravarti, *Descriptions of Birbhum* (Calcutta, 1916-1919), vol. II, pp. 67, 72, and plate 26.

As explanations for the attraction of non-Buddhist Bengali masses to Islam two arguments were generally proffered. One referred to the nebulous structure of the rather recently introduced Hinduism in the region, and the other underlined the social oppression and degradation inherent in the Hindu caste system.

In the Muslim dominant areas in Bengal, it is said, "the bulk of the inhabitants had not been fully Hinduized at the time of the Muhammadan conquest," and were "thus more easily brought under the influence of Islam."[56] The Muslim invasion "found Hinduism resting on weak and uncertain foundations" with "but a feeble hold over the minds and affections of the great bulk of the inhabitants."[57] On the other hand, "these huge masses" found themselves occupying "the position of serfs to a superior race" who had overcome them by "brute physical force" and in whose system "no social place could be found for them." They were "merely the hewers of wood and drawers of water for a set of masters" in whose eyes they were "unclean beasts and altogether abominable." The Muslim conquerors were not "altogether unwelcome" among these people because they "brought with them a religion and social system" under which "they might occupy a rival, if not equal, position to that of their late masters."[58] Islam attracted them not only because it "proclaimed the equality of all men" but also because it was "the religion of the race, keeping in subjection their former oppressors."[59] The convert to Islam "could not of course expect to rank with the higher classes of Muhammadans" but "he would escape from the degradation" which the caste system imposed on him. He would no longer be "scorned as a social leper; the mosque would be open to him; the Mulla would perform his religious ceremonies, and when he died he would be accorded

[56] Risley, *Imperial Gazetteer*, vol. I, p. 474.
[57] Beverley, *Census Report (1872)*, p. 133.
[58] *Ibid.*
[59] Wise, *Notes on the Races*, p. 5.

a decent burial."[60] The *brāhman* held out "no hopes of a future world to the most virtuous helot," while the *mullāh* "not only proffered assurances of felicity in this world, but of an indefeasible inheritance in the next."[61]

There is an element of contradiction in these two explanations. It is somewhat difficult to reconcile the idea of a weak and uncertain Hinduism, holding feeble command over the local populace, with that of the brutal oppression under a rigidly organized caste system. Besides, the interconnection between caste and conversion in the subcontinent, though indubitable, does not present itself in history as simply as many would have us believe. In its simplistic version the caste theory has to contend with some difficult questions. To begin with, the discriminatory and oppressive features of the caste system were, of course, not unique in Bengal, and hence cannot in itself have any special claim in the large conversions there. On the contrary, in some other areas of India in which the caste system operated with far greater rigidity and force, the Muslim share in the population was much lower than in Bengal. Besides, the relative laxity of the caste structure and the weakness of brāhmanism in pre-Muslim Bengal, as mentioned above by some observers, are well-acknowledged matters of Bengal history. Finally, the strong persistence, even through the present century, of caste values, practices, and organizations among considerable sections of the Muslim converts, especially those of the functional or occupational groups, is also likely to modify a simple view of the caste system as a factor in their transfer of religious affiliation. In the early nineteenth century Buchanan-Hamilton observed "a

[60] Gait, *Census Report (1901)*, pp.169-70; also cf. "The real cause of the spread of Islam in Bengal was its great inherent quality which fascinated the educated and enlightened Hindus and offered equality, justice and a status of respectability in society to the degraded and persecuted humanity." (Rahim, *Social and Cultural History*, vol. I, p. 70.)

[61] Wise, *Notes on the Races*, p. 6.

practical ascendancy" of the idea of caste over Muslims in parts of Bihar and Bengal.[62] By the end of the century and the beginning of the next, the situation appeared unchanged. In 1883, James Wise noted that the governing committees called *panchāyats* conducted affairs of individual Muslim occupational groups.[63] Similar councils of Muslim occupational groups were also recorded by the census of 1901. These were called differently in various districts, *pradhān* in Jessore, *mandal* in Murshidabad and 24-Parganas, and *mātbar* in Dacca. Those functional groups were also recorded "as strongly endogamous as the members of the Hindu castes."[64] In 1896, a Muslim observer of the phenomenon noted:

> Certainly Islam does not recognise class distinctions but places the whole humanity on one common platform of universal brotherhood . . . yet paradoxical though it may seem, people among Muhammadans do ask "so and so what caste is he?" . . . there are classes among the Muhammadan population who are divided according to their trade and calling. The Dhuniyas, the Jolahas and the Kunjras, the Darzis and many others, too numerous to mention, who have their own peculiar customs and are governed by their rules of "panchayats." . . . There are some classes who hold in great regard the custom of early marriage. Forced widowhood although prohibited by religion is rather the rule than the exception.[65]

A number of years later a non-Muslim observer of Islam in Bengal reiterated the same situation:

[62] M. Martin, *The History, Antiquities, Topography, and Statistics of Eastern India* (compiled from Buchanan MSS. in the East India House, 1807 to 1814) (London, 1838), vol. III, p. 150.

[63] *Notes on the Races*, pp. 32-35.

[64] Gait, *Census Report (1901)*, pp. 439-42.

[65] M.M.M. Khan, "Social Divisions in the Muhammadan Community," *The Calcutta Monthly*, I, no. 1 (July 1896), p. 3. Also M. A. Wali, "On the Origin of the Chaklai Mussalmans," *JASB*, LXVIII (1899), pt. 3, no. 1, in which the writer discussed the origin of a "segregated" and "polluted" Muslim group dealing in fish in the district of Jessore in eastern Bengal. See further Nur al-Husain Qāsimpuri, *Muslim Jāti-tatta* (Bogra, 1926); Muhammad Yāqub Ali, *Jāter Badāi* (Simuliya, 1926) and his *Musalmāner Jāti-bhed* (Chātuganj, 1927).

Caste prejudices have left their mark upon many. There are about thirty-five separate Moslem castes in Bengal. We use the term advisedly, for in some cases division is a clear differentiation of race, in others it means a kind of trade-guild with strong Hindu caste significance. In fact, in many instances functional groups have become so distinct that they will never intermarry, nor even dine together.[66]

And yet, in the light of much later, more extensive, and more substantial historical knowledge of the conversion process, the importance of the caste system must remain unchallenged. Highly useful historical insights into the process of conversion in Bengal, along with other regions in the subcontinent, may be derived from very much more well-documented conversion movements to Christianity and to other religions in the region in the nineteenth century and later. A broad appreciation of the important issues involved in these relatively recent conversion movements seems to be quite relevant to their medieval antecedents.

The most fundamental question about these conversions concerns the very nature and implication of the term "conversion" in the social, religious, and cultural contexts of the region. Conversion can be and has been seen in a spiritual sense of being a change of inner religious consciousness and experience, also in a social sense of "moving out of one community to another," or a "shifting of camps."[67] Conversion in this region has been noted as more meaningful in social terms than in spiritual. It scarcely involved an immediate spiritual experience and transformation, and meant "more a change of fellowship than conduct of inner life—although the latter may in time occur." The convert joined a new social group that largely defined its identity on the basis of the limit

[66] J. Talke, "Islam in Bengal," *The Muslim World* (London, New York), IV (1914), p. 12.

[67] G. A. Oddie (ed.), *Religion in South Asia. Religious Conversion and Revival Movements in South Asia in Medieval and Modern Times* (Manohar, 1977), p. 4.

on intermarriage, inter-dining, and also partly ritual observances.[68] The second significant issue relating to later conversions focuses on the close interlink between the caste structure and the conversion process. The Christian proselytizing experiences in the latter half of the nineteenth century showed how and why the trickle of conversions became a flood of mass movements into Christianity, especially its protestant missions. An analysis of the situation suggests that the missionary attitude to caste was the determinant. The egalitarian and individualistic notions of the protestant evangelists imbued them with a strong hostility to the institution of caste, which they regarded as integral to Hinduism and a hindrance to the mission. Converts were expected, therefore, to have a total break with their old social milieus. An added influence on the missionary policy was their firm belief in a downward filtration of the results of their mission. All this combined to result in only sporadic conversions at individual levels, dissensions in the church, and even reversion to Hinduism. In the latter half of the nineteenth century the large-scale mass movements in the ranks of the depressed groups clearly impressed upon the missionaries the usefulness of maintaining the traditional caste structure, retaining links between the converted and the non-converted members. The missionaries discovered to their amazement that "caste links could help rather than hinder evangelization."[69] Another significant feature of the later conversion movements, namely group rather than individual conversion, underlined the importance of the caste structure in relation to conversion. In a society where an individual counted very little outside his group, conversion inevitably tended to assume a collective form, especially among the occupational groups. The group converts were often found to preserve family and kinship ties, which not only

[68] P. Hardy, *The Muslims of British India* (Cambridge, 1972), p. 8.

[69] D. B. Forrester, "The Depressed Classes and Conversion to Christianity, 1860-1960," in G. A. Oddie, *Religion in South Asia*, p. 35.

provided much needed support and protection but were also extremely important for the purposes of marriage, commensality, and general social communication among them. The kinship ties further "provided natural avenues of communication and contact which were of considerable importance in the spread of the [conversion] movement."[70] The last but not the least significant aspect of the later conversion movements was that the depressed classes or the so-called untouchables offered the most productive source of conversion and re-conversion. In the second half of the nineteenth century, "Hardly a region of India did not have a mass movement of a depressed caste into Christianity . . . and there were similar contemporary movements into other faiths such as Islam, Sikhism, and the Arya Samaj brand of reformed Hinduism."[71] A degree of mobility within the Indian caste structure through the social and religious process of "sanskritization," involving changes in "customs, ritual, ideology, and way of life in the direction of a high, and frequently 'twice-born' caste," is now well recognized and understood.[72] For the depressed classes sanskritization remained, perhaps, the most accessible means to social improvement inasmuch as the other traditional options for social amelioration were rather limited for them. "Collective action" was negatived by their lack of "horizontal group solidarity" and "unusually fragmented character."[73] The traditional anti-caste protest, expressed in

[70] G. A. Oddie, "Christian Conversion among Non-Brahmans in Andhra Pradesh, with Special Reference to Anglican Missions and the Dornakal Diocese, c. 1900-1936" in *ibid.*, p. 83; also W. Garlington, "The Baha'i Faith in Malwa" in *ibid.*, p. 110; J.T.F. Jordens, "Reconversion to Hinduism, the Shuddhi of the Arya Samaj," in *ibid.*, pp. 153ff.

[71] Forrester, "Depressed Classes," p. 40.

[72] For a detailed analysis of the concept of "sanskritization" see M. N. Srinivas, *Social Change in Modern India* (Berkeley and Los Angeles, 1966), pp. 1-45; also his *Caste in Modern India and Other Essays* (Bombay, 1962), pp. 42-62; M. Singer, *When a Great Tradition Modernizes. An Anthropological Approach to Indian Civilization* (Delhi, 1972), *passim.*

[73] Forrester, "Depressed classes," p. 44.

medieval *bhakti* sectarian movements, was a more negative than positive step towards realizing the egalitarian aspiration of the groups. Even sanskritization for these depressed classes often appeared "a cul-de-sac" because of "concerted and efficacious rebuffs from the higher castes."[74] Moreover, sanskritization had been a fiercely competitive process, and one depressed group undergoing sanskritization impeded other comparable groups, driving the latter occasionally to non-Hindu channels.

The main features of Islamic conversion in Bengal would seem to correspond closely to the general pattern of conversion movement in the subcontinent. The earliest extant Bengali Muslim literary sources, as noted above, clearly reveal the existence of a mass of Muslim believers rather ill-grounded on and indifferent to Islamic tradition.[75] This is a good indication of initial conversion of the Bengali masses not in the sense of a "spiritual illumination," but in its usual subcontinental sense of socially "moving out from one community to another." In the course of the foregoing discussion we have noted further the weight of opinions in favor of the folk identity of the bulk of Muslim converts in Bengal.[76] Sporadic and scattered references to group conversions to Islam in Bengal and in various parts of India may be laboriously sifted from living popular local traditions and sundry other sources, as recorded in the district gazetteers, census reports, and other documents used by many writers such as Arnold, Titus, Dalton, Risley, and others.[77] The fact of mass conversions to Islam of socially unprivileged groups in Bengal is in clear

[74] *Ibid.*

[75] *Supra*, Introduction, note 7; see also *infra*, pp. 58, 68-70.

[76] *Supra*, pp. 21-30.

[77] T. W. Arnold, *The Preaching of Islam* (London, 3rd edn., 1935), *passim*; M. T. Titus, *Islam in India and Pakistan* (London, 1930; revised edn., Calcutta, 1959), pp. 41ff.; E. T. Dalton, *Descriptive Ethnology of the Tribes and Castes of Bengal* (Calcutta, 1872), p. 89 and *passim*; Risley, *Tribes and Castes*, *passim*.

accord with some general patterns of conversion in the region, and is also evidenced by limited information on the subject. The question of motivations underlying such conversions is, however, largely left to rational conjectures. There is no dearth of evidence relating to individual conversions, mostly confined to the more comfortable classes, as mentioned above.[78] The medieval Bengali genealogical literature and also some later family traditions refer to a number of Islamic conversions from upper castes, brought about by "ritual pollution" of the individuals concerned caused by accidental or deliberate infringements of commensal or marital rules and conduct. We have also cited above a few instances of conversion by religious persuasion.[79] Individual conversions were also known to have occurred because of prayers granted at the Muslim shrines or of the piety and thaumaturgic powers of the Muslim saints.[80] Material inducements were not less effective. The prospect of land settlement among cultivating groups on favorable terms, and the client's interest, under the *yajmāni* system, in the continued support of the converted patron by following his example remained a strong factor in rural conversions.[81]

Such isolated and individual conversions cannot, however, offer adequate explanation for the great preponderance of Muslims in Bengal, particularly in the rural areas. For this one has to turn to the phenomenon of mass conversion and its social context. In general terms the crucial significance of the need for and the limitation on social mobility among the unprivileged multitudes within the framework of sanskritization has been noted above.[82] The same situation underlined

[78] *Supra*, p. 23, note 16.

[79] *Ibid.*

[80] Titus, *Islam in India*, p. 48, 52-53; also Hardy, *Muslims of British India*, p. 10.

[81] Hardy, *ibid.*, pp. 10-11.

[82] *Supra*, pp. 40-41.

the importance of a social alternative in Islamization. Islamic conversion, in effect, brought little change in the social position of a particular group, as noted by several observers,[83] but as with later conversion movements, it is

> like a kind of group identity crisis, in which the group passes through a negative rejection of its lowly place in Hindu society to a positive affirmation of a new social and religious identity. This new identity does not depend on its acceptance and recognition by the higher castes; indeed, it has been chosen and is sustained despite their refusal to accept it. Only gradually does it lead to significant alterations in behaviour and occupation, and sometimes to a recognised enhancement of status.[84]

For a deeper and a clearer perception of the process of a mass movement to Islam in the region of the Bengal delta, one must set this problem in the context of the distinctive nature of the deltaic society and culture of Bengal.

The distribution of Muslim population in Bengal, with large concentrations, on one hand, in areas east of the Yamuna-Padma-Meghna line and the Meghna-Surma valley, forming a great embayment of lowland and comprising the vast areas of Mymemsingh, Dacca, and Sylhet districts, and, on the other, in the middle and lower regions of the Ganges delta proper extending over 24-Parganas, Khulna, Sundarban, Faridpur, Bakharganj, Barisal, and Noakhali, has been a significant feature of human geography of the land. The demographic particularity of these regions of deltaic Bengal consisted, as noted above,[85] in the clustering of certain predominant social groups, all occupying lower positions in the social hierarchy. The Hindu *māhiṣya*, *pod*, and *namaśudra*

[83] *Supra*, pp. 35-38.

[84] Forrester, "Depressed classes," p. 45; also J. W. Pickett, *Christian Mass Movements in India* (New York, 1933), pp. 128-29; G. A. Oddie, "Christian Conversion in Telugu Country, 1860-1900: A Case Study of One Protestant Movement in the Godavery-Krishna Delta," *Indian Economic and Social History Review*, XII, no. 1 (January-March 1975), pp. 76-77.

[85] *Supra*, pp. 25-26.

and the Muslim agriculturists and weavers, known locally as *sekh/shaikh*[86] and *julā/julāha*, respectively, constituted the overwhelming majority in these areas. The strong anthropometric correspondence between *namaśudra* and various Muslim groups has been noted above.[87] This demographic pattern fitted quite well into a significant pattern of physical changes known to have occurred in deltaic Bengal. In a deltaic region the premature decline and death of old rivers or the sudden rise and violence of new ones is rather natural. A deltaic river oscillates between its permanent banks, and while on one side there are extinct or moribund channels, on the other are active land-building ones. Delta-building consequently goes on indefinitely in this manner through the deterioration of old rivers and the emergence of new ones in tracts, which have yet to be built up and raised above the level of periodical inundations by the river system. The entire network of river-systems in Bengal has undergone great changes through the course of centuries, the most consistent and significant feature of which has been a gradual shift in the location of fertile soil from the moribund west of the delta to its mature and active eastern and southern parts.[88] This drew the aboriginal and pioneer agriculturists and settlers from the old fertile beds of the delta to the new ones. A large number of them were already pushed out of their original settlements by the later colonizers of higher culture. This appears to have been the case with the whole of the Gangetic Doab, where

[86] In all cases of alternative transliterations given, the first conforms to the original source or its actual local usage; the second is its literary and grammatical form.

[87] *Supra*, pp. 26-28.

[88] R. K. Mukerjee, *The Changing Face of Bengal—A Study in Riverine Economy* (Calcutta, 1938), pp. 4, 7-9. Cf. "From all this follows the well-known contrast between the decayed west, scarred with silted or stagnant bhils, the *disjecta membra* of dead rivers, and the active east. . . ." (O.H.K. Spate and A.T.A. Learmonth, *India and Pakistan: A General and Regional Geography* [London, 3rd edn., 1967], p. 574.)

the higher castes lived in contiguity throughout the Ganges Valley, while the unprivileged *bhar, pāsi, chāmār*, and *dosādh* of the upper plain lived in scattered clumps of houses on the brink of marshes and swamps, just like their *māhiṣya, pod, namaśudra*, and *shaikh* counterparts in the lower delta.[89]

The rainfall in the lower delta is between 60 and 95 inches, while in the rest of Bengal, excluding the northern submontane region, it is between 50 and 60 inches. The region along the Padma and the lower Meghna is backed by the Madhupur jungle, a much-dissected older alluvial terrace rising considerably above the general level. This interruption of the slope down to the sea, the ponding back of the local water by the main Ganges-Brahmaputra current, and the high rainfall combine to make the Meghna-Surma embayment perhaps the most amphibious part of Bengal during the rains. The lower tracts are flooded to a depth of 8-15 feet, and the homesteads are built on earth platforms 15-20 feet high.[90] As early as the time of the late Sen rulers the Madhyapādā Plate of Viśvarupsen mentioned a subdivision of Vanga (eastern Bengal) as *nāvya*, accessible by navigation.[91] This also is attested by some medieval sources. Abul Fazl, the court-historian of the Mughal emperor Akbar, saw rains begin in May and "continue for somewhat more than six months, the plains being under water and the mounds alone visible."[92] Slightly later Abd al-Latif, a Muslim traveller in this region observed: "For five or six months most of the land of this province [referring to Alaipur] remains under water, during which period one must use boats for the purposes of warfare, travelling or hunting."[93]

[89] Mukerjee, *ibid.*, pp. 19-23.

[90] Spate and Learmonth, *India and Pakistan*, pp. 575, 583.

[91] N. G. Majumdar, *Inscriptions of Bengal* (Rajshahi, 1929), vol. III, pp. 146, 194.

[92] Abul Fazl, *Āin*, vol. II, p. 132.

[93] Abd al-Latif, "Account," English translation by J. N. Sarkar in his "Journey to Bengal (in Persian)—1608-1609 by Abdul Latif," *Bengal Past and Present* (Calcutta), XXXV (April-June 1928), p. 144.

A more recent description in 1917 brings out the striking continuity in the situation: "In the height of the inundation no land is to be seen, and all travelling has to be done by boat. . . . Half a dozen huts are clustered together on a hillock a few yards square and the inhabitants cannot proceed beyond that hillock, whether to visit their neighbours or their fields . . . without wading, swimming, or travelling in or on something that can float. . . ."[94]

The area juxtaposed to the Bay of Bengal, including Bakharganj, Barisal, Noakhali, and extending round to Chittagong were precariously open to the constant threat of cyclonic catastrophies. The resultant economic dislocation and the indirect suffering could "hardly be estimated or exaggerated."[95]

In the most active part of the delta of the Ganges, Meghna, and Brahmaputra, comprising most of the eastern and southeastern Bengal, agriculturists, wood-cutters, fishermen, boatmen, and the like were thus pitted against a nature that was at once rich and bountiful, menacing and cruel. Pushed gradually by the influx of the new settlers and by the caprices of the rivers and the sea, they had to live and fight against a mighty array of adversaries—fierce floods, storms, brackish waters, crocodiles, snakes, and tigers. The experience of material existence in this environment was reflected in the religious beliefs characteristic of the region. It was no mere accident that the cult of the tiger-god, Dakṣin-rāy,[96] emerged and remained highly popular with the folk elements here. In the folk literature of this region, the goddess Gangā was represented as the presiding deity of the crocodiles.

In the course of time, the fertility of the mature and active deltaic regions and their gradual settlement through the stren-

[94] L.S.S. O'Malley, *Bengal, Bihar and Orissa, Sikkim* (Calcutta, 1917), pp. 8-9.

[95] Spate and Learmonth, *India and Pakistan*, p. 575.

[96] The term *dakṣin*, meaning "south," is rather significant in the geographical context.

uous efforts of the pioneering agriculturists drew representatives of the higher culture from the west. The excavation of Tamluk (ancient Tāmralipti) in the Medinipur district furnished evidence of a culture of a neolithic type, characterized by the use of polished stone axes, superseded by higher cultures from the Gangetic valley, with definite influences in pottery and terracottas.[97] The later influx of settlers in the new deltaic region resulted in "the world's highest records of rural density in certain areas in the districts of Dacca, Faridpur, Bakarganj, Tippera and Noakhali," as revealed in the early twentieth century.[98] With the gradual settlement of the region the social and cultural process of sanskritization emerged, to bring this region slowly under the ambit of the brahmanical culture. Attempts were made to superimpose brahmanical social and religious hierarchies, giving rise to a rather limited and loose *varna* social structure in the region, as noted before.[99] Simultaneously brahmanical or upper-caste attempts at assimilating folk cultures were made. This is already evidenced by the development of the cult of the tiger-god mentioned above,[100] which eventually made its way into the religion of the upper castes. One of the earliest writers on this cult to discover the tiger-god in a "plebeian" surrounding was an upper caste Hindu, Krịsnarām-dās, who received personal instruction from the god in a dream to popularize his cult.[101] A wide range of the medieval Bengali *mangal-kāvya* literature, focusing on malevolent and vindictive popular divinities, evinces clearly the vigor and tenacity with which some of the popular divinities fought for recognition from the upper castes.

[97] B. Subbarao, *The Personality of India* (Baroda, 2nd rev. edn., 1958), p. 44.

[98] R. K. Mukerjee, *Changing Face of Bengal*, pp. 61-62.

[99] *Supra*, pp. 35-36.

[100] *Supra*, p. 46.

[101] *HBL*, pp. 141-42.

Popular Bengali poetry represents these goddesses as desiring worship and feeling that they are slighted: they persecute those who ignore them, but shower blessings on their worshippers, even on the obdurate who are at last compelled to do them homage. The language of mythology could not describe more clearly the endeavours of a Plebeian cult to obtain recognition.[102]

The progress of sanskritization in the new deltaic region of Bengal was, however, rather restricted before and after the appearance of Islam on the scene, and seemed to have been affected by the changes in the courses of the rivers. It is of great consequence for subsequent developments in Bengal that the shifting of the centers of higher culture did not keep pace with that in the courses of the rivers from the moribund west to the active east. The western and northern parts of the delta have traditionally remained the seat of the hieratic brahmanical culture. Significantly enough, the first literary records mentioned the development of Vardhamānbhukti and Kankagrām between the Rajmahal hills and the Bhāgirathi (Hugli) and along the northern foothills or northern parts of Pundravardhan or Vārendra, and the early inscriptions referred to Mahāsthān on the banks of the Karatoya.[103] As Niharranjan Ray puts it:

> The strongest hold of this orthodoxy [brahmanical] was Bengal west of the Ganges at least up to the southern bank of the Ajay with its citadel presumably at Navadwipa. . . .
>
> The more east and north the country lay from the centre of Brahmanical orthodoxy lesser was, and even to-day is, its grip on the social organisation, which explains the more liberal sociological

[102] C. Eliot, *Hinduism and Buddhism. An Historical Sketch* (London, reprint, 1962), vol. II, p. 279. See also T. W. Clark, "Evolution of Hinduism in Medieval Bengali Literature: Śiva, Candi, Manasā," *Bulletin of the School of Oriental and African Studies* (London), XVII (1955), pt. 3, pp. 503-18; E. C. Dimock, Jr., "The Goddess of Snakes in Medieval Bengali Literature," *History of Religions*, I (1962), no. 2, pp. 307-21; P. K. Maity, *Historical Studies in Cult of the Goddess Manasā* (Calcutta, 1966), pp. 169-82.

[103] *HB I*, p. 3.

[social?] outlook of the upper grades of the society in Northern and Eastern Bengal and even in Lower or South Bengal.[104]

The entire drama of brahmanical revivalism and reorganization in medieval Bengal, led by Raghunāth-śiromani, Raghunandan, and others, was enacted almost exclusively in the regions of the old moribund delta. In the circumstances, the new deltaic society and culture retained in sharp contrast with the old deltaic region a considerable degree of nascency and fluidity.

There was another vital facet of life in the active part of the new delta. By the very nature of its physical particularities the region possessed strong attributes of a no man's land, comparable to a frontier society.[105] Its history down to the British period was largely marked by turbulence and rioting linked with the conditions of local geography. The inundation as it built new mud banks or destroyed old homesteads, tanks, orchards, and cultivated fields was the uncertain source of riches or poverty, and in this fluctuating environment he who risked most often gained most. This made the population full of daring and adventure, while the flood waters that destroyed all marks or boundaries between the fields were indirectly a constant source of social disorder.[106] The very nature of the lower delta precluded strong and organized administrative authorities. The British officials strongly underlined the problem of social order, and attributed it to the peculiar conditions of geography:

As soon as the river has receded the land is ripe for cultivation, and, if any delay occurs in transplanting into the liquid which the river has left, there is great danger that the river will rise again too soon for the crop to be harvested. The situation is conditioned

[104] N. Ray, "Medieval Bengali Culture—a Socio-Historical Interpretation," *The Visva-bharati Quarterly*, XI (May-July 1945), p. 47.

[105] R. W. Nicholas, "Vaiṣnavism and Islam in Rural Bengal," in D. Kopf (ed.), *Bengal Regional Identity* (Ann Arbor, 1969), p. 44.

[106] R. K. Mukerjee, *Changing Face of Bengal*, pp. 27-28.

entirely by the rapidity with which agricultural operations must begin on the land covered by water. It is this rapidity which makes determination of rival claims untenable before the cultivators have fought for the land.[107]

Taken together, the ferocity of nature and the anarchical conditions in the active delta, aggravated by the conditions of institutional inadequacies in social and cultural terms, focused on the dire need of some binding forces of authority, stability, and assurance in a largely unstable physical and social situation. The deified animistic spirits like the tiger-god, the serpent-goddess, and the crocodile-goddess found some psychological answers to the problems of the peasants, the woodcutters, the fishermen, and the boatmen of the delta, but fell short of offering counsel, guidance, decision, and authority, all so badly needed by them.

The specific demands of the new deltaic land offer some basic explanations of the great Muslim preponderance there. Islam penetrated into this region in the persons of a number of disparate Muslims who eminently succeeded in appropriating the particular roles required by the exigencies of the local frontier situations. They were covered by a general name of *pir*, which, in Bengal, embodied a far wider range of phenomena than is apparently suggested by the usual meaning and application of the term. *Pir*, a Persian word, and etymologically older, denotes "a spiritual director or guide" among Muslim mystics called *sufis*.[108] But the total range of phenomena covered by, and associated with, the nomenclature *pir* assumed in Bengal strikingly variegated forms. At the level of the Bengali Muslim folk the frame of reference to *pir* extended far beyond the range of the mystic guides, saints, and holy men, and this amorphous label came to cover a vast

[107] J. C. Jack (?), *First Report on the Survey and Settlement Operations in the Faridpur District, 1904-1914* (Calcutta, 1916), p. 56.

[108] J. Hastings (ed.), *Encyclopedia of Religion and Ethics* (Edinburgh, 1908-1926), vol. X, p. 40.

motley of popular objects of worship and supplication, not all of them being saints, or *sufis*, or religious personages, or Muslims, or even human beings. In this popular pantheon we are able to identify, besides saints and other religious personalities, apotheosized soldiers, pioneering settlers on reclaimed waste lands in deltaic Bengal, metamorphosed Hindu and Buddhist divinities, and anthropomorphized animistic spirits and beliefs.[109] The Bengali Muslim folk developed almost a cult and a pantheon of *pirs*, to whom they resorted in the trials and tribulations of their hard everyday life.

Pirs in Bengal were as ubiquitous as their numbers were legion. Their shrines were found in every nook and corner of Bengal, in desolate country lanes, in the fields and groves, in forests, and in the mountains. There were historical and legendary *pirs*, real and fictitious *pirs*, universal and local *pirs*, and old and contemporary ones. The process of popular canonization went on through the centuries. The veneration showed to them in life persisted with greater ardor after death, through visitation (*ziyārat*) to their shrines (called either *mazār* or *dargāh*). The visitation of shrines was, however, neither an uniquely Bengal nor even an Indian phenomenon. It was not also exclusively a folk monopoly. But the widely extended application of the term *pir*, as noted before, gave pirism in Bengal its distinction and context. All old and new popular objects of religious veneration and supplication were subjected to a process of folk religious transmutation that may be conceptualized as "pirification." An analysis of the religious-cultural process of pirification enables us to comprehend better the character of Islam in relation to the Muslim masses of Bengal and provides the most significant clue to the process of Islamization of the Bengali masses.

An analysis of the whole range of *pirs* known in Bengal down to the nineteenth century suggests a broad division into

[109] For further discussions on *pir* and pirism in Bengal, *infra*, Chapter 6, pp. 207-248.

one set of historical-legendary characters and another of totally fictitious and unreal elements, such as the pirified animistic spirits and Hindu-Buddhist popular deities, as noted before.[110] A more careful examination of the beliefs and traditions associated with a number of historical-legendary figures demands a further subdivision of this category into those who earned popular veneration primarily as religious preachers, or guides, or saints, and others who seemed to receive popular canonization for having performed as necessary but rather less spiritual or religious roles. The provision for the material and spiritual needs of the deltaic folk was a crucial element in the process of Islamic conversion as well as of pirification. The *avant-garde* of settlers in the deltaic frontier sought in the unstable conditions of the delta for some foci of order, authority, assurance, and faith, which were provided so successfully and gallantly by a number of Muslim adventurers and pioneering reclaimers of wastelands that the grateful people acknowledged their own debts by commending these benefactors for pirification.

Among *pirs* connected by tradition with comprehensive functions of this nature, the most well known was Khān Jahān Ali, also known as Khān Jahān Khān, whose tomb at Bāgerhāt in Khulna was one of a few most popular shrines in east Bengal.[111] At Ambarābād or Umarābād in Noakhali, there existed the shrine of Amber or Umar Shāh, who was believed to have lived in a boat to reclaim land northeast of Bhulua. His name came to be attached to the *pargana* of Ambarābād.[112] In the district of 24-Parganas Mubārak Ghāzi, popular as Mobrā Ghāzi, was a widely popular *pir*, who reclaimed the jungly tracts along the left bank of the river Hugli, and each village had an altar dedicated to him. No

[110] *Supra*, pp. 50-51; also *infra*, pp. 208ff.

[111] For an inscriptional reference to him, see A. H. Dani, "Bibliography of the Muslim Inscriptions of Bengal," no. 28, Appendix, *JASP*, II, 1957.

[112] *DGEBA, Noakhali*, p. 101.

one would enter the forest, and no crew would sail through the district, without first of all making offerings at one of the shrines. The *faqirs* "residing in these pestilential forests, claiming to be lineally descended from Ghazi," indicated with pieces of wood, called "sang," the exact limits within which the forest was to be cut.[113] Also, the Bengali folk literature, both Hindu and Muslim, underlined the wide popularity of a tradition involving Ghāzi, his close associate, and some elements of Hindu opposition. The Hindu *Rāy-mangal* literature depicts the conflict between Dakṣin-rāy, a local Hindu chief, and Ghāzi, assisted by Kālu, over the control of the active deltaic region of southern Bengal. An even battle, it was ended, we read, by a happy compromise based on territorial divisions dictated by God, appearing in a significant form, half Hindu and half Muslim.[114] The Muslim version of this tradition made Ghāzi and his closest associate, Kālu, arrive and land at Sundarban in south Bengal infested by tigers, snakes, and crocodiles. The tradition also associated them with the local wood-cutters, who owed their prosperity to the former.[115] It is significant that both Dakṣin-rāy and Ghāzi were, in their respective traditions, credited with command over tigers and crocodiles. Tradition associated three hundred and thirteen disciples with Shāh Jalāl of Sylhet, who worked and settled in widely scattered and remote parts of the region, containing shrines bearing the names of a large number among them.[116] Similar beliefs assigned twelve *pirs* to Taraf in the same region.[117] We are rather unfortunate in having no knowledge about the activities of these innumerable *pirs* who spread into the remotest corners of the new del-

[113] J. Wise, "Muhammadans of Bengal," p. 40.

[114] Kriṣnarām-dās, *Rāy-mangal*, ed. by S. N. Bhattāchārya (Bardhamān, 1956).

[115] Abd al-Karim, *Kālu-Ghāzi-Champāvati* (Calcutta, n.d.), pp. 10, 15-17.

[116] *JASP*, II, 1957, pp. 67ff.

[117] A. C. Chaudhuri, *Śrihatta*, vol. I, pt. 2, pp. 98-100.

taic areas. It is interesting to note, however, that at the turn of this century the wood-cutters, Hindu and Muslim, went in boats to certain localities in the forests called "gāis," each of which was presided by a *faqir*, and who had undoubtedly some knowledge of woodcraft. The wood-cutters worked six days in each week, for one day in the week was set apart for the worship of the sylvan deity presiding over that particular forest. The *faqir*, who was to have some personal knowledge of this supernatural personage, acted as high priest on these occasions.[118] Besides, if the beliefs associated with the particular *pirs* were any guide to their actual roles or to at least what was expected of them, most of these *pirs* were clearly identifiable in the social milieus of the new delta. Their names were invoked either as protective spirits against tigers, crocodiles, and snakes or in connection with agricultural needs. In the western and southern Bengal, especially in the Sundarban area, Mubārak or Mobrā Ghāzi[119] and Bada-khān Ghāzi or simply Ghāzi were extremely popular as possessing power over tigers. The same was believed about Sahija Bādshāh in the vicinity of the tiger-infested forest in the Pratāpgarh Pargana in Sylhet.[120] Ghāzi, mentioned earlier, his close associate Kālu, and even Khān Jahān Ali were all believed to have controlling authority over crocodiles. Shāh Kamāl with his *dargāh* in Sirājganj was renowned for his power over serpents.[121] At Astagrām in Mymensingh, no cultivator yoked cows to a plough without remembering Qutb Sāhib.[122] Mānikpir and Hājir-pir were also believed responsible for the protection of cattle.

There was another category of *pir*, whom we prefer to call

[118] *BDG. Khulna*, ed. by L.S.S. O'Malley (Calcutta, 1907), pp. 193-94.

[119] *BGD. 24-Parganas*, ed. by L.S.S. O'Malley (Calcutta, 1914), pp. 74-76.

[120] *ADG, Sylhet*, ed. by B. C. Allen (Calcutta, 1905), p. 83; A. C. Chaudhuri, *Śrihatta*, vol. I, pt. 1, p. 141.

[121] M. A. Siddiqi, *Sirājganjer Itihās* (Sirājganj, 1322 B.S./1915), p. 20.

[122] *BDG. Mymensingh*, ed. by F. A. Sachse (Calcutta, 1917), p. 38.

warrior-*pir* or martyr-*pir*. As implied in the characterization itself, tradition and other historical evidence would clearly identify them as attaining martyrdom[123] in battles against "infidel" local chiefs. An important *pir* of this category was Zafar Khān Ghāzi, mentioned in three inscriptions between A.D. 1297 and 1313 as a mighty conqueror and a "destroyer of the obdurate among infidels." Zafar Khān lost his life in action against a Hindu *rājā* of Hughli.[124] Shāh Ismāil Ghāzi, who was a military commander under a Bengal *sultān* (1459-1473), was another pirified soldier. He was known to have been beheaded by the *sultān*, who acted on the advice of a Hindu commandant that Shāh Ismail was in collusion with a Hindu *rājā*.[125] There were a few other martyr-*pirs* like Bābā Ādam Shahid of Rāmpāl in Dacca, Shāh Shafi al-Din of Chotapandua, and Shāh Anwār Quli Halwi of Phurphurā in Hughli, Tāj Khān of Hijli in Medinipur, Rāhā-pir of Mangalkot in Bardhamān (Burdwan), Turkān Shahid of Sherpur in Bagura, and Makhdum Shāh Daula Shahid of Shāhzādpur in Pabna.

In our assessment of the roles, on the other hand, of the essentially religious elements among *pirs*, the importance of two institutional innovations in the setting of rural Bengal, namely the *pir*'s hospice (*astānah* or *khānqah*) or his tomb (*dargāh* or *mazār*), placed in the care of his followers, cannot be overlooked. *Dargāhs* "have played and are playing today the most important part. It would not be an exaggeration to say that they are the nerve-centres of the Bengali Muslim society."[126] The ubiquity of *astānahs* and *dargāhs* in Bengal

[123] The titles *ghāzi* or *shahid*, meaning "martyr," often occurring in their names bear out this point.

[124] A. H. Dani, "Bibliography of Muslim Inscriptions," inscription nos. 6, 7, and 8.

[125] Pir Muhammad Shattāri, *Risālat al-Shuhda* (a biography of Shāh Ismāil), Eng. tr. by G. H. Damant in his "Notes on Shāh Ismāil Ghāzi," *JASB*, XLIII, no. 1, 1874, pp. 215ff.

[126] A. Karim, *Social History of the Muslims in Bengal*, p. 138.

appeared natural in the light of the following observation of a *sufi* of Jaunpur, Saiyid Ashrāf Jahāngir Simnāni early in the fifteenth century: ". . . what a good land is that of Bengal where numerous saints and ascetics came from many directions and made it their habitation and home . . . in the country of Bengal what to speak of the cities, there is no town and no village where holy saints did not come and settle down.[127] The significance of *pir*'s *astānah* and *dargāh* in terms of catering to the material and religious-emotional needs of the people in the neighborhood seeking such help seemed obvious in the nature of the circumstances. To the masses of the low castes and the untouchables, who were denied direct access either to a temple or to its *brāhman* priest in a society steeped in exaggerated notions of ritual pollution, the novelty of those twin Muslim institutions with open and total access was rather attractive. These were attracted not only towards the personal and religious charisma and thaumaturgic powers of a living *pir*, but also to such memories of a dead "saint," perpetuated in his shrine by his followers. In the case of a tomb in particular, it is interesting to speculate on the possible psychological impact of the Muslim practice of burying the dead and erecting tombs, in contrast with the Hindu-Buddhist practice of consigning the corpse to flames. It also seems likely that the more popular anti-caste yogico-tantric religious groups in medieval Bengal, committed to rather esoteric psycho-physiological exercises, were unable to respond to the needs for a simpler, more emotive and personal religion. Significantly enough, it was left for the great Bengali religious leader, Chaitanya, to sound later the sweeping, levelling, intensely personal and emotional call of his Bengal vaisnavism as an alternative. If the atmosphere of these institutions was emotionally congenial for the rural folk, no less attractive were

[127] Quoted by H. Askari, "New Light on Rājāh Ganesh and Sultan Ibrāhim Sharqi of Jaunpur from Contemporary Correspondence of Two Muslim Saints," *Bengal Past and Present*, LXVII (1948), pp. 32-39.

the capacity and willingness of those institutions to offer material comforts to the people. *Khānqahs* and *dargāhs* were often supported by large or small land grants. An inscriptional reference to a *pir* credited him with bestowing "advantages upon the poor and the indigent."[128] A Bengali folk-ballad that extolled the same virtues in a certain *pir* is rather unique in offering us an insight into the *modus operandi* of a *pir* in the rural setting and also into the folk perception of his religious and social roles:

A *pir* along with five disciples (*sākret/sagird*) appears on the village pasture-ground. The *pir* clears up the place underneath a banyan tree, builds a shrine (*dargā*), and lives there. He attains a wide renown and possesses immense power (*hekmat*). He cures all sickness by applying dust, does not let anybody tell his secret, for he himself [anticipates and] tells everything in detail, makes sweets (*mewā*) of clay, uttering charms (*mantra*), and distributes among children. All are struck by his miracles (*kerāmat*) and people come in hundreds to have a glimpse of him (*darśan mānase*). Everyone's desires get fulfilled, and his name spreads far and near. Rice, banana, and *sinni* [*shirni*] continue pouring in, and there is no end to the [gifts of] fowl, goat, and pigeon. But the *pir* does not take himself even a particle of the gifts and distributes all among the poor and the famished.[129]

[128] A. A. Khan, *Memoirs of Gaur and Pandua*, ed. by H. E. Stapleton (Calcutta, 1931), p. 115.

[129] "Kanka o Lilā" in D. C. Sen (ed.), *Purva-banga-gitikā* (Calcutta, 1923-1932), vol. I, pt. 2, p. 230.

2

The Emergence of the Bengali Muslim Cultural Mediators and the Syncretistic Tradition

The indigenous and low-class origin of the Muslim masses in Bengal, and the social and cultural considerations underlying the local conversions, as discussed in the preceding chapter, were vital factors in determining the character and patterns of Islamization in the region. These factors remained in the background of the situation revealed by the earliest Muslim Bengali literary sources. This literature is characterized by an anxiety to illumine the masses of Bengali Muslims, who were found ill-grounded in their religious tradition and steeped in pre-existing non-Muslim tradition.[1] The root of this problem lay, in the agreed opinion of these writers, in the Bengali Muslims' inability to follow the religious and other works in Arabic and Persian. Their attempt to make such books available in Bengali involved a stout defiance of the orthodox opposition to reducing the sublime religious truth, enshrined in Arabic and Persian, to a "profane" and "vulgar" local language.

There was, in fact, more than a simple conflict of religious attitudes involved in this issue. The emergent situation stemmed basically from a deep social dichotomy in the Muslim community in Bengal. There, as elsewhere in India on a more reduced scale, the community was composed of both immi-

[1] *Infra*, pp. 67ff.

grants and indigenous converts, occupying, respectively, the higher and the lower rungs of the social ladder. The two sections of the community in Bengal were noted even in modern times as "structurally alien" to each other.[2] The Bengal census of 1901 recorded two main social divisions among Muslims. *Ashrāf* (sing. *sharif*), meaning "noble" or "persons of high extraction," included "all undoubted descendants of foreigners and converts from the higher castes of Hindus. . . . All other Muhammadans including the functional groups . . . and all converts of lower rank, are collectively known by the contemptuous term 'Ajlaf' [or its Bengali corruption *ātraf*], 'wretches' or 'mean people.' "[3] A much earlier expression of the consciousness of distinction between them was found in an observation made by Ihtimām Khān, the Mughal admiral in Bengal during the viceroyalty of Islām Khān (A.D. 1608-1613). Displeased with an instance of unbecoming conduct on the part of the viceroy, the former remarked to his son, Mirzā Nathan: ". . . Islām Khān is behaving with us as he would behave with the natives. . . ."[4]

History, myth, and popular ignorance all contributed to the perpetuation of this ethnic cleavage between *ashrāf* and *ātraf*. Although Muhammad did not attack the distribution of property as he found it, he attacked the traditional foundation of the Arab hierarchy, deprecating noble ancestry as of no avail in the eyes of the Lord and stressing the equality of all believers within the fold of the new faith. Despite its egalitarianism Islam

> . . . strengthened the traditional aristocratic proclivities of the Arabs by providing a new and, to the Muslim, unimpeachable basis

[2] A.K.N. Karim, "The Modern Muslim Political Elite in Bengal," Ph.D. thesis (London University, 1964), p. 225; also his *Changing Society*, passim.

[3] E. A. Gait, *Census Report (1901)*, p. 439; see also R. Levy, *The Social Structure of Islam* (Cambridge, 1957), p. 68; Govt. of Pakistan, *East Pakistan*, p. 34.

[4] Mirzā Nathan, *Bahāristān*, vol. I, p. 51.

for social distinction, *the closeness to the prophet in blood and in faith.* [Italics mine.] There was added to the pagan nobility of descent, the *ashrāf*, nobles of the prophet's line, of his clan, of his tribe, the offspring of the Meccan companions of his migration, *muhajirun*, and his Medinese helpers, *ansār.*[5]

Beyond the confines of Arabia, Islam brought similar changes in the estimate of what constituted a claim to honor, so that relationship to the Prophet, however remote, demanded serious consideration.[6] The Muslim society of Bengal was no exception.

It is sociologically interesting that a sense of aristocracy was long attached even by Hindus of Bengal to immigrants from the west of the region. The social precedence of the members of a caste was often determined by their associations with the alleged five *brāhmans* and their entourage of other castes, said to have been brought by a king of Bengal from north India. Among Bengali Muslims, ancestry traceable to the west, to Arabia, Persia, Afghanistan, or Central Asia, broadly extending over the Muslim world of Arab and Ajam and sometimes even to northern India, was reckoned as *sharif* ancestry. The west is nearer to Arabia and therefore nearer to the Prophet and his religion. In the Muslim society of Bengal, according to a very recent survey of some Muslim aristocratic families in then East Pakistan, "Nobility was determined by immigration from the west in direct proportion to the nearness in point of time and distance in point of land of origin from Bengal to [sic] Arabia."[7] In reference to some aristocratic families in Dacca included in the same survey it is noted that "all the families claim foreign ancestry and their ancestors were said in most cases to have come into Bengal from Delhi

[5] G. E. Gruenbaum, *Medieval Islam: A Study in Cultural Orientation* (Chicago, 1946), p. 199.

[6] Levy, *Social Structure of Islam*, p. 68.

[7] A. M. Khan, "Research about Muslim Aristocracy in East Pakistan. An Introduction," in P. Bessaignet (ed.), *Social Research in East Pakistan*, Appendix, p. 22.

obviously with the ruling class. Instances of direct immigration from the Persian Gulf areas are also not wanting."[8] A similar report from a neighboring district came a few years earlier in 1956:

I have got report from Barisal that generally six Muslim families are regarded as the most sharif or khandan families in the district of Barisal. Of these six Muslim feudal sharif families of Barisal, two families lay distinct claim to foreign ancestry and people also regard them as such. It is claimed that the ancestors of one of these two families came to Barisal from somewhere outside Bengal (in Bengal if somebody comes from outside Bengal, i.e. from the northern India, that is thought to be a sufficient claim to foreign ancestry; and if it is from Arabia, Persia, Afghanistan or Central Asia, it is all the better). It is claimed that the ancestor of the other family came from Medina, Arabia. Because of such a distinct claim to foreign ancestry of the above two feudal families, they are regarded as the most sharif in comparison to the rest.[9]

The place of highest honor traditionally occupied by *saiyids*, related to the Prophet by blood, is clearly borne out by epigraphic and literary sources.[10]

The obvious social importance attached to foreign extraction gave rise to a natural tendency to claim fictitious foreign ancestry by aspirants to social position: ". . . the honour and respect paid to the foreign ruling and privileged classes gave to the foreign and non-Indian extraction of a Muslim the highest claims to social distinction. People began to *discover* [italics mine] for themselves as far as possible a foreign an-

[8] *Ibid.*, p. 28.

[9] Karim, *Changing Society*, p. 134.

[10] See A. H. Dani, "Bibliography of Muslim Inscriptions," inscription nos. 75, 78, 81, 83, 85, 116, 121, 137-38; Saiyid Alāwal, *Sapta Paikar* (DMS 647: sl 499); fol. 8; Mirzā Nathan, *Bahāristān*, vol. I, Introduction, xxiii; C. Stewart, *History of Bengal*, pp. 176, 381; Ghulām Husain Salim, *Riyāz al-Salātin*, Eng. tr. by Maulavi A. Salam (Calcutta, 1902), p. 285; Ghulām Husain Tabatabāi, *Siyar al-Mutaākhirin*, Eng. tr. by Hāji Mustafa (Calcutta, 1926), vol. II, pp. 166-85; *MBS*, p. 170.

cestry."[11] The late-nineteenth-century census records provide a direct insight into this protean process of seeking social ameliorations through ethnic discoveries. In 1872 the total claimants of foreign origin for the whole of Bengal, including Purnia and excluding Calcutta, was 266,378 (of whom 232,189 were *shaikhs*, 23,126 *pathāns*, 9,858 *saiyids*, and 2,205 *mughals*) against a total Muslim population of 17,609,135, while by 1901 over 19.5 million, out of a total Muslim population of over 21.5 million in Bengal proper (excluding Sylhet and Cachar), were returned as *shaikhs*. In the district of Noakhali alone, there were then 862,290 aliens distributed as 819,290 *shaikh*, 1,300 *saiyid* and 1,000 *pathān* in a total Muslim population of 865,709.[12] The social oddity and distortion inherent in the situation could not have failed to become targets of social satires. A Persian couplet gave air to such social concerns: "The first year we were butchers, the next Shaikhs: this year, if prices fall, we shall become Saiyads."[13] The Bengalis voiced their own: "What is only *ullā* or *tullā* in the beginning, becomes *uddin* later on; then, if the tide of fortune turns, *māmud* in the end of the name comes at its beginning."[14] The name alterations suggested in the saying were best illustrated by the successive changes of the name of a hypothetical Mehr Allāh, who had first become Mehr-Uddin (al-Din), then Mehr-Uddin Muhammad, and, finally, Muhammad Mehr-Uddin. This particular pattern of social mobility was also facilitated by the fact that the claim to foreign extraction was often buttressed by other usual concomitants of nobility such as wealth, land-control, or feudal status.[15] Conversely, this might explain the paradox recorded

[11] K. M. Ashraf, *Life and Conditions of the People of Hindustan* (New Delhi, 2nd edn., 1970), p. 107.

[12] Gait, *Census Report (1901)*, pp. 170ff.

[13] Quoted by E.A.H. Blunt, *The Caste System of Northern India* (London, 1931), p. 184.

[14] Gait, *Census Report (1901)*, pp. 172-73.

[15] A.K.N. Karim, *Changing Society*, p. 132; Levy, *Social Structure of Islam*, p. 68.

by the census officials that "in some places many of the Mughuls and Pathans are regarded as Ajlaf (commoner)."[16] Thus an amalgam of fact and fiction reinforced by material power provided the framework for upper class Muslim social exclusiveness.

The social hiatus was rendered less negotiable by the massive cultural barrier placed between them. Those who claimed alien lineage derived cultural sustenance from the same direction. For people with undoubted alien ancestry, even intervening centuries of naturalization often failed to mellow the intensity of their emotional and cultural attachment to the west. The extra-territorial *ashrāf* cultural ethos was clearly observed in a section of the Muslim community in Bengal even in the nineteenth and the twentieth centuries. Saiyid Amir Ali, the distinguished Muslim leader in Bengal, compared the Mahomedans of Northern India, descending "chiefly from the Mahomedan settlers from the West who had brought with them to India traditions of civilization and enlightenment," to the Muslims of Eastern Bengal, who were "chiefly converts from Hinduism" and "still observe[d] many Hindu customs and institutions."[17] Referring to the "genuine Ashraf descendants of Arab . . . or Ajam . . . who have not hitherto contracted marriages . . . with any other class," Maulawi A. Wali, a late-nineteenth-century Bengali Muslim scholar with marked *sharif* leanings, remarks:

> If any ancient culture and civilization are to be sought among the Musalmans, they should certainly be sought among the members of this class. The other classes may become very prosperous, but such higher qualities as uprightness, independence, honesty, and implicit reliance on God (Islam) can hardly be expected from them, and must be sought among the members of the genuine Arab families. . . . As no Brahman concerns himself about the controversies between Baidyas and Kayasthas, so no Ashraf Muhammadan of India cares what the majority of the Muslims are called. To them they are wine-vendors, weavers etc., with all their pretensions. Some

[16] Gait, *Census Report (1901)*, p. 439.

[17] *The Moslem Chronicle* (Calcutta), January 28, 1905, p. 193.

of the writers go so far as to say that they are not truly Musalmans, but for political and other reasons it is well that they should be called Muslims.

Wali also found both "high and low" calling themselves *ashrāf* on account of their foreign origin. But, according to him, the offspring of those among the *ashrāf*, who "contracted marriages contrary to the law of *Kufv* with Indian converts," were "looked down upon by the blue-blooded Ashraf in the same way as the Europeans of our day look upon the Eurasians and Firingis."[18] The Bengali Muslim press in the late nineteenth and the early twentieth centuries often expressed concern at "the sense of Brahmanism among high-born Muslims," who were given to "social exclusiveness" and "cultural and educational monopoly" and were also gripped by the "fear" that the commoners "might aspire after the aristocratic status."[19] In parts of Murshidabad, Birbhum and Bardhaman the commoners were regarded by the "high-born" as "even less than dogs and jackals."[20] The alien cultural self-perception of the *ashrāf* that indulged in "dreaming of Baghdad, Bokhara, Kabul, Qandahar, Iran, and Turan, while sleeping in . . . the huts amidst the mango groves and bamboo forests of Sylhet in Bengal" was held up to ridicule.[21]

[18] M. A. Wali, "Ethnographical Notes on the Muhammadan Castes of Bengal," *Journal of the Anthropological Society of Bombay*, VII, no. 2 (1904), pp. 98-113.

[19] Muhammad Maiz al-Rahmān, "Samāj-chitra," *Al-Islām* (Calcutta), V, no. 5 (*Bhādra*, 1326 B.S./1919); see also Editor, "Samāj-kālimā," *Islām Prachārak* (Calcutta), II, no. 2 (*Jyaiṣtha*, 1299 B.S./1892); Saiyid Imdād Ali, "Ashrāf-Ātraf," *Saogāt* (Calcutta), VII, no. 5 (*Pauṣ*, 1336 B.S./1929); Maulawi Shafi al-Din Ahmad, "Ābhijātya gaurav (Ashrāf-Ātraf)," *Sāmya-vādi* (Calcutta), I, no. 1, 1329 B.S./1922. See also M. N. Islam, *Bengali Muslim Public Opinion as Reflected in the Bengali Press 1901-1930* (Dacca, 1973), pp. 248-52.

[20] Manir al-Jamān Islāmābādi, "Samāj-samskār," *Al-Islām*, V, no. 8 (*Agrahāyan*, 1326 B.S./1919).

[21] Abd al-Mālik Chaudhuri, "Banga-sāhitye Śrihatter Musalmān," *Al-Islām*, II, no. 6 (*Āśvin*, 1323 B.S./1916); also Hamid Ali, "Uttar Banger Musalmān sāhitya," *Bāsanā* (Rangpur), II, no. 1 (*Baiśākh*, 1316 B.S./1909).

The exaggerated importance attached to alien origin so permeated Bengali Muslim society that Muslims in Bengal fell logical victims to their own myth, claiming for themselves an alien culture, if not origin, and being so regarded by all others.[22] In 1896 Yaqinuddin Ahmed noted:

> In Calcutta the Hindus are called Bengalees by every Mahomedan who has never travelled beyond the Mahratta Ditch [built to protect the city against Maratha incursions in the eighteenth century], as if such Mahomedans, by the fact of their professing the faith of the Great Arabian Prophet have a right to be non-Bengalees.[23]

In many parts of Bengal, rural and urban, a Hindu was, and perhaps even now is, a "Bengali" and a Muslim simply a "Musalmān." The predominantly Hindu locality was often called a *Bāngāli-pādā* (the Bengali quarter), and the predominantly Muslim quarter was simply a *Musalmān-pādā*.[24]

A natural concomitant of foreign lineage was the religious-cultural dimension of *ashrāf-ātraf* social polarity,[25] and a basic component of *ashrāf*'s alien cultural orientation was their contemptuous disregard for and hostility to the local Bengali language in favor of Arabic, Persian, and later, the composite language of Urdu. William Adam's Education Reports in the 1830s focussed on this issue.[26] William Hunter referred in 1871 to Bengali language "which the educated Muhammadans despise. . . ."[27] In 1873 Niam al-Din spoke of "the

[22] For both Muslim and Hindu assumptions, see A. Hayat, *Mussalmans of Bengal* (Calcutta, 1966), p. 97.

[23] *The Moslem Chronicle*, 11 April 1896, p. 164.

[24] A. M. Khan, "Research about Muslim aristocracy," p. 25.

[25] The common man's perception of the *ashrāf* as setting the religious-cultural norms of Islamic life in a local context is attested by an empirical study covering the Bengali Muslim society as recently as 1968. See A. Mia, "Influence of Urban Technological Development on Common Man's Islam in Pakistan." Ph.D. thesis, Case Western Reserve University, 1968, pp. 48-49.

[26] W. Adam, *Reports on the State of Education, Third Report* (1838), pp. 149, 213-14.

[27] W. W. Hunter, *The Indian Mussalmans* (Calcutta, reprinted from the 3rd ed. of 1876, 1945), p. 178.

accomplished men" in Bengal who did not take themselves to the Bengali books and did not "like their children to read them." The Bengali books were, in fact, forbidden by many.[28] A little later James Wise observed: "The Arabic and Persian classics, containing as he [a *sharif*] thinks all that is worth knowing, are his daily study . . . while English and Bengali are foreign languages to him."[29] Syed Amir Ali, a *sharif* himself, noted of the upper-class Muslims in Bengal that they "speak Urdoo, though not with the same purity as a native of Lucknow or Delhi."[30] According to Yaqinuddin Ahmed, ". . . hitherto the Muhammadans of Bengal had leaders who tried their utmost to belong to the North-West. They talked Hindustani, imitated Delhi and Lucknow manners, but in spite of that they were Bengalees."[31] The Bengali Muslim press even as late as 1930 made reference to the alien cultural outlook of the *ashrāf* in Bengal: "Though being raised in the lap of Bengal for many centuries and though they have heard Bengali from the lips of their mothers for ages the Bengali Muslims have not still learnt to love the Bengali language. The language and the country both still seem foreign to them. . . ."[32]

In 1927 a Bengali Muslim spoke of "many" co-religionists who were "ashamed and humiliated to recognize Bengali as their mother-tongue" in apprehension of undermining their prospects for the aristocratic status. He also amused himself with the notional exigency of 25 million Muslims in Bengal

[28] Muhammad Niam al-Din, *Zubdat al-Masāil* (Calcutta, 1873), vol. I, Introduction.

[29] "Muhammadans of Bengal," p. 62.

[30] Quoted in the *Nineteenth Century* (London), XII (1888), p. 200.

[31] *The Moslem Chronicle*, 11 April 1896, p. 165.

[32] Abd al-Majid, "Bānglā-bhāṣā o Musalmān," *Moyājjin* (Calcutta), II, nos. 9-10 (*Āṣādh-Śrāvan*, 1337 B.S./1930); see also Editor, "Nur al-Imāner āpil,"*Nur al-Imān* (Calcutta), I, no. 3 (1307 B.S./1900); Hamid Ali, "Musalmān sāhitya." Khadim al-Islām Bangabāsi, "Bāngālir mātri-bhāṣā," *Al-Islām*, I, *Kārtik*, 1322 B.S./1915), no. 7.

emigrating in search of a land where Bengali was not to be found and where *sharif* status was consequently assured.[33] There was further reference to the religious decree, *fatwā*, issued by the Muslim divines castigating Bengali as the "language of Hindus," and also to the prevailing prejudice against the holy books, like the *Qurān* and the *hadith*, being translated to Bengali as well as against any Islamic matter being discussed in this language.[34]

It was not so much a question of *ashrāf* ignorance of Bengali, as of their attitude towards it as a vehicle of their own religion and culture. It may seem unlikely that the bulk of the descendants of the Muslim immigrants in Bengal, leaving aside the entire body of the successful local contenders for the aristocracy, were ignorant of the local language. Ma-huan, a Chinese traveller in Bengal in the beginning of the fifteenth century, who moved closely in the official and ruling circles, observed: "The language in universal use is Pang-Kie-Li (Bengali); there are also those who speak in Pa-enl-si (Farsi-Persian)."[35] In addition, some of the Muslim *sultāns* and other members of the Muslim ruling class in pre-British Bengal were credited with patronizing Bengali literature.[36] Significantly enough, their patronage was confined to the Hindu writers on Hindu religious themes. The attitudes of the *ashrāf* were marked by a total rejection of the local language as their own religious-cultural medium. The pioneering Muslim Bengali writers on Islamic tradition came up against these deep-seated and dominant *ashrāf* prejudices and values, and

[33] Tasaddak Ahmad, "Sabhā-patir abhibhāṣan," *Śikhā* (Dacca), I (*Chaitra*, 1333 B.S./1926).

[34] Abd al-Malik Chaudhuri, "Śrihatter Musalmān."

[35] Ma-huan, "Account of the Kingdom of Bengala," English tr. by G. Phillips in *JRAS*, article no. xiv, 1895, p. 530.

[36] *BSI*, vol. I, pt. 1, pp. 103, 128, 252-57; *HBL*, pp. 80-81; also S. Sen, *Madhyayuger Bānglā*, pp. 16-17; *HBLL*, p. 12; also D. C. Sen, *Banga Bhāṣā o Sāhitya* (Calcutta, 8th ed., 1949), pp. 138, 152-54; *MBS*, pp. 36-38; Tarafdar, *Husain Shāhi Bengal*, pp. 249-51.

left traces in their manuscripts of tensions, both internal and external. Shāh Muhammad Saghir fought against his feeling of "sin, fear, and shame" associated with his literary venture in Bengali on an Islamic tradition. He spoke of the apprehension and blame associated with an attempt at writing religious books in Bengali.[37] Another prolific *pir*-writer of great standing among his followers and also among the following generations, Saiyid Sultān, who showed remarkable concern for the helpless people "born in Bengal and unable to follow Arabic," found himself "blamed," for having composed his *magnum opus* in Bengali, *Nabi-vamśa*, or the Line of the Prophets, a history of the creation and of the prophets from Adam to Muhammad. For his critics the attempt amounted to making the book "Hinduized."[38] Shaikh Muttalib, who wrote on Muslim religious laws, *fiqh*, found difficulty in getting over his sense of "sin" for having rendered "Islamic religious matters into Bengali."[39] Abd al-Nabi, who spoke of the "mental anguish of the people, unable to follow the story of Amir Hamza in Persian," was also rather "apprehensive about incurring the wrath of the lord" for having rendered "Islamic matters into Bengali."[40] Shaikh Parān, father of Shaikh Muttalib and a contemporary of Saiyid Sultān, composed, "for the people to follow in Bengali," his work on one hundred and thirty Islamic mandatory observances, *farz*, "on the basis of a Persian work."[41] Another contemporary of Saiyid Sultān

[37] *Yusuf-Zulaikha*, quoted in *MBS*, p. 58.

[38] *Shab-i Mirāj* (DMS 433: sl 490), fol. 259; also *MBS*, p. 161. The ms. used by me does not support M. E. Haq's rendering, accepted by all, that Saiyid Sultān was stigmatized a "hypocrite" (*monāfek/munāfiq*) by his critics. Instead of "I am called a monafek . . ." (*monāfek bale more . . .*), as Haq reads it, I have "the monāfek calls me . . ." (*monafeke bale more . . .*).

[39] *Kifāyat al-Musalli* (DMS 578: sl 69), fol. 102; also quoted in *DCBM*, p. 61, and *MBS*, p. 198.

[40] *Hamza-Vijay*, quoted in *DCBM*, p. 3, and *MBS*, pp. 214-15.

[41] Quoted in *MBS*, p. 163. Our MS. attributed to him (DMS 193: sl 94) is without a title. This has been introduced as *Kaidāni Kitāb* or a Book on Islamic Observances in *DCBM* (p. 80) and as *Nasihat Nāma* in *MBS* (pp. 163-64).

and Shaikh Parān, Hāji Muhammad, alluded to the contemptuous attitude of some sections of Muslims towards Bengali language.[42]

The potent and rather disturbing consequences of the situation arising essentially from the linguistic cleavage, namely the inability of Bengali Muslims to follow books in Arabic and Persian, the resultant problems concerning appreciation of their own religious and cultural traditions, and their ultimate reliance on pre-existing non-Muslim Bengali traditions were clearly brought out in the early Muslim Bengali writings. There was "no dearth of *kitābs* in Arabic and Persian" which were "for the learned alone, and not for the ignorant folk." The latter in the circumstances were "unable to grasp a single precept of their religion" and remained "immersed in stories and fictions." "In every house the Hindus and Muslims" took themselves "with avid interest" to the Hindu epic, the *Mahābhārat*, rendered into Bengali by Kavindra-parameśvar in the second quarter of the sixteenth century, and "no body [thought] about *Khodā* and *Rasul*."[43] The appeal of the other Hindu epic, *Rāmāyan*, to Bengali Muslims was attested by Vrindāvan-dās in the middle of the sixteenth century: the story of Rām was heard "respectfully even by *yavans* [Muslims]" and they were "in tears to hear about the predicament of Śri Raghunandan [Rām] at the loss of Sitā [Rām's wife]."[44] The picture of the Bengali Muslims, wallowing in "sinful activities," due to lack of adequate knowledge of Islam contained in non-Bengali *kitābs*, emerges very clearly and consistently in these early Muslim writings in Bengali.[45] One of the later writers in the eighteenth century,

[42] *Nur Jamāl* (DMS 374: sl 260), fol. 2 mc.

[43] Saiyid Sultān, *Nabi-vamśa*, quoted in *MBS*, pp. 142, 161.

[44] Vrindāvan-dās, *Chaitanya-bhāgavat*, quoted in S. Sen, *Madhyayuger Bānglā*, p. 48.

[45] Hāji Muhammad, *Nur Jamāl*, fol. 2 mc; Khwandkār Nasr Allāh Khān, *Musār Suwāl* (DMS 68: sl 338), fol. 2 mc; Muhammad Khān, *Maqtal Husain*, quoted in *MBS*, p. 190; Shaikh Muttalib, *Kifāyat*, fol. 7a; Abd al-Hakim, *Shihāb al-Din Nāma* (DMS 406: sl 246), fol. 77b; Saiyid Alāwal,

Hayāt Mahmud, wrote in reference to his native village Biśilā in the Ghorāghāt region in north Bengal, where his "forefathers were settled from a long time":

It pains me day and night to see that none knows much about religious commandments in my village. They do not grasp the truth of the religion (*din*) and have no knowledge of the *Qurān*, the *kitābs* and other provisions for guidance in all situations. With this daily experience, I have set upon myself to write the message of *din* in the name of Allāh.[46]

The social-cultural polarity between the *ashrāf* and the *ātraf* and its consequences as delineated above merely surfaced a deeper fissure in the cultural continuum of Bengal. The cultural tradition in pre-Islamic Bengal may be clearly conceptualized in terms of "great" and "little" traditions. "High" Hinduism or "Sanskritic" Hinduism, alongside the popular yogico-tantric *nāth*, *dharma*, and *sahajiyā* cults, in addition to hosts of other popular objects of veneration and supplication, constituted the religious scenario. The perpetual contact and the fundamental continuity between the great and the little traditions, stemming from the primary and indigenous nature of the cultures, presented a marked and significant contrast to the nature of Islamic contact with Bengal. The intrusive and exogenous character of orthodox *sunni* Islam in the cultural milieu of Bengal forced a breach in the cultural continuum of the great and the little traditions, of the gentry and the peasantry, and of the town and the village—a breach that was further widened by the *ashrāf*'s social and cultural exclusiveness, fortified by the linguistic apartheid. The perpetuation of the total absence of cultural contact and communication between these two major segments of the Muslim community posed ultimately a serious threat to the entire religious structure and organization of the community in Bengal. The sit-

Saif al-Muluk-Badi al-Jamāl, quoted in A. Sharif (ed.), *Tuhfa* by Saiyid Alāwal, p. 62; Muzammil, *Niti-śāstra*, pp. 5-6.

[46] Hayāt Mahmud, *Hitajnān*, p. 7 (text); see also his *Sarva-bhed*, p. 3 (text).

uation, left alone, might eventually result in a totally unbridgeable gap between the two, in a potentially dangerous isolation of the great mass of the community, and in a possible re-absorption of this differentiated and isolated majority into the amorphous sponge-like body of Hinduism. The danger inherent in the situation was poignantly echoed much later in the soul-searchings of a nineteenth-century *sharif*. Worried about the future of the Muhammadans of Bengal, he confessed:

> The refusal or inability of the higher Mosalmans to adopt the Bengali has greatly affected the relation between them and the lower Mosalmans. We do not learn the Bengali—whilst our lower orders cannot learn the Persian, cannot learn even the Hindustani. There are thus no means of fellow-feeling or of acting together. The knowledge we possess does not reach down to our lower neighbors—our character, ideas and habits of thought do not affect them.[47]

The break of cultural continuity between the great and little traditions, or between the elite and the folk traditions of Islam in Bengal, called for urgent action and mediation to revive cultural dynamism through interpenetration and cross-fertilization of ideas between them. In "the social organization of tradition," Robert Redfield identified the distinct role of the "cultural specialists devoted to mediating between Great Tradition and Little."[48] Milton Singer, in his analysis of the structure of Hindu tradition, focussed on the leading personalities who, "by their identification with the great tradition and with the masses," were in a position to "mediate the one to the other."[49] The sixteenth and the seventeenth centuries

[47] "Saeed," *The Future of the Muhammadans of Bengal* (Calcutta, 1880), quoted, *The Calcutta Review*, LXXII (1881), pt. 2, no. 7, vii.

[48] R. Redfield, "The Social Organization of Tradition," *The Far Eastern Quarterly*, XV, no. 1, (1955), p. 15.

[49] M. Singer, "The Cultural Patterns of Indian Civilization," *The Far Eastern Quarterly*, *ibid.*, p. 24. Cf. Arnold Toynbee's concept of the "cultural broker" in the intelligentsia that emerges "to solve the problem of adopting its life to the rhythm of an exotic civilization to which it has been forcibly annexed or freely converted." ("Disintegrations of Civilizations," pp. 154-58.) For an

in Bengal saw the emergence of a number of Muslim cultural mediators engaged, consciously or unconsciously, in the great task of mediating Islam to the masses of its Bengali believers. To these mediators Bengali Muslims owed not only their earliest literature in Bengali but a very rich legacy of highly creative and varied syncretistic tradition as well.

The social background of the mediators is a significant question that remains, regrettably enough, rather obscured by the paucity of adequate information. A few broad observations are, however, warranted. The mediators comprised both the descendants of immigrant families and those of indigenous converts. Despite the dominant social process of "ashrāfization" and the resultant tendency towards discovering and fabricating foreign ancestry, as noted above, there is no reason for regarding them all as of spurious origin. There were quite a few *saiyids* among these writers, such as Mir Saiyid Sultān and his grandson, Mir Muhammad Shafi, Saiyid Alāwal, Saiyid Murtaza, Saiyid Hamza, Saiyid Nur al-Din, Saiyid Muhammad Akbar, and also some Afghans such as Daulat Wazir Bahrām Khān, Muhammad Nawāzish Khān, Nasr al-Allāh Khān, Muhammad Khān, and Sābirid (Shāh Barid?) Khān. Also, there were a very large number of them bearing the doubtful title of *shaikh*, a few of whom at least could well have been of foreign origin. The mediators with foreign ancestry, however, stood apart from the *ashrāf* partly because of their lack of the economic power base of this class in the land, and largely for the reason of their effective alienation from the exclusivist cultural outlook of the same class. Apart from their pioneering role in the matter of Bengali language, the Muslim Bengali mediators revealed a strong sense of re-

---

illuminating discussion of this historical phenomenon, with particular reference to Modern Bengal and its "cultural intermediaries between the foreigner and their own people," see D. Kopf, *British Orientalism and Bengal Resistance*, pp. 1-2, 279.

gional affiliation and attachment in their writings. To Saiyid Sultān "mother land" was "holy" and the "very thought" of her was "heart-rending."[50] Muhammad Muqim compared his place, Chattagrām (Chittagong) to "heaven."[51] Daulat Wazir Bahrām Khān considered Bengal itself as "enchanting," while his own town Fatehābād was an added "embellishment," the "sight" of which brought a sense of "fulfilment."[52]

In professional terms many of the mediators were popular religious preceptors and guides introduced as *pirs* by themselves or by their disciples, while some held offices, secular or religious, largely under the local authorities. In the first category we include Afzal Ali, a resident of the village of Miluyā in the district of Chattagram, who was a *pir* himself, also being the son of a *pir*, Bhangu Faqir, and a disciple of a *pir*, Shāh Rustam. Afzal Ali appears to have been a contemporary of Alā al-Din Firuz Shāh (A.D. 1532-1533), son of Sultān Nusrat Shāh (1519-1532). Perhaps the most outstanding writer-mediator, Saiyid Sultān, was also a highly popular and esteemed *pir*, with a great number of disciples including another important writer, Muhammad Khān, who composed *Maqtal Husain* at the instance of his spiritual guide and as a continuation of the latter's colossal work, *Nabi-vamśa*, on the succession of the prophets ending with Muhammad. Sultān belonged to the noted Mir or Saiyid family of Chakraśālā in the district of Chattagram. His son, Saiyid Hasan, was a *pir*-guide to another important writer, Shaikh Muttalib, and his grandson, Mir Muhammad Shafi, a *pir*-writer himself, received mystical instruction from Hāji Muhammad, one of the greatest Bengali Muslim expounders of mystical principles. Shaikh Muttalib's father, Shaikh Parān also contributed to the mystical literature in Bengali. Shāh Akbar was a *pir* with a considerable following. Saiyid Murtaza, a disciple of

[50] *Shab*, fol. 229.
[51] *Gul-i Bakāwali*, quoted in *MBS*, p. 139 note.
[52] *Laili-Majnu*, pp. 6, 9 (text).

Saiyid Shāh Abd al-Razzāq, was a noted *pir* in Murshidabad in west Bengal. His death anniversary (*urs*) is still held at his own village, Suti, for three consecutive days. Another *pir*-writer, Shaikh Chānd, was a spiritual disciple of a noted mystic guide, Shāh Daula of Tripura, in east Bengal. Ali Rajā, alias Kānu Faqir, earned a great deal of popularity as a Bengali Muslim mystic in the eighteenth century. A disciple of Shāh Qiyām al-Din, Ali Rajā left a long line of spiritual descendants, among whom Muhammad Muqim was noted as a writer on Islamic tradition in Bengali. Muqim's *Gul-i Bakāwali* has been a valuable source of information on some of our cultural mediators.[53]

Among writers of the second category, that is those who were service-holders, we have Shāh Muhammad Saghir, who, on his own admission, was in the employ of the great King "Gyechh." E. Haq has rather doubtfully identified the king concerned with Ghiyāth al-Din Azam Shāh (A.D. 1389-1410), and all others accept it without question. For reasons given elsewhere, this identification appears extremely dubious. It is more likely that Saghir flourished at a much later period.[54] Zain al-Din seemed to receive the patronage of a chief, Yusuf Khān or Yusuf "Nāyaka." Here again E. Haq offers a rather doubtful identification of this Yusuf with the crown prince of Bengal, Yusuf Shāh, later to become Sultān Yusuf Shāh (A.D. 1478-1481).[55] Muhammad Muqim, mentioned above, was employed in the secretariat of a local *zamindār*. Chānd Qāzi served as the *qāzi* of Nabadvip under Sultān Husain Shāh (A.D. 1493-1519). Sābirid Khān's family was involved in the revenue administration and carried an official title, *mahallik*. The father of Shaikh Mansur was a *qāzi*. Daulat Qāzi, born in a *qāzi* family at Sultānpur in Chattagram, was pa-

[53] *MBS*, pp. 72-73, 143-46, 168, 178, 191, 197-98, 201, 248-49, 278-84; see also A. Sharif, *Saiyid Sultān*, pp. 48-60, *passim*.

[54] *MBS*, pp. 56-57; see also *supra*, Introduction, pp. 13-14.

[55] *MBS*, pp. 60-62; see also *supra*, *ibid*.

tronized by Ashrāf Khān, the military chief of the king of Rosāng, Śri Sudharmā (A.D. 1622-1638). Alāwal, one of the greatest poets of medieval Bengal, was the son of the *wazir* of Majlis Qutb, the Mughal governor of Fatehābād. He was wounded in a naval engagement with Portuguese pirates and was taken to Arakan. There he started life as a cavalry member of the royal bodyguard of King Thādo Mintar (A.D. 1645-1652). Later, he received patronage from the highest officials in the Arakan government.[56]

Irrespective of their social background the cultural mediators were clearly set apart, first, by their shared concern for disseminating "Islamic" knowledge and tradition among the masses of the co-religionists; secondly, by their common diagnosis of the source of the malaise in the linguistic cleavage; and, finally, by their courageous attempt to force a break with the dominant alien cultural orientation of the *ashrāf* and orthodoxy by having chosen to adopt the indigenous Bengali language as the cultural vehicle for the majority of the local Muslims. Many of these mediators, especially the *pir*-writers among them, brought a sense of pious religious obligation to bear upon their task. Saiyid Sultān addressed himself to the Bengali Muslim folk in a somewhat grandiose style:

> Muslims of Bengal, you all listen to me. May you all be engaged in pious deeds to please the Lord. . . . The learned who live in the land but do not expound the truth for you are destined to be castigated to hell. Should people commit sins, the learned will be taken to task in the presence of Allāh. I am born in the midst of you and so I have to talk to you about religious matters. Allāh shall accuse: "all you learned ones there did not stop people from committing sins." . . . When God calls for you about your good and bad deeds, you may very well plead before Him that you took recourse to the *guru*, who did not warn you. God shall chastise me much more than you. I am ever haunted by this fear, and driven by this, I composed *Nabi-vamśa* to take people away from sin.[57]

[56] *MBS*, pp. 281, 69-70, 75, 222, 236-37, 242-43.
[57] *Shab*, fols. 258-59.

The note of concern and anxiety for the fate of the masses of their co-believers is quite evident in their writings. But how far it stemmed solely from a sense of moral and religious obligation is not altogether clear. The situation involved, as already pointed out, a danger more immediate and material than an apprehended indictment on the day of judgment. The total absence of communication between the two sections of the community of believers and of contacts between the exogenous great and the endogenous little traditions had been of more immediate, direct, and urgent concern. Popular religious leaders like Saiyid Sultān, having direct concern with and knowledge of the Muslim masses in their capacity as *pirs*, could not but become increasingly anxious about the situation, and try to prevent their community (*umma*) from falling apart. Furthermore, there is evidence to show that the pressure often built up from the bottom, and that subsequent development was a mere recognition of this pressure. Shaikh Muttalib's version of the circumstances of the composition of his colossal work on Muslim canonical laws reveals that people, unable to follow religious injunctions in Arabic, approached the learned Maulawi Rahamat Allāh at the conclusion of a congregational prayer, respectfully with clasped hands, and sought his intervention in the matter of getting a religious manual produced in Bengali so that they could "perform duties according to scriptures." The task of "rendering the injunctions in Bengali" was entrusted to Shaikh Muttalib by Maulawi Rahamat Allāh, who asked him to shed all his "apprehensions" in the matter.[58]

It required formidable moral courage and will on the part of those Muslim authors of religious works in Bengali in the sixteenth and seventeenth centuries to defy this crushing weight of power and tradition. Only a few among them could shake it off completely, while most of them were apologetic for

[58] Shaikh Muttalib, *Kifāyat*, fols. 6-8.

their deviation or sought to rationalize it. Shāh Muhammad Saghir needed to take a "firm resolution" against the feelings of "sin, fear, and shame" associated with his task. He alluded to people's uninhibited "indulgence" in various sorts of literature but found them "afraid" of writing Islamic religious books (*kitāb*) in Bengali, and also apprehensive of being "blamed" for it. He reassured himself: "I have thought about this subject and have come to realise that such fears are false. If what is written is true, it does not matter what language it is written in."[59] Shaikh Muttalib failed to achieve the same degree of conviction: "I am sure that I have committed a great sin in that I have written the Muslim scriptures in Bengali. But this I am sure of in my heart, that the faithful will understand me and bless me. The blessings of the faithful shall involve great virtue, and merciful Allāh will forgive my sin."[60] A similar lack of conviction resulting from a sense of conflict was revealed also in Hāji Muhammad:

> Do not undertake anything that is forbidden. If you do not abide by the religious injunctions the end is all suffering. I am unable to write in the Hindu script but made an effort to give some knowledge to the people. . . . Do not ignore it because of its Hindu script. Why should you ignore the precious matters revealed in Bengali letters? These matters have been expounded by *pirs* and here is a fragment of that knowledge for people to seek at any cost and at any time. Do not feel sick to see it in Bengali language.[61]

Abd al-Nabi moved a little further: "I am afraid in my heart that God may be angry with me for writing Muslim scriptures in Bengali. But I reject the fear and firmly resolve to write in order to do good to the common people."[62] Saiyid Sultān took a firm stand, based both on reason and theological sanction. He said that the language that God gave to one was

[59] Shāh Muhammad Saghir, *Yusuf*, quoted in *MBS*, pp. 58-59.

[60] *Kifāyat*, fol. 102; also *MBS*, p. 198.

[61] *Nur Jamāl*, fols. 2ff.; also quoted in A. Sharif, *Saiyid Sultān*, pp. 309-10.

[62] *Vijay-Hamza*, quoted in *MBS*, pp. 214-15.

one's "precious gem," and added: "I know from Allāh that He wills to reveal the truth in the particular language of a land. The prophet speaks one language and the people another. How are we to follow the dialogue, then?"[63] But the most resolute defense came from Shāh Abd al-Hakim:

> Whatever language a people speak in a country, God understands that language. God understands all languages, whether the language of Hindus or the vernacular language of Bengal or any other. . . . Those who, being born in Bengal, are averse to Bengali language [*Bangabāni*] cast doubt on their birth. The people, who have no liking for the language and the learning of their country, had better leave it and live abroad. For generations our ancestors have lived in Bengal, and instruction in our native language is, therefore, considered good.[64]

The flood-gates of Muslim Bengali literature were thrown open by these new Muslim cultural mediators, and through them poured waves of literary works of religious import to fertilize the mind of Bengali Muslims for the following centuries. Bengali forced its recognition as the local vehicle, while Arabic and Persian continued to draw the traditional respect associated with Islamic religion and culture. This attitude was clearly evidenced by the following remarks of one of the greatest Muslim champions of Bengali language, noted above, Shāh Abd al-Hakim: "Arabic learning is the best of all. If you cannot learn Arabic, learn Persian to become aware of what is good in the end. Should you find yourself unable to master Persian, you must study the scriptures in your own language."[65]

In this new venture the Muslim cultural mediators could have referred to a precedent in Bengal history. Earlier, the hieratic brahmanical culture that raised a wall of elite exclusiveness in Sanskrit language was forced to come to terms

[63] *Shab*, fol. 259.

[64] *Nur Nāma*, quoted in *MBS*, pp. 205-206.

[65] *Shihāb al-Din Nāma*, quoted in *DCBM*, p. 250, and also in *MBS*, pp. 208-209.

with the little traditions of Bengal through the recognition and adoption of local Bengali language. To the Hindu *elite*, Sanskrit was the "divine language" (*deva-bhāṣā*), while the local language was variously called, *deśi-bhāṣā*, *laukik*, or *lok-bhāṣā*, and *parākrit* or *prākrit-bhāṣā*. Even in the beginning of the nineteenth century the *pandits* used to call it *Gaudiya-bhāṣā*. The specialists on Bengali language and literature are of the opinion that the use of the term *Bāngālā* for the language cannot be found earlier than the nineteenth century.[66] This view is to be modified in the light of the evidence of the Muslim Bengali literature. A number of Muslim Bengali writers in the late sixteenth and seventeeth centuries, such as Saiyid Sultān, Shaikh Muttalib and Abd al-Hakim, referred to the language as *Banga-bhāṣā* and *Banga-bāni*.[67] Whatever its name, the contemptuous attitude of the Hindu *elite* to the local language found a striking parallel in *ashrāf*'s contempt for the same. By the *pandits* Bengali was "despised as a Prakrit dialect fit only for demons and women, though it arose from the tomb of the Sanskrit."[68] The cultural monopoly of the Sanskritists was, however, already undermined in pre-Islamic Bengal by the *Mahāyāna* Buddhist *siddhā*-writers, who composed religious songs in proto-Bengali sharply critical of the brahmanical ritualism, formalism, pedantry and pride in birth.[69] The Buddhist *siddhāchāryas* had set in motion a process which was carried farther, on one hand, by the patronage to Bengali literature by the *sultāns* and, on the other, by the

[66] *BSI*, vol. I, pt. 1, pp. 6-7.

[67] Quoted in *MBS*, pp.154, 198, 205; also *supra*, pp. 77-78.

[68] *Friend of India* (Serampore), IV, p. 152.

[69] The antiquity of these songs, known as *charyā-giti* or *charyā-pada* or *charyā-koṣ*, is somewhat controversial. While Muhammad Shahid Allāh and his followers trace them back to the seventh and eighth centuries A.D., S. K.Chatterji and P. C. Bagchi place them roughly between the tenth and twelfth centuries. In recent years the claim for this literature as being proto-Bengali has also been challenged on behalf of other neighboring languages such as old Hindi, old Maithili, old Oriya, and old Assamese.

writers on the popular gods and goddesses in Bengal who produced a gigantic mass of literature called *mangal-kāvya*, glorifying their respective deities. The Hindu Bengali society gave birth to its cultural mediators entrusted with the task of bringing their great and little traditions closer. To these Hindu mediators medieval Hindu Bengalis owed not only Bengali translations of the Sanskrit epics and purānic mythologies, but also a religious acceptance and a literary recognition in Bengali of a great variety of popular cults and traditions. The Hindu mediators in medieval Bengal, just as their Muslim counterparts, remained apologetic of their breaking away from the tradition. Mādhav Āchārya in the middle of the sixteenth century wrote: "*Bhāgavat* in Sanskrit is not followed by all. Hence I wish to render it into the popular language [*lok-bhāṣā*] in the right spirit."[70] Rāmchandra Khān in the same century tried to explain his venture in terms of the need to provide for the "ignorant." Kavi-śekhar besought his learned readers not to "ridicule" his work being written in *laukik-bhāṣā*.[71]

In securing an effective place for Bengali in the religious-cultural world of Bengali Muslims, the Muslim mediators had overcome only the first obstacle. If the diagnosis of these writers had been confined to language alone, they could not possibly have come to grips with the problem at its grass-roots. The language alone was not capable of bringing the religion closer to the masses. If the medium of cultural communication was to be intelligible to the people, its idioms and symbols should be no less so. Islam, in its austere doctrinal forms, came to consist in the minds of the folk believers in Bengal of a few essential beliefs and observances, with little or no emotional content. These could scarcely satisfy the manifold popular demands on a religion, especially in a land where history and fiction, myth and legend, faith and superstition,

[70] Quoted in *BSI*, vol. I, pt. 1, p. 6.

[71] *Ibid.*

supernatural and real, spirit and matter were all intermingled and interchangeable. Garcin De Tassy in his interesting *Mémoire* (1831) on Indian Islam took particular note of its vast accumulation of innovations and accretions, especially at the popular level, and attributed them to "the too great simplicity of Islam for a country, where an idolatrous and allegorical religion" prevailed.[72] The masses of Bengali Muslims, hindered by the linguistic barrier and unfamiliar with the new religious and cultural symbols in the framework of the conservative type of Islam, found access to the spiritual and cultural heritage of the new religion, as a source of moral sustenance, denied to them. The problem, then, was not merely confined to making available to the masses manuals for formal religious observances in their own language. They needed more from their religion: they needed a religion that could epitomize their whole world of cultural values and forms. The religious-cultural perceptions in this folk world of Bengal, as perhaps in many other folk societies, were dominated by an instinctive search for divinity, religiosity, and godliness in the supernatural and the fantastic. The greatness was not associated in their minds with what remained subjected, like themselves, to the universal processes of nature. The truth of their religion was to be vindicated, not so much through theological or metaphysical polemics, as through the ability of its heroes to rise to superhuman and supernatural heights. The dogmas of Islam fell far short of meeting the demands of their passion for traditions in which they could hear about the glorious and miraculous exploits of the champions of their religion. They knew next to nothing about their new idols, who remained prisoners in the "ivory tower" of Arabic and Persian literatures, whereas the entire cultural atmosphere of Bengal was saturated with the traditions of the *Mahābhārat*,

[72] M. G. De Tassy, *Mémoire sur les Particularités de la Religion Musulmane dans l'Inde* (Paris, 1831), p. 9; English extract in the *Asiatic Journal* (Calcutta), VI (1831, N.S.), pt. 21, p. 353.

the *Rāmāyan*, nāthism, and the *mangal-kāvya*, centering around the exploits of Manasā, Chandi, Dharma, Śiv, and hosts of minor religious personalities or spirits. The Muslim masses could not live in a cultural void, and they held on, as observed before, to what was already before them—the inexhaustible source of traditional Bengali ballads and folklore, and religious and mythological traditions of diverse kinds. Hence the situation demanded much more than a rendering into Bengali of what was in Arabic and Persian. This would have been a comparatively easy and fairly mechanical undertaking. The more daunting task, which lay ahead of them, was to make their religious traditions available to the Muslim folk in terms familiar and intelligible to them. This meant breaking sharply with the traditional conservative approach and bringing Islam into line with the cultural traditions of the people.

It is interesting that this is precisely what emerges out of their literary efforts, though none of them mentioned this as part of his objectives. They harped on the people's inability to follow Arabic and Persian religious works and the resultant need for making such works available in Bengali. Some of them even named particular Arabic or Persian works which were being translated. But it does not take more than a casual glance to recognize how deeply indigenous elements had penetrated into these works, allegedly of translation only. Works primarily of a liturgical and didactic nature did not naturally provide much scope for re-creation. Works of this type dealt with matters like prayers (*namāz*), ablutions (*wazu*), the ceremonial bath (*ghusal*), fasting (*roza*) in the month of *Ramazān*, purification by sand (*tayammum*), funerals (*janājah*), and so on. These conformed closely to standard Islamic prescriptions of the *Hanafi* school of law, generally followed by the *sunni* majority in the Indian subcontinent.[73] The scope of the

[73] Among works of this type the following seem typical: Afzal Ali, *Nasihat*; Shaikh Parān (untitled); Khwandkār Nasr Allāh Khān, *Musār Suwāl*, and also

present study precludes this particular type of writings from our purview. All other categories of these mediators' thoughts and writings were thoroughly syncretistic and permeated by indigenous religious and cultural notions, idioms, nuances, and symbols. The following three chapters on the historical-mythical, cosmogonical-cosmological, and mystical-esoterical matters deal with the three facets of their syncretistic contributions.

---

his *Hidāyat al-Islām* (DMS 689: sl 565) and *Sharia Nāma* (cited in *MBS*, pp. 175-76); Shaikh Muttalib, *Kifāyat*; Saiyid Alāwal, *Tuhfa*; Khwandkār Abd al-Karim, *Hazār Masāil* (DMS 109: sl 569); Shāh Abd al-Hakim, *Shihāb*; Hayāt Mahmud, *Hitajnān*; Muhammad Ali, *Hairāt al-Fiqh* (DMS 646: sl 558; Bengali composition in Arabic script); Muhammad Jān, *Namāz Māhātmya* (DMS 189: sl 239); Saiyid Nur al-Din, *Musār Suwāl* (DMS 188: sl 196); also his *Qiyāmat Nāma* (DMS 526: sl 81); see Introduction, *supra*, p. 11, for calling the same work *Rahat al-Qulub*; his *Hitopadeś* or *Daykāt* (DMS 387: sl 202), see Introduction, *supra*, p. 11, for some confusion about this work; Muhammad Qāsim, *Hitopadeś* (DMS 140: sl 559).

Part II: Text

A. THE SYNCRETISTIC GREAT TRADITION

3
History—Myth

The literary area to engage the attention of the mediators most was that of the historical and mythical tradition. A survey of the entire range of the Muslim Bengali literature under study reveals the predominance and the great popularity of these historical-mythical writings. Further, an internal examination of this particular type of composition points to its total correspondance in both form and spirit to the prevailing tradition of long and continuous narrative poems in Bengali, known variously as *mangal-kāvya, vijay-kāvya*, or simply as *pānchāli* or *pānchālikā*. The old and middle Bengali literature assumed two general forms: the lyrical and the narrative. The Muslim writers adopted both: the lyrical Muslim *pada*-compositions of esoteric-mystic import[1] and the long narrative poems with historical, mythical, and romantic content. The Bengali narrative poems of both Muslim and non-Muslim authorship were composed in syllabic *payār*, or short couplets, and *tripadi* verse, or long couplets with two caesura. The *payār* couplets, which formed the bulk and helped to forward the story, were musically recited by the principal singer, generally called *mul-gāyan*, or *bayāti*, by Muslims of the eastern Bengal.[2] The songs in *tripadi* and also in *payār*, known as *nācādi* or dance-style, were sung by the principal singer, supported by the associated singers, known as *dohār* or *pāli* or *pāl-dohār*. The leading singer recited or sang the

[1] See *infra*, Ch. 5, Section II.

[2] Abbās Ali, *Gulzār-i Islām* (Dacca, 1288 B.S./A.D. 1881), p. 61; M. Islām, *Kavi Heyāt*, p. 201.

story and passed on the refrain (*dhuyā*) to his men, who repeated it in chorus. He wore a bell-anklet and a wristlet, carried a chowrie in his right hand, a pair of small cup-cymbals in the left, and a small drum, *khanjani* or *khanjuri*, made of lizard skin and tied under his left arm.

The narrative poems in the new Indo-Aryan languages, west of Bengal, were again of three types: the historical, the romantic, and the religious poems. In Bengal the grand religious narrative poems received far greater attention than the historical or the romantic. The narrative poems other than those glorifying the activities of popular deities and deified heroes are not found in Bengali until introduced by the Muslim writers.[3] The Muslim narrative historical and mythical writings were, however, not divorced from religious considerations, and were indeed prompted by the same religious impulse as that underlying the Hindu *mangal-kāvyas* celebrating and vindicating the popular deities. The Muslim narrative writer in Bengali sought to transmit to the Bengali Muslim masses the cultural heritage of Islam, woven around the activities of Islamic historical, legendary and mythical heroes. His object seemed to wean Muslims away from *mangal*-literature by creating for them in Bengali an Islamic substitute based on Muslim history and myth. In effect the Muslim heroes and heroines were either substituted for *mangal*-deities, or found their rightful place in the familiar world of the *mangal*-pantheon. This led to literary ventures, centered around the Prophet, his descendants and followers, mostly in imaginary terms designed to cater to the popular demand for the supernatural, miraculous, and fantastic. The lives of Mu-

[3] See S. Sen, *Islāmi Bānglā Sāhitya* (Calcutta, 1951), *passim; HBL*, pp. 18ff.; *HBLL, passim*. There is reason to believe that some good deeds of the Pāl and the Sen rulers of pre-Muslim Bengal were sung in verse. Except for a few couplets preserved in a sixteenth- or seventeenth-century work written in mixed Sanskrit and Bengali, Bengal has entirely lost its early historical compositions. (See *HBL*, pp. 19-20.)

hammad, his daughter Fātima, his grandsons Hasan and Husain, and his followers were embroidered lavishly with fictitious adventures and exploits to reduce them to some replicas of their *mangal* counterparts. Saiyid Sultān's monumental work, *Nabi-vamśa*, containing a biographical account of the prophets from Adam to Muhammad, was perhaps intended as a national religious epic for the Bengali Muslims in which history and myth freely coalesced.[4] Muhammad Khān, one of Saiyid Sultān's disciples, carried the work of his master forward by bringing down the story to the tragedy of Karbalā, in which the Prophet's grandson, Husain, lost his life.[5] There was also outright recourse to legendary and mythical heroes. A semi-historical person named Hanifā, believed to be a son of Ali, the Prophet's son-in-law, became the center of many heroic and supernatural exploits, which people wished to hear.[6] In close resemblance to the legend of the Bengal *vaiṣnav* leader Chaitanya (A.D. 1486-1534), an utterly fictitious story relating to the kidnapping and eventual rescue of Hasan and Husain, grandsons of the Prophet, found its way into the Muslim Bengali literary tradition.[7] Amir Hamza, uncle of Muhammad, emerged as another popular hero, whose imaginary military exploits provided much religious-cultural nourishment to the folk believers.[8] If the Muslim writers of narrative poems cherished the ulterior object of reconstructing a religious-cultural tradition for the Bengali Muslims,

[4] Saiyid Sultān, *Nabi-vamśa* [several fragmented MSS of the work consulted].

[5] Muhammad Khān, *Maqtal*.

[6] Muhammad Khān, *Muhammad Hanifār Ladāi* (DMS 286: sl 357); Abd al-Alim, *Muhammad Hanifār Ladāi* (DMS 101: sl 369); Amānullāh, *Muhammad Hanifār Ladāi* (DMS 175: sl 368); Saiyid Hamza, *Jaiguner Puthi* (DMS 135: sl 147), and also its printed version (Calcutta, 1878); Faqir Gharib Allāh, *Sonābhān* (DMS 570: sl 538).

[7] [Anonymous], *Imām-churi* (DMS 65: sl 18).

[8] Abd al-Nabi. *Vijay-Hamza* (DMS 342: sl 2); Saiyid Hamza, *Amir Hamzār Qissā* (DMS 711: sl 10); Faqir Gharib Allāh, *Amir Hamzār Punthi* (Calcutta, 1867).

they were able to advance their cause further by their pioneering contribution to romantic narratives in Bengali based on Perso-Arabic and even Indian materials. The romantic narrative poems on popular Perso-Arabic themes like Yusuf-Zulaikha, Laila-Majnun, Saif al-Muluk-Badi al-Jamāl, Lālmati-Saif al-Muluk, Gul-i Bakāwali, Zeb al-Muluk-Samarokh, and also on Indian themes such as Padmāvati, Vidyā-Sundar, Sati Maynā-Lor-Chandrāni, and Manohar-Madhumālati remained as popular in the middle Bengali period as later in the nineteenth and twentieth centuries, when they were turned out on a large scale by the cheap Bengali Press of Battalā.[9]

Apart from this general impression of relevance and congruity of the Muslim Bengali narrative writings in the cultural atmosphere of the narrative tradition in Bengal, a detailed analysis of the contents of this particular type of Muslim writing reveals more subtle and penetrating attempt by their authors to present Islamic tradition in terms meaningful to the world of the Bengali believers. An interesting part of their endeavor was to reduce the Islamic struggle against infidelity in general to that against Hinduism. The Prophet Muhammad's mission in Arabia was presented as an anti-Hindu call. His antagonistic uncle, Abu Jahl, appeared as "the chief of the Hindus"[10] and addressed his God as "Brahmā,"

[9] Shāh Muhammad Saghir, *Yusuf-Zulaikha* (DMS 125: sl 12); Abd al-Hakim, *Yusuf-Zulaikha* (DMS 425: sl 15); Faqir Gharib Allāh, *Yusuf Zulaikha* (DMS 557: sl 17) and its later printed edition (Calcutta, 1880); Daulat Wazir Bahrām Khān, *Laili-Majnu*; Saiyid Alāwal, *Saif al-Muluk-Badi al-Jamāl* (DMS 179: sl 522); Donā Ghāzi, *Saif al-Muluk-Badi al-Jamāl* (DMS 319: sl 524); Tamizi, *Lālmati-Tāj al-Muluk* (DMS 651: sl 451); Sharif Shāh, *Lālmati-Saif al-Muluk* (DMS 321: sl 448); Abd al-Hakim, *Lālmati-Saif al-Muluk* (DMS 321: sl 448); Muhammad Muqim, *Gul-i Bakāwali* (DMS 417: sl 97); Muhammad Nawāzish Khān, *Gul-i Bakāwali* (DMS 427: sl 98); Saiyid Muhammad Akbar Ali, *Zeb al-Muluk-Samarokh* (DMS 418: sl 142); Saiyid Alāwal, *Padmāvati*; Sābirid Khān, *Vidyā-Sundar*; Daulat Qāzi, *Sati Maynā-Lor-Chandrāni*; Muhammad Chuhār, *Azab-shāh-Samarokh* (DMS 358: sl 11); Saiyid Hamza, *Madhu-mālati*, ed. by S. A. Ahsān (Chattagrām, 1380 B.S./1973); Shaikh Sadi, *Gada-Mallikār Puthi* (DMS 573: sl 106).

[10] Saiyid Sultān, *Shab*, fol. 22.

"Viṣnu," and "Niranjan."[11] Reminiscent of the legends of Moses and Kriṣna, Abu Jahl came to know of the prospective birth of Muhammad and of his mission, and tried various means to destroy Muhammad before and after birth. On his birth Muhammad was kept concealed, while another boy was substituted for him. Abu Jahl took him for Muhammad, son of Abd Allāh, and strongly rebuked him for abjuring his ancestral faith in Hinduism and for leaning towards Islamic ways. Jahl, bent upon flaying the boy to death, declared his intention of taking the boy initially through a process of Hinduization:

> I shall first of all reconvert you to Hinduism, which will bring you merits on your death. If you adhere to the life of your own people, you will be rewarded in the next life. I shall first draw an image on your forehead. Secondly, I shall make you wear a sacred thread. Thirdly, I shall take you scrupulously through all rites and ceremonies. Fourthly, I shall let you have a ritual bath and prayer, and finally, you will be consigned to the flames.[12]

The birth of Muhammad shook and startled the Vedic king of gods, Indra, and other Hindu gods in heaven. Indra's royal canopy broke, and the throne rolled over. The gate to Indra's heaven was blocked; the gods were bewildered and unable to ascend to heaven.[13] From his station in Medina the Prophet despatched in all directions mighty warriors, who "brought back the severed heads of Hindus wherever they found them." The legendary sword, *zulfaqār*, which the Prophet's son-in-law, Caliph Ali, received "by the command of Allāh" and which possessed the magical power of sucking up "all water in the seas" and of burning out "hills and jungles" extending over "a distance that one could cover in a seven days' journey," caused Hindus to "fly in terror."[14] The

[11] *Ibid.*, fol. 92.
[12] *Ibid.*, fol. 22.
[13] Hayāt Mahmud, *Ambiyā*, p. 123 (text); also his *Hitajnān*, p. 3 (text).
[14] Hayāt Mahmud, *Jang*, pp. 4-5 (text).

non-Muslim country of Iraq under king Jaykum, who fought against the invading Muslim army, led by the Prophet himself, was presented as a Hindu land. The guardian-deity of the kingdom was called "Gosāi" (Goswāmi, i.e., Viṣnu), to whom the king desired to sacrifice the Muslims.[15]

The attempt to bring the characters of Muslim tradition closer to the religious-cultural milieu of Bengal also took the form of searching for parallels in the Hindu purānic and epic traditions. The simplest device for making the figures of Muslim tradition known to the local people was to introduce them along with their Hindu parallels. The motive underlying this attempt was often to vindicate the Muslim hero, drawn into a comparative frame along with his Hindu counterpart. But the dominant object seemed to make both appear natural in the complex of the Bengali religious-cultural tradition. The great war between Ali and Jaykum, the infidel king of Iraq, was compared to those of Rām and the *pāndavs* of the Indian epics, the *Rāmāyan* and the *Mahābhārat* respectively. The heroic fight between Ali and Janā, son of Jaykum, found Indra "astounded" and the other Hindu gods and demons "trembling" to watch the fight. In the face of a battle like this the Hindu epic heroes such as Kripāchārya, Birāt and Abhimanyu were certain to "take to their heels."[16] The heroism in this duel was said to be far greater than even the celebrated fight between Rām and Rāvan of the *Rāmāyan* fame, and a hundred times greater than the great war of Kurukṣetra of the *Mahābhārat*.[17] Janā was "an archer equal to Pārtha [Arjun]." He was also like Brahmā "in power," Karna "in generosity and righteousness," and Yama as "a veritable exterminator." Ali's great gift in archery was of the order of the celebrated archers of Hindu tradition such as Bhiṣma, Dronāchārya, and Aśvatthāman. One Muslim warrior was as

[15] Zain al-Din, *Rasul*, fol. 11.

[16] *Ibid.*, fols. 38, 42, and 47; also Sābirid Khān, *Rasul-vijay* (DMS 377: sl 434); Donā Ghāzi, *Saif*, fol. 219 mc.

[17] Donā Ghāzi, *ibid.*

"huge and frightful" as Kumbhakarna.[18] Another resembled Bhim "in valour."[19] Yusuf of Egypt was idealized as a ruler, and even Rām, the epitome of the Hindu ideal of paternalistic kingship, was "unable to rule his kingdom in Yusuf's manner." Karna and Bali, two proverbial donors of Hindu tradition were "no match" for Yusuf in his generosity.[20] Amir Hamza sat among his warriors "like Indra amidst gods." Saiyād, the beloved of Amir Hamza, was as exquisite as Tilottamā, and even Śachi, the most beautiful wife of Indra, was "no comparison" for her. Amir Hamza and Rupa Bānu were "as well-matched as Śiv and his consort, Pārvati."[21] Badi al-Jamāl at her first sight of Saif al-Muluk found him far more handsome then Kām-dev, the Hindu god of love. For the marriage festival of Badi al-Jamāl her father sent out invitations to all celestial mythical beings of Hindu tradition, namely *dev*, *gandharva*, *rākṣas*, *dānav*, *yakṣa*, and *daitya*, and also Indra, Yam, Varun, and Kuver. Saif al-Muluk came out of the palace on the morning after his marriage, met a number of Hindu divinities, such as Śiv, Brahmā, Indra, Yam, and Varun, and paid his respects to them. In return he received boons from them. Śiv placed all lower spirits at Saif's command. Indra granted him the vigor of youth and the protective guidance of the nine planets. Brahmā promised him eternal safety from fire. Varun put water, cloud, and thunderbolt at his disposal. Yam promised to eliminate Saif's chances of unnatural death and disease. Other gods also bestowed various boons for "improvement of his memory and ability for action and knowledge."[22] Iblis of Muslim tradition found, though somewhat inappropriately, a parallel in Nārad of the Hindus. One was as crafty and indulgent in mischief-making as the other. But, while the former enjoyed leading the be-

[18] Zain al-Din, *Rasul*, fols. 9, 13, 36, 44, 51, 53.

[19] Saiyid Sultān, *Shab*, fol. 213.

[20] Shāh Muhammad Saghir, *Yusuf*, fol. 75.

[21] Abd al-Nabi, *Vijay*, fols. 819, 821, 836.

[22] Donā Ghāzi, *Saif*, fols. 110, 140, 142, 145.

lievers astray from the path of Allāh, Nārad throve in playing off the members of the Hindu pantheon one against the other.[23] Āmina, wife of Abd Allāh and mother of Muhammad, surpassed in beauty Vidyādhari, a nymph in Hindu tradition.[24] Even a white elephant in a Muslim myth excelled Aiyrābat, the great white elephant belonging to Indra.[25] Fātima assumed the popular robe of the mother in a land where the cult of the mother-goddess or *śakti* in scores of female deities virtually dominated the religious life. Hayāt Mahmud began writing his *Jang Nāma*, having desired to take the feet of Fātima on his head.[26] Saiyid Murtaza addressed Fātima as "the mother of the world."[27] A more direct association of Fātima with the concept of *śakti* may be found in some later compositions. Pāglā Kānāi, a Muslim poet in the nineteenth century, identified Fātima with "mother Tārā" or "mother Tārini" and prayed to her for the deliverance of her father's (Muhammad's) community of believers (*umma*):

> Oh mother, . . . Pāglā Kānāi, who is of no consequence, cries for you with every breath; please cast a little shadow of your feet on me; Oh mother, take me to your feet. Oh mother Tārā, the redeemer of the world, Oh mother Tārini, you shall appear as the saviour of Muslims when Isrāfil will blow his horn, when everything will be reduced to water, and when your father's community will sink into water without a boat.[28]

Fātima was also compared to the goddess Kāli and considered more virtuous: ". . . mother Kāli is virtuous indeed, she stood on her husband's chest! Did my gracious mother [Fātima]

[23] Saiyid Sultān, *Nabi*, fol. 135 mc; also his *Shab*, fols. 29, 35; Hayāt Mahmud, *Ambiyā*, p. 34 (text).

[24] *Shab, ibid.*, fol. 10.

[25] Donā Ghāzi, *Saif*, fol. 142.

[26] *Jang*, p. 1 (text).

[27] Saiyid Murtaza, actually untitled ms. catalogued as *Yog Qalandar* (DMS 547: sl 394), fol. 1.

[28] Quoted in Bengali original in M. Islām, *Kavi Pāglā Kānāi* (Rajshahi, 1366 B.S./1959), p. 55.

ever trample Ali?"[29] Others sought to achieve their purpose by casting the Arab daughter of the Prophet into the mould of a Bengali beauty.[30] During his ascent to heaven, Muhammad passed through many wiles and temptations and, among other things, "turned his eyes away" from a damsel as beautiful as Rādhā, the beloved of Kriṣna.[31] On his journey back to the earth Muhammad was greeted and worshipped at successive stages by the Hindu presiding spirits of the cosmos. At the final stage he met Mount Sumeru of the Hindu mythology, exchanged greetings, and set off for his own land.[32]

The most significant part of the attempt to reduce the polarity between the endogenous and exogenous traditions relates to the anxiety of the mediators to bring the Prophet himself in line with the comparable symbols of the Hindu tradition. A striking attempt was made to identify the Islamic concepts of *nabi*, a receiver of the divine message, and *rasul*, who received from God a book in addition to the message, with the Hindu concept of *avatār*, an incarnation of God Himself. The Qurānic recognition of *nabi* being born in different lands at different times provided a semblance of identity between the Islamic and Hindu concepts. They, however, compromised a great deal to reconcile the two. That "*nabi* is one who is called *avatār*" it was a mere logical extension of this position to regard and present Muhammad as "the incarnation of God Himself" (*Muhammad rup dhari nij avatār*) and as "a manifestation of his own self" (*nij amśa prachārilā*).[33] On his ascent to heaven (*mirāj*), as Muhammad took his ground uneasily in the presence of Allāh, the latter com-

[29] Quoted in Bengali original, *ibid.*, p. 145. In Hindu tradition, Śiv, the consort of Kāli, got himself trampled by the latter in attempting to stop her frenzied march of destruction.

[30] Shaikh Tanu, *Fātimār Surat Nāma* (DMS 133: sl 302), *passim*.

[31] Hayāt Mahmud, *Ambiyā*, p. 182 (text).

[32] Saiyid Sultān, *Shab*, fol. 160.

[33] Sultān, *Nabi*, fol. 22 mc; also E. Haq, "Kavi Saiyid Sultān," *Sāhitya-Pariṣat Patrikā* (Calcutta, 1341 B.S./A.D. 1934), no. 2, p. 50.

forted him: "I created you of my own body. You and I have always been one single form. Your body is not any different from Mine."[34] The identity of *nabi* and *avatār* was further designed to incorporate some of the Hindu incarnations of God, such as Kriṣna and Rām among the prophets preceding Muhammad. Such innovations could not but pose serious theological problems, which the mediators sought to resolve by reconstructing the Hindu myths and even creating new ones. The most obvious question concerned the avatāric incarnation of God, as noted above. It is interesting that while an attempt was made, on one hand, to reduce Muhammad to God's own self, the Hindu *avatār* Kriṣna, on the other, was boldly depicted as God's messenger; consequently, the entire attempt may be seen as one of achieving their object by interchanging the contents of the concepts of *nabi* and *avatār*. The second serious problem presented by the assimilation of *avatār* was its iconic character, which was in sharp conflict with the declared mission of a *nabi*, as stated by the Muslim writer, to "redeem people from sin" and "forbid worship of images." In the case of Kriṣna there was the added difficulty associated with his love-dalliances extolled in the *vaiṣnav* tradition. The attempt of the Muslim myth-maker to get around these problems is clearly revealed in Saiyid Sultān's ingenious treatment of the Krisna-myth in his gigantic work on the story of the prophets down to Muhammad.

Kriṣna, according to Sultān, was born at a time when there was no *nabi* among the people, when the descendants of Qābil reigned, and when vices like adultery and drunkenness prevailed. Hence God decided to create a person capable of enforcing recognition of the supremacy of God alone, adherence to his commands, and prohibition of image-worship. The evil-minded Iblis[35] became apprehensive about his own future in

[34] Sultān, *Shab*, fols. 151-52 mc.

[35] Iblis and Nārad are, as noted above, often identified, the names interchanged, and occasionally presented in the conjoint form of "Iblis-Nārad."

the event of the end of image-worship. He visited in disguise King Kamsa, warned him against the potential enemy in Krişna, and urged him to kill Krişna, who had, in the meanwhile, been growing in his mother's womb. All attempts of Kamsa and Iblis to kill Krişna before and after his birth proved unsuccessful. Krişna grew into an attractive, handsome person, and seduced married women, including his most beloved, Rādhā, who sought amorous pleasures with him. Krişna was awakened to his senses and divine mission by a stern warning from heaven. He withdrew himself totally from this amorous life, leaving his women companions to adore his image and sing of his love-dalliances with them. Saiyid Sultān's outraged sense of morality and decency at the persistence of this mode of worship of Krişna among his (Sultān's) contemporaries found clear expression:

> The women folk continue to sing these songs. This despicable practice prevails in this land where the virtues of adultery are proclaimed. What merit is there in it? Why is such practice advocated at all? Young women are disturbed to hear about this. Young men and women take their lesson from Hari [Krişna] that adultery is no sin, and so, they will commit it in the name of Hari. No good results can accrue from such deeds.[36]

Krişna himself was mortified to find his people indulging in sin and worshipping his image as the supreme spiritual object, and decided on returning to heaven. His subsequent flight to heaven on the wings of the mythical bird, Garuda, is rather similar in details to Muhammad's ascent to heaven on the back of the celestial horse, Borāk. Krişna was, however, refused entry into paradise, insulted, and beaten back on account of his self-indulgence, corruption of his followers, and failure to prevent worship of his own image. He returned crestfallen to his people and advised them to refrain from worshipping his image along with Rādhā's. His sermon

[36] *Nabi*, fol. 331.

fell on deaf ears, as Iblis-Nārad re-emerged and continued to confound people by justifying the need for image-worship.[37]

The intended effect of identifying *avatār* with *nabi* was further heightened by the presentation of Muhammad within the chronological framework of Hindu mythology. The Hindu concept of the four ages *(yugs), satya, tretā, dvāpar*, and *kali*, found ready acceptance among the Muslim writers.[38] The Hindu concept of *yug* is integral to that of *avatār*, God having manifested Himself as different *avatārs* in different *yugs* to redeem mankind. Men in the present age, *kali-yug*, are destined to become sinful and unrighteous before being redeemed by the Savior of this particular age, namely *kali-avatār*. Significantly enough, Muhammad was introduced as *kali-avatār* by the Bengali Muslim writers: ". . . concealed in the *arsh*, he [Muhammad] became manifest in *kali* and was born in Abd Allāh's family. . . . Muhammad *nabi*, let it be known, is the *kali avatār*."[39] Saiyid Sultān mentioned a "prophecy": "Muhammad shall become the *nabi* in the age of *kali*."[40] Sultān also put in the mouth of Muhammad himself:

> In the end Allāh made me *paighambar*. This keeps me in constant anxiety and alarm. The *umma* will be sinful in the *kali* age and will perform neither justice nor righteousness. . . . How to keep the *umma*, committed to my charge, upright in the *kali* age is my perennial concern, and my body is getting emaciated and burnt out.[41]

In this general setting of the concept of *nabi* identified with *avatār* and associated with *kali-yug*, the story of Prophet Muhammad's life was told in the locally popular form of the purānic and *mangal-kāvya* traditions. The supreme object of securing a receptive audience prompted these writers to move

[37] *Ibid.*, fols. 313-39.

[38] *Ibid.*, fol. 133; also his *Shab*, fol. 257; Hayāt Mahmud, *Hitajnān*, p. 155 (text).

[39] Mahmud, *ibid.*, pp. 3, 33.

[40] *Nabi*, fol. 133.

[41] *Shab*, fol. 257.

unfettered by conditions of purity, either historical or religious. It was not history or reason but the hero and his religion that were to be vindicated for simple believers, not theologians or scholars.

Muhammad's mother Āmina, represented as the princess of Arabia[42] or of Mecca,[43] fell in love with Abd Allāh at first sight from the balcony of her palace. She sent for him and brought him into the privacy of her bolted room. She pined for the sweet aroma emanating from the divine light (*nur*) concealed in Abd Allāh's body even without his own knowledge, and proposed to marry him. This was followed by some "amorous play" between them ended by a secret marriage in the *gandharva* style, a Hindu form of marriage effected simply by exchange of garlands between the couples.[44] The marriage was attended and sanctified by four Muslims brought from the town and four hundred thousand *firishtahs* sent by God. Jibrāil read the marriage agreement, Mikāil served as the attorney, and Isrāfil and Izrāil as the witnesses. Seven months later, Āmina's pregnancy was revealed. This caused a fight between Āmina's father and Abd Allāh, in which the former was killed. On the death of this "king" the "claim to Mecca" passed to Abu Jahl. About this time an astrologer named Yusuf predicted that Āmina would give birth to Muhammad, who was desined to terminate the traditional order. Alarmed at the prospect of losing his throne, Abu Jahl tried various means to kill Muhammad in his mother's womb. At one stage the midwife, who was employed for this purpose, was "warned" by the unborn baby, and, while trying to remove the foetus, she was also bitten by him and not released until she pronounced the articles of Islamic faith. Undaunted, Abu Jahl vainly tried strong persuasion with Abd Allāh to get rid of his wife and child. In return he offered Abd Allāh

[42] Hayāt Mahmud, *Ambiyā*, p. 117 (text).

[43] Sultān, *Shab*, fol. 14.

[44] *Ibid.*, fol. 11; Hayāt Mahmud, *Ambiyā*, p. 118 (text).

as many beautiful damsels as he liked.[45] Frustrated in all his attempts, Abu Jahl remained watchful of Muhammad's birth, making arrangements for the immediate possession of the newborn baby. Allāh sent four *firishtahs* to comfort Muhammad. Accordingly, Jibrāil assured Muhammad full safety and asked him to come out. Muhammad decided to do so at night and, after his birth, the midwife, appointed to deliver Muhammad to Abu Jahl, saved him by replacing her own newly born son. Muhammad's substitute, assured by Jibrāil that he would become the first martyr of Islam to be received in heaven, was brought to Abu Jahl. The boy repeatedly told Abu Jahl about the oneness of God and foiled all Abu's attempts to humiliate and kill him until he was himself ready for his death and went straight to paradise.[46]

The birth of the Prophet of Islam was followed by the visit to Āmina and the newborn of all the previous prophets and their consorts, such as Ādam and Hauwā; Shish and his wife, Nuh; Ibrāhim and his two wives, Sarah and Hājira; Shukra, the beautiful wife of Musā; and Maryam, mother of Yusuf.[47] The celestial virgins (*hurs*) came to greet the last of the prophets with pitchers full of water.[48] They gave him a ritual bath, clothed him in the choicest garments, and offered prayers. Ādam and Hauwā took Muhammad on their laps with great affection.[49]

The subsequent development of the story of Muhammad followed the general pattern of hagiological writings as typified by the Perso-Arabic tradition of *Qisas al-Ambiyā* (the Story of the Prophets). The broad outline of Muhammad's historical life was colorfully embroidered with a great variety

[45] Mahmud, *ibid.*, p. 122 (text); Sultān, *Nabi*, fols. 14-17.

[46] Sultān, *ibid.*, fols. 18-24.

[47] An obvious confusion with Isa or Jesus.

[48] A popular Hindu ritual observance generally connected with the celebration of an auspicious occasion.

[49] Sultān, *Nabi*, fol. 29.

of legends and myths, extolling his divine and supernatural person.

During his upbringing at the home of his uncle, Abu Tālib, Muhammad, while tending goats with other boys, hit an intransigent goat with a stick. Allāh, disapproving of such anger in the Prophet, sent Jibrāil to rip open Muhammad's body, take his heart out, and purge it of "desire, anger, greed, attachment, etc."[50] According to another version, two white birds carried Muhammad on their wings to perform this purge by taking out the heart and washing off its impurities.[51]

The eyes of Ali remained closed since birth, and opened as he was placed on the lap of Muhammad and as the latter called out Ali's name.[52]

Khadija was attracted to Muhammad, when she saw "the clouds forming an umbrella over the head of *Rasul*" and "the trees prostrating on the ground touching his feet."[53]

While chasing a runaway cow, Umar came to accept the divine nature of Muhammad. The cow, introducing herself as the servant of Muhammad, impressed on Umar the futility of his opposition to her master, Muhammad, while Umar found himself unable to cope with Muhammad's servant.[54]

A blind Arab, opposed to Islam, got back his vision by unknowingly applying "dust of *Nabi*'s feet" to his eyes. He, on becoming aware of his action, later refused to accept the Prophet's mercy and made successive attempts to destroy his newly acquired vision, but with no success. He came to see the divine nature of Muhammad and embraced Islam.[55]

Muhammad was kept as a hostage for a deer captured by an infidel Arab until the deer, needing to feed her starving

[50] *Ibid.*, fol. 41.
[51] Mahmud, *Ambiyā*, p. 129 (text).
[52] *Ibid.*, p. 131 (text); Sultān, *Nabi*, fol. 43.
[53] Sultān, *ibid.*, fol. 45.
[54] *Ibid.*, fols. 68-69; Mahmud, *Ambiyā*, pp. 147-48 (text).
[55] Sultān, *ibid.*, fol. 84; Mahmud, *ibid.*, p. 160 (text).

yearlings in the forest, had come back. The young deer refused milk from their mother because she kept the Prophet a hostage for them. They all returned to the Arab just as he was about to kill the hostage.[56]

Muhammad was credited with great miraculous feats to vindicate his religion and prophethood to his opponents, especially Abu Jahl and his followers. They all approached him for proof of his religion and prophethood. They required him to turn a stone into a tree with two long branches, one spreading eastward and the other westward, with flowers and birds, and *kalima* written on every leaf. Muhammad, assisted by Jibrāil, performed the tasks to the last detail.[57]

Abu Jahl invited people to his palace to listen to an idol uttering anti-Muslim invectives. Muhammad, determined to destroy this evil plan, started for the palace and on the way met a group of fairies,[58] or, alternatively, *gandharvas*,[59] who divulged the secret of the idol to him. A Hindu fairy or Iblis himself, living inside the idol, was responsible for this blasphemy. Thanks to Muhammad, a Muslim spirit took over the idol, positioned itself inside it, and surprised and disgraced Abu Jahl in the midst of a large gathering by proclaiming the glory of Allāh and Muhammad and denouncing Abu Jahl and idolatry. Humiliated and outraged, Abu Jahl dumped the idol into a heap of garbage, an act which was followed by a large number of conversions to Islam.[60]

On another occasion Muhammad, challenged by Abu Jahl, broke the moon into two parts with a stroke of his finger, made one part of it enter his right sleeve and the other his left, and then took the two out of the opposite sleeves. The

[56] Sultān, *ibid.*, fols. 84-89; Mahmud, *ibid.*, pp. 161-63 (text).
[57] Mahmud, *ibid.*, p. 156 (text).
[58] *Ibid.*, p. 163 (text).
[59] Sultān, *Nabi*, fols. 89-91.
[60] *Ibid.*, fols. 91-93; Mahmud, *Ambiyā*, pp. 163-64 (text).

moon spoke in his presence, giving pious advice, and finally the Prophet restored the broken parts, reunited, to the sky.[61]

Abu Jahl did not believe Muhammad's ascent to heaven and sarcastically doubted if the Prophet even knew the direction in which the heavenly seat of *bait al-muqaddas* lay. Jibrāil instantly brought forth *bait al-muqaddas* itself on the spot for Muhammad and put the disbelievers to shame.[62]

During the Prophet's flight to Medina the cave in which he and Abu Bakr took shelter for a night was kept, at the instance of Allāh, concealed from their pursuers by a spider, which quickly covered the entrance with a thick web, and by a couple of pigeons, which hatched their eggs at the entrance. A snake sheltering in a hole inside the cave tried to come out to pay its homage to the Prophet, but found Abu Bakr blocking its way and bit him. Muhammad cursed the snake and cured Abu Bakr with the application of his saliva.[63] During the war between Muslims and Meccans, Ali was also cured of his eye trouble by the Prophet's saliva. Surāq, son of Jasim, pursuing Muhammad on a fast-running horse, was rendered immobile by the hooves of his horse getting stuck in the rock.[64]

Iblis joined the Meccan army against Muhammad, and Allāh sent Jibrāil, Isrāfil, and Mikāil with three thousand fighters to reinforce the Muslim army, leaving no other choice for Iblis than to desert the field of battle. He, however, tried a trick on the Muslim soldiers. He appeared to them in a dream as a beautiful woman, sexually exciting them to the point of ejaculation. The infidel enemies had already cut off the Muslims' water supply, and the lack of water rendered them unable to wash up and ritually purify their unclean

[61] Sultān, *ibid.*, fols. 100-102; Mahmud, *ibid.*, pp. 168-70.
[62] Mahmud, *ibid.*, pp. 208-209 (text).
[63] *Ibid.*, p. 213 (text); Sultān, *Nabi*, fol. 169.
[64] Sultān, *ibid.*, fols. 169, 223; Mahmud, *ibid.*, p. 214 (text).

bodies. The matter was reported to the Prophet, who brought on the rains with his prayers to Allāh.[65]

Instructed by Allāh, Jibrāil gave Muhammad the secret of success in his war against Jews. On Jibrāil's advice Muhammad threw a handful of dust at the enemy, the specks multiplying by hundreds of thousands to blind the enemy and give victory to the Muslims.[66]

In the end Jibrāil, accompanied by Izrāil, came to tell Muhammad about his imminent death. While Muhammad bade farewell to his kith and kin and other believers, both angels disappeared. As the moment of the Prophet's death drew near, Izrāil reappeared to take his life. Muhammad requested him to wait until Jibrāil returned. Jibrāil appeared with all *firishtahs*, and Izrāil took the soul out of his body. The corpse of the Prophet was bathed, and Jibrāil himself applied the sweet perfume. The funeral prayer of the Prophet was performed by Allāh himself in heaven.[67]

The process of acculturation of Muslim tradition was further stimulated by attempts of our writers to set the characters, situations, and stories in the natural geographical, social, and cultural milieus of the land. The entire atmosphere of these narratives was saturated with local color. The local landscape, flora and fauna, food and dresses, music and amusements, customs and values—all conjured up the image of Bengal and imparted an air of congruity and reality to their stories.

The river Nile in Egypt was introduced as the Ganges. To seduce Yusuf, Zulaikha sent her bewitching companions to Vrindāvan, celebrated in Hindu tradition for the love-dalliance of Krișna, Rādhā, and the companions of Rādhā.[68] During his victorious march, Amir Hamza fought against the

[65] Sultān, *ibid.*, fols. 179-80, 184-85; Mahmud, *ibid.*, p. 217 (text).
[66] Sultān, *ibid.*, fols. 251-53.
[67] Saiyid Sultān, *Wafāt-i Rasul* (DMS 138: sl 41), fols. 1-23.
[68] Shāh Muhammad Saghir, *Yusuf*, fols. 24, 32.

king of Gauda-deś, that is, Bengal, and subsequently converted him to Islam. He also marched against, subdued, and converted the king of Rosāng in the south of Chattagrām in Bengal. Reference was also made to the Himalayan peak of Kailās.[69]

The landscape of Egypt, recreated with the natural phenomena typical of the Bengali scene, contained blossoming *ām* (mango) and *jām* (blackberry) trees, exuding fragrance all around, and *bhramar* (bees), floating in the air in search of romance with flowers. Of flowers, *champā (michelia campaka)*, *yuthikā* (jasmine), and *golāp* (rose) dominated the entire landscape. The Hindu calendar month of *Agrahāyan* brought with it the exotic aroma of the ripened *śāli*, a variety of rice plant, the myriad shades of the blossoming spikelets of all other varieties of rice plants, and the chirping of the parrots and other birds like *khanjanā*, *doyel*, and *pāpiyā*, enlivening the landscape. Elsewhere in these writings there are references to flowers like *mādhavi*, *mālati*, *nāgeśvar*, *ketaki*, *bak*, *bhumikeśar*, and *tagar*.[70]

The food was no more alien to the local tastes. Muhammad and his wife, Khadija, enjoyed a grand meal that included rice, *ghee* (clarified butter), and sweet *dadhi* (curds).[71] Khāqān, the warrior-prince of Iraq, enjoyed a sumptuous dinner, which included rice and several curries, finishing with camphor, betel-leaves, and betel-nuts. The meal was followed by *āchman*, a Hindu ceremonial ablution.[72] Hauwā, Ādam's wife, entertained her husband with *sandeś*, a popular Bengali sweet. Muhammad was asked about the first item of food offered to a believer in paradise. He was inclined to fish, especially its

[69] Abd al-Nabi, *Vijay*, fols. 804, 945, 1067-1074. In Hindu tradition Mt. Kailās is believed to be the abode of god Śiv.

[70] *Ibid.*, fol. 827; Saghir, *Yusuf*, fols. 17-18, 50, 52-53; Sultān, *Shab*, fol. 147; Donā Ghāzi, *Saif*, fol. 167 mc.

[71] Sultān, *ibid.*, fol. 53.

[72] Sābirid Khān, *Rasul*, fol. 16 mc.

cerebral parts. The Prophet's answer, chosen by the Bengali writer, seemed significant in the light of the proverbial Bengali liking for fish, for its brain in particular.[73]

Furthermore, the cosmetics and dresses of the alien characters in these stories did not present any contrast with the local situation. Zulaikha and her female companions used for self-decorations vermilion (*sindur*), sandal-paste (*chandan*), and perfumes of *aguru*, a variety of scented wood highly valued among Indian cosmetics. Their hair was done in a locally appreciated style, called the *kabari-khonpā*. While making love to his wife with a Hindu name, Bidhu-prabhā, Ibn Amin of Egypt, had his body smeared by the vermilion and collyrium (*kājal*) that she used.[74] Badi al-Jamāl beautified herself with collyrium, sandal-paste, and vermilion.[75] The presents of the Abyssinian ruler to Muhammad included sandal-wood, vermilion, and the scented wood of *aguru*. The bridal decorations of Fātima made use of these items and also of colored powders (*ābir*).[76] On Saif al-Muluk's desertion of the royal palace, his royal father gave up food and garbed himself in the style of a *yogi*, thus expressing his loss of worldly desires.[77]

The locally familiar social etiquettes were freely attributed to these alien Muslim characters. Ali offered his respect to the Prophet by prostrating himself. Muhammad greeted him by kissing and embracing.[78] Since Umar recognized the divine mission of Muhammad, he prostrated himself at the feet of the Prophet and bowed down in *aṣṭānga*, a local mode of paying utmost respect.[79] Saif al-Muluk honored his father-in-law by prostrating himself and kissing his shoes. Sāhābān,

[73] Sultān, *Shab*, fols. 171-72.
[74] Saghir, *Yusuf*, fols. 17, 50, 74.
[75] Donā Ghāzi, *Saif*, fols. 11 mc, 29 mc, 93 mc.
[76] Sultān, *Shab*, fol. 173.
[77] Donā Ghāzi, *Saif*, fol. 310.
[78] Sābirid Khān, *Rasul*, fols. 4 mc, 21 mc.
[79] Sultān, *Shab*, fol. 75.

father of Badi al-Jamāl, blessed her by touching her forehead.[80]

The social ceremonies like marriage were largely molded in the local cast. The marriage of Ibn Amin and Bidhu-prabhā took place in a *svayamvar* gathering, in which the bride chose her husband from the assembled people and received him with garlands. Aziz, the king of Egypt, rode a palanquin to the place of the bride, Zulaikha. The band playing on the occasion comprised all locally known instruments such as *dhāk, dhol, dandi, kāsi, mandirā, mādal*, and *tabalā*.[81] The marriage of Badi al-Jamāl was preceded by her father's sending out letters of invitation, asking, in a typical Bengali manner, for "good wishes or blessings as appropriate for the persons concerned." During the marriage celebration her companions revelled in throwing colored powders at one another or putting betel leaves[82] into each other's mouths. The ceremony itself commenced, in the Hindu manner, at the auspicious time (*śubha-lagna*), with the women-folk making the ritually auspicious sound (*śubhadhvani*). Young vivacious women, carrying clay lamps in their hands and golden pitchers on their heads, added luster to the occasion. Some threw plain or rose water at one another, some chewed betel-leaves, and some sang *dhāmāli*, a type of erotic song in Bengal. The bride was carried by her friends and given a bath, as in the case of Hindu brides in Bengal, with water collected previously by them in pitchers during a highly stylized type of erotic song called *sahelā* or *juluā*. After her bath Badi al-Jamāl was dressed in gorgeous apparel and glittering jewels and decorated with sweet perfumes and cosmetics. Her palms were colored red, which was a north Indian custom.[83] At the marriage cere-

[80] Donā Ghāzi, *Saif*, fols. 7 mc, 139.

[81] Saghir, *Yusuf*, fols. 51-52, 74.

[82] Betel leaves and betel nuts are traditionally significant objects in social-ritual performances in Bengal.

[83] Donā Ghāzi, *Saif*, fols. 140-42.

mony of Ibn Amin and Bidhu-prabhā, women threw various kinds of flowers, delightfully scented water, wisps of grass (*durbā*), and paddy (*dhānya*), *durbā* and *dhānya* or *dhān*, being two more objects of great social-ritual significance in Bengal. Zulaikha after her marriage was accompanied by her midwife to the place of her husband, a practice not uncommon in Bengal and elsewhere in India.[84] The marriage ceremony of Fātima also witnessed a number of these local practices. Her bath, preparatory to the marriage, was preceded by the application of perfumes to her body and followed by the usual decorations and ceremonial feeding, as practiced locally, with honey, ghee, yoghurt, sugar, and fruit. The marriage-songs, *sahelā*, formed a no less significant part of this celebration, and fireworks and theatrical performances were additional features of Fātima's marriage festivities.[85]

The glorification of the military exploits of the Muslim heroes formed a significant aspect of this narrative literature and an important link in the attainment of their overall objects of vindicating Islam. The Muslim warriors in these writings often fought with weapons well known in the Hindu mythological tradition. In one of the wars of Prophet Muhammad, *gāndiv*, the divine bow of Arjun famed in the Mahābhārat war, was used. The divine missile of the god Brahmā called *brahmāstra* was also used.[86] The Muslim warrior Umiya hurled it against the army of the Persian king Noshirwān, causing a fire that consumed even the tusks of elephants. In the same war the Muslim army deployed "the arrow of Dadhichi."[87] At the battle of Uhud a leader of the infidel Meccan army used the *ardha-chandra-vān*, the crescent arrow of Hindu mythology, which was intercepted and cut in two by the Muslim commander. Abu Sufyān, the leader of the Mec-

[84] Saghir, *Yusuf*, fols. 13, 75.
[85] Sultān, *Shab*, *passim*.
[86] Zain al-Din, *Rasul*, fol. 17.
[87] Abd al-Nabi, *Vijay*, fols. 943, 1087.

can unbelievers, shot at his enemies with *agni-vān*, the fire-arrow, but the latter intercepted it before it could reach its mark.[88] Against the army of the king of Iraq the Muslims used, among other weapons, *divya-vān* (the divine arrow), *śel* (disc), *gadā* (club), and *khadga* (scimitar).[89] The various musical instruments forming part of the Muslim war-bands were those locally known and popularized by Hindu epics and legends. These were *jaya-dhol, dhāk, mridanga, ghāghari, śankha, sānāi, dandi, kāsi, dundhuvi, mandirā, mādal*, and *tabalā*.[90]

The similes, metaphors, idioms, and imageries used in these writings were characteristically familiar in the Bengali literary tradition. The nose of the Muslim beauty was compared to the sesame flower (*til-phul*), and the eyes to those of the bird *khanjanā*. The curved nose found its analogy in the beak of a hawk (*khaga-nāsā*). Badi al-Jamāl's tender arms excelled even the lotus stalks. The enchanting black mole on her face was like a bee on the lotus. The eyebrows earned comparison with a pair of bows, and the teeth to pomegranate seeds. The lover and the beloved were to each other as the bee to the flower or the insect to the flame. The idea of the passionate look of love was conveyed by the imagery of the dove gazing at the moon. Saiyād's pangs of separation from his beloved were no less intense than Lorak Rājā's on his separation from Chandrāni.[91]

The stories were often set in the local motifs. The Muslim hero on the eve of a great battle was equipped with the coats of mail and weapons previously used by earlier prophets and warriors, exactly as figures of the Hindu pantheon were armed

[88] Sultān, *Shab*, fols. 182, 199.

[89] Sābirid Khān, *Rasul*, fols. 3, 9, 26.

[90] Zain al-Din, *Rasul*, fols. 19-20, 51.

[91] Sultān, *Shab*, fols. 147, 827; Donā Ghāzi, *Saif*, fols. 18, 37 mc, 117, 120; Abd al-Nabi, *Vijay*, fol. 822. The Lorak-Chandrāni romantic tradition, popular in Bengal and in northern India, found its Muslim Bengali poets like Daulat Qāzi and Saiyid Alāwal to write on this theme. The work, begun by Daulat Qāzi, was completed by Alāwal. (See Daulat Qāzi, *Sati Maynā*.)

by Hindu divinities with their own weapons.[92] For his great combat with Noshirwān, Amir Hamza assumed the bracelet of Ādam, the robe of Khalil, the waist-band of Ishāq, the whip of Ismāil, and the bow of the great warrior Rustam.[93]

Even popular local fairytale motifs were occasionally adopted. A beautiful girl was captured by a demon, who kept her hidden in a casket placed in a jar. The jar was concealed deep under the sea. The girl could be recovered from the clutches of the demon only by breaking the jar and killing thereby the demon.[94] A similar Bengali folktale motif of a pair of wise birds, named Byāngamā and Byāngami, who were capable of looking into the future and warning the hero or heroine of the piece against the impending danger, was introduced in the story of *Yusuf-Zulaikha* where Zulaikha received the right advice from these birds.[95]

[92] Cf. the tradition of the goddess Chandi being armed by other divinities on the eve of her great battle with the demon king Mahiṣāsur.

[93] Abd al-Nabi, *Vijay*, fol. 851.

[94] Donā Ghāzi, *Saif*, fol. 166 mc.

[95] Saghir, *Yusuf*, fols. 3-4.

4
Cosmogony—Cosmology

The cosmogonical ideas presented in the mediators' writings were also strongly permeated by indigenous influences. The non-Muslim local ideas of this category formed part of the *mangal* literature and were drawn from various religious-sectarian sources popular in and outside Bengal, such as the dharmist, the nāthist, and the purānic. The Muslim stream of cosmogonical thoughts and beliefs embodied in these Bengali writings flowed generally from the Islamic cosmogonical tradition nurtured in the Judaeo-Christian environment in West Asia. And yet the Muslim and the non-Muslim traditions in Bengal strikingly converged on each other. This correspondence was as much due to a general process of cultural interaction between India and the Islamic world as to the specific influence of non-Muslim Bengali ideas on the Bengali Muslim writers on cosmogony.

Apart from being the last revelation in time and, therefore, symbolically the synthesis of all the traditions before it, Islam spread geographically over the middle belt of the world, and consequently became the historical heir to many of the earlier civilizations of Western Asia and the Mediterranean world which contributed to the remarkable efflorescence of Islamic arts and sciences. With the establishments of the Abbāsid caliphate (A.D. 749), translations of Greek, Syriac, Pahlavi, and Sanskrit scientific works became available in Arabic, with the result that in addition to the earlier schools of grammarians, poets, traditionalists, commentators, historians, and *sufi* ascetics, all of whom relied almost entirely upon the Islamic revelation for their knowledge, there now began to appear new schools which drew from non-Islamic sources as well. The new schools ranged from the logicians and rationalists like *mutazilis*, to the astronomers and mathematicians, and finally to the followers of the more esoteric forms of the Greek, Alexandrian, and Chaldean sciences connected with the Sabaean community in Harrān.[1] During the caliphate of Mansur (A.D. 754-75) and Harun al-Rashid (A.D. 786-809) some Indian scientific works were translated into Arabic partly from the Persian or Pahlavi translations, and the rest from Sanskrit. The astrology of the *Brahma-siddhānta* of Brahmagupta, which was translated from Sanskrit under Mansur with the assistance of Indian scholars, was known even before Ptolemy's *Almagest*.[2] Jabir ibn-Haiyān, the most celebrated of all Muslim alchemists, claimed to have been acquainted with the sciences of the Hindus.[3] The direct contact with the Buddhist monasteries in eastern Persia, Transoxiana, and Balkh also facilitated the process.[4] It was, however, through the keen intellectual curiosity of individual scholars like al-Biruni that notions of Indian science and philosophy found their way into Islamic tradition. He was one of the most significant contributors to the formulation of Islamic cosmogonical and ontological principles.[5]

The general correspondence between Indian and Islamic cosmogonical ideas may be noted under the three following

[1] For a general historical background of the Islamic sciences and the means of transmission of the ancient sciences to the Muslims, see D. D. O'Leary, *How Greek Science Passed to the Arabs* (London, 1948); M. Meyerhof, "On the Transmission of Greek and Indian Science to the Arabs," *Islamic Culture* (Hyderabad), XI, no. 1, Jan. 1937, pp. 17-29; G. Sarton, *Introduction to the History of Science* (Washington, 3 vols., 1927-1948), vols. I-II.

[2] T. J. De Boer, *The History of Philosophy in Islam*, Eng. tr. by E. R. Jones (London, Luzac, 1933), p. 9.

[3] S. H. Nasr, *An Introduction to Islamic Cosmological Doctrines* (Harvard, 1964), p. 38.

[4] R. A. Nicholson, *The Mystics of Islam* (London, 1914), p. 16.

[5] S. H. Nasr, *Islamic Cosmological Doctrines*, p. 111.

headings, the creator and creation, the primal or cosmic elements, and the cosmic principle and process.

The Creator and Creation[6]

Ancient and medieval cosmological sciences shared in common the recognition of the unity of nature which all of these sciences sought to demonstrate and upon which they were all based. This unity was the natural consequence of all unity of the divine principle, which formed the basis of all the ancient "greater mysteries" and which, either veiled in a mythological dress or expressed directly as a metaphysical truth, was to be found as the central idea in nearly all traditional civilizations. The question of the unity of the divine principle and the consequent unity of nature remained particularly important in Islam, where the idea of unity (*tauhid*) overshadowed all others and remained at every level of Islamic civilization the basic principle upon which all else depended. The ancient cosmological sciences were for the most part based upon the unity of nature and the search for the transcendent cause of all things and were, therefore, far from un-Islamic, even if they antedated the historical manifestations of Islam. It was this common search for a demonstration of the unity of nature among ancient cosmological sciences that brought them closer to the Islamic revelation and made them easily assimilable into its perspective. Apart from a small number of investigators inspired by Greek philosophic ideas, the Muslims who engaged in the pursuit of science did so like the Hebrews, with a view to discovering in the wonders of nature the signs or tokens of the story of God.[7]

Khalq is the term applied in the *Qurān* to God's creative activity, which includes not only the original creation *ex nihilo* but also the making of the world and of man and all that

[6] This particular issue is treated later in depth in a slightly different context. (*Infra*, Chapter 5, pp. 149-59.)

[7] R. Levy, *Social Structure of Islam*, p. 460.

is and that happens. To express the relation and contrast between the creator and creation, the terms *haqq* and *khalq* are respectively used.[8] The nature of the relation between the two and the corresponding problem of transcendence (*tanzih*) and immanence (*tashbih*) of God were long debated by theologians and mystics in Islam. The answer, of mystics in particular, was sought in a balance between absolute transcendence and total immanence.[9]

The significance of this compromise from the cosmogonical stand-point may be viewed in the process of gradual "individualization" and "qualification" of the absolute from the state of bare potentiality to one of unity in multiplicity. In sufic parlance this was known as the gradual descent (*tanazzul*) of the absolute from what was in the initial stage a bare potentiality, purely negative and supra-existential (*al-amā*), through a stage where the divine consciousness moved to the realization of its thought and knew itself as the transcendent unity (*ahdiyat*), to the third stage of oneness in multiplicity (*wahdat*), or *haqiqa al-Muhammadiya*, or *nur al- or nur-i Muhammadiya*, as this particular stage was often called.[10] The sufic model of this triad was but a different version of what the Muslim rationalists, metaphysicians, and theologians had already put in the form of the absolute, the universal intellect, and the universal soul. According to them, the first thing that the creator called into existence was intellect, an extremely perfect and excellent substance in which the form of all things was contained and from which other beings proceeded by stages. In the writings of the *Ikhwān al-Safā* God was sometimes placed above being, while in other instances they implied that being was divided into God and universe.[11]

[8] The *Qurān*, *sura* (2:159), (11:59), (67:3).

[9] *Infra*, pp. 149ff.

[10] R. A. Nicholson, *Studies in Islamic Mysticism* (Cambridge, 1921), pp. 94-95.

[11] Nasr, *Islamic Cosmological Doctrines*, p. 53n.

This led some philosophers and many mystics to the assumption that before the manifestation of his creation "the eternal creator was concealed in God."[12] Philosophers like Fārābi and Ibn Sinā laid the basis for the development of the sufic notion of creation by establishing a connection between *nur* or the divine light[13] and the intellect, the former being communicated to the latter at the first instance by the prime cause, the creator. Around the nuclear concept of *nur*, *sufis* developed their elaborate doctrine of *nur-i Muhammadiya*, or *nur-i Muhammadi*, believed to have been created before all things.

The concept of the aforesaid triad bears a striking similarity, on one hand, to the neo-Platonic triad of the one, the divine mind and the all soul, and, on the other, to that of its Hindu counterpart consisting of the absolute (*brahman*), the creative spirit (*iśvar*), and the world spirit (*hiranya-garbha*), representing respectively God as unmanifest potentiality, God as creative power, and God as immanent in this world. The integral nature of the supreme reality was symbolized in the *Taittiriya-upaniṣad* by the concept of *tri-suparna*, where the absolute was conceived as a nest from which three birds emerged, namely *iśvar*, *hiranya-garbha* and *virāj*. The Hindu metaphysical and cosmogonical ideas make a clear distinction between the absolute quality-less aspect of the supreme being, which can be described only negatively, and its self-conscious being, representing his will as the creator. The vedantic conception of the ultimate reality or the *brahman* has two aspects—the unqualified inactive absolute aspect and the qualified active aspect called *iśvar*. While the absolute remains unconcerned with the material world, *iśvar* in association with

[12] L. Massignon, *La Passion d'al-Hallaj*, p. 657, cited by De Boer, *History of Philosophy in Islam*, p. 893.

[13] The idea that God is light and reveals Himself as such in the world and to man is very old and widely disseminated in Oriental religions as well as in Hellenistic gnosis and philosophy. See De Boer in M. Th. Houtsma *et al.* (eds.), *Encyclopaedia of Islam* (Leyden and London, 4 vols., 1913-1936), vol. III, p. 955.

māyā calls the illusory world into existence. The absolute in its unqualified aspect is not the creator of the universe, being neither existent nor non-existent.[14] According to the *Manu-samhitā*, the *Hari-vamśa*, and the *purāns*, God himself was born in "the golden germ" as Brahmā or the creator-God.[15] In keeping with this general trend of cosmogonical thought, popularized especially through the purānic channel, medieval Bengali Hindu writers made consistent reference to Dharma or Niranjan, who himself being produced by the supreme lord was responsible for the rest of creation.[16]

The Primal or Cosmic Elements

Hindu and Islamic cosmogonies shared a common ground also in respect to their notions of the primordial elements. The concept of creation *ex nihilo* was practically unknown to the ancient world. It is present neither in Babylonian, nor Jewish, nor Egyptian, nor Greek tradition, and its existence in Iranian thought is at least problematical. On the other hand, "the keenest philosophers of antiquity, the Hindus, evolved the idea as early as the *Rigved*, even though but vaguely. . . ."[17] The concept of creation *ex nihilo* as understood in Hindu cosmogony does not, however, refer to the creation of being from non-being. The absolute is non-dual (*advaita*). This does not mean that the absolute is non-being; rather, it means only that it is all-inclusive and that nothing exists outside it. So reference to creation *ex nihilo* in Hindu cosmogonical system has to be understood only as creation out of a state of non-existence of primal elements coeval with the primal state of being in unmanifest potentiality.

[14] S. Radhakrishnan, *The Principal Upanisads* (London, 1953), pp. 35-37, 63, 65-66.

[15] S. Radhakrishnan, *Indian Philosophy* (London, 1923), vol. I, p. 100.

[16] S. B. Dasgupta, *Obscure Religious Cults of Bengal as Background of Early Bengali Literature* (Calcutta, rev. ed., 1962), pp. 312, 314, 319-20.

[17] L. H. Gray in J. Hastings (ed.), *Encyclopaedia of Religion*, vol. IV, p. 126; also pp. 156-67.

Islamic cosmogony, consistent with its cardinal doctrine of non-duality of God, similarly stressed on the creation of the world *ex nihilo*. Inspired by this outlook, the Muslim cosmologists such as al-Biruni made a total discount of the view of the eternity of the world, as advocated by the Greek philosophers.[18] According to Baizāwi: "God could create absolutely *ex nihilo*, as He created the heavens and earth, or from matter already existing, as He created all that lies between the heavens and the earth."[19] The part of the above statement postulating "matter already existing" underlined, however, the presence of some dualistic elements in Islamic cosmogony. The earlier traditions developed such ideas. According to al-Tirmidi, Allāh was "in the clouds" before creation, and he created "in darkness."[20] This reference to "darkness," with corresponding notions of "light," tended to produce the suspicion of dualism akin to that in Manichaeanism between *nur* and *zulmat* as the eternal principles until the monistic doctrine of light of the neo-Platonists in the ninth century was found compatible with Islamic monism and was integrated into it.[21] In the later tradition, the process of creation was elaborated with speculations about God's throne and primeval water.[22] The primeval water played a significant role in Islamic cosmogony as in many other ancient traditions. According to the *Qurān* (21:31; 24:44), all living things were created from water, but man was created of clay (15:26; 23:12ff; 35:12) and the *jinn* of fire (15:27). The subsequent development of Muslim cosmology totally dispensed with all dualistic incompatibilities.

[18] Nasr, *Islamic Cosmological Doctrines*, p. 116.

[19] Commentaries on the *Qurān* (*sura* 5:20), cited by Levy, *Social Structure of Islam*, p. 465.

[20] *Tafsir* (*sura* 11:1), cited by T. J. De Boer in M. Th. Houtsma *et al.* (eds.), *Encyclopaedia of Islam*, vol. II, p. 892; also *Imān*, *bāb* 18, and *sura* 29:8, cited De Boer, *ibid.*

[21] De Boer, *ibid.*, s.v. *Nur*, vol. III, pp. 955-56.

[22] The *Qurān*, *sura* 11:9.

Long before this, Hindu cosmogony went through a similar process of development from its original dualistic to its later monistic position. In the *Rig-ved* itself, to which the beginning of Hindu monism is traced, the cosmogonical ideas derived from "various bases" were not "mutually reconciled," nor were they "considered or even suspected to be incompatible." The primordial *nihil* often reduced to primeval water and/or primeval darkness.[23] The *Satapatha-brāhman* (11:1:6) says: "In the beginning the universe was water, nothing but water." The *Brihad-āranyak-upaniṣad* (5:5:1) puts it more emphatically that water alone was in the beginning, Satya arising from water, Brahmā from Satya, Prajāpati from Brahmā, and the gods from Prajāpati. According to the *Taittiriya-brāhman* (1:1:3) and the *Taittiriya-samhitā* (5:6; 7:1,5), Prajāpati was born in a lotus leaf, in water which existed in the beginning. The purānic literature also represents the supreme being as floating in the primordial water and hence known as Nārāyan. Thus the notion of primordial elements, with suggestions of their being coeval with the creator, appeared in the earlier stages of both Hindu and Muslim cosmogonical thoughts. But both systems in the course of their development divested themselves of the dualistic elements and projected the concept of creation *ex nihilo*. Both Hindu and Muslim literatures of medieval Bengal harped consistently on a theme of creation *ex nihilo*.

The Cosmic Principle and Process

The cosmic process and the principle underlying creation constitute another area that marked the convergence of Islamic and Indian cosmogonical ideas. One of the most potent metaphysical principles underlying almost all systems of Indian cosmogony—Hindu, Buddhist, and Jain—is the passive and the active or the static and the dynamic aspects of reality as revealed through the process of creation. The *sāmkhya* phi-

[23] W. N. Brown, "Theories of Creation in the Rig Veda," *Journal of the American Oriental Society*, LXXXV (1965), pp. 23ff.

losophy exercised a seminal influence on the development of all these cosmogonical systems. *Puruṣ* in the *sāmkhya* system is taken to be the unchanging principle of pure consciousness, while *prakriti* or *pradhān* is the primordial cosmic substance. Creation proceeded from *prakriti* in contact with *puruṣ*. Through this contact the essence of one transmitted to the other, and the creative process was set in motion. This particular nature of the philosophical concepts of *puruṣ* and *prakriti* gave rise to the tendency to regard *puruṣ* as male and *prakriti* as female and their contact as the union which gave birth to the universe.

Islamic cosmogony is similarly based on the principle of an active-passive dichotomy within the universe. The dichotomous nature has also been construed in terms of masculine-feminine duality. As number two and three in the hierarchy of beings, standing just below the creator, the universal intellect and soul become the principles of the whole universe; the duality upon which things are based returns to them in one way or another. In reference to the duality of form and matter, light and darkness, spirit and body, cause and effect, it is said that "the duality refers to the Intellect and Soul which contain in themselves the active and passive principles through which the life and activity of the Universe can be understood."[24] Creation is the "dynamic" and "feminine" aspect of the divine. It possesses in itself an "active" and "masculine" aspect which is called nature and which is the source of all activity in the universe; and a "passive" and "feminine" aspect which appears as the "matter" or "inert" base of this activity. With respect to God, the intellect is purely passive, in obedience, tranquillity, and permanent desire for union with the divine principle. The universal soul in turn remains passive and feminine with respect to the intellect.[25]

Islamic cosmogony, especially in its sufic orientation, also

[24] Nasr, *Islamic Cosmological Doctrines*, p. 56.

[25] *Ikhwān al-Safā*, *Rasāil*, vol. III, p. 188, cited by Nasr, *ibid.*, pp. 53-56.

makes use of the symbolism of love (*ishq*) to show the attraction between God and the universe. The creator is, in fact, the only beloved (*mashuq*) and the only object of desire (*murād*). The power of this yearning (*shawq*) is made the very cause of the coming into being of things and the law governing the universe.[26] That creation proceeds from the desire of the creator is also a motif common in Hindu cosmogonical thought. In the *Taittiriya-brāhman* (1:1:3), the *Taittiriya-samhitā* (7:1:5), and the *Brihad-jābālopaniṣad* (1:1) the universe proceeds from the "desire" of Prajāpati. In the *Nrisimha-purva-tāpani* it is said: "All this remained as water along (without any form). Only Prajapati came to be in the lotus-leaf. In his mind arose the desire, 'let me create this' (the world of names and forms)."[27] The cosmogonical notions in middle Bengali literature, both Hindu and Muslim, were, as treated below, deeply permeated by the concept of love (*prem*) or desire (*kām*) of the creator.

A balanced appreciation of the endeavor of Muslim mediators in this particular area demands an adequate understanding of the aforesaid agreement and convergence between classical Islamic and Indian cosmogonical traditions. There were unquestionable elements of an indigenous character permeating their cosmogonical thoughts. On the other hand, their contributions in respect to the elements which both of these systems held in common were directed toward careful and selective use of Islamic materials to suit local interests and needs.

The most significant aspect of their effort was the large accent on the mythological rather than on the scientific or speculative side of cosmogony. It is important to bear in mind that cosmogonical myths were not stressed or encouraged in Islam,[28] though later tradition constructed an elaborate imag-

[26] Nasr, *ibid.*, p. 53.

[27] S. Radhakrishnan, *Principal Upanisads*, pp. 35n, 37.

[28] Cf. "In conformity with the non-mythological perspective of Islam, al-

inary superstructure with the scanty materials supplied in the *Qurān*. Whatever place speculative ontological ideas found in the cosmogonical thoughts of Bengali Muslims, they were derived almost entirely from the mystic-sufic notions of the godhead *vis-à-vis* creation. This brings us to the other important facet of their cosmogonical writings, namely, the dominant strand of sufic cosmogony. Apart from its speculative implications, the *sufi* ideas about the creator and creation also gave birth to some conceptual developments within the mythical tradition, which the Bengali Muslim mediators not only accepted but also often adapted to the demands of local beliefs. Almost invariably they adopted the sufic concept of the universe's proceeding from the love of God through the creation of *nur-i Muhammadi*, with a significant difference in the fact that the abstract sufic concept of *nur* assumed in their writings a clearly anthropomorphized and mythical form. Consequently, the sufic concept of *nur-i Muhammadi* re-emerged in the mediators' cosmogonical writings in its anthropomorphized and personalized form of Nur Muhammad.[29] Created by the lord, Nur Muhammad in his turn brought the whole world into existence from the drops of perspiration (*gharma, ghām*) appearing in the different parts of his body. In the creation of Nur Muhammad the mystic notion of love found favor with these writers. The divine love was epitomized in the relationship between Allāh and Nur Muhammad, the latter being called the friend or lover (*sakhā, mitra*) of the former. Unable to "enjoy" or "realize" himself in the infinite void, God created Nur Muhammad of his own self.

The corresponding Hindu Bengali notions of creation underlined the initial emergence of Dharma or Niranjan from

---

Biruni rejects the mythological cosmology of the Hindus." (Nasr, *Islamic Cosmological Doctrines*, p. 134.)

[29] For this reason we have, in our discussion, referred to Nur Muhammad in this personalized form, unless it is otherwise indicated in the text concerned.

the unmanifest lord's own self, and the entire creation following later from the work of Dharma or Niranjan. The idea of primordial beings created from the perspiration of the lord was also prevalent among the Hindus. For the dharmists, Ādyā-śakti, the personalized feminine form of the primordial creative energy, was produced from the perspiration of the lord.[30] The notion of desire underlying the process of creation was a pervasive Indian cosmogonical thought which found prominence in Hindu Bengali writings.[31]

The state of the unqualified absolute, containing the potency of creation, was consistently emphasized by the Bengali Muslim writers. God was mentioned as having no beginning, end, abode, and existence. He was formless and indivisible. The state of non-existence was one without the directions of right, left, high, and low. The potential character of the primordial non-existence, as distinct from non-being, was stressed. The supreme being was omnipresent, not a void, but a manifestation of the formless in non-existence. Creation was not possible without the lord, Niranjan, who is ever concealed like the formless in the form, the heat in the fire, the hardness in the clay, the drops in the water, and the rays in the sun and the moon.[32] There was

> no land, nor water, nor the earth—no form in the void. The earth, heaven and hell, were all enveloped in darkness; there was neither the sky, nor the moon, the sun, the stars . . . no fresh clouds, air and fire . . . nor rivers, jungles, oceans . . . the universe was bereft of everything . . . and there was God alone.[33]

The lord stood as the form in the void at the beginning and was like the form lying in concealment in the formless. The

[30] Rāmāi Pandit, *Śunya-purān*, ed. by C. C. Banerji (Calcutta, 1335 B.S./A.D. 1929), *Sriṣti-pattan* (section), pp. 1-42; also S. B. Dasgupta, *Obscure Religious Cults*, pp. 317, 320.

[31] Dasgupta, *ibid.*, pp. 315-16; S. Radhakrishnan, *Indian Philosophy*, vol. I, p. 102.

[32] Saiyid Sultān, *Nabi*, fol. 1 mc.

[33] Shaikh Zāhid, *Ādya*, pp. 1ff.

form and the formless were united as one in the divine essence.[34]

The process of gradual "becoming" or "manifestation" or "descent" of the absolute, as presented in this literature, took the character of the triad. The triad represented a basic unity, the form and symbolism of which were variously drawn. The divine essence contained these elements in an unmanifest unity, and the separation of them in the process of actualization of the supreme being disturbed the cosmic equipoise and set the process of creation in motion. This idea stood very close to the *sāmkhya* system, in which the cosmic process flowed from the disturbance in the equilibrium in the nature of *prakriti*, consisting of the three qualities (*guns*) of the intelligence stuff (*sattva*), the energy (*rajas*), and the inertia (*tamas*).[35] Some of the Muslim writers directly mentioned the three qualities or *guns*, by virtue of which the creator performed the functions respectively of creation (*srijan*), preservation (*pālan*), and destruction (*samhār*). The separation of "the three qualities from the one" resulted in "many from the three."[36]

The actual form of the triad, symbolizing the unity of godhead, found various representations in these writings. A differentiation, clear or vague, between the unqualified absolute state (*ajnān*) and its conscious state of being (*jnān*) was generally maintained. The conscious was immanent in the unconscious as the fragrance in the flower. The unconscious state was compared to one of rest and passivity akin to the static aspect of reality. It was also depicted as a state of deep slumber, from which the supreme being was awakened by ego or consciousness (*chaitanya*).[37]

The entire theme, beginning with the conscious and active

[34] Shaikh Chānd, *Tālib*, fol. 8 mc; Shaikh Parān (untitled), fol. 1 mc; Ali Rajā, *Āgam*, fols. 29-33, 47, 73-74; also his *Jnān-sāgar*, fols. 83, 129.

[35] S. Radhakrishnan, *Indian Philosophy*, pp. 502-03.

[36] Saiyid Sultān, *Nabi*, fols. 1 mc, 3 mc; Ali Rajā, *Āgam*, fol. 3.

[37] Sultān, *ibid.*, fol. 2 mc; Sultān, *Shab*, fol. 1 mc; Shaikh Chānd, *Tālib*, fol. 8.

aspect of the godhead down to the creation of Nur Muhammad, who was the final link in the chain of the triad and was the direct source of the creation, remained a common theme of these writers. Different writers used, however, varied symbolism to express the same idea.[38]

Some attempted to reduce the concept of the triad to the symbolic interrelations of Ahad, Ahmad, and Muhammad. God created Ahmad as the personalized active principle of the absolute undifferentiated state of Ahad: "Allāh is the supreme one, Ahad, without a second. . . . He made Ahmad from Ahad. . . . You should know both Ahad and Ahmad as one."[39] The esoteric identity and importance of the Perso-Arabic letter, *mim*, and its Bengali equivalent, *ma*, were stressed. The letter, when added to Ahad, made Ahmad and Muhammad as well.[40] One *mim* gave birth to three names in the three worlds: "The name Ahmad was remembered in heaven, that of Muhammad on earth, and that of Mahmud by the snakes in hell."[41] An attempt was also made to find corresponding ideas in the Hindu system. Ahad was equated with Hindu Ādya, and Ahmad with Anādya. The analogy was carried further, and in the making of Anādya from Ādya was seen the importance of the additional Bengali letter *na*, from which the origin of Nārāyan or Viṣnu was derived in the same way as the letter *mim* formed the name of Muhammad. The symbolism of *mim* was also used to introduce the concept of *nur*. The letter *mim*, which distinguished between Ahad and Ahmad and made Muhammad, could be substituted by *nur*. *Nur*, split into two, could make both Ahmad and Muhammad, and the *nur* of the latter was the cause of the creation.

[38] Sultān, *Nabi*, fol. 3; Sultān, *Shab*, fol. 1; Chānd, *ibid.*, fols. 7-9; Shaikh Parān, fol. 1; Mir Muhammad Shafi, *Nur-Qindil* (DMS 143: sl 236), fol. 2; Muhammad Khān, *Maqtal*, fol. 1.

[39] Hayāt Mahmud, *Hita*, p. 6.

[40] Hayāt Mahmud, *Ambiyā*, p. 8.

[41] Mahmud, *Hita*, p. 6.

Others made direct recourse to the Hindu symbols of the triad, represented by the sounds of *ākār* (*ā*), *ukār* (*u*), and *makār* (*ma*) combined into *om*: "As *ākār* is born of *nirākār* [formless], *ukār* is formed by the combination of *ākār* and *nirākār*. Thereafter, *makār* emerges between *ākār* and *ukār*."[42]

As regards the motive force in the actualization of the divine, the generality of our writers mentioned the absolute solitude of the supreme unmanifest, unable to self-realize.[43] Shaikh Zāhid referred to God's "loneliness" and consequent "unhappiness."[44] Ali Rajā dwelt at length on the mystic principle of duality uniting in the one. There was no love and dalliance in the state of the absolute, and the creative spirit could not have been expressed without the dual self.[45] The idea of cosmic desire and love was also underlined. God having projected his image looked at himself, as it were, on a "mirror," was overpowered with "desire" and filled with self-love. In the fashion of the Hindu symbolic triad, God discovered himself in *ukār*, on which he remained in contemplation. The formless and the formal aspects of the divine essence were compared to the Hindu tāntric notions of Bhāvak and Bhāvini respectively:

> Bhāvak, as it were, is plunged in the sea of Bhāvini. Bhāvak knows the bliss of love. . . . The bee alone knows the value of the lotus. . . . The bee is perpetually steeped in honey; so is Bhāvak in the mind of Bhāvini. The formless is consumed by love.[46]

The symbolism of Bhāvak and Bhāvini was also extended to cover the relationship of Allāh and Nur Muhammad, created out of the former's *nur*. Nur Muhammad was created in the likeness of God, as reflected in the mirror before him.

[42] Ali Rajā, *Āgam*, fols. 4-5; also Sultān, *Shab*, fol. 1.

[43] Cf. *Brihad-āranyaka-upaniṣad* (1:4). ". . . as there was nothing but himself, he felt no delight, and therefore 'made this, his Self, to fall in two, and thence arose husband and wife.' " H. Jacobi in J. Hastings (ed.), *Encyclopaedia of Religion*, vol. IV, p. 157.

[44] *Loc.cit.*

[45] *Āgam*, fol. 3.

[46] *Ibid.*, fols. 5-6, 10; also Sultān, *Nabi*, fols. 2-3 mc.

Shaikh Zāhid, one of the earliest known Bengali Muslim poets, made a striking departure from the otherwise common Muslim theme of the creation of Muhammad from Allāh's *nur*. He mentioned the "loneliness" of the lord, and the creation of the "friend" of God, due to this reason, but remained conspicuously silent about the *nur* or "light" of God. His version of the creative process ran strikingly close to the local tradition. It may seem "easy to detect a few *sufi* elements" in the cosmogonical ideas of Zāhid, as maintained by Tarafdar.[47] God, according to Zāhid, took his own "seed," a potential "image of his own self," and "deposited" it in the inaccessible "cosmic ocean." The reference to the "friend of God" and his creation in the "image of God" may suggest the influence of the sufic concept of "the perfect man," *insān-i kāmil*, who is the image of God. The *Qurān* also mentions the creation of Ādam in the image of Allāh. A close examination of the text in the wider context of Zāhid's total cosmogonical perspective as well as a knowledge of the Hindu cosmogony do not, however, warrant any easy conclusions. The extract under consideration contains three component elements: a. The seed (*rati*) of the lord; b. the potential image of the lord in the seed; c. deposition of the seed in the cosmic ocean. All of these were integral to the indigenous cosmogonical system. Tarafdar has taken the word, *rati*, for "love or passion,"[48] while we prefer to read it as "seed" or semen. His reading does not make much sense in reference to the third element in the text, concerning "deposition." On the other hand, the ideas of the seed of the Lord, which contained his image and from which followed creation, and its deposition in the waters were quite popular Hindu notions found in many Bengali cosmogonical accounts of purānic and *mangal* origin. Apart from the concept of *hiranya-garva* (the golden germ) emerging as the creator from primeval waters and the associated idea of *brah-*

[47] M. Tarafdar, *Husain Shāhi Bengal*, p. 202.
[48] *Ibid.*, pp. 199, 202.

māṇḍa, or the cosmic egg,[49] there is more direct reference in the *Manu-samhitā* (1:8-9)[50] to the seed of the creator, containing his own potency, being deposited in the primeval waters:

> He (*Svayambhu* i.e., the divine Self-existent), desiring to produce beings of many kinds from his own body, first with a thought created the waters, and placed his seed in them. That (seed) became a golden egg, in brilliancy equal to the sun: in that (egg) he himself was born as Brahmā,[51] the progenitor of the whole world.

Finally, excepting the reference to the "friend of God," there is nothing in the cosmogonical ideas of Shaikh Zāhid to infer sufic inspiration. On the contrary, the striking absence of the idea of *nur*, so important in the sufic thoughts and so common with other Bengali Muslim writers, tends to discourage the sufic view. The rest of his cosmogonical discussion revealed clear indebtedness to the ideas of popular Hindu tradition, such as the creation of primordial waters from the joy of the creator, air from his speech, fire from his anger, earth from the "soil" of his friend's body, and, finally, the creation of gods (*dev*), demons (*asur*), ogres (*rākṣas*) and others, culminating in the creation of mankind.

The concept of *nur* dominated, as already noted, the cosmogonical perception of the Bengali Muslim writers. Some sought to introduce this idea with the help of the Hindu symbolism of *jyoti*, the divine candescence: "What is divine candescence for us is called Nur Muhammad in Arabia."[52] One thing they all believed in common was the anthropomorphic character of *nur*. *Nur*, in its physical form of Nur Muhammad, remained the direct source of the entire creative process. The writers, however, lacked a consensus on the ac-

[49] H. Jacobi in J. Hastings (ed.), *Encyclopaedia of Religion*, vol. IV, p. 156.

[50] Cited, *ibid.*, p. 158.

[51] Bühler's translation, quoted by Jacobi, gives *Brahman*, which appears rather misleading in the context. The god Brahmā, not the impersonal absolute, is referred to here. It may be noted here that the text mentions Brahmā.

[52] Sultān, *Nabi*, fol. 3; also Saghir, *Yusuf*.

tual form of this cosmic process flowing from Nur Muhammad. Most of them attributed the individual objects of creation to the drops of perspiration, appearing in the body of Nur Muhammad.[53] Some made no particular reference to perspiration but traced the same objects to *bindus* or drops of a liquid substance, oozing from *nur* or from Nur Muhammad himself.[54] And yet others found the origin of the different objects of creation in various parts of the body of Nur Muhammad.[55]

The notion of creation from perspiration is intriguing. The Muslim writers themselves offered either mystical-metaphorical or purely materialistic explanations of its nature. Most of them account for the perspiration as being caused by God and Nur Muhammad, gazing at each other in love, after the former created the latter in His loneliness.

> Having recreated himself in the form of [Nur] Muhammad, God keeps contemplating the latter's form. . . . The formless becomes immersed in love. . . . As he looks on intensely in love, perspiration results from love. And from [Nur] Muhammad's perspiration follows everything else.[56]

In the words of another writer: ". . . [they] look at each other in love. From the heat (*tej*) of the feeling of love both perspire. Thereafter, the lord without beginning and quality creates the world from the water of perspiration."[57]

An altogether different explanation of perspiration in Nur Muhammad came from Mir Shafi and Diwān Ali. As Nur Nabi or Nur Muhammad was created in darkness, God remained unconscious. On regaining consciousness He was struck by the luminous figure of Nur Nabi and lost His conscious-

[53] Sultān, *Ibid.*, fols. 3ff; Sultān, *Shab*, fols. 1ff; Shaikh Parān, fols. 3ff; Ali Rajā, *Āgam*, fols. 6-7.

[54] Hayāt Mahmud, *Ambiyā*, pp. 8ff.

[55] Shaikh Chānd, *Tālib*, fols. 9 mc ff.

[56] Sultān, *Shab*, fol. 1; Sultān, *Nabi*, fol. 3; also Shaikh Parān, fol. 1.

[57] Ali Rajā, *Āgam*, fols. 6-7.

ness again. On His second recovery God enquired about Nur Nabi's identity, but found no answer. He then moved forward to embrace him. Struck, as it were, by thunder, Nur Nabi moved away in different directions, followed by God. Finally, God elicited the answer from him: "You and I remained together in darkness under the same name."[58] He asked God to call him by that particular name. God addressed him as Nur Muhammad. Nur Muhammad was very tired after this physical exertion and perspired profusely.[59]

This particular concept of perspiration resulting from the physical exertions of the creator had a clear parallel in the Bengali *Dharma-mangal* literature of the followers of Lord Dharma. In the most popular dharmist book, *Śunya-purān*, Dharma was presented as perspiring after running around the world, and Ādyā-śakti, the personified primordial energy, as emerging from his perspiration.[60] In a song of Dharma, a girl emerged from his perspiration. He was attracted to her, but she tried to escape, hotly pursued by him.[61]

A variant of the perspiration theory was offered, as mentioned above,[62] by some writers who attributed creation to unspecified liquid drops (*bindus*) rather than to perspiration. Nur Muhammad shook his body, at the instance of God, to produce 124,000 *bindus* oozing out of it, which gave birth to 124,000 prophets. In the same manner other *bindus*, trickling out of the different parts of Nur Muhammad's body, resulted in the creation of various objects and spirits.[63] A second variant of the liquid theory referred to the tears shed by Nur Muhammad, who was unable to see God, causing a "stream of water" from which creation ensued.[64] A further view of

[58] Mir Muhammad Shafi, *Nur*, fols. 2-4.
[59] *Ibid.*, fol. 4; Diwān Ali, *Nur Nāma* (DMS 546: sl 404), fols. 2-5.
[60] Cited, S. B. Dasgupta, *Obscure Religious Cults*, p. 313.
[61] Cited, *ibid.*, p. 317.
[62] *Supra*, p. 128.
[63] Hayāt Mahmud, *Ambiyā*, p. 9.
[64] Shaikh Chānd, *Tālib*, fols. 9ff.

creation in relation to Nur Muhammad mentioned different parts of his body without reference to either perspiration or *bindu*.[65]

The notion of the cosmic process, hinged on perspiration, water, *bindu*, or some liquid substance, seemed on the whole as pervasive as it was intriguing. Material reasons like the physical exertions of Nur Muhammad or the rather esoteric explanation of the "heat" (*tej*) of love between God and Nur Muhammad, as offered by some writers, seem nonetheless enigmatic. Shared by both Hindu and Muslim creation-myths in Bengal, this particular motif indeed calls for some basic explanations. Various suggestions can be made.

First, the myth in question may be regarded as a metamorphosed survival of a much older tradition of creation proceeding from primeval waters which was as popular in the Judaeo-Christian-Islamic cosmogony as in the Indian.

Secondly, the extensive use of the term *bindu* by the Bengali Muslim writers raises another possibility. The concept of *bindu* forms one of the most cardinal doctrines of Hindu *tantra*. The tāntric *advaitavād*, quite in line with the vedāntic and *sāmkhya* notions of the supreme reality, recognizes a distinction between the inactive transcendent and the active immanent aspects of the same, as represented by *śiv* and *śakti*. *Śiv* and *śakti* represent two aspects of the divine unity, *brahman*, also called *śiv-śakti*. When the supreme being desires to be "many," this results in what is known as *sadriśaparinām*, in which the supreme *bindu* appears. This *bindu* or *avyākta*, the sprouting root of the universe, is called the supreme *bindu*, *parābindu*, to distinguish it from that aspect of itself which is called *bindu-kārya* and appears as a state of *śakti* after the differentiation of *parābindu* in *sadriśaparinām*.[66] Again, the concept of *nāda-bindu* is integral to all religious systems in-

[65] *Ibid.*, also Hayāt Mahmud, *Ambiyā*, pp. 8ff.

[66] J. Woodroffe, *Shakti and Shākta* (Madras and London, 3rd edn., 1929), pp. 380-89, 397-400.

spired by the yogico-tāntric ideas, especially nāthism.[67] The contemporary *nāth* literature of Bengal attached great importance to this concept, having associated it with the fundamental concept of the moon, also called *bindu*, and the sun, called *rajas*, the former representing *śiv* as the supreme state of pure consciousness and the latter *śakti* as the active principle in the cosmic process.[68] The idea of *bindu* as a potent factor in the creation could not possibly have been absent in the minds of these Bengali Muslim writers on the subject, who appear, even otherwise, so well acquainted with the yogico-tāntric ideas. They did not find much difficulty in adapting the Islamic idea of *nur*, the first attribute of God, to the Hindu concept of *jyotirmmay*, as stated above.[69] But the yogico-tāntric concept of *bindu* had no comparable Islamic symbol. The Bengali Muslim mediators adopted, therefore, the only course open to them, namely, grafting *bindu* on *nur*.

Finally, perspiration and *bindu* may, in the context of the creation-myths, very well be seen to belong in the common Indian mythological continuity of water-emission-fertility. The metaphor of love between God and Nur Muhammad here makes it even more explicit.[70]

The details of creation, whether or not proceeding from Nur Muhammad, and if from him, whether or not from his perspiration, varied a great deal. There was no measure of agreement or consistency among these writers in the matter of creation of individual objects, but no discerning reader can help being struck by the extent of the penetration of indigenous ideas and symbols. From perspiration resulted *tribhuban*, the three worlds; *brahman-jnān*, the supreme knowledge

[67] K. Mallik, *Nāth-sampradāyer Itihās, Darśan o Sādhanpranāli* (Calcutta, 1950), pp. 486-510.

[68] S. B. Dasgupta, *Obscure Religious Cults*, p. 237.

[69] *Supra*, p. 127.

[70] I am indebted to Professor Edward C. Dimock, Jr., University of Chicago, for this particular suggestion.

of the *brahman; mahāmantra*, the mystical syllable; the four *veds*; the fourteen *śāstras*, the scriptures; the twenty-seven *brahmāndas*, the cosmic orders emerging from the cosmic eggs; *jivātmā*, the vedāntic individual soul; and *paramātmā*, the supreme soul.[71] The Hindu divinities were included in the lists of creation from *bindu* and perspiration of Nur Muhammad. Brahmā emerged from the *bindu* on the left ear, Viśvakarmā from perspiration on the nose, 30 million members of the Hindu pantheon from the *bindu* on the belly, and the sages from the lower abdomen. Reference was also made to the creation of Mārichi, "the creature of fire."[72] Ādam's creation was preceded by 6,325,000 years covering "the four ages," a Hindu mythological belief.[73] Nur Muhammad, on his creation, was placed by God inside a divine lamp, *qindil*. Later, those who offered *pranām*, a Hindu mode of paying respect, to Nur Muhammad at the time and ignored him later, were born as "unbelievers among Muslims," and those who failed to do it at the time but did it in the end became "Muslims in the rank of the Hindus."[74]

The yogico-tāntric ideas and symbols, especially in their nāthist formulations, occupied a significant place in the cosmogonical writings of the Bengali Muslims. The origin of the sun and the moon and other objects in relation to the mystico-physiology of the creator were clearly indicative of the indigenous influence. The sun and the moon possessed highly symbolic meanings in the esoteric yogico-tāntric discipline. The place or seat of the moon in the mystical physiology of a tāntric *yogi* was in the cerebral region, just below *sahasrār*, the lotus of a thousand petals, and the sun was sit-

[71] Ali Rajā, *Āgam*, fol. 7.

[72] Mir Shafi, *Nur-Qindil*, fols. 7-8.

[73] Saiyid Sultān, *Nabi*, fols. 3-4. The traditional Hindu concept of the four ages (*yug*), namely, *satya, tretā, dvāpar,* and *kali*. The standard Hindu formulation given in Manu is 4,320,000 years for the four ages.

[74] Sultān, *Shab*, fols. 2-4.

uated in the navel region of *mulādhār*, the lowest plexus in the yogico-tāntric physiology.[75] Some Muslim mediators traced the moon's origin to Nur Muhammad's perspiration appearing in the region just below the forehead. The origin of the sun was attributed to the *bindu* in the mind. The stars were born of perspiration all over the forehead. *Chandra*, the moon, was itself taken in its mystico-physiological sense. The twelve houses of the zodiac (*rāśi*) were said to originate with the twelve *bindus* on the left side of *chandra* in the cerebral region, and twenty-seven asterisks, *nakṣatra*, with the same number of *bindus* on the right side of *chandra*. The four aspects of *chandra* known in the yogico-nāthist tradition such as *ādi-chandra*, *nij-chandra*, *unmatta-chandra*, and *garal-chandra* were also mentioned.[76] Ideas were often divested of their indigenous appearances and presented through Islamic symbols. The moon was regarded as belonging to the "part" of Allāh and the sun to that of *nur*, and the two as having grown from the same "semen." Indigenous ideas relating to creation sometimes found parallel Islamic concepts. The creation of the mystical sound of *kun* and of the two Perso-Arabic letters of *kāf* and *nun*, through which the absolute, *karim*, was made known, presented instances of this kind. The Hindu concept of *śabda-brahman*, the concept of the supreme truth manifested in a mystical sound like *om*, provided the closest parallel.[77]

The mythological aspect of cosmogonical thoughts found significant emphasis in the mediator's writings, revealing a clear and often direct assimilation of indigenous tradition. The fire was compared with the divine light, *nur*, and discredited. Allāh was displeased with the fire that claimed, despite its smoke, the distinction appropriate to *nur*, and chas-

[75] For a more detailed discussion of the yogico-tāntric influence, see *infra*, pp. 163ff.

[76] Mir Muhammad Shafi, *Nur-Qindil*, fols. 4-7.

[77] Shaikh Chānd, *Tālib*, fols. 8ff.

tised it by making a part of it impure and unbelieving (*kāfir*). Later, Allāh took pity on the repentant fire, purged it of its impurities and sins, and finally made Mārichi of Hindu mythology out of the purified fire. The descendants of Mārichi peopled the earth for 60,000 years, but were eliminated thereafter by God for becoming sinful. *Asurs*, the demons of Hindu mythology to follow, lived for another 30,000 years and were replaced for their immorality by the "asvagan." In the same manner the latter were removed after 10,000 years, and God decided to create Ādam, who represented the microcosm of the universe. In his body were located, among other things, the yogico-tāntric nerves like *idā*, *pingalā*, and *triveni*, or *suṣumnā*, as well as the four *chandras* of the nāthist tradition.[78]

A more direct attempt was made to forge a link with the Hindu myth on the origin of music. While the "four *veds*" and the "fourteen scriptures" were attributed to God's own self, the six scales (*rāg*) and the thirty-six sub-scales (*rāgini*) of the Hindu tradition were created from the body of Nur Muhammad. God invested him with the whole range of both esoteric and exoteric knowledge. But later, when Ali sought the same esoteric truth from the Prophet,[79] his father-in-law, the latter disregarded him on the ground that he would find himself unable to bear it and might very well jeopardize his own life because every piece of the esoteric truth was as intolerable as the heat produced by the "millions of suns." He succeeded, however, in receiving his esoteric instruction from the Prophet by virtue of his absolute faith in the mercy of the latter. Ali's practice of this newly acquired knowledge produced an all-consuming fire in his heart. Unable to withstand it, Ali pleaded with the Prophet to relieve him of this

[78] *Ibid.*

[79] Many mystical schools in Islam regard Ali as the repository of esoteric knowledge and the same idea is found in other Muslim Bengali writers as discussed below. (*Infra*, pp. 160ff.)

"supreme knowledge." The Prophet advised him to choose a dense forest for denuding himself of this fearsome knowledge. Ali obeyed his command and occasioned a great fire in the forest. The "mountain-king" caused a "stream of his tears" to quench the fire and the thirst of the creatures afflicted by it in the forest. While all other creatures perished by drinking this water, Hanumān, the great primate of the epic *Rāmāyan* fame, acquired the highest knowledge in the art of music.[80] Ali went back to the forest to discover the full development of and become thoroughly adept in the whole range of indigenous vocal and instrumental music, like the six *rāgs*, thirty-six *rāginis*, eight rhythms (*tāl, tāli*), and sixty-four sub-rhythms, percussion instruments of *dhol* and *mridanga*, string instruments of *setārā* (sitar) and *dotārā*, wind instruments of flute and *sāhnāi*, and sundry other instruments such as *karatāl* (cymbals), *kamsa* (gong), *ghantā* (bells), and *pināk* (conch shell). On Ali's return the Prophet, who found music no longer a secret knowledge, asked the former to pass it on to the god Śiv, who is traditionally regarded as the repository of esoteric knowledge (*āgam*) in Hinduism. Śiv, in his turn, entrusted the knowledge to Nārad, the sage who is credited in Hindu mythology with the systematized elaboration of the art of music. Nārad entertained the heavenly court with the music, and subsequently popularized it among mortals.[81]

The most elaborate attempt to accommodate indigenous creation-myths was made by Saiyid Sultān.[82] His was a re-

[80] "The introduction of Hanumāna does not seem readily intelligible in the context. But apart from his popular image as a great warrior, Hanumāna is also known as a *yogāchāra* for his power in magic or in the healing art, and *rajata-dyuti*, 'the brilliant.' The *Rāmāyana* says, 'The chief of monkeys is perfect; no one equals him in the *śāstras*, in learning, and in ascertaining the sense of the scriptures. . . .' " Quoted by J. Dowson, *A Classical Dictionary of Hindu Mythology and Religion, Geography, History and Literature* (London, 8th edn., 1953), p. 117.

[81] Diwān Ali, *Nur Nāma*, fols. 5-12.

[82] *Nabi*, fols. 4ff.

markable effort to use Hindu cosmogonical myths as a foil to the advent of Ādam and Muhammad, "the last of the prophets." Sultān accepted, as noted before,[83] the Hindu concept of the four ages, though on his own terms. The four ages were believed to have intervened between the creation of the earth and that of Ādam. He compressed into this span a series of Hindu mythological characters, together with, though very rarely, certain figures disfavored in Islamic tradition, underlying overtly or covertly their failure and ineffectiveness. The whole gamut of the four ages was represented as a period of gestation for the true divine messenger, a period of divine trials and experiments, during which the world repeatedly solicited to God for the right kind of divine messenger, a request persistently ending in disappointment until God decided to create Ādam. God at first created a fire without smoke, whence a primal male called Mārij/Mārichi, devoted to God, emerged. From the left part of Mārichi was born a woman; a divine message proclaimed her creation only for Mārichi. The two thereafter became known among Hindus as Iśvar and Pārvati. This was followed by the birth of Brahmā, Viṣnu, Jān, Jārn, and Azāzil, the last being a fallen *firishtah*, condemned by God for his refusal to pay respect to Ādam. Azāzil became responsible for the birth of *surs* and *asurs*, the former being placed in heaven and the latter in the atmosphere between heaven and the earth. Then began a series of appeals by the world to God for a capable and worthy protector,[84] in response to which God first sent *daityas*. The latter failed to live up to expectation and began indulging in adultery, drunkenness, forcible appropriation of property and cow-slaughter.[85] Unable to bear these sins, the world appealed to God and received an *asur* prophet, who was killed before long by his fellow *asurs*. Thereafter 800 prophets were sent

[83] *Supra*, p. 98.

[84] This is very similar to the legend about the origin of the first king in the Hindu epic, *Mahābhārat*.

[85] Sultān, *Nabi*, fols. 4-8 mc.

in succession by God to redress the situation, but they were all opposed and eliminated by *asurs*. Now *surs* were sent down to the world by God, and a fierce struggle between *surs* and *asurs* ensued. The former, outnumbered by the latter, sought God's help, and *firishtahs* were despatched to their rescue, resulting in the total annihilation of *asurs*. After a brief period of peace and happiness *asurs* took themselves to a life of ease and sin, and, on the world's further request, God replaced them by *firishtahs*, who set the tone of a religious and moral life. The world was re-populated by the pious descendants of *firishtahs*, who became known as *dvijas* or twice-born, that is *brāhmans*. After a period of virtuous life, even *dvijas* tended to become lax in piety. God desired to reinforce their faith by disseminating the supreme knowledge of *nur* through the vedic scriptures (*ved-śāstra*). The four *veds*, namely the *Rig*, the *Sām*, the *Yajur*, and the *Atharva*, were given respectively to Brahmā, Śiv, Viṣnu, and Hari (Kriṣna). The four *veds* "witnessed the ultimate appearance of Muhammad at God's will."[86] People, unable to read the *veds*, remained confused until a *firishtah*, hidden behind "the veil of space," instructed *dvijas* in the art of reading. With the knowledge of the *veds*, people continued to serve God faithfully until the waves of time washed away all their good works. On the world's solicitation, God sent down this time a *yogi*, clad in a tiger-skin, with matted hair, a serpent wound around his head, a string of skulls around his neck, ashes all over his body, and seated on a bull.[87] Given to ascetic exercises and virtues, even this *yogi* failed to rise above passion, and he gave away his beloved, in a feat of drunkenness, to an *asur*, though she was recovered later after a great battle.[88]

[86] *Ibid.*, fols. 9-16 mc.

[87] *Ibid.*, fol. 18 mc. The *yogi* in this description is clearly identifiable with god Śiv.

[88] There is a tradition involving Śiv against an *asur*, named Andhakāsur, in a battle caused by the *asur*'s desire for Pārvati, the consort of Śiv. A pro-

Saiyid Sultān, hereafter, introduced a number of mythical figures, who were clearly identifiable with the various incarnations (*avatārs*) of Viṣnu such as Mina (the fish), Kurma (the tortoise), Barāha (the boar), Nara-simha (the lion-man), Vāmana (the dwarf), followed by Paraśurām, Rām, and Krişna.[89] As a Muslim, Sultān did not, however, regard them as God's own "incarnations," after the Hindu tradition, but as his creations. He began with a "mighty king" who violated the words of a sage and thereby caused a deluge resulting from the sage's curse. A huge boat sheltered the king and a pair of all species of creatures. When a severe storm threatened the safety of the boat, God saved it by having it supported on the back of a fish.[90] Similarly, God prevented the world from sinking down, on two other occasions, once with the help of a tortoise and with a boar, on the other. The world was further relieved of a tyrant and a sinner called Hiranyakaśipu, who was killed by Nara-simha created by God for this purpose. Thereupon a king named Bali became so powerful as to threaten the kingdom of the gods. The gods appealed to the lord, who created a dwarf. Bali agreed to the dwarf's request for granting him the amount of land that the latter could cover in his three steps. The dwarf's first step covered the entire world, the second reached the nether world, and the third was placed on the head of the king, under the weight of which Bali went down to the nether region.[91] This

---

tracted battle joined in by many gods, goddesses, and demons, it ends in Andhakāsur's death and the defeat of the demons. (*Matsya-purān*, chapter 179, and *Varāha-purān*, quoted by T. A. Gopinatha-Rao, *Elements of Hindu Iconography*, New York, 1968, vol. I, pt. 2, pp. 379ff.)

[89] Sultān, *Nabi*, fols. 19-25 mc.

[90] The reference here is very likely to the seventh Manu of the Hindu mythology, to the voyage of Nuh or Noah, and finally to the "fish incarnation."

[91] Sultān's version differs slightly from the traditional Hindu one in which the Vāman-*avatār* stepped over the heaven and the earth in two strides; but then out of respect to Bali's kindness he stopped short, and left to him *pātāl*

was followed by the appearance of a *brāhman* who caused the decapitation of his mother.[92] Sultān disapproved of him on two counts: first, matricide, and, secondly, the special guilt attached to the slaughter of a *brāhman*, and added: "The mother is superior to the father, for it is the mother who nurses children from infancy. The act of beheading the mother can never be justified even for an exalted person."[93] The world was next found complaining to God about another divine messenger, clearly alluding to Rām, whose conduct was not beyond reproach. He went to the forest in self-exile to honor the words of his "father" (i.e., Daśarath, the king of Ayodhyā), and so, when his father died in his absence, the son was of no consequence to him. During the exile, he lost his "wife" (i.e., Sitā), kidnapped by a "demon" (i.e., Rāvan, the king of Lankā), but he lost his judgment too, as he certainly did not help the task of his wife's recovery by allying himself with Sugriv against his more able brother Bāli, whom Rām ultimately killed at the instigation of Sugriv. Sultān further disapproved of Rām's rejection and desertion of his wife after the recovery, despite a fire-ordeal to which she was subjected to prove her chastity during her captivity. The act of deserting especially a pregnant woman in the woods, infested by wild animals and ogres, could not be condoned in a divine being. Sultān convinced himself: "Had Sitā fallen into the ogre's hands, the sin of killing a woman would attach to Rām. Had she been devoured by tigers or bears, the entire world would talk about this scandal."[94] Moreover, Sitā's death would have resulted in the death of two more, that is the unborn twins of Rām and Sitā, whom the latter was carrying at the time. Even though Rām did not believe Sitā, it was unbe-

or the nether region. (J. Dowson, *Classical Dictionary of Hindu Mythology*, p. 42.)

[92] The reference is to Paraśurām-*avatār*.

[93] Sultān, *Nabi*, fol. 22 mc.

[94] *Ibid.*, fol. 23 mc.

coming of him not to find her a safer place. There was no wise man around Rām, Sultān convinced himself, to advise Rām against this unjust act. The failure of Rām-*avatār* of Viṣnu brought the story down to the failings of perhaps the most popular incarnation of God, namely Kriṣna. Sultān's treatment of the Kriṣna legend has been rather elaborately discussed before in the context of the historical-mythical writings of the Bengali Muslim mediators.[95]

This long catalogue of the personified world's unhappy experiences with the divine messengers was a cleverly devised foil used by Saiyid Sultān to present the story of the creation of Ādam and a succession of other prophets recognized in Islam, culminating in the emergence of Muhammad, the seal, or the last of the prophets. Sultān's conviction in his faith was unmistakably reflected in words attributed to God, who at last appeared resolute on ending all experiments and uncertainties:

> Let this be known for certain
> That I shall create Ādam:
> And from Ādam
> I shall maintain creation.[96]

[95] *Supra*, pp. 96-98.
[96] Sultān, *Nabi*, fol. 25 mc.

5

Esoterism—Mysticism

SECTION I: THE MAINSTREAM

Esoterical and mystical matters formed a major area of the mediators' literary preoccupations. As in the realm of history, myth, and cosmogony, the mystical concerns of the Bengali Muslim writers offered a total impression of accord and identification with their corresponding non-Muslim local tradition. A critical evaluation of the extent of local impact on this mystical literature is clouded by the universality and affinity of all mystical quests and also by the controversial nature of communication between India and Islamic mystical systems.[1] In point of fact, however, a student of Bengali Muslim mystical thought and practice can easily avoid both these debatable areas. The Islamic and indigenous elements in these writings remain very clearly distinguishable and self-evident. There is very little scope for any confusion and disputation concerning the sources of the two sets of mystical ideas, concepts, and practices, as revealed in this literature, one classical Islamic and the other yogico-tāntric. We should not, for instance, have much problem in distinguish-

[1] Following Tholuck, Von Kremer, Dozy, Goldziher, and Max Horten, R. C. Zaehner (*Hindu and Muslim Mysticism* [London, 1960], pp. 86ff.) notes effective Indian influence on sufism. A. J. Arberry (*Sufism. An Account of the Mystics of Islam* [London, 1950], *passim*), on the other hand, concurs with Nicholson, Massignon, and Moreno in repudiating this claim. Aziz Ahmad (*Studies in Islamic Culture*, p. 118) goes further in observing the "general trend of exclusiveness of Sufism in India from Hindu mystical schools, with which it had so much in common" and also "the merely occasional, more negative than positive contact of the two mystical systems on the Indian soil."

ing between the established sufic concepts of *manzil* (stage) and *maqām* (station), on one hand, and the yogico-tāntric concepts of *chakra* (nerve-plexus), *nādi* (nerve), *āsan* (posture), and *mudrā* (gesture), on the other. And it is largely in this clearly identifiable form that the mystical thought of the mediators found its expression. A discerning reader of these writings can identify two distinct attempts by the mediators: one the introduction of classical sufic ideas, often diluted with indigenous matters; the other a direct and outright absorption of locally popular mystical formulae, symbols, and techniques of yogico-tāntric origin, to be more fully examined below.[2]

Almost all major facets of a mystical system known in contemporaneous Bengal are found in Bengali Muslim writings, characterized by a massive penetration of indigenous matters. The contents of these writings may be classified broadly as follows:

A. Mystical Speculations
   a. The Path
   b. The Deity
   c. The Guide
B. The Mystical Discipline: Practices and Techniques
   a. The Stages and Stations
   b. The Psycho-Physiological Culture: the Microcosm.

A. Mystical Speculations

a. The Path. In Islam, as in other doctrinal religions, the recognition of mysticism as a personal and esoteric approach has been grudging and gradual. The pressure of adherence to the fundamentals of a canonical religion and the growing need of an essentially personal and loving deity for an individual believer were not easy to reconcile. The demand on a Muslim believer to conform to the orthodox *sharia* initially imposed a severe constraint on the growth of a mystical approach (*tariqa*) in Islam and constituted a source of grave tension among the believers. Islam owed it to the brilliance

[2] *Infra*, pp. 177ff.

of al-Ghazāli (d. A.D. 1111) that gnosis (*marifa*) found its theological basis and sanction in orthodox Islam.[3] And yet the debate continued throughout the Muslim world, and conflict persisted in the mind of individual believers, who often tried to resolve the problem in accordance with their personal spiritual and emotional concerns.

The Muslim authors of the mystical literature in Bengali squarely faced this issue. They considered the implications of a dichotomous position between exoteric and esoteric approaches and generally stressed the supreme merit of the latter. It is characteristic of these writings that the classical Islamic mystical terminologies like *tasawwuf* and *sufi* found no single mention. *Darweshi*, *faqiri*, and *tariqa* were terms generally used by Muslim Bengali writers to contrast the mystical path with the formal *sharia*. "No greater merit," writes one, "is found anywhere else than *darweshi*." The Prophet had reportedly "admitted in a *hadith*" that he "begged of the lord the virtue of *faqiri*," that "great love" existed between a *faqir* and himself and that both moved in the "same direction." None but a *faqir* would have "access" to and "success" with Allāh.[4]

Of greater significance is the free use of indigenous terms and concepts to underline the difference between scriptural and mystical positions. *Sharia*, representing the exoterical and formal aspects of Islam, was identified with Hindu *śāstra* or scripture, and the *Qurān* and the Hindu *purān* were cited as examples of this. The terms often used to designate esoterism are *āgam*, a Hindu tāntric name for the secret truth; *yog-pantha*, the yogic way; *siddhi-pantha*, the path leading to the attainment of yogic goal; and *ultā* or *bimukh-pantha*. Both *ultā* and *bimukh*, meaning "reverse," have reference to the "regressive culture" advocated by the popular yogico-tāntric cults in Bengal.

Marifa (gnosis), writes Ali Rajā, is "what we call *āgam*"

[3] R. C. Zaehner, *Hindu and Muslim Mysticism*, pp. 170ff.
[4] Shaikh Mansur, *Sirr Nāma* (DMS 569: sl 460), fols. 9, 13.

and *sharia* is "open and known," while *āgam* is "hidden" and "the secret Vrindāvan of the lord."[5] *Yog* is the "command of God" and the "eternally concealed truth"; *śāstra* like the *Qurān* and the *purān* are "incapable of leading to the path of *yog*." The "thorough memorization of *śāstra*," "continuous reading" of the same and of the *Qurān* "for a hundred years" cannot have a person "so purified as the foremost among the *faqirs*."[6] Concerned with "the rights and wrongs," *śāstra* is unable to offer "the vision of Allāh." People are "ordained in the *Qurān*" to adhere to "the way of *yog*," and God is certain to withold his own vision from the person who managed to reach heaven by virtue of his great piety, but failed to adopt *yog*. Caught between the "opposite pulls" of śāstric duties and *yog*, individuals, whether a king or a learned *pandit*, are denied of salvation. There is no room for "dualism in the worship of God," and even the "worship of a tree with an undivided devotion" will achieve self-realization. The knowledge of the theologians is rooted in the *śāstra* and not in the esoteric truth of the *faqiri*. The foremost among *pandits* is no more than a "servant of a *faqir*."[7] The mystical truth is kept hidden and confined because of its "supreme merit" and also for the complexities involved in understanding the nature of the "regressive way" which require a realization of the interchangeability and the essential sameness of what are apparently dissimilar and opposed such as right and wrong, sadness and happiness, front and rear, high and low, fire and water, Muhammad "as a man" and "a man as the *paighambar*," "man as God" and "God as man."[8]

Another facet of the attempt to vindicate the mystical approach was to identify and emphasize love (*prem*) as the essence of the entire creative process. The ultimate truth is not

[5] Ali Rajā, *Āgam*, fol. 26. "Vrindāvan" here refers to the secret union of Lord Krişna and Rādhā in the gardens of Vrindāvan.

[6] Ali Rajā, *Jnān*, fol. 208.

[7] *Ibid.*, fols. 215-18.

[8] *Ibid.*, fols. 115, 194.

embodied in "the written words of *śāstra*" but in "the lesson of love received at the core of one's heart." The "supreme love" is like "nectar," while "the four *veds* and the fourteen *śāstras* are as dry as wood."[9] The "abode of love" is not for the learned *ālim*. Neither knowledge nor meditation is fruitful without love.[10] Love is the essence of the divine nature, and there is God where there is love. The "throne" of God, extending over the "three worlds," is consecrated by love. The whole creation is the result of God's love, and no single particle of it is devoid of his love. Love sustains it all, and all will die with it. God "in the name of Iśvar" is "immersed, and concealed in the cosmic ocean of love." The creation is the sea, creatures are like fishes in it, and love is the net to draw them together. Love binds and holds the creation in a unity: the fire in love with the air, earth with water, heaven with the earth, water with sea, fish with water, the night with the moon, and the day with the sun. Love is to the world "just as a tree is to its roots, the bee to a lotus, the mind to the body, the breath to the heart and a male to a female."[11]

Following from the place of love in the cosmic process, the reality was conceived in dual forms. Love is "never realized without a couple."[12] God created the world "in duality." He was "alone in the beginning" and made his "dual in Muhammad with love." Together they were "like *bhāvak* and *bhāvini*," the dual representations of the creative truth in yogico-tāntrism. God stands in the same relationship to his worshipper and lover and accepts the latter as master and himself as servant:

> Nārāyan Hari [the Krișna incarnation of Vișnu] appeared in every age in human form as a devotee of Rādhā and to act with her. Daśānan [Rāvan] was devoted to Mandodari. Rām-nārāyan [Rām incarnation of Vișnu] to the beauty of Jānaki [Sitā], and the chief

[9] *Ibid.*, fols. 116-17.
[10] Ali Rajā, *Sirāj Qulub* (DMS 388: sl 203), fols. 1-2.
[11] Ali Rajā, *Jnān*, fols. 101-102, 109-11.
[12] *Ibid.*, fol. 100.

of gods [Indra] to Śachi. . . . Zulaikha was attracted to Yusuf and Amir Hasan to Zainab. . . . Diwān Hāfiz was drawn to a harlot, . . . and Bu Ali Qalandar to handsome Mubārak. . . . There is no love without beauty, no devotion without feeling, no feeling without an object and no salvation without realisation of the object. The first of the prophets, Ādam, had fallen into the well of love with Hauwā. Śiv, among gods, was a great devotee of Gauri. . . . Prophet Muhammad was devoted to the great beauty of Āyisha. Whether men, fairies, animals, birds, insects, or plants, there is salvation for none without the nectar of love.[13]

Despite the strong emphasis placed on love and esoterical truth, the importance of formal knowledge (*ilm*), revelation, and adherence to *sharia* was not overlooked. Even in Ali Rajā's religious perception, which is so thoroughly permeated by yogico-tāntric influence, *sharia* lies at "the very root," and is essential to the realisation of the āgamic truth.[14] Those who are capable of living up to the "norms set by the Prophet" are only "worthy of taking to the yogic path." True *faqiri* is not divorced from the Prophet's rules of conduct. The Prophet scrupulously covered his body in all conditions, and a true *yogi* has no need to flaunt his "matted hair." There are no external signs of a *yogi*. He never approaches people for favor or help. Only a pseudo-*faqir* is given to thaumaturgic deception. A mere particle of hypocrisy or malice in a *yogi* is enough to undo his spiritual accomplishments.[15]

The importance of formal observance and piety for a Muslim was more firmly stressed in other writings. An uninitiated Muslim who is unable to distinguish between the right (*bhāla*) and the wrong (*manda*), and between the sanctions (*halāl*) and the prohibitions (*harām*), is in no position to "recognize God" and doomed to a "spiritually barren" life. Allāh is immanent in knowledge, as a sweet fragrance and as butter in milk. There is no butter without milk, nor rain without

[13] *Ibid.*, fols. 104-109.
[14] *Āgam*, fol. 22.
[15] Ali Rajā, *Jnān*, fols. 203, 209, 219.

clouds; neither can there be a *faqir* without formal knowledge. Knowledge is either open (*zāhir*) or hidden (*bātin*). The former is comparable to milk and the latter to butter produced from it. None in the past became a true *faqir*, "without formal knowledge." A *faqir* without it is like "an unbeliever."[16]

The essential interdependence between *sharia* and *tariqa*, and the importance of the former as a basic prerequisite for the latter were recognized. The spiritual journey of a believer begins with the "attainment of the *manzil* of *sharia*"; not before this can he "step forward" to *tariqa*. The way to the attainment of Allāh is through prayers (*ibādat*) at the *manzil* of *sharia*, repentance (*tawba*) before prayers, and observance of all Allāh's prescriptions (*farmān*), and of the distinction between *harām* and *halāl*.[17] Strict adherence to the *Qurān* and the *hadith* is urged for *faqirs*.[18] Although God is not visible, his words in the *Qurān* rule the world, just as, in the Prophet's absence, his rules of pious conduct are to be found in the *hadith*. It is incumbent on all believers, including *faqirs* and *darweshes*, to abide by the scriptual observances of *namāz*, *roza*, *hajj*, and *zakāt* as a preliminary to the adoption of *tariqa*.[19]

A close examination of these writings reveals their authors straining to reconcile the popularity of the mystical discipline with the pressures of conformity with the more basic and formal demands of the *sharia*. Consequently, their positions were sometimes inconsistent and contradictory. Ali Rajā's thoughts, as discussed above,[20] betrayed this dichotomous position. While he concedes the primacy of *sharia* as being "the root of all," he leaves no doubt about his personal quest for

[16] Hayāt Mahmud, *Hitajnān*, pp. 35-36.
[17] Hāji Muhammad, *Nur Jamāl*, fols. 102 mc.
[18] Shaikh Mansur, *Sirr*, fol. 4.
[19] *Ibid.*, fols. 4-5, 14-18.
[20] *Supra*, p. 146.

the esoteric truth, in the realization of which the distinction between God and man loses its meaning—a notion that was long proscribed by orthodox *sufis* as the heretical concept of *hulul* or anthropomorphism of God.[21] The general sufic recognition of the four *maqāms* in a mystic's journey, namely *sharia, tariqa, haqiqa*, and *marifa*, not only found its way into these writings, but our authors also made a great effort to underline the essential continuity and interdependence of these stages. Elaborate similes and metaphors were used to this end. *Sharia* is compared to a lamp, *tariqa* to its wick, *haqiqa* to the oil, and *marifa* to the ignition.[22] *Tariqa* is not born without *sharia, haqiqa* without *tariqa*, and *marifa* without *haqiqa*. *Sharia* is the father, *tariqa* the infant, and *marifa* the preceptor (*guru*). While *sharia* is creation, *tariqa* the humanity, *haqiqa* the Prophet, and *marifa* God. The body represents *sharia*, the mind *tariqa*, the breath *haqiqa*, and God *marifa*. *Sharia* forms earth, *tariqa* the seas, *haqiqa* water, and *marifa* the fishes. *Sharia* is like a cow, *tariqa* its milk, *haqiqa* the butter, and *marifa* the clarified butter. While the soil makes *sharia*, the roots are *tariqa*, the tree itself is *haqiqa*, and the flowers are *marifa*.[23]

Attempts were also made to resolve the problem concerning the interrelationship of doctrinal and mystical aspects of the religion by moving away from a position of interdependence to one of independence of the two. The four mystic stages are compared to the "four sides of a house," the "four avenues leading to the same city," the "four different approaches to the same pond," and the "same fruits in four separate trees."[24]

From the complete independence to the essential oneness

[21] Ali al-Hujwiri, *Kashf al-Mahjub*, Eng. tr. by R. A. Nicholson (London, latest edn., 1967), pp. 131, 260ff.

[22] Hāji Muhammad, *Nur Jamāl*, fol. 2 mc.

[23] Ali Rajā, *Āgam*, fols. 22-24.

[24] *Ibid.*

of them all is a further step which some writers welcomed as an answer to the dilemma facing them:

> The fruit grows from the tree,
> and the tree again from the fruit. . . .
> The egg comes from the bird,
> and the bird again from the egg.
> "All is one"—is the essence of truth. . . .
> *sharia* and *marifa* are essentially one.[25]

b. The Deity. The nature of the deity, with particular reference to the relation between God and man, forms a significant component of the mystical speculations of the Muslim mediators in Bengal. While Islam, generally speaking, inculcates the transcendental and dualistic nature of the godhead, it is significant that the generality of the Bengali Muslim writers stressed the immanent character of God within a monist-pantheistic framework. And yet, in view of a fair degree of compatibility between Indian and Islamic mystical speculations on the nature of the deity in relation to man, one is advised to use some caution in drawing facile conclusions about the local impact on Bengali Muslim ideas. It is, therefore, necessary and useful to examine the Bengali Muslim thought on the subject in the larger context of Indian and Islamic speculations on God and man.

Islam has used the pair of terms, *haq* and *khalq*, to distinguish between God as the creator and the world. God's superiority over man and the world is apparent in the *Qurān*, and in Islamic theology the distance between the creator and creatures is strongly emphasized. In general, it is concluded from the transitory character of this world that its creator is eternal. In the school of the orthodox Asharite theology the absolute transcendence of God with respect to the world (*tanzih*) and the infinite gulf separating *khalq* from *haq* is emphasized to such a degree that the individual nature of things, as

[25] *Ibid.*, fols. 24-25.

well as nature as a distinct domain of reality, melts away in the absolute power of the creator. But the Asharite theological position was assailed from three directions: the rationalist *mutazilis*, the philosophers, and the mystics. According to the *mutazilis*, God only creates what is good, and man is responsible for his own actions. God's will is a kind of intermediary between the creator and the created world. Al-Jahiz felt that God could not destroy the created world.[26] Among the philosophers, the more neo-Platonic school, like the *Ikhwān al-Safā*, and also the more Aristotelian one, represented by Ibn Sinā (d. A.D. 1037) and Ibn Rushd (d. A.D. 1198), both regarded God only as the first cause, but stressed many intermediaries existing between his activity and the temporal world. The latter went so far as to regard the development of the intellectual and material world as proceeding by stages and without beginning and parallel. *Sufis* stressed the continuity between the divine principle and its manifestation. Without denying the absolute transcendence of God, they maintained that, since there could not be two absolutely distinct orders of reality, the finite must somehow be identical with the infinite. While they regarded this world simply as a ladder to God, they could intensify the spiritual life of the soul up to the feeling of god-like creative activity. The Qurānic passages (38:72), where it is said that Allāh, after forming man, breathed his spirit (*ruh*) into him, helped to reduce the gulf between the creator and creatures.[27]

In the struggle against the *mutazilis* and the speculative philosophers, the orthodox *sunni* doctrine developed along the lines suggested by the mystics. The bond between the orthodox Asharite beliefs and the gnostic-mystic speculations was formed in al-Ghazāli, as mentioned above. According to him, God and man are not simply related as creator and creature.

[26] De Boer in M. Th. Houtsma *et al.* (eds.), *Encyclopaedia of Islam*, vol. II, p. 892.

[27] Also *sura* 15:29; *ibid.*

The world is divided into "the material spatial world" (*ālam al-khalq*) and "the non-spatial world of angels and human spirits" (*ālam al-amr*).[28] As a member of the world of spirits, man in his essence shows similarity to God. In *Kimiyā-i Saādat*, al-Ghazāli lent the immense weight of his authority to two doctrines: that "the soul and God are one thing" and that "God and Universe are co-terminous."[29] The Muslim thinkers, especially at the sufic level, were very keen about striking a correct balance between the transcendence and immanence of God. They were drawn to the concept of *tanazzulāt*, or the descent of the absolute, the process by which the absolute, from the state of bare potentiality, gradually becomes "qualified" until it reaches the plane of unity (*wahdat*) in multiplicity—the one in many. The doctrine which in the popular mystic parlance was known as *wahdat al-wujud*, or *tauhid-i wujudi*, or the unity of being, was first formulated by Ibn al-Arabi (d. A.D. 1240) and further systematized by al-Jili (d. A.D. 1355). For Ibn al-Arabi, "the existence of created things is nothing but the very essence of the existence of the Creator."[30] He held that "things necessarily emanate from divine prescience in which they pre-existed as ideas" and that "the soul by an inverse involution logically constructed reintegrate the divine essence." In other words, "all Being is essentially one, as it all is a manifestation of the divine substance," and hence different religions are identical.[31] According to al-Jili,

> His manifestation interpenetrates all existences and He manifests His perfection in each atom and particle of the Universe. He is not multiple by the multiplicity of the manifestations, but He is one in the totality of manifestations. . . . And the mystery of this permeation is that He created the Universe out of Himself. And He is not divided into parts but everything in the Universe by

[28] The *Qurān, sura* 7:72; De Boer, *ibid.*

[29] R. C. Zaehner, *Hindu and Muslim Mysticism*, pp. 170-71.

[30] L. Massignon in M. Th. Houtsma *et al.* (eds.), *Encyclopaedia*, vol. IV, p. 684.

[31] D. S. Margoliouth in *ibid.*, vol. II, p. 362.

reason of His perfection has the name of creatureliness as a loan. Not as some suppose, that it is the divine attributes which are lent to the creature . . . for that which is lent is nothing but the relation of creaturely existence to the attributes and verily Creative Existence is the source of this relation. . . .

The Universe is like ice, and God, the Magnified and Exalted, is the water, which is the origin of this ice. The name "ice" is lent to that frozen thing and the name "water" is the right name for it.[32]

The pantheistic theory of the Ibn al-Arabi, also called "existentialist monism" by Massignon, remained largely popular with the Muslim mystics, despite the inveterate opposition of orthodoxy, spearheaded by Ibn Taimiya (d. A.D. 1328) and Alā al-Daula Simnāni (d. A.D. 1336).[33] According to Simnāni, the goal of the *wujudiya* was "a very low order of *Mukashifa* (mystic revelation), belonging to the earliest stages in the mystic journey."[34] Further,

Creation is a gift of the Almighty. *Mumkin ul-Wujud* (Contingent Being) can therefore in no circumstances be one with the Holy Being of *Wajib ul-Wajud* (Necessary Being). The *Malul* (effect) can never become the *Illat* (ultimate cause). It is impossible to become one with the *Zat u-Sifat* (Being and Attributes). The most Holy God is the bestower of *Wujud* (existence) to all that is *Maujud* (existent). . . . Creation is a reflection and not a manifestation of the Divine Being and that existence is separate from, and external to, essence.[35]

This sufic doctrine, as opposed to that of *tauhid-i wujudi*, became popular as *wahdat al-shuhud* or *tauhid-i shuhudi*. In India, as elsewhere, both these schools of thought fought hard for supremacy. The *wujudi* ideas of Ibn al-Arabi were dis-

[32] Al-Jili, *Insān al-Kāmil*, Eng. tr. by J. W. Sweetman (London), vol. I, p. 28.

[33] L. Massignon, *loc.cit.*

[34] S.A.A. Rizvi, *Muslim Revivalist Movements in Northern India* (Agra, 1965), p. 37.

[35] Alā al-Daula Simnāni, *Al-Urwā li Ahl al-Khalwā*, fols. 112, 25-26, quoted, *ibid.*, pp. 38-39.

seminated by Fakhr al-Din Ibrāhim Irāqi (d. A.D. 1289), Shaikh Sharaf al-Din Yahyā Manyari (c. A.D. 1350), Masud Bak (d. A.D. 1397-1398), Shaikh Ashrāf Jahāngir Simnāni (d. A.D. 1436), and the leaders of the *Shattāri* mystic order such as Shāh Abd Allāh Shattāri (d. A.D. 1485) and Shaikh Muhammad Ghaus (d. A.D. 1562-1563).[36] On the other hand, Saiyid Muhammad Gesu Darāz (d. A.D. 1422) and, much later, Shaikh Ahmad Sirhindi (d. A.D. 1624) opposed the doctrine of *tauhid-i wujudi*. But the ideas of Ibn al-Arabi found a fertile ground in the monist-pantheistic spiritual climate of India and steadily "went on increasing" there; *wahdat al-wujud* came to be "regarded as the dominant system of mystic thoughts."[37] The medieval *bhakti* or devotional movement, leavening the spiritual ground of India for eclectic developments, and the liberal forces fostered by the Mughal policy of "peace with all" (*sulh-i kul*) stimulated greater interest in and appreciation of Hindu and Buddhist mystical speculations on the godhead, facilitating the predominance in Indian Islam of the *wujudi* doctrine of one in many.

The ontological speculation of mystics in Islam had interesting parallels in India. The transcendence or immanence of the creator was a seminal question in Indian thought systems since the *upaniṣads*. Indian commentators offered divergent interpretations of the upanisadic speculations and laid the basis for different schools of speculative thought:

The various commentators upon the Upanishads belonging to different schools of thought, and yet each interested to secure for himself the support of the Upanishads, have been fighting with one another for the last twelve hundred years or more to prove that the

[36] Rizvi, *ibid.*, pp. 43-53, 62-64. In the course of his journey, Shāh Abd Allāh Shattāri came to Bengal, and Shaikh Muhammad Alā, subsequently known as Shaikh Qazān Shattāri, accepted his discipleship and proved himself one of his most noted disciples. The *Shattāris* put great emphasis on ascetic exercises, like the *yogis*, and studied *yog* and the monist (*advaita*) philosophy of Samkar. (*Ibid.*, pp. 62-63.)

[37] *Ibid.*, p. 59.

Upanishads are exclusively in favor of one party as against the others. Thus some contend that the Upanishads teach that Brahman alone exists and all the rest that appears is false and illusory. Others hold that the Upanishads favor the doctrine of modified duality of man in God and of God in man. Still others maintain that the Upanishads give us exclusively a doctrine of uncompromising duality. And so forth. Passages have often been twisted and perverted, and many new connections and contexts have been introduced or imposed upon the texts, to suit the fancy or the creed of the individual commentator.[38]

An analysis of various Indian schools of thought reveals a variety of notions ranging from Samkara's perfect non-dualism (*advaita-vād*), through Rāmānuja's modified non-dualism (*viśiṣṭādvaita-vād*), to pure dualism (*dvaita-vād*)—all forming parts of the speculative heritage of India. In the light of our brief observations above[39] on Muslim mystical speculations on the godhead, it is to be noted that the dominant Muslim mystical notion of *wahdat al-wujud*, advocating a position of qualified dualism achieved through the mediating role of the soul between God and man, found a close Indian parallel in Rāmānuja's system of modified non-dualism. The role of "the unitive experience" of the soul in both systems was equally determining. In the words of a great exponent of the *wujudi* school, al-Jili:

While every appearance shows some attribute of reality, man is the microcosm in which all attributes are united, and in him alone does the Absolute become conscious of itself in all its diverse aspects . . . the Absolute, having completely realised itself through the medium of human nature. . . . Hence the upward movement of the Absolute from the sphere of manifested Essence takes place in and through the unitive experience of the soul. . . .[40]

[38] S. N. Dasgupta, *Hindu Mysticism* (Chicago, 1927), p. 53.

[39] *Supra*, pp. 149ff.

[40] Quoted by R. A. Nicholson, *Studies in Islamic Mysticism* (Cambridge, 1921), pp. 84-85.

On the other hand:

The kernel of Rāmānuja's teaching . . . is . . . to realize the nature of one's immortal soul as being unconditioned by time and space and to see all things in the soul and the soul in all things, is inherent in all men naturally, and it is a godlike state. But this is not to know God: to know God is to love him, and without a passionate and all-consuming love there can be neither communion nor union with the beloved. Any mystical state which is one of undifferentiated oneness is the experience that one individual soul enjoys of its own individual self: it has nothing to do with God. Thus in any form of mystical experience from which love is absent, there can be no question of God: he is absent too. To interpret the experience as being identical with the One or the All is absurd; beguiled by the beauty and apparent infinity of its own deep nature, the liberated soul—so Rāmānuja holds—mistakes the mustard-seed for Mount Meru, the drop for the sea.[41]

In the Muslim mystical literature in Bengali the dualistic notions of the *shuhudi* school of Islamic mysticism were characteristically absent. To the extent that the immanent rather than the transcendental character of God was projected in these writings, this is familiar to the mystical world of Bengal, dominated by the monistic and pantheistic notions of the deity.

God's immanence was clearly brought out by a number of the mediator-writers, with the help of telling similes, metaphors, and analogies. In the words of Saghir: "You and I are but fruit and flowers, God being the roots of the tree. . . . You should search for the roots in the fruit, just as the ocean is to be sought in a single drop [of water]."[42] To Saiyid Sultān, God remains ever concealed as "essence in matter, heat in fire, hardness in clay, drops in water, and rays in the sun and the moon."[43] He is "unmanifest in the manifest,"

[41] Zaehner, *Hindu and Muslim Mysticism*, p. 85.

[42] Shāh Muhammad Saghir, *Yusuf*, fol. 27.

[43] *Nabi*, fol. 1 mc.

"the fragrance in the flower," and "omnipresent." The "attributes of the form" are there in the "shadow," and yet "the shadow cannot be penetrated." The water shapes itself after the pitcher. The pitcher full of water and the water in the pitcher make a unity. Mobility and staticity are but two different names for what is essentially a single phenomenon.[44]

Ali Rajā appeared to offer the most forceful articulation of the immanent and pantheistic nature of the godhead. The infinite and the formless essence of God, he said, "beggers description." Who could "penetrate" his "real nature"? He keeps the secret of his essence from everyone and is revealed to people only in his manifest forms. People are "deceived" by his "transitory attributes." The lord assumes forms to play his cosmic sports (*lilā*). He is like the puppeteer, pulling the strings and making the puppets do all the acts, while the puppets get the name for it. The world is like the puppets, transient and conditional. The lord's hidden nature is "known" through supra-knowledge (*bijnān*) and manifest only in knowledge (*sujnān*). The "pure and subtle body" of the lord penetrates every atom of creation. The three worlds of heaven, earth, and nether region constitute, as it were, the lord's body (*tanu*). He is fire, air, water, and clay—all in himself. All the prophets were the lord himself in their respective incarnations. The body of Ādam was made of clay by God, who lived in it as the creative power. God is the tree of which the creatures are branches. There is one God and countless people, just as a single tree bears many fruits. If he is the skin covering the human body, he is also the flesh beneath it. It is none else but God who hears in the "form" of ears, sees in the form of eyes, speaks in the form of mouth, holds in the form of arms, walks in the form of feet, and knows all in the form of mind.[45] Ali Rajā also made use of the Hindu concepts of *paramātmā*, or the supreme soul, and *jivātmā*, or

[44] Sultān, *Jnān-chautisā* (DMS 366: sl 153), fols. 1-2 mc.

[45] Ali Rajā, *Āgam*, fols. 29-33, 47, 73-74.

the individual soul, or the self, to underline God's immanence. *Paramātmā* is distinct from the human body, which is the abode of the *jivātmā*. The former is, however, in eternal contact with the mind in the body. Ali Rajā's pantheistic beliefs urged him to eschew violence against the living creatures, for they all proclaimed "the glory of the creator."[46]

A total obliteration of distinction between the creator and creatures did not elicit ready response from some other writers. They could not help facing the full theological implications of a position of unqualified pantheism for Islam. Shaikh Mansur made direct reference to the widely popular and contentious case of Mansur Hallāj (d. A.D. 922), "the foremost among the saints" who "completely lost his self-consciousness" and "declared himself God." The writer concerned himself with the rationale of the saint's blasphemy. He found his answer in the belief that God himself spoke through the saint, or else "who dares call himself God." Had a man so pretended, "his head must at once be severed from his body." Shaikh Mansur reminded his readers that "the religion of Islam" is not a polytheistic affair (*kāfiri āchār*) and that it is "the Hindu scriptures, the four *veds*, the twenty-two *purāns*, and the fourteen *śāstras* which teach that a person in the contemplation of Brahmā becomes Brahmā himself."[47]

The most brilliant exposition of God's qualified immanence was offered by Hāji Muhammad, who, like Saiyid Sultān, was a leading religious leader.[48] He identified God's attributes in the creation, but drew a clear distinction between the creator and creature—the lord and the servant (*bāndā*). Significantly, even Hāji Muhammad did not see this distinction in terms of strict dualism. God unites pure essence (*zāt*) and attributes (*sifat*) in himself, just as the bird is concealed in the egg and the tree in the seed. He is simultaneously mani-

[46] Rajā, *Jnān*, fols. 83, 129.
[47] Shaikh Mansur, *Sirr*, fols. 3-4.
[48] *Supra*, p. 73.

fest and unmanifest and also omnipresent. He is the flower, the fragrance, and the bee all at the same time; at once the insect and honey; milk, butter, and the churner to make the butter; the male, the female, and the neuter; the eater and the food. God takes the form of a sufferer in hell (*dojakhi*) and also enjoys bliss in the form of a dweller in heaven (*bihisti*). He takes the forms of the four angels to perform their respective duties.[49] The notion of dichotomy between the Islamic faith and disbelief (*kufr*) was, to Hāji Muhammad, "confusing," for the "truth" is "one and indivisible." In "Hindu view" God is, as though, "personified" in Muhammad, and "one becomes Brahmā in the contemplation of Brahmā." Similar "sanctions" are not lacking in Islamic scriptures. A mystic, after having attained the *maqām* of *lāhut*, the final stage in the sufic spiritual journey, "perceives nothing but Allāh within and without himself." Allāh is all, and all is he. He is near, and far, and everywhere.

Hāji Muhammad's concern, in the final analysis, was, on one hand, to reject a total identity of the creator and creatures and, on the other, to reduce their polarity to a supreme monistic unity. He mentioned the cyclic process of creation as exemplified in the seed, giving birth to the tree and the tree to the fruit and seeds again. This underlined that "the one is three and the three is one." The one is not "affected" by the other, and "the death of the fruit is not the end of the tree." Each drop of water in the sea, the sea itself, and the waves of the sea make "a unity" bound by a causal relation, but one is not called the other. The lord and his servant stand in "a similar relationship." Allāh, the creator of his *bāndā*, is "not subject to the sufferings and conduct of the *bāndā*."

Despite his attempt to differentiate between God and man, Hāji Muhammad's monistic faith finally triumphed over his dualistic concerns. The *bāndā* is finally a mere name of Al-

[49] Hāji Muhammad, *Nur Jamāl*, fol. 5 mc.

lāh.[50] The *pir*-writer expounded his final thoughts on the nature of the godhead with the help of a striking analogy drawn from the mundane experiences of life in rural Bengal:

As people talk in the village market a motley of noises result; a person, listening to it all at a distance, hears nothing but one harmonic noise combining all. This is the key to the truth: one is many and many is one. This particular truth attained through the mystic stage of *marifat/marifa* does not let one see anything but God alone.[51]

c. The Guide. A highly exalted and venerable status, often purported to be of divine nature, attributed to the mystic guide, variously called *pir, murshid, shaikh*, or *guru*, is another characteristic feature of these mystical writings. The importance of a spiritual guide in rightly directing an aspirant to the mystical truth was no less in Islam than in the Indian concept of *guru-vād*, or the truth of the religious preceptor (*guru*). The preceptor-disciple relationship, popular as *pir-muridi* in Islam, found its Indian parallel in the widely prevalent *guru-śiṣya* or *guru-chelā* phenomenon. The position of *pir*, or *murshid*, or *shaikh* in sufism was, however, vitally different from that of the Indian *guru*. *Guru* was worshipped by the disciple as a divine incarnation. But the sufic attitude in this regard, even in its most liberal expression, did not go beyond looking upon the mystic guide as an object of contemplation, whereby the ego or the self-consciousness of the disciple was merged in the mentor's as a step toward the ultimate mystic communion with the deity. In sufic parlance, the pursuit of the mystic object of this first stage is called *rābita* and that of the second is *murāqiba*, while the attainment of the first is known as *fanā fi-shaikh* and of the second is *fanā fi-Allāh*.

Bengali Muslims' adoration of the mystic guide, as reflected in this literature, was unqualified and boundless, and

[50] *Ibid.*, fols. 5-6, 8 mc.
[51] *Ibid.*, fol. 10 mc.

provided a striking parallel with the local non-Muslim attitudes to *guru*. In many instances, the term *guru* was used either exclusively or alongside the Perso-Arabic equivalents, like *pir*, *shaikh*, and *murshid*. Besides, Prophet Muhammad was presented as the final repository of the esoterical truth and Ali as receiving secret instruction from him as an example of the perfect disciple.[52] It cannot be overlooked here that the god Śiv is regarded in Hindu esoteric tradition as the primal source of the secret truth of *āgam*, and his consort Pārvati, or some other divine being, as its first recipient. Finally, the idea and the image of the mystic preceptor was conveyed, as in all other areas of the mediator's concern, through direct reference to Hindu tradition and symbols.

Guru, to Saiyid Sultān, is "the supreme Iśvar," and there is "no equal for him in the three worlds."[53] Sultān had Muhammad as Ali's mystic guide, and Ali addressed Muhammad as Iśvar and said:

> You are the land, the water and the seven seas; the sustainer of the earth and my father; you are the moon, the sun, the sky, the trees, the creepers, both poise and motion; you are Niranjan, Śyām and the name of Viṣnu.[54]

Hayāt Mahmud urged the "worship of the feet of *guru* with a firm resolve," for the latter himself is "the faith (*dharma*), Brahmā and the fulfilment of all actions," and "it is a life without meaning not having a *guru* to worship."[55] Zain al-Din wished to take on his head the dust from the lotus-feet of his *pir*, Shāh Muhammad, compared his "beauty" to that of Madan, the Hindu cupid, and expressed his inability to speak of his "endless virtues."[56] Shaikh Chānd was inclined

[52] Shaikh Chānd, *Tālib*, fol. 4; Ali Rajā, *Jnān*, fol. 1; Saiyid Sultān, *Jnānpradip* (DMS 365: sl 152), fol. 6 mc.

[53] Sultān, *ibid.*, fol. 3 mc.

[54] *Ibid.*, 6 mc.

[55] *Hitajnān*, p. 38.

[56] *Rasul*, fol. 29.

to "dispose" himself at the feet of his *murshid*, Shāh Daula, and begged the latter to carry him through this world.[57] Saiyid Sultān, a renowned *pir* himself, was highly exalted by one of his desciples, Muhammad Khān, who compared him to Abu Bakr in piety, Umar in the conviction of his faith, Uthmān in humility, Ali in knowledge, Hasan in beauty, Hamza in bravery, and Hātim in liberality. Muhammad Khān indicated his eagerness to ignore the pleasures and the wealth of life and of heaven in order to be able to place and worship the lotus-feet of his *pir* on his head.[58] Ali Rajā spoke of his *pir*, Qiyām al-Din in the same vein. His "greatness" is "boundless" and his beauty "unqualified." He is "the grace of the world, the light of heaven on the earth, and the lamp of [Ali Rajā's] own heart."[59] Representing the "supreme knowledge," he is Iśvar, and there is "no greater friend in the three worlds." One should regard no one as equal to his *guru*. The blessings of fulfilment (*siddhi*) and liberation (*mukti*) result from his compassion. The secret knowledge should never be revealed to the disciple until he successfully emerges through the twelve years of disciplinary tests under the *guru*, and the latter is entitled to withhold aspects of knowledge from his *śiṣya* (disciple) until the disciple attains "a pure mind." A person "turning away" from his preceptor finds no prospect of redemption, and no greater sinner exists than one who has fallen out with his *guru*.[60] Once chosen, the *pir* is to be "served after the manner of the lord himself." Though immersed in the thought of God, none can reach the lord without following the words of his *pir*. It is the supreme duty (*mahā dharma*) of the *murid* to respect his *pir*'s command, even though it is "wrong." *Pir*'s secret message must never be "assessed with anyone else." A day's service under *pir*'s feet yields "the piety

[57] *Tālib*, fol. 4.
[58] *Maqtal*, fol. 1.
[59] *Sirāj*, fol. 2; also his *Āgam*, fol. 1.
[60] Ali Rajā, *Jnān*, fols. 90-93.

attained in a thousand years." It is incumbent on a disciple to respond to his *pir*'s call "even in the midst of offering the prayers." This invests him with "greater spiritual merits than *namāz*." Faithlessness (*kāfiri*) dogs the footsteps of one without a *pir*, and he eventually finds his *pir* in Iblis.[61]

There were even sterner and more fearsome warnings for people without a preceptor. Such a person is destined on his death to be "seized" by Izrāil, who will make him drink "a bowl of urine" and beat him with an iron rod. Even the slightest "disregard" shown to the *murshid* is punished by consigning the culprit to hellfire.[62]

Intertwined with this general spirit of apotheosizing the mystic preceptor were attempts to present his role in a more rational perspective. The intercessory or the mediatory role of the mystic guide were occasionally stressed. Some argued that "the form and essence of Allāh is beyond knowledge and description" and hence the "*guru* alone is empowered to reveal it in part."[63] Without his "spiritual guidance" a traveller in the mystic way is "likely to go astray."[64] To know the *pir* in the first instance is the way of "knowing God." The *pir* takes to the safety of the shore "a drowning man in the sea of life."[65]

Nonetheless, a rather critical self-perception of the guide's role was not lacking, and it came from the quill pen of the popular *pir*-writer, Saiyid Sultān. Citing a case where a *guru* seduced one of his female disciples, earned great opprobrium, and committed suicide, Sultān advised a prospective disciple to enquire about the *guru* of his choice from the latter's neighbors. "A good soul" cannot but "care" for his neighbors. The body of the *guru* is like "a clay pot that has to be turned into

[61] Shaikh Mansur, *Sirr*, fols. 6ff.
[62] Mir Muhammad Shafi, *Nur-Qindil*, fols. 4, 6.
[63] Hāji Muhammad, *Nur Jamāl*, fol. 4 mc.
[64] Abd al-Hakim, *Chāri Maqām-bhed* (DMS 408: sl 247).
[65] Shaikh Mansur, *Sirr*, fols. 6ff.

gold through the fire of *karma*." He should also "meditate continually on the great name of *ajapā*."[66] Having obtained satisfaction from the initial enquiries about the prospective guide, the candidate should directly "approach" and "confront" him with "all the doubts" of a spiritual seeker. Once the *pir* proves himself equal to the task, the seeker should have "no hesitation in accepting his discipleship."[67]

B. *The Mystical Discipline: Practices and Techniques*

A substantial part of the Muslim mystical literature in Bengali was devoted to the actual practices and techniques of the discipline. As with speculative mysticism, so with mystical techniques, the relevant literature presents classical sufic notions alongside syncretistic models, based either on local dilution of exogenous materials or direct absorption and assimilation of indegenous culture. The local influence on the mystical practices was, as already noted, predominantly of the yogico-tāntric nature. The wide popularity of these ideas among Bengali Muslims is evidenced not only by these writings under study but also by two other Muslim compositions, in which the respective authors resorted directly to Hindu religious traditions influenced by the yogico-tāntric ideas. One is Shaikh Faiz Allāh's *Gorakṣa-vijay*,[68] which is a direct contribution to the *nāth* tradition. The other is Shaikh Chānd's *Hara-Gauri Samvād*,[69] which makes a thorough exposition of the yogico-tāntric ideas, adopting the tāntric and nāthist motif of the revelation of esoteric ideas put into the mouth of Hara or Śiv, in response to the enquiries of his consort Gauri.

It is rather difficult to identify the channel through which

[66] *Ajapājap* or *hamsa-mantra*, also known as *mahāmantra*, associated with inhalation and exhalation, is highly regarded in the yogic-nāthist system of meditation. (K. Mallik, *Nāth-sampradāyer Ithihās*, pp. 459-60.)

[67] Saiyid Sultān, *Nabi*, fols. 54-55.

[68] Ed. by Munshi A. Karim (Calcutta, 1324 B.S./1917).

[69] DMS 559: sl 556; also ed. in A. Sharif, *Sufi Sāhitya*, pp. 27-40.

these ideas influenced the minds of these Muslim writers. Medieval Bengal witnessed the emergence and nourishment of various cults and sects influenced by yogic and tāntric ideas, such as Buddhist *sahajiyā*, nāthism, *vaiṣnav sahajiyā*, and, to some extent, *bāul*. Naturally enough, there was much that these cults held in common, for example, the supreme importance attached to the mystic initiator (*guru*), as already examined, the importance of the human body as the microcosm of the universe (*dehatattva*), and the resultant psycho-physiological culture (*kāyā-sādhanā*). And yet it appears that the yogico-tāntric ideas of the Muslim writers were largely derived through the nāthist channel, as evidenced by a large stock of nāthist terminologies in their writings. We have also noted above that one of the earliest and the most popular works on the *nāth* tradition was written by a Muslim, Shaikh Faiz Allāh. In addition, the *nāth* stress on yogic psycho-physiological exercises, in contrast with the *sahajiyā* preoccupations with tāntric sexual symbols and techniques, drew Bengali Muslims generally closer to nāthism than to other esoterical disciplines in Bengal.

Significantly enough, the nāthist literature in Bengali is the only medium through which the ideas of tāntric *yog* and *hatha-yog* were popularized in medieval Bengal. The emergence of *hatha-yog* itself was linked with the name of the most popular *nāth* divinity, Gorakṣa-nāth or Gorakh-nāth.[70] While the other forms of *yog*, such as *mantra-yog, lay-yog*, and *rāj-yog* are rather philosophical, laying stress on the final arrest of the mental processes, leading to liberation from the whirl of existence, the primary emphasis of *hatha-yog* is on the physiological culture, conducive to immortality initially in a perfect

[70] To Gorakh-nāth is attributed a work named *Hatha-Yog*, which is no longer extant. The term *hatha-yog* soon came to be the collective designation for the traditional formulae and disciplines aimed at the perfect mastery of body. (M. Eliade, *Yoga. Immortality and Freedom* [London and N.Y., 1958], pp. 228-29.)

body (*siddha-deha*) and finally in a divine body (*divya-deha*).[71] The yogic texts contain the promise and prescription for a state of perfect (*siddha*) body free from disease, decay, and death, the attainment of which is called *siddhi* or immortality and forms the supreme object of yogic exercises. In the realization of this supreme yogic goal, a perfect control over the mental processes is considered an indispensable pre-condition. And from this particular need follow a host of patent yogic psycho-physiological exercises, relating, on one hand, to control of nerves (*nādis*), nerve-plexuses (*chakras*), ducts, sinews, and muscles, and, on the other, to retention of *semen virile* (*virya*) with the help of respiratory techniques (*prānāyam*), physical postures (*āsan*), gestures (*mudrā*),[72] and other yogico-tāntric practices. *Nādis* and *chakras* perform the most vital role in the mystical physiology of the yogico-tāntric system. The vital energy, in the form of "the breath" (*vāyu*), circulates through the nerves, and the cosmic energy exists, in a latent state, in the *chakras*. The control of the vital wind (*vāyu*) finds a prominent place in the nāthist literature in Bengali. Though six nerve centers or plexuses (*ṣat-chakra*) are commonly mentioned, there are seven of them:[73]

First, *mulādhār*, situated at the base of the spinal column between the anal orifice and the genital organs (sacrococcygeal plexus). It has the particular form of a red lotus with four petals.

Second, *svādhiṣthān*, situated at the base of the male genital organ (sacral plexus). It has a lotus with six vermilion petals.

Third, *manipur*, situated in the lumbar region at the level of the navel (epigastric plexus). It has a blue lotus with ten petals.

Fourth, *anāhata*, situated in the place of the heart. It has a red lotus with twelve golden petals.

[71] S. B. Dasgupta, *Obscure Religious Cults*, pp. 218-19.

[72] In *hatha-yog, bandha* or *mudrā* designates a position of the body to "immobilize" the *semen virile*. (*Hatha Yoga-Pradipikā*, vol. III, pp. 61-63, cited M. Eliade, *Yoga*, p. 211.)

[73] Eliade, *ibid.*, pp. 241-43; A. Avalon (pseudonym), J. Woodroffe, *The Serpent Power* (London, 1919), pp. 103-80.

Fifth, *viśuddha*, situated in the region of the throat (laryngeal and pharyngeal plexus). It has a lotus with sixteen petals of smoky purple.

Sixth, *ājnā*, situated between the eyebrows (cavernous plexus). It has a white lotus with two petals.

Finally, *sahasrār*, situated at the top of the head (cerebral plexus) with a thousand petalled lotus, head down.

Nādis are countless. The majority of the yogico-tāntric texts enumerate only ten: *idā, pingalā, suṣumnā, gāndhāri, hastijihvā, puṣā, yaśasvini, alambusā, kuhu*, and *śankhini*, of which the first three are more significant than the others in the yogico-tāntric system.[74] An extremely complex system of homologies has been elaborated around them. *Idā* and *pingalā* are often identified with *prān* (inhalation) and *apān* (exhalation), the moon and the sun, *som* (nectar) and *agni* (fire), and Śiv and *śakti*. The quintessence of the visible body in the form of *som* or the celestial nectar is reposited in the moon in *sahasrār*. There is a curved duct known as *śankhini*, also called *banka-nāl* in the Bengali literature, from the moon below *sahasrār* up to the hollow in the palatal region through which *som-ras* passes, and the mouth of the curved duct is also called "the tenth door" (*daśam-dvār*). It is through the yogico-tāntric practice of *khechari-mudrā* that the *yogi* saves the nectar from being trickled down into the fire in the navel region and dried up.

Dominating the entire background of the esoteric disciplines in medieval Bengal was, therefore, the idea of the supreme importance of the human body exalted as a microcosm, and the consequent emphasis on the psycho-physiological culture. An all-embracing and elaborate structure of homologies—cosmic, theological, natural, and physical—was effectively used to illustrate the subtle truth of the mystic physiology. The microcosmic view, examples of which have been found all over the world from ancient times, was evidenced in India

[74] Eliade, *ibid.*, p. 237; Avalon, *ibid.*, pp. 113-14.

in the vedic age. The Buddhist *sahajiyās* in Bengal gave clear expression to this idea. In the words of Saraha:

Here (within this body) is the Ganges and the Jumna, here the Gangā-sāgara (the mouth of the Ganges), here are Prayag and Banaras—here the sun and the moon. Here are the sacred places, here the *Pithas* and the *Upa-pithas*—I have not seen a place of pilgrimage and an abode of bliss like my body.[75]

Kānhā-pād located the mount Sumeru in the body.[76] The idea was carried to its farthest point in tāntrism, where this cosmo-physiology received an elaborate treatment. The sensory activities were magnified, and the parts of human body and the physiological functions were identified with the cosmic regions, stars, planets, gods, and so on. *Hatha-yog* and *tantra* transubstantiated the human body by giving it macranthropic dimensions and multi-layered homologization for "realization."[77]

The mystical ideas in particular reference to the techniques and practices of the discipline, as found in the Bengali Muslim writings, show the strong influence of many of these ideas and practices of indigenous bio-mental culture. The local elements are not hard to detect, but any such attempt should take prior note of two relevant considerations. First, an analytical dissection of the divergent sources of a mystical knowledge, in which all diversities finally come to lose their angularities in the totality of a unitive mystic experience, may offer a false rather than an authentic perception of this mystic phenomenon. Secondly, there were Islamic parallels, as mentioned above,[78] to some of the indigenous mystic matters. The microcosmic view of the individual is an important instance.

[75] Quoted by P. C. Bagchi, *Materials for a Critical Edition of the Old Bengali Charyāpadas: a Comparative Study of the Text and the Tibetan Translation* (Viśva-bhārati, 1956), pt. 1, nos. 47, 48; S. B. Dasgupta, *Obscure*, p. 89.

[76] Dasgupta, *ibid.*, p. 14.

[77] M. Eliade, *Yoga*, p. 236.

[78] *Supra*, pp. 141ff.

Great importance was attached in classical sufism to man as the embodiment of all qualities and attributes of the supreme being. "Man is the microcosm," said Jili, "in which all attributes are united, and in him alone does the Absolute become conscious of itself in all its diverse aspects."[79] In the words of Jalāl al-Din Rumi, "The mosque that is built in the hearts of the saints is the place of worship for all, for God dwells there."[80] Similarly, sufism shares with the Indian systems some notions and practices associated with mystical physiology. *Sufi* techniques, relating to *zikr*, or repetitions of God's name, performed in conjunction with the regulation of bodily postures and respiratory devices, and also with the help of the concept of *latifa*, or "centers," in the human body, where different kinds of divine light (*nur*) is said to descend during the practice of *zikr*, offer close parallels to the yogico-tāntric concepts and practices discussed above. Efforts have also been made to trace the growth of some of these sufic techniques to Indian influence. Eliade believes that "the regulation of bodily postures and breathing techniques is owing, at least in part, to Indian influences," and adds:

> We must emphasize the mystical physiology assumed by the practice of *dhikr*; there are references to "centers" and subtle organs, to a certain inner vision of the human body, to chromatic and acoustic manifestations accompanying the various stages of the experience, etc. Respiratory discipline and ritual enunciation play an essential role; the process of concentration is not unlike the yogic method.[81]

Gardet examines the relation of *zikr* with *japa-yog*, and compares the "*zikr* of the tongue" (*zikr-i jali*) with *dhāranā* and the "*zikr* of the heart" (*zikr-i khafi*) with *dhyān*.[82]

[79] Quoted in R. A. Nicholson, *Islamic Mysticism*, p. 84.

[80] *Mathnawi*, quoted in R. A. Nicholson, *The Idea of Personality in Sufism* (Cambridge, 1923), p. 78.

[81] M. Eliade, *Yoga*, pp. 216-17.

[82] L. Gardet, "La Mention du Nom Divin (*Dhikr*) dans la Mystique Musulmane," *Revue Thomiste* (Paris), vol. LII (1952), p. 670 and LIII (1953), p. 205; also *ibid.*, pp. 216, 408 (note vi, p. 6).

Regardless of the sufic indebtedness to Indian mysticism, the influences of the locally popular yogico-tāntric ideas on Bengali Muslim mediator-writers are evident and incontrovertible. Local influences appeared in various forms and proportions. The indubitable sufic concepts were often diluted with local symbols, and, where symbolism was found inadequate, unqualified use of indigenous materials occurred. The most significant expression of yogico-tāntric influence related to the objects underlying the psycho-physiological exercises discussed in this literature. A number of these writers made unambiguous reference to hatha-yogic objects of the bio-mental culture. There are frequent references to the term *yog*, *yog-siddhi*, and *sarva-siddhi*. The practitioner's goal of a perfect (*siddha*), indestructable (*akṣay*), and immortal (*amar*) body was stressed. The psycho-physiological practices are thought to bring "health" and "grace" to the body, "great longevity," and also to keep the "body free from disease" and "the shadow of death" away from it. With regular practices of this kind "the tree never grows old." With reference to specific practices, we are told that some mystical "postures" are aimed at warding off "eighty-four diseases," the number having a great deal of mystical significance in nāthism. The mystical "gestures" like *śitali-mudrā* confer "perfection" (*siddhi*), and *bharjari-mudrā* enables the practitioner "to defy Yam [the Hindu god of death]." The culture of "nerves," assured the "continued life of the old," while the retention of *semen virile* contributes to "beauty, strength, long life, and eye power." The respiratory controls not only increase "longevity" and transforms a body that "does not perish in fire or water," such practices also help to obtain *bākya-siddhi*, "the supreme feet [of God]" and "a vision of Allāh."[83]

The mediators' notions of the mystic discipline and tech-

[83] Abd al-Hakim, *Chāri Maqām*, fols. 2-4; Saiyid Murtaza (untitled), fols. 1-7; Saiyid Sultān, *Jnān-chautisā*, fols. 2-4, 10-14 mc; Shaikh Mansur, *Sirr*, fols. 31-36. See also *infra*, pp. 181-83.

niques may be broadly categorized, as already suggested, under "the stages and stations" and "the psycho-physiological culture: the microcosm."

a. The Stages and Stations. The sufic concepts of the four stages (*manāzil*, sing. *manzil*) and the four corresponding stations (*maqāmat*, sing. *maqām*)[84] follow directly from the notion of the mystic's journey (*safar*) or path (*tariqa*) to the "beloved" God, in which the mystic is a traveller (*sālik*). The Bengali Muslim writers discussed in largely classical sufic terms the four stages of *sharia*, *tariqa*, *haqiqa*, and *marifa* as well as their corresponding stations of *nāsut*, *malkut*, *jabrut*, and *lāhut*. The attitudes and duties, incumbent on the mystic traveller, appropriate to each stage and station were clearly delineated.

Generally speaking, the integral and interdependent nature of the four stages were stressed.[85] We have already cited some examples of the notion of interdependence of *sharia*, and *tariqa*. *Sharia*, to one of the writers, is a "boat" of which *tariqa* is the "sail," *haqiqa* the "anchor," and *marifa* the "rudder."[86] To another, *sharia* is "lamp," *tariqa* is "wick," *haqiqa* is "fuel," and *marifa* is "ignition." The "three together, without the other, cannot function" and "there is light only when all the four come together."[87] The importance of the preliminary stage of *sharia* was, however, particularly emphasized, along with the strict obligation of performing the basic observances of this stage and its station of *nāsut*. In addition to "the five essentials of Islam," namely "fasting, prayer, pilgrimage, almsgiving, and the faith," repentance (*tauba*) preparatory to meditation (*ibādat*), observance of the distinction between permitted (*halāl*) and prohibited (*harām*) food and of other

[84] The terms *manzil* and *maqām* are often interchanged in the Muslim Bengali writings.

[85] Hāji Muhammad, *Nur Jamāl*, fol. 1 mc; Abd al-Hakim, *Chāri Maqām*, fol. 1.

[86] Hakim, *ibid.*

[87] Hāji Muhammad, *Nur Jamāl*, fol. 1 mc.

injunctive commandments (*farmān*) of God were strongly urged. The realization of the distinction between one's own belongings and those of another, the need for ritual cleanliness, and contemplation on the implications of the faith (*din*) and of being a believer (*mumin*) were also advocated.[88]

The "complete mastery" of the stage of *sharia* and of the station of *nāsut* leads to the next stage of *tariqa* and the station of *malkut*. The traveller at this stage loses all "hunger and thirst," and transcends the feelings of "desire, anger, greed, and attachment" and also of "malice and envy."[89] The practitioner must have discarded his illusion of reality (*māyā*) and all "evil thoughts."[90] The body, purged of them, is "as pure as *firishtah*," who are stationed at *malkut*. The mind is absorbed in the contemplation of God and loses the "consciousness of self." The "body" is "in the open," while the "mind" focusses "on what is concealed." This state of mind marks the realization of the station of *malkut*. The essence (*sifat*) of man leaves the human attributes of the *nāsut* station behind and emerges in the form of "the essence of a *firishtah*" to become at one with it in a "divine body."[91]

The traveller can never, however, "rest" here at this stage, and "moves on to the next stage of *haqiqa* to attain the state of *jabrut*." Here he finds himself in the world of spirits (*ārohā*/*arwāh*, sing. *ruh*) and comes to realize his "own self" as "at one with the supreme soul." The bright irradiance of the light (*nur*) of the spirits totally blurs the distinction between the self and the non-self. This stage beggars description.[92] The essence of Allāh is "infinitesimal" and "inexpressible," and a *guru* alone is capable of revealing some of the truth.[93]

The attainment of the station of *jabrut* in the stage of *haqiqa*

[88] *Ibid.*, fols. 1-2 mc; Saiyid Sultān, *Jnān-pradip*, fols. 1-2.
[89] Muhammad, *ibid.*, fol. 2; also Sultān, *ibid.*, fol. 2.
[90] Sultān, *ibid. Māyā* is the Hindu concept of the illusion of reality.
[91] Hāji Muhammad, *Nur Jamāl*, fols. 2-3 mc.
[92] *Ibid.*, fols. 3-5 mc.
[93] *Ibid.*, fol. 5 mc.

leads the mystic traveller to the penultimate stage of *marifa* with its station of *lāhut*. Here he is invested with the power of miracles (*karāmāt*, sing. *karāmat*) and offered the vision (*didār*) of Allāh. But many *faqirs* are lured by the thaumaturgic powers attained at this stage, and are consequently denied the vision of Allāh. Prophet Muhammad alone is the guide to the truth of *marifa* embracing the entire cosmic process of genesis (*utpatti*) and doom (*pralay*).[94]

Within this general conceptual framework of the sufic stages and stations, other Bengali Muslim mediators introduced further elements, which, if of Islamic origin, fitted well into the milieus of indigenous mystical concepts and practices or were otherwise derived directly from the latter sources. In his discussion of psycho-physiological practices associated with the culture of sufic *manzils* and *maqāms*, Abd al-Hakim clearly traversed Islamic and indigenous grounds. Not only did he use the term *yog* in reference to those practices, as noted before,[95] the very title of his work, *Chāri Maqām-bhed*, meaning the "piercing" or "penetration" of the four *maqāms*, is also strongly suggestive of the central yogico-tāntric concept of *ṣat-chakra-bhed* or the piercing of the six nerve-plexuses. He made frequent references to the "sun" and the "moon" representing the right and left nostrils. The sun and the moon, in both Hindu and Buddhist *tantra*, symbolize the two significant mystical nerves on the right and the left, also known as *idā* and *pingalā*, and their union is generally regarded as the union of the two currents of the vital wind, *prān* (inhalation) and *apān* (exhalation). Hakim frequently advocates the yogic practice of *kumbhak*, or retention of the inhaled air, the most important aspect of yogic exercises.

The station of *nāsut* in the stage of *sharia*, writes Hakim, is the abode of the *firishtah* Jibrāil, living in the form of a peacock in the midst of radiant waves of light. The place has

[94] *Ibid.*
[95] *Supra*, p. 169.

three colors—red, white, and yellow. The mystic seeker is urged to contemplate his own face which is but a "reflection of the soul." The image of the mystic preceptor (*murshid*) is also to be "mentally perceived." With the help of *zikr* the seeker wipes clean the mirror of his mind, in which he observes "the lord of the subtle body." The mind is turned away from all distractions to the internalized "cry of Allāh" at the heart. The *zikr* of Allāh is followed by continuous repetitions of the sound *hu hu*. All other sounds are banished from the ears, as is the thought of food from the mind. The mystic assumes a squatting posture (*āsan*) with both hands on his knees, and performs *kumbhak*. The air from the lower region of the navel is drawn upwards to the heart. He also spends his time offering *namāz* and reading the *Qurān* in solitude.[96]

At the next station of *malkut*, the air arising from "a green star located at the root of the navel," blows incessantly in the mystic's body through the nerve channels. The heart is central in the control of the air, with two passages on its right and left, the former being "the abode of the sun" and the latter is "graced by the presence of the moon." *Firishtah* Isrāfil, in a form of the size of a grain, presides over this station, gazing at the root of the navel. The performance of *kumbhak* and contemplation on the *murshid* are important in mystic practice even at this stage. During inhalation the first part of the Islamic creed (*kalima*), "there is no god" (*lāilāha*), and during exhalation the second part, "but Allāh" (*illallāh*), are repeated. "Longevity" increases in direct proportion to the degree of retention of the inhaled air. The culture of this mystic "path" gives the practitioner "vitality" to his body as well as *bākya-siddhi*.[97]

Firishtah Mikāil, in the form of an elephant, presides at the *maqām* of *jabrut* in the third *manzil* of *haqiqa*. Here there is perennial water that contains the reflection of the moon.

[96] Abd al-Hakim, *Chāri Maqām*, fol. 2 mc.
[97] *Ibid.*, fols. 2-3.

This is the "source of intelligence," and the brain, which is the size of a pearl, is deposited in the head. The technique of meditation here is to contemplate the pearl conceived as a "lake" in order to establish the identity of the "gross" and the "subtle" visions. In this state of mind it is transformed into a mirror in which the image of the *murshid* is observed. This is followed by *zikr*, performed with two thumbs touching the ears, and the fore, the middle, and the little fingers reaching respectively to the eyes, the nostrils, and the lips, while one of the heels is pressed against the anus. With the head lowered, the mystic performs *kumbhak*, and encounters his *ātmā*. The image of the *ātmā* becomes at one with the mystic's own. All profane feelings of desire, anger, greed, and attachment are eschewed, and "the image of Allāh" appears in his vision.[98]

The final station of *lāhut*, presided over by the *firishta* Izrāil "in the form of a tiger," is the "seat of fire." The body contains a "well of fire," burning like charcoals. The place is illuminated by "a bright star." Smoke comes incessantly out of the well and air from the smoke. The fire, on one hand, causes "hunger and thirst," and remains, on the other, the source of "power, strength, and sexual virility." An individual continues to live as long as the fire exists in the body, and the "desertion of fire from the body" brings his death. An effective practitioner at this *maqām* turns his mind away from the "falsity of the world" and looks at "the mirror of his own mind" with the help of *zikr*. This enables him to acquire a "divine" or subtle vision and observe "a red star." The aspirant's meditation, preferably "in solitude," is aimed at a constancy of the image of the *firishtah* and his own *murshid* in his mind, which is now thoroughly purged of all "unclean matters." The practitioner has now prepared himself "to find Allāh." One should, therefore, learn "the practice of *yog*,"

[98] *Ibid.*, fol. 3.

adds Hakim, and "attain mastery of the four *maqāms*." This keeps him free from the "great sins" and earns him *bākya-siddhi*.[99]

If Abd al-Hakim located the sufic *manzils* and *maqāms* in the mystic's own body, Saiyid Murtaza went a step farther to identify their position in the body with the yogico-tāntric *chakras*, or nerve-plexuses. His ideas on the mystic formulae and techniques offer the strongest evidence of local influence.

Murtaza identifies the station of *nāsut* with *mulādhār-chakra*,[100] as "it is called in *yog*." Like Hakim, he regards this part of the mystical physiology as the "seat of the eternal fire,"[101] but unlike him mentions Izrāil as the presiding *firishtah* of this station. Here the *kalima* is the appropriate *zikr* performed with "closed ears and eyes" by the practitioner. The latter must be "watchful" that the fire, which makes "an immortal body," is kept alive by the yogic practice of contractive pressures created at the anal root. The sound of *anāhuta/anāhata* is always in the mystic's ears which constitute "the main outlets for the soul." The air is also always there in the *mulādhār*, and there is a "lamp" burning there, revealing an image for meditation. The *śakti* of Śiv must remain "confined" to this place. The mind is kept pure with the help of the *zikr* of *lāilāha*, followed by that of *illallāh* nine times in succession. This is to be concluded with the *zikr* of *rasulallāh*.[102]

The station of *malkut*, "in the navel region," presided over by Isrāfil, is identified with the yogic *manipur-chakra*. The nose forms the "gateway" to this station. The mystic must learn about the movements of five different types of air blowing in this part of the mystical physiology. As long as there

[99] *Ibid.*, fol. 4.

[100] For a description of *mulādhār-chakra*, see *supra*, p. 165.

[101] In yogico-tantrism "the sun" is regarded as the source of "the fire" in this part of the body.

[102] Saiyid Murtaza, fols. 1-3.

is air, there is life. The mystic places his chin on his throat, the right leg on the left thigh, and concentrates on "the tip of the nose." This arrests "the breath" within the body. The mystic observes "an image" of the soul. One who is able to visualize it all forever is capable of "foretelling" events. Having attained this, the mystic fixes his attention on "a star" positioned in "the region of *manipur*." *Firishtahs*, *surs*, and *asurs* inhabit the place. The sun and the moon occupy, respectively, the right and the left sides of the body, and the air is to be confined to the left nostril during the day, and to the right during the night. From his *guru* the practitioner should learn "the great secret name" concealed in the *kalima*, to which he must resort. This results in *yog-siddhi*, and Allāh bestows "very long life."[103]

The *maqām* of *jabrut*, presided over by Mikāil, is located in the cerebral region. The eyes constitute its "doors." There is "an ever-flowing stream" in the region of the heart that keeps the body "steady." The practitioners know it as the reservoir lake of the celestial nectar (*amrit-kunda*),[104] and it makes the drinker "indestructible and immortal." This is also the source of "cognitive intelligence" and regarded in mystics' circle as *ājnā-chakra*. There are golden lotuses fully blossomed in the water. *Paramātmā* and *jivātmā* exist there in an unitive state, as the light in the lamp in relation to its oil. It is in this form that Allāh's supreme companion, Nur Muhammad (Nur-i Muhammad),[105] resides here. There is a "white lotus," "a pearl" in the lotus, and Nur-i Muhammad inside the pearl. The place also contains *ādi-chandra* and *mul-chandra* or *garal-chandra* (both of nāthist origin). The mystic attains his purpose at this station as he obtains a vision of Nur-i Muhammad.[106]

103 *Ibid.*, fols. 4-5.

104 A popular yogico-nāthist concept, using it in the sense of the ambrosia and quintessence of the body.

105 *Supra*, pp. 114-15, 121.

106 Saiyid Murtaza, fols. 6-7.

He moves next onto the final station of *lāhut* in the region of the heart, which is the abode of fire under the guardianship of the *firishtah* Jibrāil. Known to the *yogi* as *anāhata-chakra*, the *maqām* of *lāhut* reveals the nature of the supreme being to the seeker with the help of the yogic practices of "sealing the tenth door,"[107] as well as continuous remembrance of *ajapā-jap*, which gives him "an inviolability." The supreme being gazes at his own form and produces "the sweat"[108] from which Nur-i Nabi is created. *Paramātmā* and *jivātmā* remain merged in each other as two "luminous substances." The lord resides in "the thousand petalled lotus," and a seeker should look into his own heart. The mystic aspirant here has also to contend with Iblis and his companions like "desire, anger, greed, and attachment." The mind is to be "purged" of them before the "vision of Lord Niranjan" appears in "the clean mirror of the heart." This is to be achieved with the *zikr* of *lāilāha* and by drawing the "air" upwards and transferring it from "one nerve to another." Finally, the *zikr* of *illallāh*, should be "hurled" against the "sinful creature," Iblis, and this *zikr* is accompanied by "slow exhalation."[109]

b. The Psycho-Physiological Culture: the Microcosm. The supreme importance of the microcosmic body in the mystical writings of the mediators has been noted above.[110] An analysis of this literature reveals that the microcosmic body is invested with elements derived from three sources: general or universal, Islamic, and local. An analytical dissection of its nature tends, however, to violate the spirit of unity underlying the mystic thought and experience. There is an additional problem relating to matters deriving from what we have called

[107] In the *hatha-yog* the body consists of "ten doors," the tenth being the cerebral region and known as *brahma-randhra*. The nāthist ideal is to close these ten doors and drink, with the help of *khechari-mudrā*, the ambrosia, oozing out of *sahasrār*.

[108] For the cosmogonical significance of "sweat" (*gharma*) in both Hindu and Muslim Bengali literature, *supra*, pp. 121-22, 128-31.

[109] Saiyid Murtaza, fols. 8-9.

[110] *Supra*, pp. 166-67.

"general or universal" sources. Although not particularly Islamic or local, these elements have been introduced in either Bengali or Perso-Arabic terms and symbols, thereby creating the difficulty of attributing them to particular sources.

The entire universe is located in the human body: nine planets, twelve houses of the Zodiac, the sun, the moon, the stars, the air, fire, water, clay, the sky, and the nether regions.[111] The seven days of the week are also there, occupying particular parts of the body: Sunday (Ravi) in the navel, Monday (Som) in the brain, Tuesday (Mangal) in the eyes, Wednesday (Budh) and Thursday (Guru or Vrihaspati) in the heart, Friday (Śukra) in the "semen," and Saturday in the *nād-chakra*.[112] Of the four elements in the body, air is in the navel, fire in the brain, water in the hair, and clay in the heart.[113]

The body also contains the empyrean (*arsh*) and the throne of Allāh, the divine tablet (*lauh*) and the pen (*qalam*), the seven heavens, the seven hells, Iblis and his "four companions."[114] The rivers, noted in Islamic tradition, such as the Furāt or the Euphrates, the Rud or the Oxus, the Nil or the Nile, Saihun or the Jaxartes, the Jaihun or the Bactrus, and the Kulsum are traced in the body.[115] Mansur, again, identifies them with the six rivers known in Hindu tradition, namely the Ikṣu, the Ratnākar, the Sindhu, the Nabani, the Kṣirod, and the Dadhi. He also compares "the rocks and hills" on the surface of the earth with "the bones in the body" and identifies "the spinal cord" with Mount Sumeru, a favorite symbol in the yogico-tantric system.[116] Ādam's body

[111] Shaikh Mansur, *Sirr*, fol. 24; Shaikh Zāhid, *Ādya-parichay*; Shaikh Chānd, *Tālib*, fols. 8-9; Hayāt Mahmud, *Hitajnān*, pp. 33-34.

[112] Mansur, *ibid.*, fols. 24-26.

[113] Shaikh Chānd, *Tālib*, fol. 8 mc.

[114] *Ibid.*; Hayāt Mahmud, *Hita*, pp. 33-34.

[115] Mahmud, *ibid.*, pp. 34-35; Shaikh Mansur, *Sirr*, fol. 26.

[116] Mansur, *ibid.* See also Kānha-pād, *Dohā-koṣ*, *supra*, p. 167.

epitomizes the whole creative process.[117] The four *maqāms* are also found in the particular parts of the body: the nose is the location of *nāsut*, the mouth of *malkut*, the ears of *jabrut*, and the eyes of *lāhut*, each *maqām* being presided over by one of the four great *firishtahs*.[118] A seeker should "worship" his *murshid* to realize the truth contained in his body. The body possesses a lotus, which itself contains a "jewel." The jewel possesses a "brilliance," the latter a "heart," the heart a "king," the king the *nur* (the divine light), and the *nur* contains "the abode of God." This is visualized in "the mirror of the heart." A room is illumined by a "lamp" that needs "oil," a "wick" and its "ignition." The body bears the "proofs" of the room, the lamp, the oil, the wick, and the ignition.[119]

The body is also said to contain various elements of Hindu tradition. The four "ages" of Hindu mythology, namely *satya, tretā, dvāpar*, and *kali*, are to be found in the body. The local rivers—the Gangā and the Bhāgirathi—flow across the body. Along with the four *kitābs* (the four revealed books of the *Psalms*, the *Old* and the *New Testaments*, and the *Qurān*, the four *veds* (the *Rig*, the *Sām*, the *Yajur*, and the *Atharva*) are also located in the body.[120] Saiyid Sultān traces the *Sām-ved*, the *Yajur-ved*, and the *Atharva-ved* to the ears, the navel, and the mouth, respectively. The twelve houses of the Zodiac, located in the body, correspond to the six yogico-tāntric *chakras*: aries and taurus are in the *mulādhār*, gemini and cancer in the *svādhistān*, leo and virgo in *manipur*, libra and scorpio in the *anāhata*, sagittarius and capricorn in the *biśuddha*, and aquarius and pisces in the *ājnā-chakra*. The "six seasons" are also located in the six *chakras*.[121] The homologization of the *maqāms* and the *chakras* by Saiyid Murtaza have

[117] Shaikh Chānd, *Tālib*, fol. 8 mc; Hayāt Mahmud, *Hita*, p. 34.
[118] Chānd, *ibid.*, fol. 10 mc; also Saiyid Murtaza, *supra*, pp. 175-77.
[119] Hayāt Mahmud, *Hita*, p. 35.
[120] Shaikh Zāhid, *Ādya-parichay*.
[121] Saiyid Sultān, *Jnān-pradip*, fols. 9-10 mc.

already been noted.[122] "The four parts of the moon," known among nāthists as *ardha-chandra*, *nij-chandra*, *unmatta-chandra*, and *rohini-chandra*, are associated, respectively, with the brain, the breath, the blood, and the hair of Ādam.[123]

Various parts of the microcosmic body are also associated with different forms of prayers (*ibādat*).[124] The prayers of the mouth are recitation of God's name, continuous reading of the *Qurān*, and utterance of "kind, truthful," and "pleasant" words. The prayers of the ears consist in hearing about the lord, listening mindfully to the *Qurān* and to the "supreme sound" that contains "the secret of long life and health." The prayers of the eyes is to observe the power and majesty of God, and that of the nose is to control breath as a means of getting a vision of the inner soul. Copying the Qurānic verses, writing the myriad names of Allāh, making gifts to the needy, and flashing the sword at the unbelievers are all prayers of hands. The prayer of the heart is to ponder and contemplate the greatness of God, and also to know one's own self. The prayer of stomach consists in taking nothing but permitted (*halāl*) food, and of the feet in undertaking the pilgrimage of *hajj* to Mecca, in visiting the *murshid* on foot, and in walking along the path of Islam. Even the genital organ is associated with particular forms of prayer, such as abstaining from promiscuous sex relations and not coveting another man's wife.

The whole system of bio-mental culture is, however, based on an elaborate concept of a "mystical" physiology. It is essentially mystical inasmuch as the references to physiological matters are of mystical rather than of biological import. The mystical anatomy detailed in this literature is more meaningful in the context of the pursuit and attainment of mystical objects than as a description of the human physiology. The body is said to consist of "eighteen" matters, ten of which are

[122] *Supra*, pp. 175-77.

[123] Shaikh Chānd, *Tālib*, fol. 9 mc.

[124] Shaikh Mansur, *Sirr*, fol. 21; Saiyid Sultān, *Jnān-pradip*, fol. 2 mc.

derived from God and the rest from parents, mother contributing flesh, blood, skin, and hair, and father giving bones, nerves, brain, and semen. From God are derived breath, heart, intelligence (*aql*), the faith (*imān*), and faculties of seeing, hearing, speaking, and smelling. All this forms the eighteen *maqāms* in the body, which also contains "ten doors"—an established yogico-tāntric concept—in the two ears, two eyes, two nostrils, the mouth, the genital organ, and the anus.[125] Shaikh Mansur alludes to "four hidden doors" as well, but prefers not to divulge them.[126] There is further reference to "seventy-two compartments (*kothā*)" in the body, set apart by the bones, another highly popular yogico-tāntric notion.

The nerves (*nādi*) in the mystical body form a vital component of the system. There is very little agreement, however, among these writers about the details of the nervous system. One mentions only four central nerves in the cerebral region, which cover the rest of the body. They are named *abd al-rahim*, *abd al-karim*, *abd al-qahr*, and *abd al-zabar*, and said to be of black, white, red, and green colors respectively.[127] Another mentions two thousand and seventy nerves in the body, of which twelve are the principal ones, divided equally between the right and the left side of the body.[128] Shaikh Chānd refers to sixty thousand nerves but reduces them to three hundred and sixty basic ones, of which three called *ingilā*, *pingilā/pingalā*, and *tripini* are the most important.[129] Significantly enough, these three nerves, also known as *idā*, *pingalā*, and (as mentioned before) *suṣumnā*, form an all-important triad in the yogico-tāntric mystical culture, and are often compared to the three rivers—Gangā, Yamunā, and

[125] Mansur, *ibid.*, fols. 23-25; Sultān, *ibid.*; Hayāt Mahmud, *Hita*, p. 35; Shaikh Chānd, *Tālib*, fol. 14 mc.

[126] Mansur, *ibid.*, fol. 25.

[127] Shaikh Parān (untitled), fol. 18 mc.

[128] Hayāt Mahmud, *Hita*, p. 41.

[129] *Tālib*, fol. 14 mc.

Sarasvati—meeting at their confluence at Tripini or Triveni. These three, along with several other popular nerves of the yogico-tāntric system, are cited also in other Muslim works. Of the total "three hundred and sixty," Shaikh Mansur identifies "ten" major nerves, namely *idā*, *pingalā*, *suṣumnā*, *gāndhāri*, *hasti-jihvā*, *puṣā*, *śankhini*, *pakṣini*, *masā*, and *kundali*. The first seven in Mansur's list appear clearly in their yogico-tāntric forms, but the last three are, in yogico-tāntric parlance, called *yaśasvini*, *alambusā*, and *kuhu*. There is, according to him, an eleventh nerve called *brahma-nādi*, running along the spinal column, on the either side of which stand *idā* and *pingalā* as two "poles." *Hasti-jihvā* and *śankhini* lie in the cerebral region, *masā* in the center of the mouth, *suṣumnā* and *pakṣini*, respectively, in the right and left ears, *gāndhāri* and *puṣā*, respectively, in the left and right eyes, and *kundali* in the genital organ.[130] Even for Saiyid Sultān, who traces "seventy thousand" nerves in the body, ten are most important, and his list of names includes many of yogico-tāntric origin.[131] He resorts to the yogico-tāntric homolization of *idā* and *pingalā* with the "moon" and the "sun."[132] Following the same tradition, he also identifies *ingilā* with the river Gangā and *pingalā* with "Jabunā" (Jumnā or Yamunā), while the river Sarasvati, writes Sultān, is "in the middle with the name of *susamā* [*suṣumnā*]."[133] The wise men call it the confluence

[130] Shaikh Mansur, *Sirr*, fols. 25-26.

[131] *Jnān-pradip*, fol. 10 mc. In our ms. the names other than *ingilā*, *pingalā*, *gāndhāri*, *hasti-(jihvā)*, *alambusa*, and *sakṣini* (*śankhini*) cannot be deciphered at all. But M. R. Tarafdar (*Husain Shāhi Bengal*, pp. 205, 371) provides the rest of the names as *kuhu*, *pusā*, *yaśasvini*, and *payasvini*.

[132] Our ms. has "sea" or "waters" for "sun." But we accept M. R. Tarafdar's (*ibid.*) reading of *divākar* (sun) as being fully consistent with the use of the other word "moon" in this particular context.

[133] Here we suggest a rational emendation of what seems a copyist's confusion. The ms. has it *surāsur* ("gods and demons") for Sarasvati. Tarafdar (*ibid.*) misses the point and offers a literal translation of the line that strikes me as rather incongruous: "The nerve running between the god and the demon is called Susumnā." Sarasvati for *surāsur* does appear wholly consistent with

of "tripini," and a "bath" taken at this place "washes away the sins of a million years."

The culture of nerves went hand in hand with the application of respiratory techniques, the pursuit of which, writes Sultān, confers "eternal life." The "fire" in the body is kept burning by "air," and one lives on as long as the fire remains unextinguished. It "destroys all" adversaries and is to be kept alive by "consuming fresh air."[134] The nerves are vitally connected with the respiratory techniques. *Ingilā* contains the breath and has "thirty subsidiary nerves" while *pingalā* has "forty-one." Knowledge of the *śankhini*, which is "curved at three points," removes "the fear of death." The ten major nerves are attached to the "ten doors" in the body, *pingalā* and *idā* being connected respectively to the right and left ears. Air blows from the other seven nerves through *suṣumnā*. The breath is held in the left nostril, to be transferred to the right nostril and then to the middle and the most vital nerve *suṣumnā*, the seat of "Ārdhya [Ādyā]-śakti." It is first taken to the left ear, brought back carefully to *tripini* in the middle, and then passed out through the right ear.[135] The air is drawn in *purak* as "a thread enters the opening of the needle." With the gradual dilating of the passage a great deal of air comes in, producing "a sound" as it rises up. The sound stills the mind, then the mystic aspirant perceives a luminous substance emerging from the sound. The mind is lost in the contemplation of the light, which is nothing but "the feet of the lord."[136]

---

the contextual background, involving the use of the terms Gangā, Yamunā, and, a little later, Tripini or Triveni, which is regarded as the confluence of all three of them, as already mentioned.

[134] Saiyid Sultān, *Jnān-pradip*, fol. 3 mc; also Shaikh Mansur, *Sirr*, fols. 31-36.

[135] Sultān, *ibid.*, fol. 10 mc. Ādyā-śakti is the primordial goddess in the tāntric system.

[136] *Ibid.*, fols. 3-4, 10 mc. M. R. Tarafdar reads *pantha* or "path" for *pada* or "feet" of the lord. (Tarafdar, *Husain Shāhi Bengal*, pp. 206, 370.) Our ms. clearly shows the latter word.

The physical postures and gestures were vital components of the psycho-physiological discipline, as already noted. Not only the *āsans* and *mudrās* prescribed in the Muslim Bengali literature are of indigenous origin, but the specific yogico-tāntric objectives underlying these practices also find clear acceptance. Certain *āsans* are advocated with the particular object of averting "eighty-four diseases," which is a very popular nāthist idea. Some other postures and gestures are recommended because the successful practitioner is "dreaded by gods and nymphs alike" and becomes "omnipresent"; his body is not "perished in fire and water," and he attains the "supreme feet of the lord," power over the consequences of all his "utterances and actions" and finally "complete loss of self-consciousness."[137]

The lotus-posture (*padmāsan*), with the chin resting on the chest, the left leg placed on the right, the hands resting on the knees, and the mind fixed on the nose, is highly recommended. A variant of *padmāsan* involves placing the left heel on the right thigh, touching the bottom of the pelvic region, and concentrating the mind on the middle of the eyebrows. As a means of transcending the process of physical decay, the Bengali Muslim mystic literature refers to the highly complex nāthist practice called *khechari-mudrā*, which involves the turning of the tongue back to the root of the cerebral region, reaching for the source of the divine nectar. Another gesture called *mahā-mudrā* consists in placing the chin on the chest, pressing the left foot against the anus, and holding the right leg with two hands. This is accompanied by the performance of the yogic practice of *kumbhak*, or retention of the inhaled air. *Mul-mudrā* puts similar stress on pressing the left heel against the anus, placing the right leg on the left, and finally pushing the air up through the alimentary canal by applying repeated pressures. With the help of *śitali-mudrā*

[137] Sultān, *ibid.*, fol. 14 mc.

the practitioner transfers the air inhaled through *purak* to the navel and then further down the stomach. The *bharjari-mudrā*, the mastery of which empowers one to defy Yam, the Hindu god of death, concerns the control of the *semen virile*; and "secrecy" and "caution" are urged in its practice.[138]

Ali Rajā's ideas of psycho-physiological culture claim some distinction insofar as he attaches supreme importance to the mind. A great *faqir*, according to him, is one who regards "the three worlds" as "no different from the mind." The mind itself is the "body." The "king" of the mind is both servant and God (Iśvar), both Allāh and Prophet Muhammad, both preceptor and disciple, both learned and ignorant, and heaven, hell, the earth, the empyrean, the throne of God, the divine light (*nur*), and a devoted *yogi* like Śiv and Brahmā, "the lords of mendicants."[139] The mind contains a "light," and the latter produces a great sound called *anāhata-śabda*, which is the key to the fulfilment of all objectives.[140] The heart, which is shaped like a lotus-bud, radiates what is by far "the greatest name of the lord" ever written in the scriptures like the *purāns*, the *veds*, and the *Qurān*. Twelve years of meditation on "the source of the sound" still the sound as well as the mind. The composure of the mind results in a "steady body," which becomes the object of physical culture. Among the *siddhās* the sound is known as *param-hamsa* or *ajapā*. It may be noted here that *hamsa* or *ajapā* are central in the yogico-tāntric system. The two syllables *ham* and *sah* are often taken to represent exhalation and inhalation or even Śiv and *śakti*. *Param-hamsa* is realized by meditation on the name of *hamsa*.[141] The "power" of the sound or the name of *hamsa*, according to Ali Rajā, purifies both body and mind. There is "no superior" mode of worshipping God to *ajapā*,

[138] *Ibid.*, fols. 10-14 mc.
[139] Ali Rajā, *Āgam*, fols. 55-57.
[140] Rajā, *Jnān*, fol. 132.
[141] K. Mallik, *Nāth-sampradāyer Itihās*, pp. 459, 468.

which is "the root" of all knowledge, while others are like "branches and flowers." The body contains a "lake" and the confluence of *tripini*, comprising *hamsa*, *purak*, and *rechak*.[142]

The mystic's concern for a perfect body also focussed on the need to control the *semen virile*, which was believed to be associated with physical vitality. The Bengali Muslim writers identified the Arabic words *mani* and *nutfa* with the Bengali words for semen such as *chandra*, *ritu*, *śukra*, and *virya*. *Mani*, writes one, confers "beauty, strength, longevity, and visual power."[143] Another attributes "strength, intelligence, and knowledge" to semen. Just as a man "owes his life to semen," it can also "cause his death." A tree cannot stand without its roots, a fish cannot live without water, and there is "no day" without the sun. So a body cannot exist without semen.[144] It is like a "treasure" in the body and an ocean of the "divine nectar." The "abuse of this wealth" through uncontrolled sexual enjoyment renders the body "weak and without energy." The vision is rooted in *mani*, and copulation steals the light from the eyes. The "store-keeper" of semen in the body is *khemāi*, entrusted with the charge of preserving semen against temptations of love.[145] A *yogi* is not advised to indulge much in sexual acts; the less he does, the more enriched become his yogic accomplishments. He is permitted to copulate only on some specific days determined by the position of the moon.[146]

The Muslim writers believed that the judicious use of this "wealth" in the body depended on a clear knowledge of the changing location of physical desire (*kām*) in the body following from the variations of the lunar position (*tithi*). On the day of the new moon it is found under the foot; on the first day of the bright moon, in the toe; on the second day, on the

[142] Ali Rajā, *Jnān*, fols. 133-39.
[143] Shaikh Mansur, *Sirr*, fol. 36.
[144] Rajā, *Jnān*, fols. 178-79.
[145] Mansur, *Sirr*, fols. 37-38.
[146] Rajā, *Jnān*, fol. 180.

top of the foot; on the third, in the ankles; on the fourth, in the knees; on the fifth, in the thighs; on the sixth, in the region of the anus and genital organ; on the seventh, in the navel; on the eighth, in the wrists; on the ninth, in the heart; on the tenth, in the throat; on the eleventh, in the mouth; on the twelfth, in the nose; on the thirteenth, in the eyes; on the fourteenth, in the forehead; and on the fifteenth, in the cerebral region. The position of *chandra* in the body is also believed to change each day in the week. On Monday it is placed in the anus; on Tuesday in the navel; on Wednesday in the heart; on Thursday in the throat; on Friday in the mouth; on Saturday in the eyes; and on Sunday in the head.[147]

SECTION II: THE MUSLIM "VAIṢNAV" LYRICAL LITERATURE

The syncretistic spirit of Bengali Muslim mysticism assumed another characteristic form in a large corpus of lyrical compositions written by them in the popular middle-Bengali *pada* (short song) style of *vaiṣnav* origin. Ranging from the sixteenth down to the early years of the present century, these Muslim *pada* compositions have been gradually recovered and published in relatively old and recent compilations of Bengali *padas*.[148] My own investigation in this area has revealed the name and work of another Muslim *pada* writer (*pada-kartā*) named Alam, not included in the lists known so far.[149]

The nature of these Muslim *pada* compositions is not easy

[147] Mansur, *Sirr*, fols. 37-38; Shaikh Chānd, *Tālib*, fols. 12-14.

[148] J. Bhadra, *Gaur-pada-tarangini* (Calcutta, 1903); S. C. Rāy, *Pada-kalpa-taru* (Calcutta, 1905); also his *Aprakāśita pada-ratnāvali* (Calcutta, 1920); C. C. Vandopādhyāy, *Vidyāpati, Chandidās o anyānya Vaiṣnav Mahājan Gitikā*; R. M. Mallik, *Musalmān Vaiṣnav Kavi* (Calcutta, 1895); V. S. Sanyāl, *Musalmān Vaiṣnav Kavi*, 4 vols. (Rajshahi, 1906); Y. M. Bhattāchārya, *Bānglār Vaiṣnav-bhāvāpanna Musalmān Kavi* (Calcutta, 1356 B.S./A.D. 1950); and A. Sharif, *Muslim Kavir Pada-sāhitya* (Dacca, 1961).

[149] *Sāhitya-Pariṣat Patrikā* (Calcutta), no. 2 (1314 B.S./A.D. 1907).

to determine, as various writers on the subject would have us believe. Broadly speaking, the Hindu commentators had not only regarded these compositions as direct Muslim contributions to the tradition of vaiṣnavism, but also accepted their authors as *vaiṣnavs* themselves.[150] Undeniably, the entire atmosphere of this literature is saturated with characters, places, objects, images, symbols, and nuances, characteristic of *vaiṣnav* tradition and of *vaiṣnav* lyrical literature as well: the love dalliances of Rādhā and Kriṣna; the *gopinis* (the milkmaids); Lalitā and Biśākhā, the two closest companions of Rādhā; the standing annoyance of Rādhā in her *nanadini* (the sister-in-law); the bemusing flute of Kriṣna; places like Mathurā, Vrindāvan, Gokul, and Braja; the river Yamunā or Kālindi or Kāliyā; the *kadamba* tree under which Rādhā and Kriṣna frequently engaged in amorous sports; and, finally, the festival of *phāgu*, *phāg*, or *holi* in which Rādhā, Kriṣna, and all their friends amused themselves by smearing one another with colored powders—are all there in the Muslim *pada* compositions.[151] And yet any facile assumption of the *vaiṣnav* identity of this literature and their authors is totally unwarranted for several reasons. First, a critical analysis of the literature reveals that a fair proportion of the Muslim poets merely used *vaiṣnav* symbolism to express their own mystical urges and concerns, as we shall fully examine below. Secondly, even where the writers fully adopt a pure *vaiṣnav* tradition as a literary theme, we cannot establish a necessary co-relation between their personal faith and their literary interests and objectives. Some of the greatest Hindu *pada* writers themselves

[150] Svāmi Bhumānanda, "Vaiṣnav Musalmān," *Bangaśri* (*Chaitra*, 1344 B.S./A.D. 1937, p. 387 and *Baiśākh*, 1345 B.S./A.D. 1938, p. 502); R. K. Śāstri, "Kriṣna-bhakta Musalmān," *Pratibhā*, *Kārtik*, 1328 B.S./A.D. 1921, p. 265; P. L. Dās, "Musalmān vaiṣnav kavir dharmamat," *Arghya*, vol. IV (1324 B.S./1917), p. 425.

[151] Shaikh Faiz Allāh, *Rāgmālā* (DMS 545: sl 403), fols. 7-16; Y. M. Bhattāchārya, *Musalmān Kavi*, pp. 39, 44-48, 52-53, 59, 67, 69, 73, 77, 80-81, 88-89, 95, 98, 101-103.

were not adherents of the *vaiṣnav* faith. Vidyāpati of Mithilā was not a follower of Viṣnu, but a *smārta-panchopāsak*, who composed verses on Śiv and Gauri as well as on Kriṣna and Rādhā. Badu Chandidās, the author of the celebrated work on Kriṣna, was a worshipper of the goddess Bāśali or Chandi. Thirdly, certain Bengali Muslim writers chose other Hindu traditions without becoming necessary converts to the particular cults. Shaikh Chānd, already noted as a dominant mediator-writer on mysticism, wrote also on the tradition of Śiv and *śakti*.[152] Besides, some writers chose more than one Hindu tradition as literary themes. Shaikh Faiz Allāh, for example, is credited with literary pursuits of nāthism as well as vaiṣnavism.

The Muslim critics of this literature, on the other hand, are generally predisposed to attach nothing more than allegorical and symbolic meanings to these mystical compositions couched in *vaiṣnav* terms and forms. E. Haq not only does not view the Muslim *pada* as essentially sufic in spirit; he goes to the extent of characterizing the totality of the Bengali literature on *Gaudiya* (Bengali) vaiṣnavism as "fully impregnated with the spirit of *sufi* literature" under "a Hinduistic veneer." Rādhā and Kriṣna of the Bengali *vaiṣnav* literature are, in his opinion, imbued with the "form and essence" of the sufic concepts of *āshiq* (lover) and *mashuq* (beloved), of *sāqi* (the cup-bearer) and *bat* (wine), or of *shama* (lamp) and *parwāna* (moth). Haq also notes close resemblance between *vaiṣnav* lyric and *sufi ghazal* in respect of their "content and style," between the *vaiṣnav* concepts of *biraha* (separation) and *milan* (union), on one hand, and the sufic notions of *hijrān* and *biśhal*, on the other. Haq's views on the *vaiṣnav* literature stem from his general opinion that Bengal vaiṣnavism, as enunciated by Chaitanya (A.D. 1486-1534) and his immediate followers, owed most of its basic features to su-

[152] *Hara-Gauri Samvād* (DMS).

fism. He claims that the strong monistic attitude in Bengal vaiṣnavism is "the legacy of Islam," that its anti-caste tendency is the result of "the influence of Islam," and that the *vaiṣnav* concept of *prem* (divine love) indicates the influence of the *sufi* concept of *ishq*. He also asserts that the *sufi* practice of *halqa*, referring to "an assembly of persons met together for the purpose of devotional exercises through the medium of *dhikr*, accompanied by *samā* or musical performance," "perfectly resembles" the *vaiṣnav* practice of *nām-samkirttan* or *kirttan*, involving congregation, singing God's name (*nām*), with the help of music and dance, leading to an ecstatic condition called *daśā* in vaiṣnavism and *hāl* in sufism.[153]

Islamic influence on Bengal vaiṣnavism or on the medieval *bhakti* movement in general is not very easy to determine. It is a truism that the *bhakti* movement cannot be studied without reference to Islam and sufism in contemporary India. But one must guard against an uncritical tendency to interpret the origin and growth of this religious phenomenon exclusively in terms of Islamic influence. On a close analysis the movement appears more complex and heterogenous than it is generally assumed, and reveals at least two distinct variants. The earlier is a linear development of the Indian devotional tradition, anteceding the spread of sufic influence in India. This refers to the devotional impulses in the Ālvār *vaiṣnav* movement in South India, continued and developed further in the works of Rāmānuj (d. A.D. 1137), Mādhav (d. A.D. 1278), Nimbārk and Nāmdev (the fourteenth century A.D.) and Tukārām (b. A.D. 1608). The other variant of the *bhakti* movement was rather different from this in that it originated later and was, in essence, syncretistic, cosmopolitan, and more populist. The latter drew as much upon sufic as on indigenous devotional mysticism. Its *raison d'être* was to stress the unity of the godhead, transcending the artificial barrier of religious

[153] *MBS*, pp. 50-53; also M. E. Haq, *A History of Sufism in Bengal* (Dacca, 1975), pp. 268-81.

pluralism, and to provide a common ground for people of all religious and social affiliations to meet and unite. Unlike the other clearly Hindu *bhakti* tradition, the protagonists of syncretistic devotionalism like Kabir (c. 15th century A.D.), Nānak (A.D. 1469-1539) and Dādu (A.D. 1544-1603) were not concerned with the revitalization of Hinduism or, for that matter, of any particular religion.

Bengal vaiṣnavism of Chaitanya clearly belonged to the main stream of Hindu *bhakti* tradition.[154] Its fundamental tenets grew from "the general course of development of the *Vaiṣnava* faith in India." The two most fundamental elements forming "the texture of Bengal vaiṣnavism" are "derived more or less from vaiṣnavism in general," the first and foremost being "the general doctrine of *Bhakti*, or emotional service of love and devotion as a means of spiritual realisation." The other, no less important, is "the Kṛṣṇa cult, intimately connected with it, as forming the ground of this devotional attitude."[155] In addition, the *vaiṣnav* theology, in its attitude to the godhead and in its concept of divine love, follows very closely in the tradition of Rāmānuj-Nimbārk rather than of the dominant *wujudi* concept of sufic thought in India, as we shall see more fully below. The Islamic context of Bengal vaiṣnavism is indubitable, but then one cannot attribute this multi-faceted religious phenomenon to this particular factor alone. A detailed examination of the social and religious background of Bengal vaiṣnavism reveals its revivalist character formulated in response to three major concerns of contemporary Bengal: the challenge of Islam, particularly in its mystical form; the orgiastic excesses of *śākta-tāntriks*; and the arid

[154] S. K. De, *Early History of the Vaiṣnava Faith and Movement in Bengal* (Calcutta, 2nd ed., 1961), p. 2; F. Hardy, "Mādhavendra Puri: A Link between Bengal Vaiṣnavism and South Indian *Bhakti*," *Journal of the Royal Asiatic Society of Great Britain and Ireland*, no. 1 (1974), pp. 23-41.

[155] De, *ibid.*

intellectualism and dry ritualism of the subtle logicians of the *navya-nyāy* school centered in Nabadvip.[156]

As we turn to the limited question of Islamic impact on Bengal vaiṣnavism, Haq's observations seem grossly uncritical and over-simplified. The problem of interaction between Hinduism and Islam with particular reference to mysticism is complicated by several unresolved issues, as partly noted earlier in the chapter.[157] First, an apparent similarity between Hindu and Islamic practices or beliefs may, in effect, conceal a basic conceptual difference. Secondly, even where agreement is substantial, the problem of independent origin arises. Finally, as a distinguished historian so succinctly observed in this connexion:

> . . . the process of interaction may be complicated by a double movement. Original Hindu influences, for example, may have passed over into Islam; the movement or process that resulted from this may then in turn influence Hinduism, causing a rather different phenomenon. Mysticism . . . provides a possible illustration. . . . It is . . . quite possible that the Islamic mystics, the sufis, had been directly or indirectly influenced by Hindu thought and institutions before the conquest of India. Hinduism in the fifteenth century, then, was receiving in an elaborated form what it had already given to Islam.[158]

The *sufi* practice of *zikr* is an instance. We have noted above Haq's attempt to cite it as the source of the *vaiṣnav* practice of *nām-kirttan*.[159] On the other hand, Louis Gardet and Marcia Eliade attribute some essential features of *zikr* to original Indian hatha-yogic influence, as also discussed before.[160] Again, the *vaiṣnav* practice of singing God's name to the accompani-

[156] T. Raychaudhuri, *Bengal Under Akbar and Jahangir* (Delhi, 2nd impression, 1969), pp. 132-33.

[157] *Supra*, pp. 167-68.

[158] S. M. Ikram, *Muslim Civilization in India*, ed. by A. T. Embree (New York, 1964), pp. 123, 125.

[159] *Supra*, p. 190.

[160] *Supra*, p. 168.

ment of music and dance, the origin of which is traced by Haq to the *sufi* practice of *samā*, did have a clear precedent in the devotional exercises, involving the song, dance and ecstasy of the southern *vaiṣnav* Ālvārs. About the middle of the ninth century A.D. Nammalvār wrote: "We have seen the devotees of the sea-hued Krishna enter the world in rich abundance, sing His glory, dance in ecstasy and prosper." Further

> Come, all ye lovers of God, let us shout and dance for joy with oft-made surrenderings. Wide do they roam on earth singing songs and dancing, the hosts of Krishna who wears the cool and beautiful Tulsi, the desire of the Bees. . . . These hosts of the Lord of Discus. . . . And sweet are their songs, as they leap and dance, extending wide over earth.[161]

Similarly, a clear precedent for congregational hymn singing (*samkirttan*) is evidenced by the *Bhāgavat-purān*.[162]

None of the two extreme and conflicting views on the nature of the Muslim *pada* literature—the *vaiṣnav* and the sufic view—can, therefore, be exclusively adopted. Faced with the problem, J. M. Bhattāchārya is led to a six-fold categorization of this literature, which has also been adopted by E. C. Dimock, Jr.[163] The six categories are:

1. Pure *vaiṣnav* poetry, in which the quality of devotion and poetic style make the poem indistinguishable from one written by a Hindu *vaiṣnav*.
2. Philosophical poetry, in which ideas neither specifically Hindu nor specifically Muslim are expressed with the help of imagery drawn from the Rādhā-Kriṣna story.
3. Poetry which employs the names Rādhā and Kriṣna to designate not the Rādhā and Kriṣna of *vaiṣnav* text and belief, but an abstract God.

[161] Quoted in J.M.S. Pillai (ed.), *Two Thousand Years of Tamil Literature* (*An Anthology*) (Annamalainagar, 1959), p. 335.

[162] Bangavāsi edn. (11:5:32).

[163] E. C. Dimock, Jr., "Muslim Vaiṣnava Poets of Bengal," in *Bengal Regional Identity*, ed. by D. Kopf (Michigan, 1969), pp. 25ff.

4. A purely secular poetry of love.
5. Poetry on Chaitanya.
6. Poetry using subsidiary *vaiṣnav* themes, but without clear mention of Rādhā, Kriṣna, or Chaitanya.

This classification is diffuse, overlapping, and inadequate in providing for a clear basis of differentiation. It may be amply illustrated by a few specific instances. Bhattāchārya's anthology contains a piece by Chānd Qāzi:

You do not know how to play the flute. You play it at the wrong times. You care nothing for me. When I am sitting with my elders, you call me with your flute. I could die of shame. You play it on the farther bank. I hear it here. I am an unlucky girl; I don't know how to swim.

If you find the bamboo clump from which this flute was made, tear it up by the roots and throw it into the river Cānd Kāzi [Chānd Qāzi] says, I hear the flute, my life ebbs from me—I shall not live, unless I see my Hari.[164]

Both Bhattāchārya and Dimock have taken this particular *pada* as an example of "pure *vaiṣnava* poetry" of their first category, in which Rādhā addressed herself to Hari or Kriṣna. E. Haq has, on the contrary, chosen it as a fine specimen of sufic mysticism using *vaiṣnav* symbolism.[165] Another *pada* attributed to Ārkum/Arqam is interpreted by Dimock in terms of the *vaiṣnav* theological demand "for the unitary God to become two, in order to express his nature which is love." It runs:

The water of the sea blows in the strong wind; it whirls as spray, it fills the wind, it falls again on the land, and finally once more flows to the sea. Kind mingles with kind in the waves' play: you are I, and I am you—I know this in my heart. The tree is born in the seed; how can the seed contain the tree? From one, two come, because of love.[166]

[164] Original in Y. M. Bhattāchārya, *Musalmān Kavi*, no. 40, Eng. tr. by Dimock, *ibid.*, p. 27.

[165] *MBS*, p. 52.

[166] Ārqam, *Haqiqa-i Sitārā*, p. 12, original quoted in Y. M. Bhattāchārya,

Dimock's *vaiṣnav* identification may seem highly suspect in view of the undisputed sufic parallel in the concept of Nur-i Muhammad, according to which God in his absolute and undifferentiated essence (Ahad) was unable to realize himself alone, and hence divided his own self into Ahmad and Muhammad or Nur-i Muhammad, and bound them in love, as already discussed.[167] Again, the following composition by Irpān/Irfān is cited as an example of "a purely secular poetry of love":

> Day and night it draws my life away; I cannot live without him. Tell me, friend, what shall I do? My friend, without him there is no help for this body of mine—I need him—and, thus dependent, I drift upon a sea of sorrow. If I find him I shall keep him captive, holding his feet. The youthful Irpān says, He holds a flute; and with its charm he has stolen my tender life.[168]

It is hard to see how this particular piece could be more "secular" than many other compositions not included in this category. Rather, the *vaiṣnav* motif is here much less obscure than in many of its kind. The beloved here holds a flute, as does Kriṣna, and the lover, like Rādhā, bares her heart to her friend on her separation from the beloved. And yet Irfān, in the guise of a lover, may symbolize the longing of the mystic soul for God.

The universality of the mystical urge and the eclectic and syncretistic ethos of the mediator-writers often made it hazardous to determine the nature of these poems in absolute terms. One cannot, however, ignore the obvious truth of their Muslim authorship. A student of this literature must take cognizance of the fact that these mystic concerns were expressed by writers who were Muslims by faith. Without in-

---

Musalmān Kavi, p. 21, Eng. tr. by Dimock, "Muslim Vaiṣnava Poets," pp. 27-28.

[167] *Supra*, pp. 121, 123-24.

[168] Original quoted in Y. M. Bhattāchārya, *Musalmān Kavi*, no. 20, Eng. tr. by Dimock, "Muslim Vaiṣnava Poets," p. 30.

controvertible proofs it is unreasonable to look beyond their mystic yearnings as Muslims. A careful analysis of a poem often reveals its Islamic identity under a *vaiṣnav* or another veneer. A good example of this kind is a *pada* attributed to Musā, in regard to which Dimock maintains that "the terminology, the setting, the condition of the speaker are all *Vaiṣnava*," but "the expression could be that of any human, separated from his God."[169] The universality or even the *vaiṣnav* "setting" of this poem cannot be doubted. But it is more important to note here, what Dimock overlooks, how clearly the Muslim identity of the writer is revealed in his reference to the "day of judgment" in the concluding line of the poem:

If one knows a *rasika*, one has to love him. If one gives her life to other than a *rasika* she dies while still alive. I know my friend to be a *rasika*, and I a woman indifferent to the world. My heart burns in the fire of *prema*, and there is nothing left for me but death. My heart burns in the fire of *prema* for my cruel friend. The day has passed in hope and longing, night has turned into dawn not knowing him, not drowning in this cruel love; if one loves a man, she searches for a more-than-human love. Who creates this love is drowned in it. The lowly Muchā [Musā] says: My body burns in the fire of this love; but at the Day of Judgment He will be known.[170]

In other instances the sufic nature is more clearly observed. In the words of Rahim al-Din:

Oh, my dear friend, do you know what name does the flute of Śyām play? . . . If you could trace the name that the flute repeats, the lock of *lāhut* would open, and darkness would turn into light. . . . Śyām-chānd plays the flute day and night; the world is made of two letters—*kāf* and *nun*.[171] I make a union of the breath and utterances of the name [of Śyām], and meditate on the flute. And lo, Nilamani [Kriṣna] occupies the *lā mokām*. Faqir Rahim al-Din

169 Dimock, *ibid.*, p. 29; Bhattāchārya, *ibid.*, no. 76.

170 Dimock, *ibid.*; Bhattāchārya, *ibid.*

171 Kānu, the other name of Śyām or Kriṣna, is written in Persian with the same two letters, *kāf* and *nun*, strongly imbued with mystical meanings in sufism.

says, "You have a life and you have not dedicated it. The one, who has fallen a victim of love, has alone got hold of Śyām who is full of all virtues."[172]

Badi al-Jamāl's *pada* is another clear example of sufic symbolism:

> There are only two birds, one black and the other white, flying in this world. None knows about them; petty conflicts abound. The lord was a unity as he created *mim*. He created the three worlds with the tremor of his power. Everyone calls Kālā as Kālā, only I call him Śyām. Kālā conceals in himself the name of Maulā [God] himself. The sky is black, black is earth and so are air and water. The moon is black, the sun is black and so is Maulā Rabbāni. Badi al-Jamāl says, "Oh, what darkness pervades all. Save us by uniting *mim* and *āyen* [*ain*]."[173]

This does not, however, resolve all our problems about Muslim *pada*. In other instances the Islamic elements are not always as obvious as in Musā's case, and yet may very well be sufic in inspiration. This latter type of Muslim *pada* presents the greatest difficulty in determining its inspirational source. With regard to this controversial type of *pada* we suggest a line of differentiation between the product of sufic and that of *vaiṣnav* inspiration in terms of the author's attitude to the deity as the beloved.

The most dominant feature of the *pada* literature of both Hindu and Muslim authorship is the element of love binding the devotee and the deity. But the concept of love, as enunciated in Bengal vaiṣnavism is rather dissimilar to that of the popular *wujudi* school of sufism in India. With the former, the theory of love is based on a principle of duality, theological, if not metaphysical. Theologically, *vaiṣnav* recognizes a measure of duality between God as Kriṣna and the individual (*jiva*), and this principle of duality raises the question of devotion, which gradually culminates in the conception of pas-

[172] Quoted in original in Y. M. Bhattāchārya, *Musalmān Kavi*, pp. 88-89.

[173] Quoted in original, *ibid.*, p. 76.

sionate love.[174] The supreme soul is boundless and is full of intelligence itself. The individual soul is an atom having intelligence. They are necessarily linked, and this connection can never be destroyed. Krişna is the support (*āśray*), and *jiv* depends on him (*āśrita*). The relation between the two is identity as well as difference. As the bee is distinct from the honey and hovers over it, and when it drinks it, is full of it and is at one with it, so the individual soul is at first distinct from the supreme soul. It seeks the supreme soul consistently and continuously, and when through love it is full of the supreme soul, it becomes unconscious of its individual existence and is absorbed, as it were, in God. This is the ecstatic condition in which the individual soul becomes one with God, though they are really distinct.[175] This relation between the deity and the individual has been metaphysically described as incomprehensible (*achintya*); it is a relation of non-dualism, and yet of dualism, and this principle of dualism in non-dualism (*advaita-dvaita-bhāv* or *viśiṣṭādvaita* of Rāmānuj) is said to transcend cognitive knowledge. The theological concept of dualism, however, prevails, and all poetical and metaphorical descriptions of love seem to be based on this theological speculation. The sufic concept of love in its popular *wujudi* form, on the other hand, practically assumes an ontological monistic position in the doctrine of annihilation of self in God (*fanā*), as discussed above.[176] This subtle difference in the theological formulation of love in Bengal vaiṣnavism and sufism may be related to two different types of Bengali *pada* writings. With the former, man (*jiv*) has no part to play in the eternal and cosmic love-process (*prem-lilā*) between Krişna and his cosmic partner of feminine energy in the form of Rādhā. *Jiv* has no more to do in this than remain a spectator with all love and faith, enjoy its bliss, and pro-

[174] S. B. Dasgupta, *Obscure Religious Cults*, p. 175.

[175] R. G. Bhandarkar, *Vaiṣnavism, Saivism and Other Minor Religious Systems* (Varanasi, 1965), p. 85.

[176] *Supra*, pp. 151ff.

claim (*kirtan*) this *lilā* in words and music. There is no room, at least in accordance with the *Gaudiya vaiṣnav* theory, for a desire on his part to participate in the *prem-lilā* of the two, or to long for union with Kriṣna. The *vaiṣnav* lyrics of Bengal, in consequence, are conspicuous by the absence of a human longing to take part in the *Vrindāvan-lilā* or for union with Kriṣna, unlike the old *vaiṣnav* community of Ālvārs or individual devotees like Mirā Bāi.[177] On the other hand, the lyric writers, inspired by sufic ideals of love, and unrestricted by any theological demands, discovered in Rādhā's longing for Kriṣna, which was exquisitely expressed in stirring erotic emotionalism in the earlier *vaiṣnav* lyrics of Jay-dev, Vidyāpati, and Chandi-dās, a channel in which to direct the strong currents of their own anxiety, anguish, and quest for their adorable deity. Their writings, hence, tended to become allegorical and assumed symbolic character.

These divergent mystical attitudes to the deity, as reflected in the whole range of the *pada* literature of Hindu or Muslim authorship, cut across the religious affiliations of the lyricists. A not insignificant number of compositions adopting the *vaiṣnav* approach to the deity can be traced to Muslim lyricists, just as there are a number of Hindu *pada* written in the monistic spirit of the *sufi* mystics. The former explain the attempt by some observers, as mentioned above,[178] to claim Muslim *pada* writers as *vaiṣnavs*, while the latter have induced some like E. Haq to attach allegorical significance to Rādhā and Kriṣna in the *vaiṣnav pada* literature,[179] regardless of the fact that the love dalliances of Kriṣna and Rādhā are, to the *vaiṣnav* lyricists, as much a "divine allegory" as a "literal fact of religious history."[180] The latter may further ex-

[177] S. B. Dasgupta, "Bānglār Musalmān vaiṣnav-kavi," *Viśva-bhārati Patrikā* (*Māgh-Chaitra*, 1363 B.S./A.D. 1956), *passim*; also Y. M. Bhattāchārya, *Musalmān Kavi*, p. 157.

[178] *Supra*, pp. 87-88.

[179] *MBS*, p. 52.

[180] S. K. De, *Early History of Vaiṣnava Faith*, p. 223.

plain the position maintained by Dimock that the *vaiṣnav sahajiyā*, at least, are non-dualistic in their theological standing.[181]

An effective mode of differentiating between the *vaiṣnav* and the sufic spirit in the *pada* literature is provided in the colophon of this particular type of lyrical writing. On strict theological grounds the *vaiṣnav* poet is unable to identify himself with or participate in the cosmic love process of Kriṣna and Rādhā, and so his colophon assumes a distinction between the object in the divine love and the humble observer in the poet. The sufic leanings are often expressed in the poet's unmistakable effort, in the colophon, to substitute himself for Rādhā, longing for Kriṣna. Examples of this tendency are numerous. Akbar Ali writes,

My heart aches for my dear Śyām [Kriṣna]. He has pierced me with his new love. I cannot stay back in the house, for the love of Śyām-kālā and my own [love for him] burn my body out. I sleep alone in the room, and see him in dream. It is the fault of my *karma* that I do not see him as I wake up. Akbar Ali, who is a mere child, says, "My limbs are burnt in love. Oh! the adorable one, appearing in dreams, has nearly taken my life."[182]

Saiyid Murtaza echoes the same feeling:

Śyām-bandhu, you are my life. I cannot forget the great day when we met each other. I cannot suffer to be patient as I behold that face like the moon. . . . Oh, Kānu [Kriṣna], my heart, have mercy on me. Give me shelter under the shadow of your feet. . . . Saiyid Murtaza submits at the feet of Kānu, "I forsake everything and remain at your feet in life and death."[183]

Burhāni wants to "surrender" himself "at the feet of Śyām," whom it was his "good fortune to see." He entreats his "merciful friend" to give him shelter "at his feet," taking him for

[181] E. C. Dimock, Jr., *The Place of the Hidden Moon* (Chicago, 1966), pp. 23-24.

[182] Quoted in original in Y. M. Bhattāchārya, *Musalmān Kavi*, p. 39.

[183] Quoted in original by D. C. Sen, *Banga Sāhitya Parichay* (Calcutta, 1914), pt. 2, pp. 1145-6.

"a suffering lover." He advocates making a "voluntary offering of one's youth" to Śyām-bandhu.[184] Badi al-Din appeals:

You come before me and soothe my mind. . . . The music of my friend's flute makes his lady-love impatient and restless. Your flute has made me your maid and I am devoted to your feet. . . . You are the lord of my life; who else is there in the world? From whom else can I expect compassion? . . . Why do you not show yourself to your Rādhā.[185]

Fazl al-Haq says that he loves Kālāchānd (Krisna) and has suffered "immense afflictions for having cherished the name of Kālā alone ever in his mind." He asks, "Why are you so hard with me, my love? . . . You make me cry to amuse yourself as much as you wish." The poet finds himself "burnt to ashes in the fire of love." He cannot bear the "pangs of separation," as Śyām "remains hidden after making love." The poet expresses his doubt to Biśākhā about "meeting" his beloved even "in death," while he could not meet him "in life."[186] Nāzir complains that his "heart burns constantly for the sake of Śyām" and confesses that he is "drowned day and night in sins (*gunāh*)."[187] Kālā Shāh confides to Lalitā that his "friend" has turned him "mad" and that "he has departed" after "making love" to him.[188] Arqam writes:

Whom would you spend this night with, Oh, Śyām, forsaking me? The candles burn the night through over my bed-head; be kind, and please come to the lap of Rādhā. . . . Mad Ārkum says that the sweetheart does not come in the night unless there is love since childhood.[189]

Occasionally, a poet dispenses altogether with the symbolism of Rādhā as the lover and transposes himself to her position.

[184] Quoted in original by Y. M. Bhattāchārya, *Musalmān Kavi*, p. 77.
[185] *Ibid.*, p. 76.
[186] *Ibid.*, p. 73.
[187] *Ibid.*, p. 66.
[188] *Ibid.*, p. 54.
[189] *Ibid.*, p. 44.

Abd al-Bāri makes Rādhā play second fiddle in the poet's search for the beloved:

I beseech you, touch your feet, Oh Rāi, tell me where can I get the treasure of my heart? What shall I do, where can I go? I have lost Kānāi; I ask the birds and animals, trees and creepers about him; none tells me what my mind longs to know; how can I assuage my heart? . . . Why blame Providence? It is all my fate and *karma* that Abd al-Bāri spends his days in tears.[190]

Irkān/Arkān places himself in a similar position:

Rāi, with what can I win the heart of Śyām?
I do not possess that treasure in me![191]

The symbolic nature of this particular variety of *pada* is further substantiated by the fact that Rādhā, in some instance, replaces Krișna as the object of the poet's love. Ali Miyān himself affects to rival Krișna for Rādhā's love and company:

Had I got her I would have taken care of her and passed the nights in enjoyment. I would have friends to keep her company and would treat her with respect. The days would have passed blissfully. Oh, my darling, will you please listen to the proposal of Ali Miyān? Will you really go off the river bank in his [Krișna's] company?[192]

The sufic symbolism in a particular type of *pada* compositions is, therefore, unquestionable. Significantly enough, the Bengali Muslim poets of this category chose to adopt the locally popular Rādhā-Krișna motif of Bengal vaișnavism. Unlike the Muslim mystic poets elsewhere in India and outside, their Bengali counterparts were conspicuous by their indifference to the popular Islamic motifs such as Yusuf-Zulaikha, Laila-Majnun, Shirin-Farhād, Saif al-Muluk-Badi al-Jamāl, Gul-i Bakāwali, Haft-Paikār, and so on. Bengali Muslim writers no doubt made use of almost all those themes, but with a crucial difference. They stripped these stories of their mys-

[190] *Ibid.*, p. 41.
[191] *Ibid.*, p. 48.
[192] *Ibid.*, pp. 46-47.

tical content and presented them in the form of a secular romantic narrative poem—a literary genre which Bengali Muslims had the distinction of introducing into the corpus of Bengali literature.

All Muslim *padas* are, however, not symbolical in form and sufic in spirit. A significant proportion of such lyrics is devoid of any allegorical meaning and is little different from the vast body of *vaiṣnav* lyrics in respect to both content and style. They pursued almost all the different thematic categories of the *vaiṣnav* lyrical literature. More importantly, the objective of these poets, as indicated in their respective colophons, is not to seek a mystic union with the adorable deity in the manner of monistic sufism, but to "observe" and "witness," with love and veneration, the myriad revelations and realisations of the *vaiṣnav* lord. It is reasonable to assume that the Muslim *pada* writer was often drawn toward this particular form of *vaiṣnav* poem by its lyrical quality and by its potential for giving poetic expression to diverse and subtle nuances of human emotions and feelings. The *vaiṣnav* lyrical literature is minutely classified on the basis of the different stages and events in the lives of Kriṣna and Rādhā, sharply focussing on the moods and feelings appropriate for each occasion. Kriṣna's childhood (*bālya-lilā*), pastoral pursuits (*goṣtha-lilā*), beauty (*rup*), and the dawn of love in Rādhā, its gradual development, with corresponding emotive variations—*purva-rāg* (ante-love), *anurāg* (in-love), *abhisār* (secret meeting), *mān* (hurt feeling), *milan* (union), and *viraha* (separation)—and the various amorous sports of the couple like *kunja-lilā*, *naukā-vilās*, *holi-lilā*, and so on, all opened a new horizon of lyrical literature in Bengali language. The Bengali Muslim lyricists could not have been slower than their non-Muslim counterparts in responding to these new themes and techniques for canalizing various modal and emotional currents. Habib chose for himself the theme of Kriṣna's "beauty":

Lo, mother, what a beauty is Nanda-gopāl [Kriṣna]! He has a sandal-paste mark on his forehead . . . a garland of *bakul* flowers around his neck, and rings hanging from his ears. The world is seduced by his glances, and his face is matchless. He has a flute in his hands and a yellow loin cloth. . . . He stands beneath the *kadamba* tree. . . . Faqir Habib says, "Looking at Kānu is like having a full-moon rise on the forehead. My heart longs to keep him ever before my eyes and gaze at him."[193]

The theme of pastoral pursuits of young Kriṣna was taken up by Nāsir Mahmud:

With cattle in the grazing field are playing Rām [Balarām, the brother of Kriṣna] and handsome Śyām. . . . Along with Śridām and Sudām [two close companions of Kriṣna] Śyām frolics with youthful girls on the bank of the river. . . . Nāsir Mahmud seeks shelter at his feet.[194]

A few poets chose the themes of *milan*, *kunja-lilā*, and *viraha*. Shaikh Faiz Allāh wrote on the passionate union of Kriṣna and Rādhā:

They remain awake in love very late in the night. . . . He is attractively attired; Binodini [Rādhā] lies beside him. Rāi loses herself in a blissful state. With Kānu in her embrace and one's lips on the other's, Rādhā is not awake. . . .[195]

Further,

Let us go home, charming Rādhā. You are neither asleep nor awake. You have sandal-paste marks all over your body, people may see you at the break of the dawn and tease you. . . . On a bed of flowers how fast is she sleeping, snuggled in the embrace of Śyām, the shining black![196]

Mir Faiz Allāh depicts the amorous play of Kriṣna and the milkmaids:

Rādhā-mādhav [Kriṣna] is in the garden. Hari-Nārāyan [Kriṣna], who is placated even by the four-faced Brahmā, stands here in

[193] *Ibid.*, pp. 103-104.
[194] *Ibid.*, p. 67.
[195] *Rāg-mālā*, fol. 8.
[196] *Ibid.*, fol. 13.

person. The milkmaids rush in with flowers and sandal paste to throw at Govinda [Krişna]. . . . Murāri [Krişna] hides himself behind the *mādhavi* creepers. . . . [Having lost him] the milkmaids begin to cry, calling out the name of Śri Krişna. Mir Faiz Allāh says, "How beautiful is this divine *lilā*! Even a stone is dissolved at the sight of Śyām's beauty."[197]

Nāsir's was the theme of "separation." This piece is of some importance to illustrate the point, made before, that the attitude of the poet to the Rādhā-Krişna *lilā* is the determining factor in a *vaişnav* composition. Until one comes to the colophon, the anguish and longing for Krişna in Nāsir's poem may very well be taken figuratively to refer to Nāsir's own longing for God symbolized by Krişna. In his colophon, however, Nāsir clearly reduces himself to a characteristically *vaişnav* position of a blessed witness to the divine *lilā* of Krişna and Rādhā:

Where should I look for my friend? Kālā has whetted my love, augmented my suffering, and now keeps himself hidden from me. I spent all four watches (*prahars*) of the night sitting on the bed. My youth grows unbearable on me; I cannot keep it in bounds. How can I soothe my mind? Nāsir, who is unillumined, says, "Go, you darling, look under the *kadam* tree for your handsome Kānāi."[198]

Alāwal, a very gifted Bengali Muslim poet, adopts a pure *vaişnav* theme for a lyric. He writes on Rādhā's secret meeting with Krişna, going out early in the morning and returning at nightfall. For this she is taken to task by her sisters-in-law. Rādhā finds some excuses to tide over the difficulty.[199] Kabir[200] and Nāsir Muhammad[201] write beautifully on *holi-lilā*. Nāsir's colophon is marked by his devotion to Krişna and Rādhā: "Nāsir Muhammad says, "Worship the feet of Rādhā and Śyām; no delay can be excused."[202] To Masan Ali

[197] Quoted in original, Y. M. Bhattāchārya, *Musalmān Kavi*, pp. 81-82.
[198] *Ibid.*, p. 68.
[199] *Ibid.*, pp. 44-45.
[200] *Ibid.*, p. 53.
[201] *Ibid.*, p. 69.
[202] *Ibid.*

is attributed a *pada* on the boat theme (*naukā-vilās*). Rādhā, carrying pots of curds on her head to the market in Mathurā, is stopped by the ferryman, Krişna. Rādhā begs him to tell his price for letting her go. He replies: "You are the lotus and I am the bee. Let us go to the garden so that I may be satisfied."[203] Sher Chānd has a similar subject called *dān-lilā*. In his colophon, the poet entreats Rādhā to adore Krişna, who is "the essence of all virtues" and without whom "there is no way out."[204] Qamar Ali,[205] Ālim al-Din,[206] and Sahikā (Sahifā?) Bānu[207] all draw on the same theme, known as *māthur* in *Gaudiya* vaişnavism. This type of *pada* deals with the extreme sadness and suffering of both Rādhā and Krişna caused by their separation, after Krişna's departure from Vrindāvan to Mathurā to become a king. Qamar Ali asks "loving Rādhā" not to "worry," for Krişna is sure to come back to her.[208] Ālim al-Din's colophon reassures Rādhā in the same vein: "Śri Ālim al-Din says, "Listen, Oh Rādhā, you will certainly meet Krişna again."[209]

203 *Ibid.*, pp. 83-84.
204 *Ibid.*, p. 98.
205 *Ibid.*, pp. 53-54.
206 *Ibid.*, pp. 45-46.
207 *Ibid.*, p. 61.
208 *Ibid.*, p. 54.
209 *Ibid.*, p. 46.

B. THE SYNCRETISTIC LITTLE TRADITION

6

Pirism or the Cult of Pir[1]

The syncretistic tradition formulated by the Bengali Muslim cultural mediators, as examined in the three preceding chapters, presented a significant contrast with the other tradition obtained at the folk level of the Bengali Muslim society.[2] The former undoubtedly catered for the folk, as this literature was primarily aimed at them, while it originated not with the folk but with the cultural mediators of the higher social strata.[3] The latter, on the other hand, emerged clearly from the folk level itself. In addition to authorship, there were two more vital differences between these literary traditions. A mere casual glance reveals a qualitative difference in literary refinement, style, diction, and cognitive level. The literary sophistication of the mediators stands out in high relief against the simple, coarse, and rustic character of the folk literature. The other significant point of difference relates to the contents of these literatures. The object of both was the ultimate vindication, refurbishing, and diffusion of Islam as they interpreted it. But the folk writers, unlike the mediators, had very little concern with Islamic theology, lit-

[1] This particular chapter draws substantially on my essay entitled "The Pir-Tradition: A Case Study in Islamic Syncretism in Traditional Bengal," in F. W. Clothey (ed.), *Images of Man: Religion and Historical Process in South Asia* (Madras, 1982), pp. 112-41. My gratitude to New Era Publications of Madras is here acknowledged.

[2] The present writer had the good fortune of discovering a number of manuscripts of this folk-category in the motley collections of an antiquarian in the *mofussil* area of Jaynagar-Majilpur in West Bengal in 1967. (See "General Notes" under Bibliography.)

[3] For the social identity of some of the mediators, see *supra*, pp. 72-75.

urgy, mysticism, ontology, cosmogony, and even with the historical-mythical characters of Islamic great tradition. The Muslim folk literature was almost exclusively focussed on the most popular object of their veneration and supplication during the trials and tribulations of their everyday life, namely *pir*. We have already discussed at length that pirism, or the cult and the pantheon of *pir*, as evolved at the Bengali folk level, extended beyond the usual theoretical notions of veneration or even worship of mystic guides, saints, or holy men. It embraced, on one hand, disparate Muslims who received popular canonization as *pir* in recognition of their secular and religious roles in diffusing Islam in the land and, on the other, a vast motley of pirified old popular religious objects of worship, veneration, and supplication.[4] The massive dispersion, ubiquity, popularity, and heterogeneity of *pirs* in Bengal point to the seminal importance of the *pir* phenomenon in the study of Islamization in Bengal as providing a meaningful frame of reference for and a point of interaction between exogenous Islam and indigenous converts.

The Pir *Cult: the Pantheon*

We have classified the *pirs* known in Bengal into two broad groups of historical-legendary characters and of totally fictitious and unreal pirified religious objects and spirits, focussing on the contributions of the former, heterogeneous as they were, to Islamization in the form of conversion of the Bengali masses.[5] But a proper and adequate appreciation and evaluation of the folk or little tradition of Islam in Bengal underlines the significance of the nature and composition of the body of the fictitious *pirs*.

In a number of cases involving the fictitious *pirs*, some old popular beliefs and practices associated with a particular locality or a site were sought to be "Islamized" through the

[4] *Supra*, pp. 50ff.
[5] *Supra*, pp. 52-57.

protean process of pirification. In the Mymensingh district there was Āthkā-pir,[6] resorted to by people for either quick recovery from illness or escape from trouble.[7] Hājir-pir was taken to get back lost cattle. A supplicant observed a fast, took a bath, and prepared *sinni/shirni* to offer it to the *pir*.[8] Thankā-pir was believed to possess the power of regaining lost property. The rituals relating to the propitiation of this particular *pir* bore a striking resemblance to the *vrata* rites observed by the local Hindus to attain a particular desire. Tuesday and Saturday were considered auspicious for Thankā-pir. On the appointed day a part of the courtyard in the house was ceremonially cleaned. An equal number of wooden plank seats and banana leaf-tips were kept there. Each leaf-tip contained four whole betel leaves and betel nuts. The ceremony began with Islamic salutation *(salām)*, followed, in a typical Hindu *vrata* style, by recitation of a story which proclaimed the ultimate triumph and glory of the *pir* and the absolute merit of seeking his favor. Significantly enough, the story involved a *brāhman* boy blinded for ignoring Thankā-pir, where vision was restored on his submission to the *pir*. The ceremony was concluded, again in the *vrata* fashion, with the distribution of the betel leaves and nuts among the assembled people.[9]

Norā-pir's favor was solicited in order to fulfill a desire or a wish. People took vows in the name of the *pir*, tied a knot called *norā* on a wisp of grass or hay, and placed it under a banyan tree (*ficus bengalensis*).[10] The particular association of the banyan tree with this *pir*'s rituals suggests a possible pir-

[6] Significantly enough, "āthkā," in some eastern Bengali dialects, means "all of a sudden."

[7] K. K. Rāy, "Maimansimher sādhāran grihastha Musalmān paribāre anusthita kayekti sinni o āchār-niyamer vivaran." *Sāhitya-Pariṣat Patrikā*, no. 39, 1339 B.S./1932, pp. 217-18.

[8] *Ibid*., p. 229.

[9] *Ibid*., p. 227.

[10] *Ibid*., p. 223.

ification of a tree-spirit. Tree-worship was a widely prevalent practice in Bengal in the form of the worship of Bana-durgā.[11] Tree-worship in the *pir* form was known in other parts of Bengal. In the village of Giriśgangāsāgar in the Medinipur district, a banyan tree was held sacred as the supposed abode of Nekurśani-pir. Situated on the way to the local court of justice, it was resorted to by litigants in the belief that the *pir* would favor their law-suits.[12] The offerings to the *pir* usually consisted of lumps of clay, pieces of red rags tied to the branches of the tree, and sometimes clay horses. The votive offerings of red rags, tattered rags, and clay horses at the folk religious shrines had been an old and widely prevalent practice in Bengal, as in many other parts of India.[13] In Bālya-govindapur, Medinipur, there was another sacred tree, botanically a hybrid of a banyan and a pipal (*ficus religiosa*) and popularly called "makdum tree," believed to be the abode of one Makdum/Makhdum-pir. People in distress vowed to offer either *shirni* or a dishful of sugar-wafers (*bātāsā*) to the *pir*. Clay horses were also offered. According to its devotees the tree grew from a twig which was originally used by the *pir* to clean his teeth.[14]

In places, the Bengali Muslim folk made *pirs* of local non-Muslim divinities or objects of worship. In the Mymensingh district, Manāi-pir appeared as the pirified Hindu god, Kārtik, and the rites and fertility beliefs pertaining to his adoration were almost identical with those of local Kārtik celebrations (*Kārtik-vrata*). The *pir* was resorted to by unmarried

[11] See S. C. Mitra, "On the Cult of the Tree-Goddess in Eastern Bengal," *Man in India* (Ranchi), II, no. 2, 1922, pp. 228-41; also his "The Worship of the Sylvan Goddess," *The Hindustan Review*, March 1917, pp. 178-89.

[12] C. Rāya, "On Tree-Cults in the District of Midnapur in Southwestern Bengal," *Man in India*, *ibid.*, pp. 242-48.

[13] See S. C. Mitra, "Supplementary Remarks," *ibid.*, pp. 249-64; also W. Crooke, *Religion and Folklore of Northern India*, 2 vols. (London, 1926), *passim*.

[14] C. Rāya, "On Tree-Cults in Midnapur," pp. 244-48.

girls for suitable husbands and by married women desiring pregnancy. To the west of the Brahmaputra river the twentieth day of the Bengali calendar month of *Phālgun* and the nineteenth in the east were chosen for this observance, called Manāi-pir's *shirni*. By rotation one or two families in the locality took the initiative in this matter, having circulated among other families a tray containing betel leaves and nuts, the acceptance of which indicated willingness to participate in the observance. On the appointed day a high altar of clay was erected in the courtyard of a house. Four bamboo twigs at the four corners of the altar supported a canopy, while the altar was bedecked with as many earthenware pitchers (*pural*) as promised by the adorers under their respective vows. The women and the girls fetched water in the pitchers from a pond or a river, while they tied a corner of their *sāris* to each other, and all carried on their heads ceremonial trays containing vermilion, a lamp, a small quantity of paddy, and a wisp of green grass. The pitchers were placed on the altar, with a small earthen lamp on the top of each pitcher burning all through the night. On two sides of the altar eight painted and decorated earthenware pots of sweets were placed. Unlike Hindu ceremonial occasions, fowls were also ritually sacrificed. The women, who vowed for the first time in expectation of a child, offered salutation to the *pir* and kept standing with a lamp on her head until it dropped by itself. Throughout the night the womenfolk sang about the *pir*; the ceremony was concluded by the village *mullāh*'s reading out the *sura fātiha* from the *Qurān*, and by the participants' sharing the sweets among themselves. At sunrise all left for their homes, carrying back their own pitchers.[15]

In the same district, another pirified Hindu object of worship was Tinnāth-pir, who seemed no other than the *nāth* trinity, Ādi-nāth or Śiv, Matsyendra or Mina-nāth, and Go-

[15] K. K. Rāy, "Maimansimher vivaran," p. 212.

rakṣa-nāth, collectively called by Hindus Trināth (three *nāths*) or its corrupted form, Tinnāth, or Tinnāth-thākur. In the Alapsingh region, Muslims resorted to this *pir* for the recovery, on one hand, of lost cattle and, on the other, from illness. A supplicant promised the *pir* either three, five, or seven rounds (*kalki*) of hemp after the fulfillment of a particular wish. On the actual fulfillment of the wish the promised quantity of hemp or its equivalent in cash was given to a smoker of hemp to organize a ceremony for Tinnāth-pir.[16]

By far the greatest figure in this category of *pir* was Mānik-pir, whose wide recognition as the guardian-*pir* of the village folk, protecting the cattle, promoting its fertility, as well as agricultural prosperity, family health, and happiness, enshrined him in the hearts of the village folk, both Muslim and Hindu. Muslim mendicants (*faqir*) and village bards sang ballads glorifying the *pir*.[17] Mānik-pir's identity cannot be easily established. While sharing some of the characteristics of the Hindu god, Śiv, he also came close to resembling Gorakṣa-nāth. A tradition, indeed, connected Mānik with him as his disciple.[18] A song about him gave further support to this śaivite association, according to which Mānik-pir came to the house of Kālu-ghoṣ with the cry of *vam vam*, a common practice among śaivite mendicants. Kālu-ghoṣ's mother offered him five small coins in the name of Pānch-pir. Mānik refused to accept cash, and asked for milk and curds. Kālu's mother played a trick on him, as a result of which all their cattle and even the milkmaid died. The mother came to realize her folly and begged for the *pir*'s mercy. Mānik took pity on her, struck his staff (*āsā*) on the ground, and everything came back to life again.[19] The first birth of a calf in

[16] *Ibid.*, p. 229.

[17] A folk ballad on Mānik-pir is included in the second section of this chapter. *Infra*, pp. 245-48.

[18] S. B. Dasgupta, *Obscure Religious Cults*, p. 371.

[19] *Ibid.*

the west Mymensingh district was usually followed by cooking in the cowshed itself a sweet made of sugar, rice, and molasses, which was offered on a banana leaf-tip to the *pir*. Served on banana leaves, the food was later shared by the votaries, after which the used leaves were hung up on the walls of the cowshed.[20]

Pānch-pir seems another *pir* in this particular category whose identity appears rather obscured. The cult was popular with both Muslims and Hindus in and out of Bengal. The shrine of Pānch-pir was usually a small tomb with five domes, or a simple mound at the foot of either a banyan or a pipal tree. Offerings of goats, fowls, and sweetmeats were made to the *pir* to ensure birth of children, recovery from an incurable illness, or even success in a particular venture. In the forest that overgrew the old city of Sonārgāon in east Bengal, there was a very popular shrine of Pānch-pir containing five unfinished tombs.[21] Popular beliefs concerning this quintet of divinities provided no common list of names for them. The pantheon varied widely from place to place and, occasionally, stretched even to include characters ranging from Āmina Sati, a faithful wife who died along with her husband, to Bhairon, a Hindu godling.[22] Sometimes it was taken for *panjtani pāk* or five holy persons who, according to the *shia*, are Muhammad, Ali, Fātima, Hasan, and Husain, while many *sunnis* include Muhammad and the first four *khalifāhs* under the name.[23] Some have traced the cult to the five *pāndav* brothers of the *Mahābhārat* fame.[24] Wise suggests that five is a lucky number and that it may well have been used loosely as half-a-dozen is used in English.[25] Should this be so, it is not clear

[20] K. K. Rāy, "Maimansimher vivaran," p. 228.
[21] J. Wise, "Muhammadans of Bengal," p. 44.
[22] Risley, *Imperial Gazetteer*, vol. I, p. 435.
[23] Gait, *Census Report (1901)*, p. 180.
[24] Risley, *Imperial Gazetteer*, vol. I, p. 435.
[25] J. Wise, "Muhammadans of Bengal," pp. 44-45.

why we must always find a collective tomb for Pānch-pir alongside their separate individual shrines, and also why there should invariably be five shrines associated with this name. On the other hand, its wide geographical distribution and popularity in India among lower orders of both Muslim and Hindu societies tend to suggest its origin in a pre-Muslim indigenous source. Agrawālā traces the cult of Pānch-pir to the Indian cult of Panch-bir, which, in its turn, was related to the widely popular ancient Indian cult of the *yakṣa*.[26] H. P. Dwivedi and S. L. Sanghavi lent support to this view by the argument that "the pronunciation of the word *bir* as *pir* is highly probable in Chulikā, Paiśāchi, or the Panjābi dialects," and that through the Panjab "Muslims brought this pronunciation with them to the east."[27]

If the identity of Pānch-pir is at least amenable to rational reconstruction, that of Bāra-auliyā (lit., twelve saints) seems almost inscrutable. In the village of Nanda-pādā in Bakharganj, the shrine of Bāra-auliyā was believed to be associated with twelve *pirs*, who came from Baghdad on the back of a fish to settle on the island of Sandvip.[28] In the absence of further information on them, we may consider the possibility, among others, of regarding them as pirified pioneering Muslim settlers.

Satya-pir added a whole new dimension to the syncretistic process of pirification. Pirification, in this particular instance, seemed to relate more appropriately to the phenomenon of sanskritization, which applied to the Hindu society, than to Islamization. On close scrutiny the Satya-pir myth and cult emerges as a brāhmanical device to absorb the increasingly popular *pir* cult. The popularity of the cult seemed to have

[26] V. S. Agrawālā, *Prāchina Bhāratiya Loka-dharma* (Varanasi, 1963), pp. 2-3, 118-43.

[27] Quoted, *ibid.*, pp. 135-36.

[28] K. C. Rāy, *Bākharganjer Itihās* (Barisal, 1895), p. 15; also R. K. Chakravarti and A. M. Dās, *Sandviper Itihās* (Calcutta, 1924), p. 11.

been greater among Hindus than Muslims, for the large majority of writings on the *pir* were Hindu contributions.[29] As was the case with other popular *pirs*, the identity of Satya-pir seemed rather obscure, indeed even more than others. Although a few shrines bearing the name could be found, an examination of the relevant literature and tradition on the *pir* categorically rejects the historicity of the *pir*. Some traditions quite arbitrarily linked Husain Shāh, a fifteenth-century *sultān* of Bengal, with the introduction of this cult.[30] Other commentators on the subject idealized it in general terms as a symbol of Hindu-Muslim syncretism.[31] In the absence of hard historical evidence we attempt to offer a possible explanation of its origin on the basis of an internal analysis of its literature.

The literary tradition on the *pir* adopted either of two motifs, the *brāhman* or the merchant motif, both aiming at vindication of the *pir* in the same way as the Hindu *mangal-kāvya* literature proclaimed the glory of particular popular divinities. The first motif involved a *brāhman* who was advised by God to worship Satya-pir, appearing in the guise of a Muslim mendicant. The *brāhman*'s refusal to accept a Muslim divine led to God's reappearance in the form of Krișna—a feat which finally convinced the *brāhman*. The second motif concerned a Hindu sea-merchant and his son-in-law, who, despite their initial scant regard for Satya-pir, were able to save their entire fleet from a storm, thanks to the steadfast devotion of the merchant's daughter to Satya-pir and the final submission of the whole family to the *pir*. Both these versions may be interpreted as underlining a process of upper-class

[29] *BSI*, vol. I, pt. 2, pp. 452-66.

[30] *HBLL*, p. 797.

[31] *Ibid.*; K. K. Datt, "Relations between the Hindus and the Muhammadans of Bengal in the Middle of the Eighteenth Century (1740-1765)," *Journal of Indian History* (Trivendrum), VIII (1929), p. 330; A. Karim, *Social History*, p. 167; M. A. Rahim, *Social and Cultural History*, vol. I, p. 338.

Hindu acceptance of the Satya-pir cult. The process was closely parallelled by the gradual recognition of popular Hindu deities by the hieratic brāhmanical order. The growing popularity of *pir* and the *pir* cult in Bengal was at once a challenge and an opportunity for the brāhmanical priestly class. The *brāhman* answer, consistent with their past tradition, was to create a cult of *pir* in abstraction in Satya (eternity/truth)-pir and to establish an essential identity of and a continuity between old and new beliefs, with a view to its final absorption. It was not without significance that there were more Hindu writers on the Satya-pir tradition than Muslim, that God appeared before the *brāhman* in both Hindu and Muslim guises, and, finally, that there was also a clear attempt to divest the cult of its Muslim associations. Vidyāpati, a *brāhman* writer, called Satya-pir God's incarnation in the present age (*kali-yug*) "in a faqir's guise."[32] An old Sanskritic text, the *Skanda-purān*, was interpolated, and Satya-nārāyan[33] emerged to dislodge Satya-pir.[34] The brāhmanical acceptance of the *pir* cult was not easily achieved. The orthodox brāhmanical reaction was positively hostile to it, as evidenced by the life of Kanka, the author of *Satya-pirer-kathā*. A *brāhman* of Mymensingh, Kanka was allegedly brought up by an outcaste *chandāl* couple, both of whom died while he was a boy of five. He was recovered by a kindly and scholarly *brāhman*, Garga, in whose care he grew up into an intelligent young man, well versed in all learning. He earned a good reputation as a poet, and was later attracted to a *pir*, becoming his disciple. On the *pir*'s instruction Kanka wrote a ballad on Satya-pir, which was "well received by both Hindu and Muslims devoted to Satya-pir." But when Garga proposed to restore Kanka to his *brāh-*

[32] Quoted in *BSI*, vol. I, pt. 2, p. 455.

[33] Nārāyan is another name of Viṣnu.

[34] One edition (Bangabāsi) of the text retains the name of Satya-pir, and another (Venkateśvara Press) does not. (See P. V. Kane, *History of Dharma-śāstra*, Poona, 1958, vol. V, pt. 1, p. 437.)

man caste, in a gathering of the *brāhmans* at his place of birth, the orthodox *brāhmans* led by Nandu vehemently opposed, on the ground of his *chandāl* upbringing and also for his receiving spiritual instruction from a Muslim. They accused Kanka of being a Muslim, and copies of his popular work on Satya-pir were "torn" and "burnt."[35]

Despite what may, perhaps, be taken as the initial opposition of the Hindu orthodoxy, the syncretistic objects of the Hindu authors of Satya-pir tradition were clearly achieved. Their attempts did not, however, meet with success, if they intended total absorption of Satya-pir into Satya-nārāyan. Satya-pir and Satya-nārāyan remained with the masses of believers as one and the same. One Muslim writer combined them both into one "Satya-pir-nārāyan" or "Ghāzi Satya-nārāyan."[36] Another found "Pir-nārāyan" sitting in Mecca.[37] A third addressed Satya-pir as Ghāzi and added: "Thou art Brahmā, Viṣnu, and Nārāyan."[38]

Between the purely fictitious and the indubitable historical *pirs* there existed a number of *pirs* of dubious origin who became associated with particular beliefs, and those beliefs often seemed more important than the *pirs* connected with them. Some of them were also known outside Bengal. In north Bengal, the beliefs and practices about Ghāzi Miyān, also called Gajnā Dulha or Sālār Chinulā, were closely associated with marriage and fertility. Ghāzi Miyān was identified with Sālār Masud, the nephew of Sultān Māhmud of Ghazni, who was known to have died in a battle against some Hindu chiefs at Bahraich in Oudh in north India. Ghāzi Miyān in Bengal was believed to have died on the day set for his marriage. The rites and beliefs associated with his ado-

[35] "Kanka o Lilā" in D. C. Sen (ed.), *Purva-banga-gitikā*, vol. I, pt. 2, pp. 265-266.

[36] Arif, quoted in *BSI*, vol. I, pt. 2, pp. 457-58.

[37] Quoted in *ibid.*, p. 462.

[38] Faiz Allāh, quoted in *ibid.*

ration in Bengal were clearly associated with marriage and fertility. The second Sunday in the second month of *Jyaiṣtha* in the Bengali calendar was set for the celebration of what was known as "the wedding of Ghāzi Miyān." Eight days before the occasion a bamboo pole, representing Ghāzi Miyān and decorated with red and white pieces of cloth and a fan, was erected on the site of the festival. Two days before the main celebration, the pole, also called "the flag of Miyān," was taken to a nearby jungle with the accompaniment of music. A large number of both Muslims and Hindus exchanged garlands with Ghāzi Miyān. On the appointed Sunday the pole was brought to the fair of Kellā-kuśi, followed by two days of festivities. A girl born as a result of the vow taken in the name of Ghāzi Miyān was ceremonially married to him. Such girls were not generally accepted afterward as brides, for it was believed that one spouse was destined to die soon after.[39]

Another example of this category was Khwāja Khizr, associated with beliefs in water-spirit. A highly controversial figure, of general renown in the Muslim world and often identified with the prophet Ilyās, Khwāja was believed to reside in the seas and waters and to ride upon a fish.[40] The people propitiated him at the first shaving of a boy, at marriages, and during the rainy seasons, by launching in rivers and tanks small paper boats, decorated with flowers and candles.[41]

There was, however, a far more popular *pir* highly and widely venerated as the guardian-spirit of waters. Known as Pir Badar, his name was invoked by every sailor and fisher-

[39] H. D. Kundu, "Śerpurer Itihās," *Sāhitya-Pariṣat Patrikā*, VII, additional no. (1307 B.S./A.D. 1900), pp. 33-35; P. C. Sen, *Bagurār Itihās* (Rangpur, 1912), pp. 107-08.

[40] The *sultāns* of Oudh, therefore, adopted fish as a crest. (See M. Th. Houtsma et al., eds., *Encyclopaedia of Islam*, vol. II, p. 865.)

[41] *Ibid.*; Gait, *Census Report (1901)*, p. 179; J. Wise, "Muhammadans of Bengal," pp. 38-39.

man starting on a cruise or overtaken by a storm.[42] Among several others, the shrine associated with his name in Chittagong was visited regularly by the local folk—Muslim, Hindu, and Buddhist. The popular belief about the *pir* was that he arrived in Chittagong "floating on a rock," exterminated the *jinns* or evil spirits infesting Chittagong and its neighborhood, and took possession of the whole country.[43] The rituals performed at the Chittagong shrine of the *pir* possessed some distinction. Situated on a hillock, the place was thought to be the spot where Pir Badar lighted his lamp. Candles were offered and burned there nightly, the cost being met by contributions from people of different religious denominations.[44]

There is no greater confusion about the identity of a *pir* than that of this enigmatic focus of popular veneration. Wide-ranging and conflicting views exist on the subject. The most prevalent opinion regards Pir Badar as identical with Shaikh Badr al-Din Badr-i Ālam, who came from Meerut in north India to live in Chittagong for some length of time and who eventually moved to Bihar, where he died about the middle of the fifteenth century and was entombed in the *Chota-dargāh* of Bihar.[45] The strong association of Pir Badar with seafaring and waters led some to identify him with Khwāja Khizr.[46] Another view on the subject is that he was a pirified Portuguese sailor, named Pas Gual Peeris Boteilho,[47] possibly a

[42] Wise, *ibid.*, p. 41; also Houtsma, *ibid.*, p. 559. The latter reproduces Wise in every essential detail, without acknowledgement.

[43] Wise, *ibid.*

[44] Gait, *Census Report (1901)*, p. 178.

[45] H. Blochmann, "The Firuzshāhi Inscription in the Chhota Dargāh, A.H. 761," note no. 38, *JASB*, vol. XLII (1873), p. 302; M. Hidayet Hussain in M. Th. Houtsma, *Encyclopaedia*, vol. I, pp. 559-60; T. W. Beale, *The Oriental Biographical Dictionary* (Calcutta, 1881), p. 216; Gait, *Census Report (1901)*, p. 178; A. Karim, *Social History*, p. 114; M. S. Khan, "Badr Maqams or the Shrines of Badr al-Din-Auliya," *JASP*, VII, no. 1 (June 1962), pp. 17ff.

[46] R. C. Hamilton, cited in Gait, *Census Report (1901)*, p. 178.

[47] J. Wise, "Muhammadans of Bengal," p. 41; also J. Beames, "The Saint

corruption of Pascual Perez Botelho,[48] who reached the shore by clinging to a raft. Others attributed a Hindu origin, a survival of the worship of the Hindu sea-god (*samudra devatā*).[49] This theory is further strengthened by the tradition that two Hindu merchants, Mānik and Chānd, built the shrine associated with the name of the *pir* in Akyab, the metropolitan town of the littoral province of Arakan in Burma.[50] Yet others strongly advocated a Buddhist origin of the *pir*, tracing him to one of the lesser Buddhas or to a *nāt*, a local guardian-spirit for Buddhists. A number of shrines, popular as *buddermokān* or *baddermokān* in the region, which are regarded as corruptions of the Arabic word *Badr-muqām* (or the abode of Badr) by many, were "called by the Arakanese Buddhamaw, *maw* being the Burmese for a promontary. . . ."[51] The absence of a final "r" in the Burmese and Arakanese speech facilitated this transposition. This does not, however, resolve the problem of derivation of one from the other.

A close examination of the nature and circumstances of the tradition and adoration of Pir Badar militates against a facile identification with an itinerant *pir* in Chittagong, Shaikh Badr al-Din Badr-i Ālam, who spent the last part of his life far away in Bihar, where he was buried, as noted above.[52] It is quite possible that the name of Shaikh Badr came in the course of time to be associated in the popular mind with a far older object of common veneration along the vast coastline of south Bengal and Burma from Akyab to Mergui. The "coast from

---

Pir Badar," *JRAS*, July-Oct. 1894, pp. 839-40; H. Beveridge, "The Saint Pir Badar," *ibid.*, pp. 840-41.

[48] Beveridge, *ibid.*

[49] R.F.S.A. St John, "Correspondence," *JRAS*, *ibid.*, pp. 149-54; also his "A Burmese Saint," *ibid.*, pp. 566-67; J.G.R. Forlong, "Bud, Bad-a-r, and Badra," *ibid.*, 1895, pp. 203-205.

[50] St John, *ibid.*; also the report (1876) of Col. Nelson Davies, the Deputy Commissioner of Akyab, cited by M. S. Khan, "Badr Maqams," pp. 19-20.

[51] Col. Parrot, quoted by R. C. Temple, "Buddermokan," *Journal of the Burma Research Society*, XV, pt. 1, 1925, p. 4.

[52] *Supra*, p. 219.

Assam to Malaya" was dotted with these enigmatic shrines, usually situated on boulders or crags at the mouths of rivers.[53] Some of the most popular shrines were located in Akyab, Sandoway, Cheduba, and Mergui. The shrines attracted people equally from different communities and creeds—Muslim, Hindu, Buddhist, and Indian, Burmese, and Chinese. At Mergui the wealthy Burmese offered "gold leaves to gild the boulders of the shrine" and the Chinese did "magical paper charms."[54] R. C. Temple, who devoted a great deal of attention to the Pir Badar phenomenon, characterized "the Buddermokāns" as "universal shrines" which were

> accepted by the Buddhists, Hindus, and Muhammadans, natives of India, Burmese and Chinese alike, which is a sure sign that they are symbols of the animistic faith which underlies all Indian religions. Their chief votaries are sailors, fishermen, and those who obtain a livelihood on the water.[55]

His concluding remarks on the identity of Pir Badar raise for us questions about the complex nature of pirism in Bengal with particular reference to its syncretistic transformations:

> There is a supernatural being, worshipped along the Burmese coast by seafarers from Akyab to Mergui at certain spots specially dedicated to him. . . . To the Buddhists he is a *nat*; to the Hindus a *deva* or inferior god; to the Muhammadan a saint; to the Chinese a spirit. His worship is precisely that which is common all over the East to spirits or supernatural beings, believed in by the folk irrespective of their particular form of professed belief, and it points, in just the same way as do all other instances, to the survival of an old animistic worship in "pre-religious" days. As in all other similar cases one of the contending local professed religions has chiefly annexed this particular being to itself, and he is pre-eminently a Muhammadan saint, legendarily that saint best known to the bulk of the Muhammadan seafaring population, namely Pir Badar of their own chief town of Chittagong.[56]

[53] G. E. Harvey, *History of Burma* (London, 1925), p. 137.
[54] M. S. Khan, "Badr Maqams," p. 32.
[55] R. C. Temple, "Buddermokan," pp. 3-4.
[56] *Ibid.*, p. 9.

The popularity of Pir-Badar was matched by another uncertain figure of popular veneration called Ghāzi Sāheb or simply Ghāzi, as noted before.[57] Believed to possess power over tigers in southern Bengal, Ghāzi Sāheb was not to be confused with Ghāzi Miyān, who was associated with marriage and fertility beliefs in northern Bengal. James Wise had identified the two and grafted the tradition of one on the other.[58] On an examination of the tradition about him, we suggested earlier the possibility that Ghāzi was a pirified pioneering Muslim settler in the tiger-infested Sundarban area of the southern and the most fluid part of the new Bengal delta.[59] Although it is difficult to determine the historical identity of this popular figure, the popular tradition about him strongly points to a historical kernel. As an example of the syncretistic little tradition of Bengal Muslims we shall examine later in some detail two popular ballads of the *pir*. Several matters in them merit attention. In both, we read about Ghāzi's marriage with a Hindu princess, whose royal father strongly opposed it and vainly tried all means to undo this union. In both, the Hindu king bore the same name, Matuk, the popular corruption of the word *mukut* or the crown, and was located in the same place, called either Khaniyā or Brāhman-nagar. The same place was popularized in the Hindu *Rāy-mangal* literature, in which Dakṣin-rāy was involved in a battle with Ghāzi and his associate Kālu for the control of the Sundarban area. In the south of the district of the 24-Parganas in the present state of West Bengal, there still exists a place by the name of Khaniyā, containing the ruins of old buildings and three tanks, one of the tanks being locally called "the tank of Matuk." In the vicinity of Khaniyā the remains of two tombs still bear association with the names of Bada-

[57] *Supra*, p. 53.
[58] J. Wise, "Muhammadans of Bengal," p. 43.
[59] *Supra*, pp. 52ff.

khān Ghāzi and Champā-bibi.[60] On the other hand, the outline of Ghāzi's life, as depicted in the folk tradition, provided a striking resemblance to that of a historical *pir*, Shāh Muhammad Māhisawār, as known from a family account left by Māhisawār's grandson, Muhammad Khān, one of the Bengali Muslim mediator poets. According to Muhammad Khān, his grandfather, who was an Arab of the Siddiq family, arrived with his friend Khalil in Chittagong, riding "on the back of a fish." There he was attracted to a *brāhman* maiden whom he wanted to marry. On the refusal of her father, the suitor arrived at the latter's house on a tiger and intimidated him into submission.[61] The points of similarity between this account and the tradition of Ghāzi are indeed striking. But a simple identification of the two may not be warranted. An examination of the popular traditions of *pirs* reveals that indiscriminate interchange of motifs was quite common. The desire to marry a *brāhman* maiden on the part of a *pir* was one of them. Renouncing the pleasures of a princely life to become a spiritual mendicant was another, which R. C. Zaehner characterized as the "renunciation motif."[62] This appears to be the case with Ghāzi, as we shall see later, and also with some other *pirs* in Bengal, such as Shāh Langar and Maulānā Shāh Daula. In the circumstances it is a little hazardous to equate *pirs'* identities on the basis of mere external similarities in their respective traditions.

The content of the Ghāzi cult in eastern Bengal underwent some substantive mutation. In this region which contained few villages "without a shrine dedicated to Ghāzi Sāhib," the latter possessed a protective power over cattle.[63] The *shirni* of rice and milk was prepared in a cowshed and offered to Ghāzi.

[60] Zain al-Din, "Bada-khān Ghāzir gān," ed. by K. Datta, *Bhāratiya Lokyān* (Calcutta), II, pts. 1-2 (1963), pp. 18-19.

[61] Muhammad Khān, *Maqtal*, fols. 2-3.

[62] Zaehner, *Hindu and Muslim Mysticism*, pp. 20ff.

[63] J. Wise, "Muhammadans of Bengal," p. 43.

In a Hindu house a Muslim was invited to prepare the sweet. They also donated rice or money to the *faqirs*, who sang about Ghāzi's influence on cattle.[64] Along the banks of the river Lakhyā in east Bengal, on the outskirts of villages, mounds of earth smeared with cowdung stood beneath grass thatches. A mound contained two knobs on the top, said to represent the tombs of Ghāzi and Kālu. On the twenty-second day after a cow had calved, the first milk drawn was poured over the mound as libation, and in times of sickness, rice, banana, and sweetmeats were offered.[65]

In addition to Ghāzi in southern Bengal, Mubārak or Mobrā Ghāzi in the Bārāsat-Basirhāt area in west Bengal and Sahijā Bādshāh in east Bengal were believed to possess controlling power over tigers.[66] There were several abodes (*maqām*) said to have been founded by Sahijā Bādshāh. Timber traders, both Muslim and Hindu, worshipped at the places; it was said that "tigers in former days used to visit these shrines on Thursday nights and eat any food left for them, without molesting the persons stopping in the Mukam."[67]

The Pir *Cult: the Beliefs*

The widespread and wide-ranging beliefs about *pirs* concerning their supernatural and thaumaturgic powers constitute a significant part of the study in the cult of *pir* and throw considerable light on the popularity of the *pir* phenomenon and thereby on the nature and importance of pirification as a component of the process of Islamization in Bengal. The belief in the capacity of *pirs* to heal, to help, and to perform other miraculous feats extended over almost the whole range of human need and imagination. The graves of saints were

[64] K. K. Rāy, "Maimansimher vivaran," p. 228.

[65] J. Wise, "Muhammadans of Bengal," p. 43.

[66] M. G. De Tassy, *Mémoire*, p. 355; *ADG. Sylhet*, p. 83; A. C. Chaudhuri, *Śrihatta*, vol. I, pt. 1, p. 141.

[67] *Sylhet*, *ibid.*; Chaudhuri, *ibid.*

visited by the farmer who had lost his cow, by the woman who desired a child or sought a cure for her sick one, and so on. Popular belief invented *pir* with both individual and shared capabilities and powers. These beliefs may be broadly grouped under two categories. One set of beliefs shows that a *pir* was regarded as not subject to the laws of physical nature that applied to everyone else, and the other reveals that he was even thought to possess command over the forces of nature.

The notion of the physical inviolability of *pirs* was typical of beliefs of this first category. Hamid Khān, a *pir*, was believed to have frustrated all attempts by a certain king to take his life. He was pitted against a tiger, drowned in the sea, consigned to the flames, struck with a scimitar, shot with arrows, and finally poisoned, but he came out unharmed.[68] Shāh Abd al-Alā, whose shrine was located in Magrāpārā in Sonārgāon, was credited with twelve years' continuous meditation in a forest, in consequence of which he was "buried up to his neck by the sand, raised by ants." This earned him a popular name, Pokāi Diwān.[69] It was said of Shāh Mahbub, alias Dātā Sāhib, of Pātharchāpuri, Suri sub-division of Birbhum that he could "remain under water through a whole year."[70] Saiyid al-Ārifin, whose tomb existed at the foot of a very old banyan tree in Kālisuri in Bakharganj, was known to be capable of floating on the water on his magic carpet.[71] According to a tradition of Pir Badar, he walked across the river Gangā on his wooden sandals.[72] In another account he came to Chittagong on a floating rock.[73] Shāh Sultān Māh-

[68] Daulat Wazir Bahrām Khān, *Laili-Majnu*, p. 11 (text).

[69] S. C. Rāy, *Suvarna-grāmer Itihās*, p. 83. *Pokā* in Bengali means "insect."

[70] *BDG. Birbhum*, ed. by L.S.S. O'Malley (Calcutta, 1910), p. 125.

[71] *BDG. Bakarganj*, ed. by J. C. Jack (Calcutta, 1918), p. 148.

[72] Jayaraddi (Zāhir al-Din?), *Mānik-pirer Jahurā [Zāhir] Nāma* (Viśva-bhārati MS. no. 216: sl 936) in P. Mandal (comp.), *Punthi-parichay* (Viśva-bhārati, 1958), vol. II, pp. 306-308; also *infra*, p. 243.

[73] Wise, "Muhammadans of Bengal," p. 41; also *supra*, p. 219.

isawār was thought to have come to Bengal riding on a fish.[74] The same was believed of Shāh Jalāl Bukhāri, a belief which was associated with the name of a place called Mahiganj (literally, the fish emporium) in Rangpur that contained a shrine believed to be his.[75]

Some of the saints were credited with instant coverage of a great distance. It was believed of Shāh Jalāl of Sylhet by his followers that he performed his "morning prayer everyday at Mecca" and also his annual *hajj* on the days of the Arfa and Id, "in as much as he vanished from the people's sight" on those days, and "no one knew whither he had gone."[76] The same kind of belief was cherished about Bābā Farid of Chittagong, who went to Mecca to offer his homage to God and "came back instantly" to Chittagong.[77] Shaikh Alā al-Haq, on the eve of his death, instructed his disciples not to perform his funeral prayers and to leave the task for Makhdum Jahāniyān. The disciples were perplexed, for Makhdum was in Sind at the time. But to their great amazement, Jahāniyān, on Haq's death, appeared on the scene and led the funeral prayers.[78] It was said about Machandali Saif of Gangāsāgar in the 24-Parganas that one day, while being shaved by a barber, he suddenly disappeared and returned shortly, dripping with perspiration. In explanation the *pir* told about a boat that ran aground, the sailors of which prayed for his assistance. Saif responded to their call and pulled the boat back to deep water. The barber laughed in disbelief, and forthwith he and his family perished.[79]

Pirs were regarded as not subject to death like ordinary mortals. Ahmad Ali, popular as Zinda Faqir and buried near

[74] Muhammad Khān, *Maqtal*, fols. 2-3.

[75] *DGEBA. Rangpur*, ed. by J. A. Vas (Allahabad, 1911), p. 146.

[76] Ibn Battutah, *Rehla*, p. 241.

[77] Muhammad Khān, *Maqtal*, fols. 1-2.

[78] Abd al-Rahmān Chishti, *Mirāt al-Asrār* (Asiatic Society of Bengal MS. 264), fol. 462.

[79] Gait, *Census Report (1901)*, p. 177.

the shrine of Khān Jahān in Bāgerhāt, was believed to have risen, while being buried, and "asked the mourners to bring his Koran."[80] The severed head of a martyred *pir* could talk. Shāh Ahmad Gesu Darāz, whose *dargāh* was located in Kharampur near Ākhāurā in Tripura, was killed fighting on the side of Shāh Jalāl of Sylhet against the Hindu king Gaudgovinda. his severed head and one of his wooden sandals (*khadam*)[81] were caught in the net of a Hindu fisherman. To his great astonishment the head began to speak. The fisherman embraced Islam and erected a tomb for the *pir*.[82] The decapitated body of the warrior-*pir* Shāh Ismāil Ghāzi, who was executed at the order of Sultān Husain Shāh, mounted on a horse and rode forth to Māndāran, where his body was thought to be buried. A tomb was later built in Māndāran by the *rājā* of Bardāh in fulfillment of his vow that he would build it for Shāh Ismāil, if he became successful in his battle against the *rājā* of Bardhamān.[83]

The person of the living *pir* possessed great sanctity in the eyes of the people. Any attempt to violate it might result in dire consequences. The Mughal emperor Aurangzeb sent Dilir Khān to execute Niamat Allāh, the religious guide of his brother, Prince Shāh Shujā. On his arrival at Gaud the Mughal commander lost his son Fateh-yār Khān, who died "after vomitting blood."[84] Sultān Ibrāhim Sharqi of Jaunpur and his *qāzi*, during the former's invasion of Bengal for the suppression of Rājā Ganeś, earned the displeasure of Shaikh Nur Qutb Ālam, as a result of which the *sultān* and the *qāzi*

[80] *BDG. Khulna*, ed. by L.S.S. O'Malley (Calcutta, 1907), p. 167.

[81] Hence, it is believed, the place is named Khadampur.

[82] Gait, *Census Report (1901)*, p. 178.

[83] *BDG. Hooghly*, ed. by L.S.S. O'Malley (Calcutta, 1912), pp. 290-91.

[84] R. K. Gupta, *Bānglār Itihās* (Calcutta, 1902), vol. II, Appendix, p. 16. A shrine called Niamat Allāh's Bāra-duāri existed at Firuzpur near Gaud. The tomb of Fateh-yār Khān was also there, near the Qadam Rasul building in Gaud. (*Ibid.*, pp. 16-17.)

were believed to have died on their return to Jaunpur.[85] Shaikh Anwār, son of Nur Qutb Ālam, was banished by Rājā Ganeś from Pandua to Sonargaon, where he was allegedly tortured to death by royal officials. It was said that Ganeś himself died as the "sacred blood" of Shaikh Anwār dropped on the ground.[86]

The beliefs concerning the special and supernatural position of *pir* not only placed them above the application of the universal laws of nature, but also invested them with powers to assume control over the forces of nature and often to override them.

The saints were believed to be endowed with unusual powers of anticipation, prophetic vision, and ability to make infallible and irrevocable statements. Sultān Ghiyath al-Din Iwaz Khalji is said to have served two *pirs* with respect and humility before he came to Bengal. The pleased divines asked him to proceed immediately to India, "where there was a kingdom allotted for him."[87] According to Ibn Battutah, Shāh Jalāl of Sylhet summoned his disciples before his death and said, "I shall leave you tomorrow, God willing. . . ." He expired the following day, and an open grave was discovered beside his body. Battutah himself was received by some of Jalāl's disciples two days before he could reach the *pir*'s hospice. This was made possible by Shāh Jalāl's premonition of Battutah's impending arrival, as he asked four of his disciples, "A traveller from the west has come to you, go to receive him!" Battutah entertained the desire of being presented with Shāh Jalāl's mantle made of goat's skin. The latter read Battutah's mind and made a gift of the mantle and a cap to

[85] G. H. Salim, *Riyāz*, pp. 112-14. It is conclusively established on numismatic and other evidence that Ibrāhim Sharqi continued to live long after his return to Jaunpur from Bengal. (H. N. Wright, *Catalogue of Coins in the Indian Museum* [Oxford, 1907], vol. II, p. 211.)

[86] Salim, *ibid.*, pp. 115-16.

[87] C. Stewart, *History of Bengal*, p. 56.

the visitor while he took leave. Jalāl also told his disciples that Battutah would eventually be dispossessed of the mantle, which was destined to come into the possession of another saint. The course of events narrated by Ibn Battutah suggested that the prophecy came true in every detail.[88]

Shaikh Anwār disturbed his father Nur Qutb Ālam in his prayers, as he came to complain about the "tyranny" of Rājā Ganeś. The enraged father cursed his son saying that "this tyranny shall cease only when thy blood shall be shed on the earth." It is said that Shaikh Anwār was tortured to death by royal officials at Sonargaon.[89]

Abd al-Latif during his visit to Bengal found, in the region of Ghorāghāt, mangoes containing "black worms as large as the gad-fly." No external marks appeared in the fruit from outside. He was told that this was the result of a curse pronounced by Nur Qutb Ālam on a village headman in the area.[90]

Shāh Pahlawān of Śekhar in Faridpur reportedly left instructions to lay his grave east to west. His wish was ignored at the time of his burial as being inconsistent with Islamic rites, and he was buried in a grave as required by the *sharia*. Next morning the grave was allegedly found pointing in the direction he wanted.[91]

Shāh Karim Ali of Jagannāthpur in Tripura was considered able to "raise from the dead."[92] The same power was attributed to Shāh Gharib, whose tomb was located in Bāraijuri near Pānśa in the Faridpur district.[93]

Therapeutic powers were widely attributed to *pirs*. Their

[88] Ibn Battutah, *Rehla*, pp. 239-40.

[89] G. H. Salim, *Riyāz*, pp. 115-16.

[90] Abd al-Latif, "Account," p. 146.

[91] A. N. Rāy, *Faridpurer Itihās* (Calcutta, 1328 B.S./A.D. 1921), pt. 2, p. 171.

[92] J. Wise, "Notes on Sunargaon," *JASB*, XLIII (1894), pt. 1, no. 1, p. 96.

[93] A. N. Rāy, *Faridpur*, vol. II, p. 172.

shrines were visited by people largely for this purpose. Shāh Mahbub of Birbhum was believed to "cure dangerous diseases by applying ashes or grass." Makhdum Saiyid Shāh Zāhir al-Din of Birbhum was also credited with miraculous control over all sorts of diseases, and his tomb was frequented by the afflicted persons who sought relief from their ailments.[94] The tombs of Khwandkār Muhammad Yusuf and his father in Magrāpārā in Sonargaon were resorted to by people who invoked in their names for relief from particular diseases.[95] The shrine of Shāh Jalāl in Sylhet preserved his used sword, called *zulfaqār*, a deer-skin for prayers, a pair of wooden sandals, two copper cups, and an egg, believed to be that of an ostrich, brought by him to this country. These objects were held in the utmost veneration by the believers, and the water used in the ritual cleaning of these objects was drunk by them for the recovery from illness.[96] Shaikh Hamid used to dip in water an edge of the shoe used by his *pir*, Shaikh Ahmad Sirhindi, and the water was believed to possess the potency of curing people of their ailments.[97] Some *pirs* were supposed to have control over particular ailments. The dust from the shrine of Alman Sāheb, near Bainchi in Hugli, if rubbed on the body, was believed to remove all kinds of rheumatic pains.[98] A *dargāh* in Noakhali earned a similar reputation in the cure of rheumatism.[99] In Bardhaman people bathed in the tank called Māine-pukur and rolled on the ground of the adjoining *dargāh* of Maulānā Hamid Danishmand, an act supposed to help to cure all kinds of skin diseases.[100] The *dargāh* of Pāgal Sāheb of Habibpur in Son-

[94] *BDG. Birbhum*, pp. 121, 125.

[95] S. C. Rāy, *Suvarnagrām*, p. 80.

[96] A. C. Chaudhuri, *Śrihatta*, vol. I, pt. 2, p. 37.

[97] Rizvi, *Muslim Revivalist Movements*, pp. 279-80.

[98] Gait, *Census Report (1901)*, p. 197.

[99] A.K.N. Karim, "Some Aspects of Popular Beliefs among Muslims of Bengal," *Eastern Anthropologist*, vol. IX, no. 1 (Sept.-Nov., 1955), p. 34.

[100] N. N. Basu, *Bardhamāner Itikathā* (Calcutta, 1321 B.S./A.D. 1915), p. 30.

argaon was visited by parents seeking remedy against dangerous diseases among their children.[101]

A number of *pirs* in different parts of Bengal were believed to exercise influence and command over animals, reptiles, and birds. The association of Mānik-pir, Ghāzi Sāheb, and Hājir-pir with the protection of cattle has already been noted.[102] Khān Jahān of Bagerhat was offered the first milk of a cow.[103] In Astagrām, Mymensingh, no cultivator would yoke cows to a plough without remembering Qutb Sāheb.[104] On the other hand, Ghāzi, Kālu, Mobrā Ghāzi, and Sahijā Bādshāh were all believed to possess command over tigers, as also noted before.[105] Ghāzi and Kālu were also invested in tradition with powers over crocodiles.[106] Majlis Sāheb and Badr Sāheb, two brothers who were buried in Kālnā, Burdwan, were also associated with crocodile spirit. It was believed that between the two tombs, almost a mile apart on the riverbank, a man was safe from any accident, and crocodiles would not attack him.[107] South of Khān Jahān's mausoleum in Bagerhat, Khulna, there was a large tank, believed to be constructed by Khān Jahān, but rather curiously called *thākur-dighi* or the god's pond.[108] This contained a large number of crocodiles which were supplicated by people and regarded as descended from the two original crocodiles, popular as Kālā (black)-pād (pāhād, i.e., hill?) and Dhalā(white)-pād, kept by Khān Jahān.[109] There was a similar crocodile named Kālā-

[101] S. C. Rāy, *Suvarnagrām*, p. 84.

[102] *Supra*, pp. 212-13, 209, 223-24.

[103] S. C. Mitra, *Yaśohar-Khulnār Itihās* (Calcutta, 2 vols., 1321-28 B.S./A.D. 1914-1922), vol. I, p. 292.

[104] *BDG. Mymensingh*, ed. by F. A. Sachse (Calcutta, 1917), p. 38.

[105] *Supra*, pp. 222-24.

[106] *Infra*, pp. 239ff.

[107] *BDG. Burdwan*, ed. by J.C.K. Peterson (Calcutta, 1910), p. 198.

[108] There are evidences that a number of *pirs*' shrines in Bengal came up on some pre-existing popular sacred sites, and similar mutations of objects of popular veneration were also in evidence.

[109] *BDG. Khulna*, pp. 166-67; S. C. Mitra, *Yaśohar-Khulnā*, vol. I, pp. 331-32.

khān in a "sacred" tank called *pir-pukur* (tank), attached to the shrine of Shāh Shafi Sultān in Pandua. Womenfolk made votive offerings to the crocodiles, attached to the shrines of Bagerhat and Pandua, "in the belief that this offering will procure them offspring."[110]

Some *pirs* were believed to possess power over snakes. Saiyid Shāh Abd Allāh Kirmani of the village Khustigiri, Suri sub-division in the district of Birbhum, was "especially renowned for the power which he had over serpents," and his name was repeated in formulae for overpowering snakes.[111] Another *pir* in this category was Shāh Kamāl of Bhuinyānānyā in Sirājganj. People poured milk and rice on the shrine.[112]

Even birds were believed to respect *pirs*. Madan-pir had a famous shrine in Netrakonā, Mymensingh, and it was said that birds never flew over it.[113]

Tradition connected a number of *pirs* to some particular trees, suggesting a grafting of pre-existing tree-cults on the locally popular *pir*. To the south of the *salāmi-darwāza* in Pandua, where Shāh Jalāl Tabrizi allegedly sat first on his arrival, was a margosa (*nim*) tree, highly regarded by people. It was believed that the tree originated from the toothpick of Shāh Jalāl.[114] Makhdum Rahim al-Din, one of the companions of Shāh Jalāl of Sylhet, was said to have left his staff at Jalālpur, which grew into a banyan tree. The custodians of his *dargāh* in Jalālpur would distribute the leaves of the tree among the visitors to the shrine. Similar beliefs attached to

110 *BDG. Hooghly*, p. 109; A. C. Gupta, *Hugli bā Dakṣin Rādh* (Calcutta, 1914), pt. 1, pp. 65-66; *BDG. Khulna*, p. 167. In the *pir*-tank of Pandua, we have another instance of Islamic appropriation of a pre-existing Hindu tank, as the tank was extended in the north-south line as required by the Hindu law-givers. In contrast, the Muslim practice was to extend a tank in the west-east direction.

111 *BDG. Birbhum*, p. 120.

112 Milk and rice were two most common offerings to snakes.

113 *BDG. Mymensingh*, p. 38.

114 R. K. Gupta, *Bānglār Itihās*, vol. II, p. 21.

Saiyid Shāh Abd Allāh Kirmani of Birbhum. It was noted about him that he left Kirman in Persia, when very young, and met Shāh Arzani, who directed him to go to Bengal. Shāh Arzani gave him a toothpick of *chambeli* wood, advising him to settle down at the place where the toothpick turned fresh and green. Shāh Abd Allāh arrived in the village Khustigiri in Birbhum, where one morning he discovered that the toothpick, left overnight under his pillows, had become green. He planted it immediately at the place, and it soon became a large tree.[115]

Several *pirs* were also related to the water-spirit. The wide popularity of Pir-Badar and Khwāja Khizr as the guardian-spirits of water has already been mentioned.[116] In the village of Firuzpur, on the bank of the river Bhairav in the Nadia district, the *dargāh* of Budā-diwān was quite popular. It was told about him that he threw into the river Bhairav everything that the people offered him, and had anyone sought anything from him, he asked Bhairav to help to fulfil the supplicant's desire.[117]

There were other ramifications of the beliefs about *pirs* controlling the forces of nature. Shāh Karim Ali of Jagannāthpur in Tripura was thought capable of causing the rains, when and wherever he pleased.[118] Ali Sabr Shāh was also connected with the making of rains. The people resorted to his shrine in Bāgiārā in the Ātiyā sub-division of the Mymensingh district, on the occasion of a drought, and poured 125 pitchers of water on the shrine in the expectation of rains.[119]

The warrior-*pir* Shāh Ismāil Ghāzi, following upon his

[115] *BDG. Birbhum*, p. 120. For similar traditions about the growth of a tree from the toothpick used by a *pir*, see C. Rāya, "On Tree-Cults in the District of Midnapur," pp. 242-64.

[116] *Supra*, p. 218.

[117] K. N. Mallik, *Nadiyā*, p. 365.

[118] Wise, *Notes on the Races*, p. 96.

[119] A. K. Maulik, *Ātiyā Parganār Itihās* (Mahedā, 1323 B.S./A.D. 1916), p. 84.

victory against the king of Assam, came to "a piece of land completely covered with water." He allegedly prayed for a piece of land to rise from the water for him to stand on and offer his prayers, and so it did.[120]

It was said about Shāh Gharib of Pānśā in the Faridpur district that he approached certain members of the Chaudhuri family of Belgāchi for alms. The latter scornfully advised him to earn his livelihood by physical labor and offered him a job of planting banana saplings in the latter's garden. Shāh Gharib cut a sapling right through the middle and planted it upside down, for which he was scolded. To everyone's amazement, however, the plant was found, the next morning, shooting from the reversed roots.[121]

Saiyid al-Ārifin of Kālisuri in Bakharganj saw a Hindu girl coming down to a river to wash a bowl of rice. He asked her to cook a little rice for him. On her refusal, she was asked to look into her vessel and was staggered to find that the rice was already cooked in there. The miracle "made her at once become a convert," and she entreated him to grant her a boon. She was promised that the particular spot would become the site of a great annual gathering to be called after her name. Since the girl's name was Kāli and she belonged to *suri/sundi* caste, the village came to be called Kālisuri and the annual fair was named after the village.[122]

Tradition had it about Alā al-Haq that once a number of *qalandars* visited his *khānqah*, bringing a cat. The cat got lost, and the *qalandars* asked Haq to find it. With a view to ascertaining his miraculous power, one of them asked him to bring the cat out from the horns of a deer, and another asked him to do it from his testicles. The *qalandar* who talked about the deer was gored by a cow, and the other died of inflammation of his testicles.[123]

[120] Pir Muhammad Shattāri, *Risālat*, p. 219.
[121] A. N. Rāy, *Faridpur*, vol. II, p. 172.
[122] *BDG. Bakarganj*, p. 148.
[123] Abd al-Rahmān Chishti, *Mirāt*, fol. 484.

The Pir *Cult: the Myths and the Folk* Pir *Tradition*

Although aspects of the *pir* cult and the beliefs about *pirs* partly cut across the social barriers in the Muslim community, it is quite evident from the foregoing discussion that the *pir* cult occupied a highly significant place in the living religion of the Muslim folk in Bengal. It comes to us as no surprise that the Muslim folk tradition was almost exclusively centered on the popular *pirs*, real or fictitious, and its object was to glorify and vindicate a particular *pir* in the manner of the *mangal* deities, seeking the *pir*'s blessing and favor. These folk ballads on *pirs* were meant for both singing and recitation, accompanied by music, in the village gatherings attended by both Muslims and Hindus. The particular *pir* was offered *shirni*, and at the conclusion of the song the food offered to the *pir* was shared by the participants. The ballad of Ghāzi ended with the following couplet:

> The *shirni* of Ghāzi is over:
> Let the Muslims invoke Allāh
> And the Hindus Hari.[124]

These narrative poems were characteristically syncretistic, clearly identifiable in the religious-cultural milieus of rural Bengal. The forms, motifs, and atmosphere of this literature exuded a strong local flavor. Hindu characters, religious or secular, freely moved into these narrations, not as parts of artificially contrived decorative motifs but by virtue of their own right as natural components of an organic system. The folk ballads, considered below, on three of the most popular *pirs* in Bengal, namely Ghāzi, Pir Badar, and Mānik-pir, are clearly illustrative of these points.

The Tradition of Ghāzi

The wide popularity and the possible identity of a *pir* called either Ghāzi or Bada-khān Ghāzi or Ghāzi-sāheb by the Bengali Muslim folk has already been noted in different con-

[124] Zain al-Din, "Bada-khān Ghāzi," p. 30.

texts.[125] We have found at least two separate folk ballads[126] on Ghāzi and his mate Kālu, which focus on Ghāzi's love for a beautiful *brāhman* princess, the strong opposition of her royal father to Ghāzi's proposal and attempt to marry her, the consequent fight between Ghāzi and the *rājā*, and the ultimate success of Ghāzi in the battle, as well as in his cherished object of marrying the princess. Despite this broad thematic conformity, suggesting a historical kernel in the story, there are differences in these two accounts. Abd al-Karim's account is more elaborate than the other, and the hero is called Ghāzi in the former and Bada-khān Ghāzi in the latter. Ghāzi's beloved princess is Champā-vati in the first and Subhadrā in the second, while the royal father, Matuk (Mukut)-rājā, is the ruler of Brāhman-nagar in the first and Khaniyā-nagar in the second. There are further differences in details, and the spirit of these traditions is likely to be captured more in their authentic reproduction in essential outline.

King Sikandar and Queen Ojufā of Bairāt-nagar were deeply distressed at the loss of their only son and child. The queen went for a stroll along the bank of the river Gangā and discovered a baby in a box floating in the water.[127] She brought the child home and named him Kālu. Later, the queen conceived, and "the fate" of the unborn child was "written on its forehead by the divine agency" in the sixth month of the pregnancy. In the seventh month, the ceremony called *sādh*, of entertaining the would-be mother with a variety of food, was performed.[128] The child born in due course was Ghāzi, who was "destined to become a celebrity in the world."[129]

Ghāzi and Kālu grew up together as inseparable compan-

[125] *Supra*, pp. 222-24.

[126] Abd al-Karim, *Kālu-Ghāzi*; Zain al-Din, "Bada-khān Ghāzi."

[127] Possible adoption of the tradition of Musā or Moses, one of the prophets (*nabi*) recognized in Islam.

[128] A popular Hindu rite in Bengal.

[129] Abd al-Karim, *Kālu-Ghāzi*, pp. 5ff.

ions, and both were firmly devoted to God and endowed with supernatural powers. The king offered the throne to Ghāzi when he was ten, but the latter declined it on the ground that his life's mission was to become "a spiritual mendicant in the way of God." The offended and enraged king tried unsuccessfully various means to chastise his disobedient son, who finally convinced his royal father of his divine powers by picking up a needle thrown into the sea, with the help of crocodiles.[130]

One night Ghāzi and Kālu left secretly the comforts of the royal palace for the life of a *faqir*.[131] They reached the wild tracts of Sundarban in the southern Bengal, where not only did tigers, crocodiles, and other wild animals offer submission to Ghāzi, but Hindu deities like Śiv, Durgā, Gangā, and Sati[132] also accepted him as a son.

Once the two friends strayed into a place called Sāfāi-nagar "in search of food." They were maltreated by its Hindu ruler named Śri-rām. Kālu prayed to Allāh to burn down the place, convert all local people to Islam, and kidnap the queen. Allāh responded to his prayers, and his wishes were fulfilled through the agency of Khwāja Khizr, the universally popular Muslim saint. The Hindu ruler offered his submission to Ghāzi, greatly honored him and Kālu, and built a mosque in the place, while, in return, the kidnapped queen was restored to the king.

At another place the two friends, tired and hungry in the course of their wanderings, received the kind hospitality of seven wood-cutters. Ghāzi repaid them with a huge quantity of gold obtained through the goddess Gangā, whom Ghāzi addressed as his maternal aunt (*māsi*).[133]

130 Ghāzi was regarded by his believers the guardian-spirit of tigers and crocodiles.

131 Cf. R. C. Zaehner's "renunciation-motif." (*Supra*, p. 223.)

132 Sati is but another name of Durgā, the consort of Śiv.

133 Abd al-Karim, *Kālu-Ghāzi*, p. 16.

This set the stage for the most central event in the tradition of Ghāzi, namely his infatuation with the Hindu princess, which involved him in a war with her father, and the final triumph of Ghāzi. The circumstances of Ghāzi's meeting with the princess diverged widely in the two accounts. In Abd al-Karim's version, while Ghāzi and Kālu slept one night in a mosque, the former was carried by a group of fairies (*pari*) to the bedchamber of Champā-vati, the daughter of Rājā Mukut of Brāhman-nagar, a place largely inhabited by orthodox *brāhmans* who "performed purifying penances at the mere sight of a Muslim." Ghāzi and the princess, however, fell in love with each other and married secretly in the Hindu *gandharva* style. They were again separated in their sleep, Ghāzi being brought back by the fairies to the mosque.[134]

In Zain al-Din's account Bada-khān Ghāzi, in the company of his close friend Kālu, was engaged in reading the *Qurān*, under the shadows of a tree on the bank of the Ganges, when he saw Princess Subhadrā, daughter of Rājā Mukut of Khaniyā-nagar, taking a ceremonial dip in the Ganges, on the Hindu auspicious day of *mahā-bāruni*. Shot by cupid's arrow, Ghāzi was immediately infatuated with love for her.[135]

In respect of subsequent developments, the two accounts present a considerable difference. From this particular point in the narratives, it may be convenient to present them separately. To pick up the thread of Karim's account, Ghāzi, first united and then separated from his beloved princess, set out in Kālu's company for Brāhman-nagar. On the way, Ghāzi was pleased to observe a number of good omens, such as a snake on his right, a lizard calling from somewhere above his head, a pregnant mother feeding her child, a rider on an elephant, a flower-girl carrying a basketful of blooms, a milkmaid carrying milk in a pitcher, women carrying pitch-

[134] *Ibid.*
[135] Zain al-Din, "Bada-khān Ghāzi," pp. 21-22.

ers full of water, and a cow suckling her calf.[136] Kālu appeared rather skeptical and wondered, "How could a Muslim marry a Hindu?" Ghāzi advised absolute trust in Allāh.[137]

In the meanwhile, the princess Champā-vati, unable to bear the separation from Ghāzi, confided in her mother, who advised her to worship Śiv and her consort Gauri. Gauri assured Champā:

> Ghāzi Pir is my sister's son;
> He shall be your husband.[138]

On his arrival in Brāhman-nagar, Ghāzi sent Kālu to the *rājā* with the proposal of marriage. The indignant *rājā* heaped humiliation on the messenger and threw him into prison. Ghāzi returned to Sundarban to raise a pack of tigers, and later attacked the *rājā*. Rājā Mukut invoked Dakṣin-rāy, the Hindu tiger-god. The latter seemed hesitant to face Ghāzi, commanding a tiger-force. Dakṣin-rāy approached goddess Gangā for a contingent of crocodiles. She told him about goddess Gauri's and her own affection for Ghāzi and advised him to persuade the *rājā* to marry Champā to Ghāzi, a marriage that was "destined to come through, despite the entire world taking a stand against Ghāzi." The tiger-god eventually obtained a 52,000-strong crocodile-force from Gangā, having resorted to the emotional blackmailing of Gangā by the threat of committing suicide. Extremely reluctant to displease Ghāzi, Gangā agreed only after Dakṣin-rāy's undertaking that the matter should not come to Ghāzi's knowledge.[139] The crocodiles were no match for the tigers, and Dakṣin-rāy, defeated and desperate, approached Gauri for an army of ghosts

[136] All were and possibly some still are widely prevalent superstitious beliefs in Bengal.

[137] Abd al-Karim, *Kālu-Ghāzi*, pp. 34-36.

[138] *Ibid.*, p. 16. Bengali Hindu maidens still worship Śiv for timely and appropriate matches.

[139] *Ibid.*, p. 58.

and goblins.[140] Gauri acceded to his request on the same undertaking as for Gangā. The attack of the invisible spirits threw the tiger-force into initial disarray, but Ghāzi mustered his army and turned the scale of the war totally in his favor with the help of thaumaturgic powers instilled in his mendicant's stick (*āsā*) and the pairs of wooden sandals. Thoroughly vanquished, Dakṣin-rāy was bound hand and foot and not released until he promised to prevail on Rājā Mukut to marry the princess to Ghāzi. The *rājā* was left with no choice other than taking the field against Ghāzi. It resulted in his crushing defeat. He agreed to solemnize the marriage of his daughter and Ghāzi and embrace Islam, before he was restored to his position with full dignity.[141]

In Zain al-Din's version, on the other hand, Bada-Khān Ghāzi's love at first sight for Princess Subhadrā was followed by Kālu's gathering information about Subhadrā and her family, at Ghāzi's instance. The latter's further instruction for Kālu to carry the marriage proposal to Mukut-rājā failed to strike an enthusiastic response in Kālu who wondered: "Who has ever heard of a marriage between a *bāmun* [*brāhman*] and a *mochalmān* [Muslim]?"[142] Urged by Ghāzi and rather apprehensive of his life, Kālu appeared at the royal court in Khaniyā-nagar, in the disguise of a *brāhman*. On the introduction of the proposed bridegroom as a *brāhman* prince, Kālu's marriage proposal came under royal scrutiny and provoked suspicion. Kālu decided to save his life from the royal wrath by a discreet disappearance from the scene. This was followed by Ghāzi himself appearing in Khaniyā-nagar and secretly tampering with the Hindu sacred texts to establish a *brāhman* origin for himself. Ghāzi's credentials and the marriage proposal were both accepted by the *rājā* on the strength

140 Śiv, husband of Gauri, is also known for his command over the spirits and ghosts.

141 Abd al-Karim, *Kālu-Ghāzi*, pp. 60-70.

142 Zain al-Din, "Bada-khān Ghāzi," pp. 22ff.

of his apocryphal scriptural sanction. The *faqirs* forming part of the bridegroom's *entourage*, assumed sacred threads and posed as *brāhmans*. Subsequently, the fraud was discovered, and the entire party, including Ghāzi and Kālu, was thrown out by the *rājā*. Ghāzi retaliated by raising his tiger-force and launching an attack on the *rājā*. Mukut-rājā was forced to submit, accept Islam, and marry Subhadrā to Ghāzi. The orthodox *brāhman* leaders of the place decided to boycott the marriage celebration and socially excommunicate the royal family for their polluting association with an "impious Muslim." Ghāzi cowed them by turning his pack of tigers loose on them. The marriage was performed with great festivities, at the end of which Ghāzi, accompanied by his wife and followers, went to Chandipur.[143]

The Tradition of Pir Badar[144]

Allāh, seated in the company of twelve *auliyā*, enquired about a competent messenger to advance his glory in the world. He desired to introduce that person as Mānik, "the *avatār* in the *kali-yug*," and to "entrust the world to his care." None among the dignitaries present, who included Hāji, Ghāzi, Muhammad, Rahim, Karim, Rasul, Pakāmbar/Paighambar, Hajjat/Hazrat, and Mādār (Shāh Madār), gathered enough courage to respond to this call of Allāh.[145] Just then Pir Badar

[143] *Ibid.*, pp. 29-30.

[144] For the identity of Pir-Badar, *supra*, pp. 218ff. This particular account is based on Jayaraddi, *Mānik-pir* (Viśva-bhārati Ms.).

[145] The name-list showed utter confusion among simple Muslim folk, regarding the characters of Islamic tradition. Hāji does not have any individual reference. Similarly, Ghāzi, unless the writer was referring to the particular character of the tradition studied above, has no personal reference. Rahim and Karim are but two additonal names of Allāh. Rasul and Paighambar are synonyms for the Prophet. Hazrat is a title used in respect, but the writer appeared, in the context, to refer to Hazrat Ali. It is also significant that a popular *pir* like Shāh Madār was considered worthy of sitting in the company of Allāh.

appeared on the scene, offered his respects to Allāh, and agreed to bear his burden.

He descended on the earth in the garb of a *faqir-murshid.* He began his journey in Delhi and thence proceeded to Lāhur/Lahore.[146] Next he arrived in Śāntipur in west Bengal and then to "Sābājār" (Shāhbazār?), where he told Golāmāli/Ghulām Ali, a locally popular *pir*, of his mission. The next point in Badar's journey was Saptagrām, well-known for "the descent of goddess Gangā."[147] On the banks of the river in Triveni, Badar found some Hindu ascetics and holymen, meditating on goddess Gangā, but unable to see her in person due to their "fickleness of mind." Pir Badar gave them the unsolicited advice to "pray with a pure heart." The audacious intrusion of Badar, "a shaven-headed faqir," was resented by them all, and they heaped insults on Badar:

> What the hell has your father to do with our worship of Gangā? . . . Where do you come from? We have been here meditating for the last twelve years; our bodies are all covered with weeds; and yet the mother of Brammā [Brahmā] has not appeared before us. How dare you make all this tall talk?

Badar was offended and determined to display his miracle-working powers. He performed ceremonial ablutions, sat on a tiger-skin,[148] and urged Gangā to make her appearance in response to his call as "an elder brother." Gangā let her Hindu

[146] One wonders if the commencement of Badar's errand from Delhi and Lahore could reflect, in his writer's mind, the advent of Islam in Bengal from its west, and/or the association of these places and that particular part of the Indian sub-continent with the glory of Islam in India. Beyond a very broad and vague awareness, the geographical knowledge of a common man such as this writer was extremely limited and confused, as evidenced by the further details of Pir-Badar's journey narrated by the writer.

[147] According to Hindu tradition, the river-goddess Gangā was persuaded by the austere penances of King Bhagirath to descend on the earth at a place called Triveni, near Saptagrām. This earned the river Gangā the other name of Bhāgirathi.

[148] Hindu *yogis*, following Lord Śiv, often meditated while sitting on tiger-skins.

worshippers have a glimpse of herself, as a result of which they immediately passed into heaven. She was, however, reluctant to appear before Badar, a *yavan*, and subjected him to various tests. He emerged successfully through all this, and then decided to chastise Gangā by tying her up in a sack. She was released only after she agreed to accept Badar as her elder brother.

Thereafter, Badar wished to build a mosque in Triveni and sent Gangā to fetch stones from Rāmeśvar-setubandha.[149] He also sent for Viśva-karmā, the divine architect of Hindu mythological tradition, and gave him betel leaves and flowers as a token of agreement to build the mosque in a single day and night.[150] Viśva-karmā persuaded Badar to arrange for delaying the daybreak. Badar instructed Niśi, the Hindu guardian deity of the night, to take care of it. While two nights passed without daybreak, Allāh became concerned that Viśva-karmā's creation might reduce the splendor of Mecca, Medina, and even "paradise" to insignificance. He sent Hazrat Ali in the form of a white crow to herald the dawn by cawing. Allāh himself forced the sun to rise. Unable to finish his contract, Viśva-karmā slipped away, leaving behind his axe and the incomplete structure.[151]

Having left the completion of the mosque to the care of Dafargā Ghāzi,[152] Badar set out for Chittagong, crossing the river Gangā on his pairs of wooden sandals used as rafts. Curiously enough, his journey took him back to Delhi, where he approached the *bādshāh* (emperor), asking for the hand of

[149] Situated in the southernmost part of India, the place is associated with *Rāmāyan* tradition. Rām constructed a bridge at this particular point to launch an attack on Rāvan, the King of Lankā and the kidnapper of his wife, Sitā.

[150] Betel leaves were often taken as a token of an agreement in Bengal.

[151] Attached to the mosque of Triveni was a curious piece of stone, often called "the axe of Viśva-karmā" and by some "the axe of Ghāzi."

[152] The Triveni mosque is associated with the name of Zāfar Khān Ghāzi, and Dafargā is a popular corruption of his name.

the princess Dudh-bibi.[153] The *bādshāh* was enraged and drove him out of the palace, heaping insults on him. Badar managed to kidnap Dudh-bibi in the darkness of night, with the help of a pack of tigers amenable to his command. Dudh-bibi agreed to marry Badar on certain conditions. She said:

> . . . I have taken a vow. In the *tretā-yug* I worshipped Rām Nārāyan; thereafter, I was a milkmaid (*gopini*) in Gokul, feeding the son of Nanda [i.e., Krișna] with butter. I should only marry the person who is able to assume the four-armed form [of Vișnu] in my presence.

Badar asked her to close her eyes, and transformed himself to Rām, with the bow in the left hand and the arrows in the right, and Rām's brother, Lakșman, held an umbrella on his head. Next he assumed the form of Krișna, holding in his hands the conch shell, the wheel, the mace, the lotus, and a garland of wildflowers, and playing the flute in the company of his brother, Balarām. He stood under a *kadamba* tree in the typically amorous posture of Krișna. This completely won over Dudh-bibi, who accepted him as her husband by putting a garland around his neck in the Hindu *gandharva* style of marriage. Next morning, Dudh-bibi's absence was noticed at the palace. People were sent in all directions after them. Badar and Dudh-bibi escaped to a forest. On the approach of the people looking for them, the couple played a trick on the searchers by transforming themselves into Rām and Sitā. Subsequently, however, they revealed their identity, and were taken back and received in the capital with "as much jubilation as followed the return of Rām and Sitā to Ajodhā/Ayodhyā." The *bādshāh* arranged a gala marriage ceremony for them. He sent for the *qāzi* and the *mullāh*, while Allāh, having come to know of all this from heaven, sent down "Hāji, Kāji/Qāzi, Mahāmad/Muhammad, Rahim, Karim, Sekh/

[153] This section of the story appears a mere modified version of the Ghāzi tradition. (*Supra*, pp. 235ff.)

Shaikh, and Fakorān/Faqorān [pl. of *faqir*]" to attend the celebration in Delhi.

Badar enjoyed the company of his wife for some time and then departed for Chittagong, leaving Dudh-bibi in tears. A couple of years later, Dudh-bibi conceived as the result of a union with Badar in a dream, as willed by Allāh. In due course Dudh-bibi gave birth to a boy, who was none other than the well-known *pir* of the Bengali Muslim folk, namely Mānik-pir. The fear of social scandal prompted the mother to place the newborn baby inside "a copper casket" and "float it in the water." A gardener named Madu/Madhu discovered it and took the baby to his home. Mānik was growing up steadily in the care of Madhu and his wife.[154] Twelve years elapsed, when Badar, stationed in Chittagong, suddenly recalled his wife and started for her home.[155]

The Tradition of Mānik-pir[156]

Mānik, or Zinda Mānik, proposed to Isa (Jesus) for a joint errand to preach their missions. Isa was reluctant to accompany him until Mānik tried him (Isa) and proved his power over sickness and disease.[157] Initially hesitant to test his power on his friend, Mānik was goaded into it by Isa's insistence. He begged forgiveness of Allāh for the consequences that were to follow from Isa's insistence, and invoked the personified affliction, Jarāsur. The latter immediately responded to the call and struck Isa down on the road with dangerously high fever.

Early the next morning some forty *firishtahs*, on their way to the place of congregational prayers, discovered Isa lying

[154] Reminiscent of the very popular legend of Moses.

[155] The manuscript abruptly ends here and appears torn.

[156] For the identity of Mānik-pir, *supra*, pp. 212-13. This particular narrative is based on Shaikh Hābil, *Mānik-pirer Gān* (JMS), fols. 1-9.

[157] Mānik-pir was often regarded by his believers as a protective power against diseases.

on the roadside. The *firishtahs* were on the horns of a dilemma, for they could ill afford to miss their prayers, nor could they leave behind a *faqir* in this dire condition. In utter desperation they prayed to Allāh for a physician. At this stage Mānik presented himself, claiming the power to cure the afflicted *faqir*. He regretted, however, not having one important ingredient for the required potion, and he asked the *firishtahs* to procure it. The *firishtahs* were horrified to know of the requirement, which was the liver of the only surviving son of a couple who had already lost seven children. Mānik was adamant, and the *firishtahs* had no choice. They travelled around many parts of the world: Mecca, Medina, Karbalā, Erān/Irān, and Torān/Turān (i.e., central Asia), but with no result. Extremely concerned and desperate, they arrived in "the city of Ārabba/Arab," found their way to the house of a poor woman who at last provided the eagerly sought after information. She referred them to a rich merchant family with a son answering Mānik-pir's description. The *firishtahs* were well-received by the merchant, who was required by his guests to promise to do whatever they asked. As the *firishtahs* stated the purpose of their visit, the merchant's family broke down. The merchant's wife offered to save her five-year-old son, Said Allāh's life with all their wealth and even her own life. The merchant painfully reminded his wife of the utter inviolability of the promise made to the *faqir*. When the son himself came to know of it all, he set aside all other considerations in favor of upholding his father's word. He was then killed with a knife, and his liver was taken out. The *firishtahs* showered unqualified praise on the merchant as the most righteous man in the world and profusely blessed him. The liver of the boy was taken to Mānik, who read "four *kālemā*/*kalima*"[158] and touched with his hand the body of Isa. The

[158] The author seems to mean that *kalima* was read four times.

latter immediately stood up. The *firishtahs* conceded that they had never experienced anything like this before.

Mānik, however, did not feel at ease until he revived the dead boy and restored him to the bewailing mother. He felt that her agony, anguish, and suffering were like "a river, breaking through its banks and reaching up to the sky. . . . Her lamentations are comparable to Kauśulle/Kauśalyā's without Rām." Mānik and Isa arrived before long at the merchant's home. The latter was filled with alarm to see a new pair of *faqirs*. They asked for some food, and the pious merchant brought them into the house. The merchant gradually told them about his family's harrowing experience, while Mānik tried to console him by referring to the Hindu tradition of King Harichandra/Hariś-chandra, sacrificing his son to uphold the will of Dharma, and of Karna, killing his son to honor his commitment. Mānik cited a few more Hindu traditions to bring solace to the bemoaning couple. He asked: "How did Śochi-/Śachi-thākurāni sustain herself when Gorā/Gaurānga [i.e., Chaitanya], having forsaken the world, left her? How did Yaśodā survive when Hari left Golok [Gokul] for Maturā/Mathurā?" Mānik asked all to prepare themselves for the burial of the boy after they had some refreshments. The Arab merchant humbly questioned the propriety of taking food in a house undergoing the ceremonial impurity (*aśuch/aśauch*) consequent upon death.[159] Mānik drew his attention to the lack of a Qurānic sanction for such a prejudice.

Thereupon the food was cooked and served to the guests alone. But Mānik and Isa refused to touch the food unless the host shared it with them. The merchant, initially reluctant to take food while his son still lay dead in the house, was persuaded by his wife to make company for the *faqirs*. The two friends, at this particular stage, asked for a fourth person to share their food. The merchant's wife, as a woman, was

[159] A widely prevalent and strong Hindu notion of ritual impurity.

unacceptable to both as a dining companion. Just as the merchant had reached the limit of his self-control, Mānik asked him to call his dead son by name. The dead son sprang to life as soon as his father complied with Mānik's instruction. The boy rushed to the eager arms of the mother. The joy and gratitude of the couple knew no bounds. They prostrated themselves at the feet of Mānik and entreated him to reveal his true identity. Isa disclosed Mānik's identity, introducing him as the son of Bādsā Karamdin (Bādshāh Karim al-Din) and Surat-bibi. In taking leave of the family, Isa urged them to remain steadfast in their faith in Mānik-pir.

Conclusion

In examining the Islamic syncretistic tradition in Bengal, we hoped to raise and answer, directly or indirectly, some basic questions about the approach to an historical study in the process of Islamization in a regional setting, the growing and developing nature of Islamization as an historical phenomenon, and the changing meaning and implication of being a Muslim in the context of the believer's social and cultural mores. The study has made it possible to draw a few conclusions.

The conventional Islamist's concern to measure the progress of Islamization at a regional level by the yardstick of classical Islam merely reduces, as already discussed at length in the Introduction, a very creative and complex process of cultural interaction between an intrusive religion and an indigenous culture to a simple, uncritical, and subjective polarity between a sort of "true" or "original" Islam and its "popular" or "folk" aberration. A culture is no less a determinant in recasting and reformulating a religion than is a religion in modifying a culture. The social and cultural contexts of the believers are seminal factors in inter- and intra-regional variations in a religion. Islam in its Perso-Arabic attire failed to elicit any meaningful response from the masses of Bengali Muslims. Consequently, their cultural mediators had not only to pull down the language barricade but also to make Islamic tradition more meaningful to the Bengali converts in syncretistic and symbolic forms.

This leads to another significant conceptual issue calling

into question the adequacy of the prevailing concepts of great and little traditions as analytical tools to probe Islam in Bengal. The classical formulation of these concepts as applied to India, basically enunciated in the context of a "single" great tradition of Hinduism, seems clearly inadequate for our investigation of the Islamic phenomenon in Bengal. There the secondary or exogenous Islamic great tradition was unable to interact with the endogenous little traditions of the region, which had been culturally continuous with the primary or indigenous Hindu great tradition for centuries. This created conditions for the construction of an alternative syncretistic model of great tradition for Bengali Muslims, restoring thereby the broken continuity between the great and little traditions of those who became Muslims. Islam in Bengal, therefore, provided an uncommon paradigm of one religion's containing two great traditions juxtaposed to each other, one exogenous and classical, and the other endogenous and syncretistic. To use the more technical terms applied in the study of cultural change, the syncretistic model offered an "orthogenetic" response of the Bengalis to the challenge of Islam, while the adoption of the classical Islamic model represented a "heterogenetic" response to the same. In a case of contact between an indigenous and a foreign culture, it has been found that the response ranges between an imitative heterogenetic pattern of total adoption of the foreign model and an orthogenetic pattern of utilizing the external stimulas to generate a momentum of change essentially from within on the basis of the indigenous culture.[1]

The interrelationship between syncretism and Islamization emerges as another significant issue from this study. The syn-

[1] For a conceptual analysis of these seminal issues involved in a process of cultural change, see G. E. von Gruenbaum, "The Concept of Cultural Classicism" in his *Modern Islam: The Search for Cultural Identity* (New York, 1964), pp. 116-22; also D. Kopf, *British Orientalism and Bengal Renaissance*, pp. 287-88.

cretistic developments in Islam have been generally condemned, particularly at the level of religious "purists," fundamentalists, and revivalists, as hindrances to Islamization. Viewed in its historical context, Islamic syncretism in Bengal would seem, on the contrary, a necessary stage in the progress of Islamization in the country. It has been our purpose to explore the making of the syncretistic tradition by the conscious efforts of the Bengali Muslim cultural mediators, with a view to disseminating Islam in a more locally familiar and meaningful form. This tradition continued to dominate the religious-cultural perception of the Bengali Muslim masses until the emergence of vigorous and even militant Islamic revivalist and purificatory movements in Bengal, as elsewhere within and without India, since the beginning of the nineteenth century, which sharpened the Islamic consciousness among Bengali Muslims, strongly condemned the syncretistic tradition, and urged suppression of non-Islamic accretions. Until the revivalist challenge the syncretistic tradition performed a significant historical function in the dissemination of Islam in Bengal, and was not, therefore, an antithesis of Islamization but a necessary stage in its historical development in Bengal. Syncretism remained as integral to the process of Islamization in the land as the subsequent revivalist, reformist, and fundamentalist contributions. It cannot also be overlooked that the purificatory ideas did not find an easy acceptance, as evidenced by a significant volume of popular *punthi* literature in the late nineteenth and early twentieth centuries, mounting a strong counterattack.[2] Also, sundry sources, coming down well into the present century, attest to the persistence of traditional beliefs and practices among Bengali Muslims.[3] Even eight years after the Partition of 1947 a

[2] *Supra*, Preface, note 16.

[3] *Ibid.* Cf. ". . . despite the reformists' eloquent claims, the rural Muslims continued with their older way of life to a marked degree. . . ." "The reformist succeeded in 'converting' only a fraction of the total Muslim population to

survey of popular beliefs among some Muslims of then East Pakistan notes:

> The life of the average Hindu cultivator is not so colourless as [that] of his Muslim counterpart. . . . At every important festival they [the Hindus] would arrange for drama (dramas which relate the stories of the Ramayana, Mahabharata, or the life of some great Hindu saint, such as Shree Chaitanya, Nityananda, etc.). Carnivals, singing, dancing, poetic fights, sports, exhibitions, shows, and many such other amusements would be arranged. The Muslim cultivator is deprived of such amusements, because they are bida'ats (or innovations) according to the Mullah's opinion. But human nature craves for amusements, so some would steal to the neighbouring Hindu village when such amusements have been arranged. But soon the "crime" would also be detected by the Mullah. The Mullah would call the meeting of the village elders and severely censure the offenders. The offenders would ask pardon and promise not to do so again, through [sic] it is almost certain that they would repeat the "crime."[4]

Finally, the Bengal phenomenon raises very fundamental questions about the meaning of Islamization. Who is a Muslim? What does it mean to "become" a Muslim? Is Islamization conterminous with "conversion"? Does conversion refer to an instant spiritual illumination? In our study we have sought answers to these questions in the context of Bengal. We have noted that conversion in Bengal, as elsewhere in South Asia, involved more an immediate "change of fellowship" than a spiritual experience. Reasons other than spiritual largely underlay man's conversion so that "becoming" a Muslim in a spiritual sense, was a gradual process, "a slow accretion of minor changes" and "not . . . a sudden, total, overwhelming illumination but a slow turning toward a new light,"

their point of view; the vast majority remained steadfastly opposed to any new dogma and faithful to the traditional system. . . ." "The practices condemned as heretical by the fundamentalist reformers a hundred years ago were found persisting at every level of Bengali Muslim society as late as the 1960s." R. Ahmed, *Bengal Muslims*, pp. 69, 70, 71.

[4] A.K.N. Karim, "Popular Beliefs among Muslims," pp. 39-40.

as observed in the case of the Islamization of Indonesia.[5] The Islamic identity of the Bengali converts acquired changing attributes in time, and may be seen to have developed in three broad stages. In its earliest stage, Islamization was no more than a change of commensal and connubial relations of the converts in a social sense, while, culturally, the dichotomy between exogenous Islamic great tradition and endogenous little traditions of the converted masses broke the cultural continuum and arrested the cultural process. This, in the second stage of Islamization of the land, necessitated the emergence of the cultural mediators and the construction of a syncretistic model of Islamic great tradition with a view to restoring the broken continuity. The syncretistic model of Islamization held its ground until in the third stage of Islamization, beginning from the early nineteenth century, the fundamentalist and the revivalist forces in Islam, stirred by a massive combination of diverse factors, sharply focussed on the need for a deeper Islamic consciousness, and launched a vigorous assault on the syncretistic and acculturated tradition. Bengal's Muslims were gradually drawn toward the heterogenetic model of classical Islam as an answer to the whole range of religious and secular problems and challenges facing the community in contemporaneous Bengal, with the consequence of widening the hiatus that already existed between the exogenous Islam and the indigenous Bengali culture and of deepening the crisis of Bengali Muslim identity.

[5] C. Geertz, *Islam Observed*, pp. 97, 105.

Bibliography

GENERAL NOTES

Bengali Muslim literature of the traditional kind in verse, both manuscripts and prints, generally known as the *punthi-sāhitya* (see *supra*, Preface, note 12) constitutes the basic primary source of this study, as noted at the beginning of the text (*supra*, p. 8). It is also noted that the manuscript materials belong primarily to Munshi A. Karim's Collection in the Dacca University Library (DMS). Muslim Bengali manuscripts are conspicuous by their significant absence from the Bengali manuscript holdings of various libraries such as Bangiya Sāhitya-Pariṣat (Calcutta), Asiatic Society of Bengal (Calcutta), Calcutta University, National Library of India (Calcutta), and Viśva-bhārati (Śāntiniketan). Among the libraries in India and Bangladesh, the National Library, Calcutta, has the best collection of the later *punthis* in print. But the British Library (formerly the British Museum), Oriental Section, and the India Office Library, London, offer together a richer collection of the same material. In the private collection of a local antiquarian, Mr. Kālidās Datta, of Jaynagar-Majilpur in the district of 24-Parganas, West Bengal, I had the good fortune of discovering a few popular folk-ballads on the *pir* tradition, which I have designated as "JMS" in my study.

Naturally enough, I have tried to draw upon sundry other sources, non-Bengali or/and non-literary, wherever possible. In a study of this nature one can ill afford to be too dogmatic about the nature of primary sources. Consequently, some relatively later and even fairly recent observations and findings with close bearing on the question of the syncretistic tradition have been profitably examined and included in the primary sources. Further, some recent works containing edited materials of primary importance have been used as both primary and secondary sources, as the case demands.

PRIMARY SOURCES

I. Bengali

A. RELIGIOUS AND SECULAR LITERATURE

Manuscript

1. Mythological—Legendary—Fictional—Historical

Abd al-Ālim. *Muhammad Hanifār Ladāi*. DMS 101: sl 369. This particular work has also been attributed to Abd al-Hakim, see DMS 386: sl 365. The confusion relating to this work is also evidenced by a colophon in the former ms., giving the name Abd al-Halim rather than Abd al-Ālim.
Abd al-Hakim. *Yusuf-Zulaikha*. DMS 425: sl 15.
———. *Lālmati—Saif al-Muluk*. DMS 321: sl 448.
Abd al-Nabi. *Vijay-Hamza*. DMS 342: sl 2.
Ādam Faqir and Zain al-Ābidin. *Abu Samār Puthi*. DMS 620: sl 6.
Ali Ahmad. *Sarup [Svarup?]-er Ladāi*. DMS 413: sl 548.
Amānullāh. *Muhammad Hanifār Ladāi*. DMS 175: sl 368.
Anonymous. *Bibi Hanifir Yuddha*. DMS 535: sl 332.
———. *Bibi Fātimār Vivāha*. DMS 619-20: sl 367a.
———. *Mallikāzādār Puthi*. DMS 359: sl 379.
———. *Imām-churi*. DMS 65: sl 18.
Ārif. *Lālmaner Qissā*. DMS 542: sl 450.
Dayāl. *Gorkha-vijay*. DMS 602: sl 115. This work on the Hindu *nāth-guru*, Gorakṣa-nāth, was sponsored by the poet's patron, Safar Ali.
Donā Ghāzi. *Saif al-Muluk-Badi al-Jamāl*. DMS 319: sl 524.
Faqir Gharib Allāh. *Yusuf-Zulaikha*. DMS 557: sl 17. Also in print, Calcutta, 1884.
———. *Sonābhān*. DMS 570: sl 538. Also printed later.
Jafar. *Shahid-i Karbalā*. DMS 615: sl 459.
Jayaraddi [Zāhir al-Din?]. *Mānik-pirer Jahurā [Zāhir?] Nāma*. Viśva-bhārati Ms. 216: sl 936.
Lengtā Faqir. *Satya-pir Pānchāli*. DMS 462: sl 539.
Manir al-Din. *Mahāru-sundari o Munirer Qissā*. DMS 505: sl 380.
Mardan. *Nasib Nāma*. DMS 44: sl 238.
Muhammad Akbar. *Gulshanbarer Upākhyān*. DMS (unnumbered): sl 585.
Muhammad Ali Rajā. *Tamimgolāl-Chatunnasilāl*. DMS 54: sl 164.
———. *Misri Jamāl*. DMS 284: sl 381.

Muhammad Chuhār. *Azab-shāh—Samarokh*. DMS 358: sl 11.
Muhammad Khān. *Maqtal Husain*. DMS 380: sl 353.
———. *Muhammad Hanifār Ladāi*. DMS 286: sl 357. Appears to be a mere part of *Maqtal Husain*.
Muhammad Muqim. *Gul-i Bakāwali*. DMS 417: sl 97.
Muhammad Naqi. *Tuti Nāma*. DMS 389: sl 170. This Bengali version of the Persian translation from the original Sanskrit was at the instance of a local Hindu *zamindār* of Chittagong.
Muhammad Nawāzish Khān. *Gul-i Bakāwali*. DMS 427: sl 98.
Muhammad Sultān. *Zahar Mohra*. DMS 130: sl 129.
Muhammad Yaqub. *Jang Nāma*. DMS 653: sl 149.
Pandit Musharraf Ali Murādpuri. *Rasa-manjari*. DMS 704: sl 435.
Parāwal [Parāgal?]. *Shāh-parir Qissā*. DMS 649: sl 458.
Sābirid [Shāh Barid?] Khān. *Rasul-vijay*. DMS 377: sl 434.
Saiyid Alāwal. *Sapta Paikār*. DMS 647: sl 499.
———. *Saif al-Muluk—Badi al-Jamāl*. DMS 179: sl 522.
———. *Sikandar Nāma*. DMS 532: sl 531.
Saiyid Hamza. *Jaiguner Puthi*. DMS 135: sl 147.
———. *Amir Hamzār Qissā*. DMS 711: sl 10.
Saiyid Muhammad Akbar Ali. *Zeb al-Muluk—Samarokh*. DMS 508: sl 138.
Saiyid Muhammad Nasir. *Benāzir—Badr-i Munir*. DMS 364: sl 334.
Saiyid Sultān. *Nabi-vamśa*. Several fragmented mss. of the work have been consulted.
Saiyid Sultān. *Shab-i Mirāj*. DMS 433: sl 490.
———. *Iblis Nāma*. DMS 269: sl 36.
———. *Wafāt-i Rasul*. DMS 138: sl 41. Also ed. by A. Ahmad. Noakhali, 1356 BS/1949.
Shāh Muhammad Saghir. *Yusuf—Zulaikha*. DMS 125: sl 12.
Shāhdat Allāh. *Hatim Tai*. DMS 340: sl 566.
Shaikh Hābil. *Mānik-pirer Gān*. JMS.
Shaikh Sadi. *Gada—Mallikār Puthi*. DMS 573: sl 106.
Shaikh Sherbāz Chaudhuri. *Fakkar Nāma bā Mallikār Hazār Suwāl*. DMS 367: sl 312.
Shaikh Tanu. *Fātimār Surat Nāma*. DMS 133: sl 302.
Sharif Shāh. *Lālmati—Saif al-Muluk*. DMS 47: sl 445.
Tamizi. *Lālmati—Tāj al-Muluk*. DMS 651: sl 451.
Zain al-Din. *Rasul-vijay*. DMS 494: sl 423. Also ed. by A. Sharif

in *Sāhitya Patrikā* (Bengali Dept., Dacca University), VII, no. 2, pp. 115-89.

2. Mystical—Esoterical

Abd al-Hakim. *Shihāb al-Din Nāma*. DMS 406: sl 246.

———. *Nur Nāma*. DMS 299: sl 231.

———. *Chāri Maqām-bhed*. DMS 408: sl 247.

Ali Rajā alias Kānu Faqir. *Jnān-sāgar*. DMS 146b: sl 9. Also ed. by Munshi A. Karim. Calcutta: *Sāhitya-Pariṣat Granthāvali*, no. 59, 1324 BS/1917. For a later edn., see Sharif, A., *Bānglār Sufi Sāhitya*, pp. 365-532.

———. *Āgam*. DMS 146a: sl 9. Also ed. by A. Sharif, *ibid.*, pp. 323-62. This is not a separate work but the first part of *Jnān-sāgar*.

Anonymous. *Darbeshi Puthi*. DMS 659: sl 213.

Bālak Faqir. *Chautisār Puthi*. DMS 613: sl 118.

Dayāl. *Jnān-chautisā*. DMS 603: sl 116.

Hāji Muhammad. *Nur Jamāl*. DMS 374: sl 260. Also ed. by A. Sharif, *Sufi Sāhitya*, pp. 139-209.

Mahsin Ali. *Maqām-Manziler Kathā*. DMS 544: sl 387.

Qamar Ali. *Padāvali*. DMS 301: sl 265.

Saiyid Murtaza. (Untitled ms. catalogued as *Yoga-Qalandar*.) DMS 547: sl 394. Also ed. by A. Sharif, *Sufi Sāhitya*, pp. 94-116.

Saiyid Sultān. *Jnān-pradip*. DMS 365: sl 152.

———. *Jnān-chautisā*. DMS 366: sl 153. Also ed. by A. Sharif, *Sufi Sāhitya*, pp. 14-20.

Shaikh Chānd. *Tālib Nāma*. DMS 694: sl 171. Also ed. in *ibid.*, pp. 43-86.

———. *Hara-Gauri Samvād*. DMS 559: sl 556. Also ed. in *ibid.*, pp. 27-40.

Shaikh Faiz Allāh. *Rāg-mālā*. DMS 545: sl 403.

Shaikh Mansur. *Sirr Nāma*. DMS 569: sl 460. Also ed. by A. Sharif, *Sufi Sāhitya*, pp. 242-307.

3. Scriptural—Liturgic—Didactic

Abd Allāh. *Nasihat Nāma*. DMS 403: sl 245.

Āin al-Din. (untitled). DMS 668: sl 576.

Akbar Ali. *Hadither Kathā*. DMS 149: sl 561.

Ali Rajā alias Kānu Faqir. *Sirāj Qulub*. DMS 388: sl 203.

Anonymous. *Nikah-mangal*. DMS 650: sl 573.

———. *Nasihat Nāma*. DMS 650: sl 573.

Ata Allāh. *Mufid al-Mumenin*. DMS 638: sl 176.

Azmat Ali. *Namāzer Kitāb*. DMS 683: sl 242.
Azmat Allāh. *Sufi Sanā-Allāhr Sifat Nāma*. DMS 404: sl 126.
Bālak Faqir. *Faid al-Muqtadi*. DMS 697: sl 307.
Faqir Asghar Ali. *Hadith-vāni*. DMS 662: sl 557.
Khwandkār Abd al-Karim. *Hazār Masāil*. DMS 109: sl 569.
———. *Dullā Majlis*. DMS 323: sl 215.
Khwandkār Nasr Allāh Khān. *Musār Suwāl*. DMS 68: sl 338.
———. *Hidāyat al-Islām*. DMS 689: sl 565.
———. *Sharia Nāma*. *MBS*, pp. 175-76.
Lokmān Ali. *Hadith-kalam-vāni*. DMS 663: sl 560.
Muhammad Ali. *Hairat al-Fiqh*. DMS 646: sl 558. A Bengali work written in Arabic script.
Muhammad Fasih. *Munājāt*. DMS 87: sl 8.
Muhammad Jān. *Namāz-māhātmya*. DMS 187: sl 195.
Muhammad Jāni. *Namāz-māhātmya*. DMS 189: sl 239. This appears no different from Muhammad Jān's work of the same title. Hence either Jān or Jāni is a copyist's confusion.
Munshi Gharib Allāh (of Dacca). *Nek-bibir Bayān*. DMS 636: sl 174.
Muhammad Qāsim. *Hitopadeś*. DMS 140: sl 559.
Muhammad Zinat. *Jagadiśvar Stotra*. DMS 655: sl 157.
Najib and Musharraf. *Ali-band*. DMS 76: sl 7.
Qāzi Badi al-Din. *Qaidāni Kitāb*. DMS 541: sl 83.
———. *Sifat-i Imān*. DMS 133: sl 121.
Saiyid Nāsir. *Sirāj Sabil bā Panther Chirāgh*. DMS 600: sl 536.
Saiyid Nur al-Din. *Musār Suwāl*. DMS 188: sl 196.
———. *Hitopadeś bā Daykāt*. DMS 387: sl 202.
Shaikh Muttalib. *Kifāyat al-Musalli*. DMS 578: sl 69.
———. *Qaidāni Kitāb*. DMS 112: sl 82.
Shaikh Parān. (untitled). DMS 193: sl 92. This untitled ms. is called *Kaidāni Kitāb* in *DCBM* (p. 80), and *Nasihat Nāmā* in *MBS* (pp. 163-64).
Sulaimān. *Nasihat Nāma*. DMS 59: sl 32.

4. Cosmogonical—Ontological

Abd al-Hakim. *Nur Nāma*. DMS 70: sl 232.
———. *Nur-farāmish Nāma*. DMS 519: sl 233. These two mss. attributed to the same author do not seem to be intended as separate works.
Diwān Ali. *Nur Nāma*. DMS 546: sl 404.

Mir Muhammad Shafi. *Nur-Qindil* or *Nur Jamāl*. DMS 143: sl 236. Also ed. by A. Sharif, *Sufi Sāhitya*, pp. 216-34.
Muhammad Hāri. *Sriṣti-pattan*. DMS 82: sl 537.

5. *Eschatological*

Ghulām Maula. *Sultān Jamjama*. DMS 12: sl 546.
Hāji Ali. *Maut Nāma*. DMS 664: sl 384.
Muhammad Qāsim. *Sultān Jamjama*. DMS 343: sl 542.
Saiyid Nur al-Din. *Qiyāmat Nāma*. DMS 526: sl 81.
———. *Rahat al-Qulub*. DMS 692: sl 437. These two mss. are only two different segments of one large work.

6. *Astrological and Superstitious*

Abd al-Ghani. *Fāl Nāma*. DMS 144: sl 305.
Husain Faqir. *Rāśi-gananār Puthi*. DMS 49: sl 38.
Muzammil. *Saad Nāma*. DMS 195: sl 119.
———. *Niti-śāstra-vārtā*. DMS 214: sl 237. Also ed. by A. Sharif. Dacca: Bānglā Academy, 1965.

In Print

1. *Mythological—Legendary—Fictional—Historical*

Abd al-Karim. *Kālu—Ghāzi—Champāvati*. Calcutta: Ghausiya Library, n.d.
Abd Allāh. *Shāh Madārer Jang Nāma*. Calcutta: the author, 1872.
Daulat Qāzi. *Sati Maynā o Lor-Chandrāni*. Ed. by S. N. Ghoṣāl in *Sāhitya Prakāśikā* (Śāntiniketan), pt. 1, 1362 BS/1955.
Daulat Wazir Bahrām Khān. *Laili—Majnu*. Ed. by A. Sharif. Dacca: Bangla Academy, 2nd edn. 1966.
Faqir Gharib Allāh. *Amir Hamzār Puthi*. Calcutta, 1867.
———. *Jang Nāma*. Calcutta, 1880.
———. *Saif al-Muluk—Badi al-Jamāl*. Calcutta.
Hayāt Mahmud. *Ambiyā-vāni*. Ed. by M. Islām, *Kavi Heyāt Māmud* [Hayāt Mahmud]. Rajshahi: Rajshahi U.P., 1961.
———. *Jang Nāma*. Ed., *ibid.*
Jayānanda. *Chaitanya-mangal*. Ed. by N. N. Basu. Calcutta: Bangiya Sāhitya-Pariṣat, 1312 BS/1905.
Kriṣnarām-dās. *Rāy-mangal*. Ed. by S. N. Bhattāchārya. Bardhamān: *Sāhitya-sabhā Prakāśikā*, no. 4, 1956.
Mālādhar Basu. *Śri-Kriṣna-vijay*. Ed. by K. N. Mitra. Calcutta: Calcutta U.P., 1944.
Mānik-rām-gānguli. *Dharma-mangal*. Ed. by B. Sānnyāl, *Mānik Gānguli o Dharma-mangal*. Calcutta, 1906.

Mukunda-rām. *Kavi-kankan Chandi*. 2 vols. Ed. by D. C. Sen *et al*. Calcutta: Calcutta U.P., 1924.
Munshi Abd al-Samād and Munshi Asir al-Din. *Hazrat Ali o Vir-Hanumāner Ladāi*. Calcutta: A. Ahmad, 1908.
Munshi Amir al-Din. *Lakṣmi—Śanir Jhagdā*. Calcutta: M. Q. Ali, 1313 BS/1916.
Munshi Asir al-Din. See above, Munshi Abd al-Samād.
Munshi Yaqub. *Jang Nāmār Puthi*. Calcutta, 1867.
Saiyid Alāwal. *Tuhfa*. Ed. by A. Sharif, *Alāwal-birachita Tohfa*. Dacca: Bengali Dept., Dacca Univ., 1958.
———. *Padmāvati*. Ed. by S. A. Ahsan. Dacca: Student Ways, 1968.
Saiyid Hamza. *Madhu-mālati*. Ed. by S. A. Ahsan. Chittagong: Bānglā Academy and Baighar, 1380 BS/1973.
Shafi al-Din. *Jang Nāma Puthi*. Calcutta, 1877.
Shaikh Faiz Allāh. *Gorakṣa-vijay*. Ed. by Munshi A. Karim. Calcutta: *Bangiya Sāhitya-Pariṣat Granthāvali*, no. 64, 1324 BS/1917.
Shuqur Mahmud. *Pānchāli* [on Mānik-chandra—Maynāmati legend]. Calcutta: G. Rasul, 1889.
Vijay-gupta. *Padmā-purān*. Ed. by B. K. Bhattāchārya. Bariśāl: Vāni-niketan.
Vipra-dās. *Manasā-vijay*. Ed. by S. Sen. Calcutta: Asiatic Society of Bengal, 1953.
Vrindāvan-dās. *Chaitanya-bhāgavat*. Ed. by S. N. Basu. Calcutta: Dev Sāhitya Kutir, 1955.
Zain al-Din. "Bada-khān Ghāzir Gān." Ed. by K. Datta in *Bhāratiya Lok-yān* (Calcutta Univ.), III, nos. 1-2, 1963.

2. *Mystical—Esoteric*

Abd al-Rahmān. *Sharf al-Imān*. Dacca, 1929.
Ālam. "Pada" in *Sāhitya-Pariṣat Patrikā* (Calcutta), no. 2, 1314 BS/1907.
Baduh Shāh alias Ghulām Imām. *Jalsāh Nāma*. Calcutta, 1873.
Bhadra, J. (ed.). *Gaud-pada-tarangini*. Calcutta: *Sāhitya-Pariṣat Granthāvali*, no. 10, 1310 BS/1903.
Muhammad Hamid-Allāh Khān. *Trān-path*. Chittagong: M.M.A. Husain, 1277 BS/1870.
Muhammad Mansur al-Din. *Hārāmani*. A monumental collection of Bengali folk-songs. 7 vols. Dacca: M. Kamāl al-Din, 1337-74 BS/1930-67.

Sharif, A. (ed.). *Madhya-yuger Rāg-tāl Nāma*. Dacca: Bānglā Academy, 1967.

———. *Bānglār Sufi Sāhitya*. Dacca: Bānglā Academy, 1969.

——— and Hāi, M. A. (eds.). *Madhya-yuger Bānglā Giti-kavitā*. Dacca: Maula Bros., rev. and enlgd. edn., 1973.

3. Scriptural—Liturgic—Didactic

Anonymous. *Saif al-Mumenin*. Calcutta, 1875.

Abbās Ali. *Misbāh al-Muslimin*. Dacca, 1871.

———. *Gulzār-i Islām*. Dacca, 1881.

Abd al-Aziz. *Tariqa-i Mahammadiyah*. Calcutta, 1283 BS/1876.

Abd al-Ghani. *Jauhar-i Maknun*. Dacca, 1880.

Abd al-Hamid Khān. *Sār-samgraha*. Maimansing, 1878.

Abd al-Jabbār. *Islām Dharma Parichay*. Calcutta, 1906.

———. *Islām-chitra o Samāj-chitra*. Gaffargaon, 2nd edn., 1914.

Abd al-Qadir. *Akhbār-i Pir-i Najdi*. Calcutta, 1874.

Afzal Ali. *Nasihat Nāma*. Ed. by A. Sharif. Dacca: Bānglā Academy, 1969.

Hābil al-Din. *Radd-i Hanafi o Mazhab-darpan*. Calcutta, 1925.

Hayāt Mahmud. *Hita-jnān-vāni*. Ed. by M. Islām, *Kavi Heyāt Māmud*. Rajshahi: Rajshahi U.P., 1961.

———. *Sarva-bhed-vāni*. Ed., *ibid*.

Māl-i Muhammad. *Hāl Ākhir-i Zamāna*. Dacca, 1876.

———. *Tanbih al-Nisā*. Calcutta, 1876.

Muhammad Abd al-Karim. *Irshād-i Khaliqiyah*. Calcutta, 1903.

Muhammad Ābidin. *Dharma-prachārini*. Calcutta, 1875.

Muhammad Basr Biswas. *Lakṣmipur Hanafi o Muhammadider Bahās*. Calcutta, 1921.

Muhammad Haidār Chaudhuri. *Ahwāl-i Zamāna*. Sylhet: the author, 1907.

Muhammad Imdād Ali. *Ku-riti Varjan*. Bariśāl: the author, 1922.

Muhammad Khair Allāh. *Sirājganjer Bahās*. Khulna: S. A. Wahid, 1926.

Muhammad Khān. *Satya-Kali Vivād Samvād*. Ed. by A. Sharif in *Sāhitya Patrikā* (Dacca: Bengali Dept., Dacca Univ.), III, no. 1.

Muhammad Kobad Ali. *Nabābpure Hanafi-Muhammadidiger Bahās*. Calcutta, 1923.

Muhammad Mallik. *Akhbār al-Marifa*. Calcutta, 1283 BS/1876.

Muhammad Maqsud Ali. *Narendrapurer Bahāse Bidati Dalan*. Narendrapur: the author, 1924.

Muhammad Naim al-Din. *Zubdat al-Masāil*. 7th edn. Karatiya: the author, 1901.
———. *Adillāh-i Hanafiyah. Radd-i Lāmazhabiyah*. Karatiya, 1904.
Muhammad Ruh al-Amin. *Dafāyel-i Mufsadin*. Calcutta, 1925.
Muhammad Tāj al-Din. *Khulāsat al-Nisā*. Calcutta, 1287 BS/1880.
Muhammad Tāj al-Islām. *Tāj al-Mumenin*. Rangpur, 1916.
Muhammad Yaqub Ali. *Jāter Badāi*. Simuliya: K. Anjumān, 1926.
———. *Musalmāner Jāti-bhed*. Chātuganja: the author, 1927.
Munshi Nāsir al-Din. *Zalālat al-Fuqrah*. Calcutta, 1878.
Nur al-Husain Qāsimpuri. *Muslim Jāti-tattva*. Bogra: Musalmān Sāhitya Samiti Karyālay, 1926.
Sakhi al-Din Ahmad. *Islām-pradip*. Calcutta, 1907.
Shāh Muhammad Kavirāj. *Del Śikṣā*. Calcutta, 1914.
Shaikh Samir al-Din. *Bidār al-Ghāfilan*. Calcutta, 1286 BS/1879.
Yusuf Ali. *Fatwā Radd-i Bida*. Calcutta: the author, 1323 BS/1916.

4. *Cosmogonical—Ontological*

Rāmāi Pandit. *Śunya-purān*. Ed. by C. C. Banerji. Calcutta, 1929. Also ed. by N. N. Basu. Calcutta: Bangiya Sāhitya-Pariṣat, 1314 BS/1907.
Shaikh Zāhid. *Ādya-parichay*. Ed. by M. M. Chaudhuri. Rajshahi: Vārendra Research Museum, 1964.

5. *Eschatological*

Mir Faiz Allāh. *Sultān Jamjama*. Ed. by A. Ghafur. Dacca: Bānglā Academy, 1969.

6. *Astrological—Superstitious*

Ghulām Farid. *Saad Nāma*. Calcutta: the author, 1878.
Muhammad Waiz al-Din. *Islāmiya-mantra*. 2 pts. Calcutta, 1895 and 1910.

7. *Miscellaneous*

A. Qādir and R. Karim. *Kāvya-mālancha*. Calcutta, 1945.

B. HISTORICAL: REGIONAL AND LOCAL ACCOUNTS AND NOTES

Bandopādhyāy, B. C. *Koch-bihār Rājyer Sankṣipta Vivaran*. 2nd edn. Calcutta, 1291 BS/1884.
Bandopādhyāy, R. D. *Bānglār Itihās*. 2 vols. Calcutta: Bengal Medical Library, 1914 and 1917.
———. "Sapta-grām," *Sāhitya-Pariṣat Patrikā* (Calcutta), no. 1, 1315 BS/1908.

Basu, J. C. *Medinipurer Itihās*. Calcutta, 1346 BS/1939.
Basu, N. N. *Banger Jātiya Itihās*. Calcutta: the author, 1900-1914.
———. *Bardhamāner Itikathā*. Calcutta: D. N. Mitra, 1915.
Chakravarti, R. K. *Gauder Itihās*. 2 pts. Pt. 1: *Rangpur*. Rangpur Sāhitya-Pariṣat, 1909. Pt. 2: *Māldaha*. A. A. Khān, 1910.
Chakravarti, R. K. and Dās, A. M. *Sandviper Itihās*. Noakhali: J. K. Chakravarti, 1923.
Chattopādhyāy, H. M. *Vikrampur*. 3 vols. Vikrampur: D. Chattopādhyāy, 1931.
Chaudhuri, A.A.A.K. *Koch-bihārer Itihās*. Vol. 1. Kochbihār: Kochbihār Govt., 1936.
Chaudhuri, A. C. *Śri-hatter Itivritta*. 2 pts. Silchar: Sarasvati Library, 1317 BS and 1324 BS/1910 and 1917.
Dāsgupta, M. M. *Śri-hatter Itihās*. Sylhet, 1903.
Gupta, A. C. *Hugli bā Dakṣin Rādh*. Pt. 1. Calcutta: L. M. Pāl, 1321 BS/1914.
Gupta, R. K. *Bānglār Itihās*. 2 vols. Calcutta: Hindu Machine Press, 1902.
Gupta, Y. N. *Vikrampurer Itihās*. Calcutta: Bhattāchārya & Sons, 1316 BS/1909.
———. *Vikrampurer Vivaran*. Dacca: Nawābpur Albert Library, 1919.
Kundu, H. D. "Śerpurer Itihās," *Sāhitya-Pariṣat Patrikā*, VII, additional no., 1307 BS/1910.
Majumdār, K. N. *Maimansimher Vivaran*. Calcutta: Sānnyal & Co., 1311 BS/1904.
———. *Maimansimher Sahachar*. Calcutta, 1908.
———. *Maimansimher Itihās*. Calcutta, 1312 BS/1906.
Majumdār, R. "Bariśāler Grāmya-giti," *Sāhitya-Pariṣat Patrikā*, XIV, no. 2, 1314 BS/1907.
Mallik, K. N. *Nadiyā Kāhini*. Rānāghāt: Nadiyā Kāhini Prachār Bibhāg, 2nd edn., 1912.
Maulik, A. K. *Ātiyā Parganār Itihās*. Mahedā, Maimansimha: G. M. Maulik, 1323 BS/1916.
Mitra, S. C. *Yaśohar-Khulnār Itihās*. 2 vols. Calcutta: Chakravarti, Chatterji & Co., 1914 and 1922.
Pati, R. N. *Keśiyādi*. Medinipur: B. C. Dās, 1323 BS/1916.
Putātunda, V. *Chandra-dviper Itihās*. Bariśāl: Sāhitya-Pariṣat, 1320 BS/1913.
———. *Nutan Banger Purātan Kāhini*. *Ibid.*, 1323 BS/1916.

Rāy, A. N. *Faridpurer Itihās*. 2 pts. Pt. 1. Calcutta: B. N. Pālit, 1316 BS/1909. Pt. 2. Calcutta: J. N. Rāy, 1328 BS/1921.
Rāy, K. C. *Bākharganjer Itihās*. Bariśāl, 1895.
Rāy, K. K. "Maimansimher sādhāran grihastha Musalmān paribāre anusthita kayekti sinni o āchār-niyamer vivaran," *Sāhitya-Pariṣat Patrikā*, no. 39, 1339 BS/1932.
Rāy, S. C. *Suvarna-grāmer Itihās*. Calcutta, 1891.
Sen, P. C. *Bagurār Itihās*. Rangpur: Bangiya Sāhitya-Pariṣat, 1912.
Sen, R. K. *Bāklā*. Kirtipāśā, Bariśāl: S. K. Sen, 1915.
Sen-sharma, K. P. *Bānglār Itihās (Nawābi Āmal)*. Calcutta, 1308 BS/1901.
Siddiqi, M. A. *Sirājganjer Itihās*. Sirājganj: Pābnā, 1322 BS/1915.

C. MISCELLANEOUS

Abd al-Ghafur Siddiqi. "Musalmān o Bānglā sāhitya," *Sāhitya-Pariṣat Patrikā*, no. 2, 1323 BS/1916.
Abd al-Majid. "Bānglā-bhāṣā o Musalmān," *Moyājjin* (Calcutta), II, nos. 9-10, 1337 BS/1930, pp. 191-94.
Abd al-Mālik Chaudhuri. "Banga sāhitye Śrihatter Musalmān," *Al-Islām* (Calcutta), II, nos. 6-7, 1323 BS/1916, pp. 329-36, 379-86.
Hamid Ali. "Uttar Banger Musalmān sāhitya," *Bāsanā* (Rangpur), II, no. 1, 1316 BS/1909.
Islām Prachārak. "Samāj-kālimā," editorial, II, no. 2, 1299 BS/1892.
Khadim al-Islām Bangabāsi. "Bāngālir mātri-bhāṣā," *Al-Islām*, I, no. 7, 1322 BS/1915.
Manir al-Zamān Islāmābādi. "Anjumān-i ulamā o samāj samskār," *Al-Islām*, V, no. 3, 1326 BS/1919.
———. "Samāj-samskār," *ibid.*, no. 8.
Maulawi Shafi al-Din Ahmad. "Ābhijātya gaurav (Ashrāf-Ātraf)." *Sāmya-vādi* (Calcutta), I, no. 1, 1329 BS/1922, pp. 29-30.
Muhammad Maiz al-Rahmān. "Samāj-chitra," *Al-Islām*, V, no. 5, 1326 BS/1919.
Nur al-Imān. "Bangiya Musalmān bhāi-bahiner khidmate Nur al-Imāner āpil," editorial, I, no. 3, 1307 BS/1900.
Saiyid Imdād Ali. "Ashrāf-Ātraf," *Saogāt* (Calcutta), VII, no. 5, 1336 BS/1929.
———. "Banga-bhāṣā o Musalmān," *Bangiya Musalmān-sāhitya Patrikā* (Calcutta), I, no. 2, 1325 BS/1918, pp. 79-87.

Sharif, A. (ed.). *Madhya-yuger Kāvya-samgraha*. Dacca: Bānglā Academy, 1369 BS/1962.

Tasaddak Ahmad. "Sabhā-patir abhibhāṣan," *Śikhā* (Dacca), I, 1333 BS/1926, pp. 7-16.

Wadud, K. A. "Bānglār Musalmāner kathā," in his *Śāśvata Banga* (Calcutta, 1951), pp. 95-112.

II. Persian—Arabic—Urdu

Abd al-Haq Dehlawi. *Akhbār al-Akhyār fi Asrār al-Abrār*. Delhi, 1332 AH/1914.

Abd al-Hamid Lahori. *Bādshāh Nāma*. *Bibliotheca Indica*, 1867.

Abd al-Latif. "Account," an English tr. by J. N. Sarkar in his "Journey to Bengal (in Persian)—1608-1609 by Abdul Latif," *Bengal Past and Present* (Calcutta), XXXV, April-June 1928, pp. 143-46.

Abd al-Rahmān Chishti. *Mirāt al-Asrār*. Asiatic Society of Bengal Ms. no. 264.

Abul Fazl. *Āin-i Akbari*. English tr. by H. Blochmann and H. S. Jarrett, 1873-1894, revised and annotated by J. N. Sarkar. Calcutta: Asiatic Society of Bengal, 1949.

Ali al-Hujwiri. *Kashf al-Mahjub*. English tr. by R. A. Nicholson. London, latest edn., 1967.

Al-Jili. *Insān al-Kāmil*. English tr. by J. W. Sweetman. 2 vols. London, 1929.

Azād al-Husain. *Naubahār-i Murshid Quli Khān*. English tr. by J. N. Sarkar in his *Bengal Nawabs*. Calcutta: Asiatic Society of Bengal, 1952.

Babur. *Tuzukh-i Baburi*. English tr. by A. S. Beveridge. 2 vols. London, 1921.

Ghulām Ali Azād Bilgrāmi. *Khazānah-i Āmirah*. 2nd edn. Kanpur: Newal Kishore, 1900.

Ghulām Husain Salim. *Riyāz al-Salātin*. *Bibliotheca Indica*, 1898. English tr. by M. A. Salām. Calcutta: Asiatic Society of Bengal, 1902.

Ghulām Husain Tabatabāi. *Siyar al-Mutaākhirin*. English tr. by H. Mustafa. 2 vols. Rev. edn. 4 vols. Calcutta: R. Cambray & Co., 1926.

Ibn Battutah. *Rehla*. English tr. by H. A. Gibb. London: Brockway Travellers' Series, 1929.

Jafar Sharif. *Qānun-i Islām*. English tr. by G. Herklot, ed. by W. Crooke. London: Oxford U.P., 1921.

Karam Ali. *Muzaffar Nāma*. English tr. by J. N. Sarkar in his *Bengal Nawabs*. Calcutta: Asiatic Soc. of Bengal, 1952.

Minhāj al-Din Sirāj. *Tabaqāt-i Nāsiri*. *Bibliotheca Indica*, 1864. English tr. by H. G. Raverty. Calcutta, 1881.

Mirzā Nathan. *Bahāristān-i Ghaybi*. English tr. by M. I. Borah. 2 vols. Gauhati (Assam): Govt. of Assam, 1936.

Muhammad Ghausi Mānduwi. *Gulzār-i Abrār*. Asiatic Soc. of Bengal Ms. no. 240.

Nizām al-Din Ahmad. *Tabaqāt-i Akbari*. 3 vols. English tr. by B. De and B. Prasad. Calcutta: Asiatic Soc. of Bengal, 1927, 1936 and 1939.

Pir Muhammad Shattāri. *Risālat al-Shuhdā*, being a biography of Shāh Ismāil. English tr. by G. H. Damant in his "Notes on Shāh Ismāil Ghāzi," *JASB*, XLIII, no. 1, 1874, pp. 215-39.

Shams-i Sirāj Afif. *Tārikh-i Firuzshāhi*. *Bibliotheca Indica*, 1890.

Shihāb al-Din Tālish. *Fathiya-i Ibriya*. English tr. by J. N. Sarkar in his *Studies in Aurangzeb's Reign*. Calcutta: M. C. Sarkar & Co., 1933. Also summary English tr. by H. Blochmann in *JASB*, XLI, no. 1, 1872, pp. 49-101.

Yahyā bin Ahmad Sirhindi. *Tārikh-i Mubārak Shāhi*. *Bibliotheca Indica*, 1931. English tr. by K. K. Bose. Baroda, 1932.

Yusuf Ali. *Ahwāl-i Mahabat Jang*. English tr. by J. N. Sarkar in his *Bengal Nawabs*. Calcutta: Asiatic Soc. of Bengal, 1952.

Ziyā al-Din Barani. *Tārikh-i Firuz Shāhi*. *Bibliotheca Indica*, 1862.

III. Sanskrit

Anonymous. *Śek [Shaikh]-śubhodaya*. Extremely doubtfully attributed to Halāyudha Miśra. Ed. and English tr. by S. Sen. Calcutta: Asiatic Society of Bengal, 1963.

Jayadeva. *Gita-Govinda*. Ed. and Bengali tr. by K. Rāy. Calcutta, 1929.

IV. English

A. OFFICIAL REPORTS AND ACCOUNTS

Adam W. *Reports on the State of Education in Bengal, 1835-1838*. Ed. by A. N. Basu. Calcutta: Calcutta U.P., 1941.

ADG. *Assam District Gazetteers*. Ed. by B. C. Allen. 3 vols. Calcutta, 1905. Vol. I: *Cachar*; Vol. II: *Sylhet*; Vol. III: *Goalpara*.

BDG. *Bengal District Gazetteers*. Calcutta: Bengal Secretariat Book Depot. *Burdwan*, ed. J.C.K. Peterson, 1910; *Bakarganj*, ed. J. C. Jack, 1918; *Mymensingh*, ed. F. A. Sachse, 1917; the following all ed. L.S.S. O'Malley: *Khulna*, 1907; *Bankura*, 1908; *Birbhum*, 1910; *Midnapur*, 1911; *Jessore*, 1912; *Hooghly*; *Murshidabad*, 1914; *24-Parganas*; *Pabna*, 1923; *Faridpur*, 1925; *Howrah*, ed. O'Malley and M. M. Chakravarty, 1909.

Beverley, H. *Report on the Census of Bengal*, 1872. Calcutta: Bengal Secretariat Press, 1872.

Bourdillon, J. A. *Report on the Census of Bengal*, 1881. *Ibid.*, 1882.

Buchanan-Hamilton, F. *A Geographical, Statistical and Historical Description of the District or Zila of Dinajpur, in the Province or Soubah of Bengal. Ibid.*, 1833.

Crawford, D. G. *A Brief History of the Hughli District. Ibid.*, 1902.

EBADG. *Eastern Bengal and Assam District Gazetteers*. Allahabad: the Pioneer Press. *Tippera*, ed. J. E. Webster, 1910; *Noakhali*, ed. J. E. Webster, 1911; *Bogra*, ed. J. N. Gupta, 1910; *Jalpaiguri*, ed. J. F. Gruning, 1911; *Rangpur*, ed. J. A. Vas, 1911.

Gait, E. A. *Report* [on Bengal]. *Census of India, 1901*, vol. VI, pt. 1. Calcutta: Bengal Secretariat Press, 1902.

———. *The Lower Provinces of Bengal and their Feudatories. Ibid.*

Glazier, E. G. *A Report on the District of Rungpore*. 2 vols. Calcutta: Govt. of India, 1873-1876.

Govt. of India. *File-Book regarding Ethnographical Researches*. India Office Ms. 532. Eur. E. 100.

———. *Return Idolatry (India). Ibid.* Ms. 499. Eur. D. 166.

Govt. of Pakistan. *East Pakistan: Land and People*. Karachi: the People of Pakistan Series no. 2, 1955.

Harington, J. H. *Harington's Analysis of the Bengal Regulations*. Calcutta, 1866.

Hunter, W. W. *A Statistical Account of Bagura*. 2 vols. London: Trubner, 1875-1877. Reprinted, Delhi: D. K. Publishers, 1975.

———. *Annals of Rural Bengal*. 7th edn. London: Smith & Elder, 1897; Calcutta: Indian Studies Past and Present, 1965.

——— (ed.). *The Imperial Gazetteer of India*. 9 vols. London: Trubner, 1881. Rev. 2nd edn., 1885-1887. 14 vols. Vol. VI: *The Indian Empire, Its History, People, and Products*. London:

Trubner, 1882. 3rd. edn. rev. and ed. by H. Risley *et al.* (See below Risley, H. *et al.*)

Jack, J. C. (?) *First Report on the Survey and Settlement Operations in the Faridpur District, 1904-1914*. Calcutta: Superintendent of Govt. Printing, 1916.

Khan, M. A. *Selection from Bengal Government Records on Wahhahi Trials, 1863-1870*. Dacca: Asiatic Society of Pakistan, 1961.

Martin, M. *The History, Antiquities, Topography, and Statistics of Eastern India*. Compiled from Buchanan Mss. in the East India House, 1807-1814. 3 vols. London: Wm. H. Allen, 1838. Vol. II: *Dinajepoor*. Vol. III: *Rungpoor*.

Mills, A.J.S. *Report on Serajgunge (in the Pabna District)*. Calcutta, 1852.

O'Donnell, C. J. *A Statistical Account of Bogra*. Calcutta, 1854.

Pemberton, J. J. *Geographical and Statistical Report of the District of Maldah*. Calcutta, 1854.

Ricketts, H. *A Report on the District of Midnapur and Cuttack*. Calcutta, 1858.

Risley, H. *The Tribes and Castes of Bengal*. 2 vols. Calcutta: Bengal Secretariat Press, 1891. Vol. I: *Ethnographic Glossary*. Vol. II: *Anthropometric Measurements*.

——— *et al.* (eds.). *The Imperial Gazetteer of India*. 3rd and rev. edn. of W. W. Hunter's (see above Hunter, W. W.). Oxford: Clarendon Press, 1907-1909. New rev. edn. 26 vols. 1931.

Sherwill, J. L. *A Geographical and Statistical Report of the Dinajpur District*. Calcutta, 1865.

Smyth, M. R. *Statistical and Geographical Reports of the District of 24-Parganas*. Calcutta, 1857.

Sutherland, H. C. *Report on the History and Statistics of the District of Backergunge*. Calcutta, 1868.

Taylor, H. *A Sketch of the Topography and Statistics of Dacca*. Dacca, 1850.

Westland, J. *A Report on the District of Jessore: its Antiquity, History and Commerce*. Calcutta, 1871.

B. NON-OFFICIAL REPORTS AND ACCOUNTS

Ahmed, B. *The Bengal Mussulmans*. India Office Tract no. 755.

Bandopadhyay, B. C. *History of Cooch Behar*. Dacca: the author, 1882.

Banerjee, R. D. "Saptagrāma or Sātgānw," *JASB*, V (NS), no. 7, July 1909, 245-62.

Barbosa, D. *The Book of Duarte Barbosa*. English tr. by M. L. Dames. 2 vols. London: Hakluyt Society, 1918 and 1921.

Beveridge, H. *The District of Bakarganj: Its History and Statistics*. London, 1876.

Chakravarti, M. R. *Descriptions of Birbhum*. 2 vols. Calcutta, 1916 and 1919.

Chowdhury, D. A. "The Mohammedans of Bengal," *The Muslim World* (London and New York: Hartford Seminary Foundation), XV, 1925, pp. 135-39.

Dalton, E. T. *Descriptive Ethnology of the Tribes and Castes of Bengal*. Calcutta: Asiatic Society of Bengal, 1872.

Das, R. C. "Village Mohammedans of Bengal," *The Muslim World*, XVI, 1926, pp. 267-71.

Deerr, W. J. "General Account of Burdwan and Culna [Kālnā]," *Church Missionary Record* (London), I, no. 10, Oct. 1830.

Fazl, S. A. *On the Muhammadans of India*. Calcutta: B.P.M. Press, 1862/1872? The date appears to be a mistake, because the author quotes an article dated 8 September 1871. India Office Tract no. 603.

Foster, W. (ed.). *Early Travels in India, 1583-1619*. London, 1927.

Fuzli Rubbee, K.B.D. *The Origin of the Musulmans of Bengal*. Calcutta: Thacker's, 1895.

Hamilton, A. *A New Account of the East Indies*. New edn., with introduction and notes by W. Foster. London: Argonaut Press, 1930.

Hayat, A. *Mussalmans of Bengal*. Calcutta: Z. Ali, 1966.

Hodgson, B. S. *Miscellaneous Essays relating to Indian Subjects*. Ed. by R. Rost. 2 vols. London: Trubner's Oriental Series, 1880.

Jones, L. B. "The Educated Moslems in Bengal," *The Muslim World*, VI, 1916, pp. 228-35.

Karim, A.K.N. "Some Aspects of Popular Beliefs Among Muslims of Bengal," *Eastern Anthropologist* (Lucknow), IX, no. 1, Sept.-Nov. 1955, pp. 29-41.

Khan, A. A. *Memoirs of Gaur and Pandua*. Ed. by H. E. Stapleton. Calcutta: Bengal Secretariat Book Depot, 1931.

Khan, A. M. "Research about Muslim Aristocracy in East Pakistan. An Introduction," in P. Bessaignet (ed.), *Social Research in East Pakistan*. Dacca: Asiatic Soc. of Pakistan, 2nd rev. edn., 1964, pp. 21-37.

Khan, M.M.M. "Social Divisions in the Muhammadan Community," *The Calcutta Monthly*, I, no. 1, July 1896.

Ma-huan. *Account of the Kingdom of Bengala*. English tr. by G. Phillips in *JRAS*, article no. xiv, 1895, pp. 523-35.

Mandelslo, J.A.D. *The Voyages and Travels of J. A. de Mandelslo . . . into the East Indies*. English tr. by J. Davies. London, rev. 2nd edn., 1669.

Mansooruddin, M. "Abstract of Muslim Folk-Songs: an Untapped source of Islamic History," *Proceedings of the First All-Pakistan History Conference* (Karachi), I, 1951, pp. 368-88.

———. "Further Muslim Folk-Songs of East Bengal," *Proceedings of the Second All-Pakistan History Conference*, II, 1952, pp. 316-25.

Marshall, J. *John Marshall in India. Notes and Observations in Bengal, 1668-1672*. Ed. by S. A. Khan. London, 1927.

Master, S. *The Diaries of Streynsham Master, 1675-1680, and other contemporary papers relating thereto*. Ed. by R. C. Temple. 2 vols. London: Indian Records Series, 1911.

Mclean, H. "Moslem Childhood in Bengal," *The Muslim World*, XXVI, 1936, pp. 291-95.

Orme, R. *History of the Military Transactions of the British Nation in Indostan*. 2 vols. London, 1803.

Parkes, F. *Wanderings of a Pilgrim in Search of the Picturesque*. 2 vols. London, 1850.

Pelsaert, F. *Remonsrantie*. English tr. as *Jahangir's India*, by Moreland and Geyl. Cambridge, 1925.

"Saeed." *The Future of the Muhammadans of Bengal*. Calcutta: Urdoo Guide Press, 1880. Review in *Calcutta Review*, LXXII, pt. 2, no. 7, 1881, iv-vii.

Sen, K. "Notes on Rural Customs of Dinajpur District," *JASB*, Letters, 3rd series, III, 1937, pp. 33-38.

Tagore, R. N. "Hindu-Musalman," *Visva-bharati Quarterly* (Santiniketan), IX (N.S.), 1943-1944, pp. 99-103.

Talke, J. "Islam in Bengal," *The Muslim World*, IV, 1914, pp. 3-19.

Wadud, A. "The Mussalmans of Bengal," *Visva-bharati Quarterly*, XIV (N.S.), 1948-1949, pp. 17-32.

Wali, Maulavi A. "Ethnographical Notes on the Muhammadan

Castes of Bengal," *Journal of the Anthropological Society of Bombay*, VII, no. 2, 1904, pp. 98-113.

———. "Note on the Hari Allah Sect," *JASB*, LXVII, no. 2, 1898, p. 112.

———. "Note on the Chitliya Faqirs," *ibid.*, pp. 112-15.

———. "On the origin of the Chaklai Musalmans," *ibid.*, LXVIII, no. 3, 1899, pp. 61-62.

———. "Note on the Faqirs of Baliya-dighi in Dinajpur," *ibid.*, LXXII, no. 2, 190, pp. 61-65.

Watters, T. *On Yuang Chwang's Travels in India*. 2 vols. London, 1905.

Wise, J. *Notes on the Races, Castes, and Trades of Eastern Bengal*. London: Harrison & Sons, 1883. Only twelve copies printed for private circulation. The British Library copy consulted.

———. "Notes on Sunargaon, Eastern Bengal," *JASB*, XLIII, pt. 1, no. 1, 1874, pp. 82-96.

———. "The Muhammadans of Eastern Bengal," *ibid.*, LXIII, no. 1, pt. 3, 1894, pp. 28-61.

Zaidi, S.M.H. "A Social Psychological Study of Fatalism in Two Villages in East Pakistan," in M. E. Haq (ed.), *Muhammad Shahidullah Felicitation Volume*. Dacca: Asiatic Society Publication, no. 17, 1966, pp. 413-22.

C. ARCHAEOLOGICAL—EPIGRAPHIC—NUMISMATIC

Ahmad, S. *Inscriptions of Bengal*. Vol. IV. Rajshahi: Varendra Research Society, 1960.

Bhattasali, N. K. *Coins and Chronology of Early Independent Sultans of Bengal*. Cambridge: W. Heffer & Sons, 1922.

———. "Some Image Inscriptions from East Bengal," *Epigraphia Indica*, XVII, 1923, pp. 349-52.

———. *Iconography of Buddhist and Brahmanical Sculptures in the Dacca Museum*. Dacca: Rai Bahadur S. N. Bhadra, 1929.

Blochmann, H. "Notes on the Arabic and Persian Inscriptions in the Hugli District," *JASB*, XXXIX, no. 4, 1870, pp. 280-303.

———. "Notes on Arabic and Persian Inscriptions, from Dinājpur, Dhākā, Dhāmrāi (N. of Dhākā), Badāon, and A'lāpur," *ibid.*, XLI, no. 1, 1872, pp. 102-13.

———. "Contributions to the Geography and History of Bengal (Muhammadan period)," *ibid.*, XLII, pt. 1, no. 1, 1873, pp. 209-310; XLIII, pt. 1, no. 3, 1874, pp. 280-309; XLIV, no. 3, 1875, pp. 275-306.

———. "The Firuzshahi Inscription in the Chhota Dargah, A.H. 761," *ibid.*, note no. 38, XLII, 1873.

Cunningham, A. *Report of a Tour in Bihar and Bengal in 1879-1880. Archaeological Survey of India*. Calcutta: Govt. of India, 1882, vol. XV.

Dani, A. H. "Bibliography of the Muslim Inscriptions of Bengal," *JASP*, Appendix, no. 28, II, 1957.

Dikshit, K. N. "Excavations at Paharpur," *Annual Report of the Archaelogical Survey of India*, 1926-1927, pp. 140-49.

———. "Excavations in Mahasthan," *ibid.*, 1928-1929, pp. 87-97.

——— and Chandra, G. C. "Excavations at Paharpur," *ibid.*, 1930-1931, pp. 113-28.

Epigraphia Indica. (A collection of inscriptions supplementary to the Corpus Inscriptionum Indicarum of the Archaelogical Survey, translated by several Oriental scholars.) Calcutta: Govt. of India, 1892-.

Epigraphia Indo-Moslemica. (Published as a supplementary part of the Epigraphia Indica.) Ed. by D. Ross. Calcutta: Govt. of India, 1908-.

Karim, A. *Corpus of the Muslim Coins of Bengal*. Dacca: Asiatic Society of Pakistan, 1960.

Khan, F. A. *Mainamati: A Preliminary Report on the Recent Archaelogical Excavations in East Pakistan*. Karachi: Dept. of Archaelogy, Govt. of Pakistan, 1963.

Majumdar, N. G. *Inscriptions of Bengal*. Vol. III. Ed. with tr. and notes. Rajshahi: Varendra Research Society, 1929.

Mukharji, R. and Maiti, S. R. *Corpus of Bengal Inscriptions bearing on History and Civilization of Bengal*. Calcutta: Firma K. L., 1967.

Sen, B. C. *Some Historical Aspects of the Inscriptions of Bengal* (*Pre-Muhammadan Epochs*). Calcutta: Calcutta U.P., 1942.

Sircar, D. C. *Select Inscriptions Bearing on Indian History and Civilization*. Calcutta: Calcutta U.P., 1942. 2nd edn., 1965.

Stapleton, H. E. "Recent Advances in Knowledge of the Early and Medieval History of Bengal," *Annual Bibliography of Indian Archaelogy*, VII, 1933, pp. 13-17.

Wright, H. N. *Catalogue of the Coins in the Indian Museum*. 2 vols. Oxford: Indian Museum, 1907.

SECONDARY SOURCES

I. Bengali

A. BOOKS

Bibliographical Works

Ahmad, A. *Bānglār Kalami-punthir Vivaran*. Noakhali, 1354 BS/1947.
Biśwās, K. K. "Prāchin Punthir Vivaran," *Sāhitya-Pariṣat Patrikā* (Rangpur), no. 2, 1314 BS/1907.
Chaudhuri, M. M. *Bānglā Punthir Tālikā*. Rajshahi: Varendra Research Society, n.d.
Mandal, P. (comp.). *Punthi-parichay*. 3 vols. Viśva-bhārati, 1951, 1958, and 1963.
Sharif, A. (ed.). *Punthi-parichiti* (compiled by Munshi A. Karim). Dacca: Dacca U.P., 1958.

General

Ahmad, W. *Bānglār Lok-samskriti*. Dacca: Bānglā Academy, 1974.
Bandopādhyāy, C. C. *Vidyāpati, Chandidās o anyānya Vaiṣnav Mahājan Gitikā*. Calcutta, 1935.
Basu, G. K. *Bānglār Laukik Devatā*. Calcutta, 2nd edn., 1969.
Basu, R. *Rājā Pratāpāditya-charitra*. Serampore, 1802.
Basu, N. N. *Banger Jātiya Itihās*. 3 vols. Calcutta: the author, 1900-1914.
Bhattāchārya, A. *Bānglā Mangal-kāvyer Itihās*. Calcutta, 3rd. edn., 1958.
———. *Bānglār Lok-sāhitya*. Calcutta, 3rd edn., 1962.
Bhattāchārya, U. N. *Bānglār Bāul o Bāul Gān*. Calcutta, 1336 BS/1929.
Bhattāchārya, Y. M. *Bānglār Vaiṣnav-bhāvāpanna Musalmān Kavi*. Calcutta: *Śrihatta Sāhitya-Pariṣat Granthamālā*, no. 6, 1356 BS/1949-1950.
Chaudhuri, M.A.W. *Śrihatte Shāh Jalāl*. Sylhet: the author, 1965.
Chaudhuri, P. *Prāchin Bānglā-sāhitye Hindu-Musalmān*. Viśva-bhārati, *Viśva-vidyā-samgraha*, no. 73, 1953.
Dās, G. N. *Bānglā Pir-sāhityer Kathā*. Barasat, 24-Parganas: Q. A. Wadud, Shahid Library, 1976.
Dāsgupta, N. *Bānglāy Bauddha-dharma*. Calcutta: A. Mukherji & Co., 1948.
Dev, C. R. *Palligiti o Purva Bānglā*. Calcutta, 1360 BS/1953.

Govt. of East Pakistan. Board of National Reconstruction, Dacca. *Muslim Sāhitya Sevak*. Dacca, n.d.

Haq, M. E. *Bange Sufi Prabhāv*. Calcutta: Mahsin & Co., 1935.

———. *Muslim Bānglā Sāhitya*. Dacca: Pakistan Publications, 1965.

——— and Chaudhuri, K. (eds.). *Abdul Karim Sāhitya-viśārad Smārak Grantha*. Dacca: Bānglā Academy, 1969.

——— and Karim, M. A. *Ārākān Rājsabhāy Bānglā Sāhitya, 1300-1700*. Calcutta: the authors, 1935.

Islām, A.K.M.A. *Bānglā Sāhitye Muslim Kavi o Kāvya*. Dacca: Book Stall, 2nd impression, 1969.

Islām, M. *Kavi Heyāt Māmud [Hayāt Mahmud]*. Rajshahi: Rajshahi U.P., 1961.

———. *Kavi Pāglā Kānāi*. *Ibid*., 1336 BS/1959-1960.

Islām, S. *Uttar Banger Lok Sāhitya*. Rangpur: A. Islam, 1973.

Jahāngir, B. R. (ed.). *Bāul Gān o Duddu Shāh*. Dacca: Bānglā Academy, 1371 BS/1964-1965.

Karim, A. *Bānglā Sāhitye Muslim Kavi o Sāhityik*. Kuṣthiyā, Bangladesh: S. A. Anwār, 1969.

———. *Bāul Sāhitya o Bāul Gān*. *Ibid*., 1971.

Kāsimpuri, M. S. *Bānglādeśer Lok-sangit Parichiti*. Dacca: Bānglā Academy, 1973.

Mallik, K. *Nāth-sampradāyer Itihās, Darśan o Sādhan-pranāli*. Calcutta: Calcutta U.P., 1950.

———. *Nāth-pantha*. Viśva-bhārati, *Viśva-vidyā-samgraha*, no. 88. 1951.

Mallik, R. M. *Musalmān Vaiṣnav Kavi*. Calcutta: S. N. Basu, 1895.

Muhammad, Q. D. *Bānglā Sāhityer Itihās*. 4 vols. Dacca: Students' Ways, 1968-1969.

——— *et al*. *Sufi-vād o Āmāder Samāj*. Dacca: Nawroz Kitābistān, 1969.

Mukhopādhyāy, S. *Bānglār Itihāser Duśo Bachhar: Svādhin Sultānder Āmal, 1338-1538*. Calcutta: Bhārati Book Staff, 2nd edn., 1966.

Rahmān, H. F. *Uttar Banger Meyeli Git*. Dacca: Bānglā Academy, 1369 BS/1962.

Rāy, N. *Bāngālir Itihās. Ādi Parva*. Calcutta Book Emporium, reprint, 1949.

Sānnyāl, B. J. *Musalmān Vaiṣnav Kavi*. 4 pts. Rajshahi: Sanātan Dharma Samiti, 1904-1906.

Śāstri, H. P. *Prāchin Bānglār Gaurav*. Viśva-bhārati, *Viśva-vidyā-samgraha*, no. 54, 1963.
Sen, D. C. *Banga Bhāṣā o Sāhitya*. Calcutta: Calcutta U.P., 8th edn., 1949.
———. *Banga Sāhitya Parichay*. 3 pts. *Ibid.*, 1914.
——— (ed.). *Purva-banga-gitikā*. 4 vols. *Ibid.*, 1923-1932.
———. *Prāchin Bānglā Sāhitye Musalmāner Avadān*. Dacca, 1940.
Sen, K. M. *Bānglār Sādhanā*. Viśva-bhārati, *Viśva-vidyā samgraha*, no. 42, 1965.
———. *Bhārate Hindu-Musalmāner Yukta Sādhanā*. *Ibid.*, 1356 BS/1950.
Sen, S. *Bānglā Sāhityer Itihās*. 4 pts. Calcutta: Bardhamān Sāhitya Sabhā, 1948-1958.
———. *Charyāgiti Padāvali*. *Ibid.*, 1956.
———. *Islāmi Bānglā Sāhitya*. *Ibid.*, 1951.
———. *Prāchin Bānglā o Bāngāli*. Viśva-bhārati, *Viśva-vidyā samgraha*, no. 12, 2nd edn., 1946.
———. *Madhyayuger Bānglā o Bāngāli*. *Ibid.*, no. 44, 1962.
Sen, U. *Prāchin o Madhyayuger Bānglā Sāhitye Sādhāran Mānuṣ*. Calcutta: Jijnāsā, 1971.
Sharif, A. *Muslim Kavir Pada-sāhitya*. Dacca: Dacca U.P., 1961.
———. *Saiyid Sultān—Tār Granthāvali o Tār Yug*. Dacca: Bānglā Academy, 1972.
———. *Madhyayuger Sāhitye Samāj o Samskritir Rup*. Dacca: Muktadhārā, 1977.
Yāzdāni, R. *Maimansimher Lok-sāhitya*. Dacca: Bānglā Academy, 1958.
Wadud, K. A. *Hindu-Musalmāner Birodh*. Viśva-bhārati, 1936.
———. *Ājkār Kathā*. Calcutta: D. M. Library, 1941.
———. *Śāśvata Banga*. Calcutta: Khurshid Bakht, 1951.
———. *Nava Paryāy*. 2 vols. Vol. I (Calcutta: Muslim Publishing House, 1926) and vol. II (Dacca: Modern Library, 1929).

B. ARTICLES

Bāgchi, Y. M. "Palli-kathā," *Sāhitya-Pariṣat Patrikā*, no. 2, 1312 BS/1905.
Bhumānanda, Svāmi. "Vaiṣnav Musalmān," *Bangaśri, Chaitra* 1344 BS/1937 and *Baiśākh* 1345 BS/1938.
Dās, P. L. "Musalmān vaiṣnav kavir dharmamat," *Arghya*, VIII, 1324 BS/1917.

Dāsgupta, S. B. "Bānglār Musalmān vaiṣnav kavi," *Viśva-bhārati Patrikā, Māgh-Chaitra* 1363 BS/1956.
Datta, K. "Bada-khān Ghāzir Gān," *Bhāratiya Lok-yān* (Calcutta Univ.), III, nos. 1-2, 1963.
Haq, M. E. "Kavi Saiyid Sultān," *Sāhitya-Pariṣat Patrikā*, no. 2, 1341 BS/1934.
Karim, A. "Kifāyatul Musallin-rachayitā Shaikh Muttaliber samay nirupan," *Sāhitya Patrikā* (Dacca Univ.), XI, no. 2.
Majumdār, B. B. "Vaiṣnav sāhitye sāmājik itihāser upādān," *Sāhitya-Pariṣat Patrikā*, no. 4, 1339 BS/1932.
Qādir, M. A. "Bānglār lok-sangit," *Śikhā* (Dacca), I, 1333 BS/1926, pp. 38-48.
Rāy, N. "Prāchin Bānglār śreni-bibhāg," *Sāhitya-Pariṣat Patrikā*, 1940.
———. "Bāngālir ādi-dharma," *Viśva-bhārati Patrikā*, 1947-1948.
Roy, A. "Islām o Bāngāli Muslim samāj: prāk-British parva," *Jijnāsā* (Calcutta), I, no. 1, *Baiśākh*, 1387 BS/1980, pp. 81-94.
Śāstri, R. K. "Kriṣna-bhakta Musalmān." *Pratibhā* (Calcutta), XI, *Kārtik*, 1328 BS/1921.
Siddiqi, A. G. "Raushan Ara," *Sāhitya-Pariṣat Patrikā*, no. 3, 1323 BS/1916.
Thākur, A. N. "Bānglār vrata." *Viśva-bhārati Patrikā*, 1354 BS/1947.
Wadud, K. A. "Abhibhāṣan" in his *Nava Paryāy*, vol. II. See Wadud, K. A., *supra*, p. 276.

II. English

A. BOOKS

Bibliographical Works, Encyclopaedias, and Dictionaries

Beale, T. W. *The Oriental Biographical Dictionary*. Calcutta: Asiatic Soc. of Bengal, 1881.
Blumhardt, J. F. *Catalogue of Bengali Printed Books in the Library of the British Museum*. London: British Museum, 1886.
———. *A Supplementary Catalogue of Bengali Books in the Library of the British Museum, Acquired During the Years 1886-1910*. London: British Museum, 1910.
——— and Wilkinson, J.V.S. *Second Supplementary Catalogue of Bengali Books in the Library of the British Museum, Acquired During the Years 1911-1934*. London: British Museum, 1939.
Blumhardt, J. F. *Catalogue of the Library of India Office*, vol. 2,

pt. 4, *Bengali, Oriya and Assamese Books, with Supplement 1906-1920*. London: India Office, 1888.

Dowson, J. *A Classical Dictionary of the Hindu Mythology and Religion, Geography, History and Literature*. London: Routledge and Kegan Paul, 8th edn., 1953.

Gibb, H.A.R. and Kramers, J. H. (eds.). *Shorter Encyclopaedia of Islam*. Leyden: E. J. Brill, 1961.

Hamid, M. A. (compiled). *Catalogue of the Arabic and Persian Manuscripts in the Oriental Public Library at Bankipore*, vol. 5, pt. 1, *Tradition*. Patna, 1920.

Hastings, J. (ed.). *Encyclopaedia of Religion and Ethics*. Edinburgh: T. T. Clark, 1908-1926.

Houtsma, M. Th. *et al.* (eds.). *Encyclopaedia of Islam*. 4 vols. Leyden and London: E. J. Brill and Luzac, 1913-1934.

Hughes, T. P. *A Dictionary of Islam*. London: W. H. Allen, 1895.

Husain, S. S. (ed.). *A Descriptive Catalogue of Bengali Manuscripts in Munshi Abdul Karim's Collection by Munshi Abdul Karim and Ahmad Sharif*. Dacca: Asiatic Society of Pakistan Publication, no. 3, 1960.

Kesavan, B. S. (ed.). *Indian National Bibliography*. Calcutta: Indian National Library, 1957-.

National Library, India. *A Bibliography of Indology, Enumerating Basic Publications on all Aspects of Indian Culture*, vol. 3, *Bengali Language and Literature*. Calcutta: Indian National Library, 1960-.

Pearson, J. D. *Index Islamicus, 1906-1955*. Cambridge: Cambridge U.P., 1958.

———. *Index Islamicus, Supplement 1956-1960*. *Ibid.*, 1962.

Storey, C. A. *Persian Literature. A Bio-Bibliographical Survey*. London: Luzac & Co., 1927.

Walker, B. *Hindu World, an Encyclopaedic Survey of Hinduism*. 2 vols. London: Allen & Unwin, 1968.

General

Acland, C. *A Popular Account of the Manners and Customs of India*. London: John Murray, 1847.

Ahmad, A. *Studies in Islamic Culture in the Indian Environment*. London: Oxford U.P., 1964.

Ahmad, Q. *The Wahabi Movement in India*. Calcutta: Firma K. L., 1966.

Ahmed, R. *The Bengal Muslims 1871-1906. A Quest for Identity.* Delhi: Oxford U.P., 1981.

Ali, H. *Observations on the Mussulmauns of India.* Ed. by W. Crooke. Oxford, 1917.

Anwar, A. *The Moslem Festivities.* Calcutta, 1892.

Arberry, A. J. *Sufism: An Account of the Mystics of Islam.* London: Allen & Unwin, 1950.

Arnold, T. W. *The Preaching of Islam: A History of the Propagation of the Muslim Faith.* London: Luzac, 3rd edn., 1935.

Ashraf, K. M. *Life and Conditions of the People of Hinustan (A. D. 1200-1550).* Calcutta: Asiatic Society of Bengal, 1935; also New Delhi, 2nd edn., 1970.

Ashraf, S. A. *Muslim Tradition in Bengali Literature.* Karachi: Karachi Univ., Bengali Literature Society, 1960.

Avalon, A. (pseudonym). See Woodroffe, J., *infra*, p. 286.

Bagchi, P. C. *Materials for a Critical Edition of the Old Bengali Charyapadas: A Comparative Study of the Text and the Tibetan Translation.* Viśva-bhārati, 1956.

Banerji, B. N. *Begams of Bengal.* Calcutta: M. C. Sarkar, 1942.

Banerji, K. N. *Popular Tales of Bengal.* Calcutta, 1905.

Basham, A. L. *The Indian Sub-continent in Historical Perspective.* London: London U.P., 1958.

Baumer, R. Van M. (ed.). *Aspects of Bengali History and Society.* Honolulu: Hawaii U.P., Asian Studies at Hawaii, no. 12, 1975.

Belnos, S. C. *Twenty-four Plates Illustrative of Hindoo and European Manners in Bengal.* London: Smith & Elder/J. Carpenter & Co., 1832.

Bentley, C. A. *Fairs and Festivals of Bengal.* Calcutta: Bengal Secretariat Press, 1921.

Bessaignet, P. (ed.). *Social Research in East Pakistan.* Dacca: Asiatic Society of Pakistan, 2nd rev. edn., 1964.

Bhandarkar, R. G. *Vaiṣnavism, Saivism and Other Minor Religious Systems.* Varanasi: Indological Bookhouse, latest edn., 1965.

——— *et al.* (eds.). B.C. *Law Commemoration Volume.* 2 vols. Calcutta and Poona: Indian Research Institute, and Bhandarkar Oriental Research Institute, 1945 and 1946.

Bhattacharya, D. *Mirror of the Sky. Songs of the Bauls from Bengal.* London: U. N. E. S. C. O., 1969.

Blunt, E.A.H. *The Caste System of Northern India with Special Reference to the United Provinces of Agra and Oudh.* London: Oxford U.P., 1931.

Bottomore, T. B. *Sociology—A Guide to Problems and Literature*. London: Allen & Unwin, 1962.

Chakravarti, C. H. *The Tantras—Studies on Their Religion and Literature*. Calcutta, 1963.

Chanda, R. P. *The Indo-Aryan Races: A Study of the Indo-Aryan People and Institutions*. Rajshahi: Varendra Research Society, 1916.

Chatterjee, A. *Bengal in the Reign of Aurangzeb, 1658-1707*. Calcutta: Progressive Publishers, 1967.

Chatterji, S. K. *The Origin and Development of the Bengali Language*. 3 vols. London: Allen & Unwin, 1970.

Chattopadhyaya, N. K. *The Yatras or the Popular Dramas of Bengal*. Calcutta. 1882.

Clothey, F. W. (ed.). *Images of Man: Religion and Historical Process in South Asia*. Madras: New Era Publications, 1982.

Coomaraswamy, A. K. *Yaksas*. 2 pts. Washington: Smithsonian Institution, 1928-1931.

Crooke, W. *Religion and Folklore of Northern India*. 2 vols. London: Oxford U.P., 1926.

Das, S. R. *Folk-Religions of Bengal: A Study of the Vrata Rites*. Calcutta: S. C. Kar, 1953.

Dasgupta, J. N. *Bengal in the 16th Century*. Calcutta U.P., 1914.

———. *Bengal in the 17th Century*. Calcutta: Calcutta U.P., 1916.

Dasgupta, S. B. *Obscure Religious Cults: As Background of Bengali Literature*. Calcutta, rev. edn., 1962.

Dasgupta, S. N. *Hindu Mysticism*. Chicago: Open Court Publisher, 1927.

———. *General Introduction to Tantra Philosophy*. Calcutta: Calcutta U.P., 1922.

———. *A History of Indian Philosophy*. 5 vols. Cambridge: Cambridge U.P., reprint, 1951.

Dasgupta, T. C. *Aspects of Bengali Society from Old Bengali Literature*. Calcutta: Calcutta U.P., 1935.

Datta, K. K. *Studies in the History of the Bengal Subah (1740-1770)*. Vol. 1. Calcutta: Calcutta U.P., 1936.

Davis, K. *The Population of India and Pakistan*. Princeton: Princeton U.P., 1951.

De Boer, T. J. *The History of Philosophy in Islam*. English tr. by E. R. Jones. London, Luzac's Oriental Religious Series, 1933.

De, L. B. *Folk Tales of Bengal*. London: McMillan, reprint, 1954.

———. *Bengal Peasant Life*. London: McMillan, reprint, 1916.

De S. K. *Early History of the Vaiṣnava Faith and Movement in*

Bengal, from Sanskrit and Bengali Sources. Calcutta: Firma K. L. later edn., 1961.

Dimock, E. C. *The Place of the Hidden Moon*. Chicago: Chicago U.P., 1966.

Dowson, J. *A Classical Dictionary of the Hindu Mythology and Religion, Geography, History and Literature*. London: Routledge and Kegan Paul, 8th edn., 1953.

Dutt, H. C. *Bengali Life and Society*. Calcutta, 1853.

Eliade, M. *Yoga. Immortality and Freedom*. London and N.Y.: Routledge and Kegan Paul, 1958.

Eliot, C. *Hinduism and Buddhism: An Historical Sketch*. 3 vols. *Ibid*., reprint, 1962.

Encyclopaedia of Islam. See M. T. Houtsma *et al*. (eds.), *supra*, p. 278.

Encyclopaedia of Religion and Ethics. See J. Hastings (ed.), *supra*, p. 278.

Frazer, J. G. *The Golden Bough*. Pt. 6, *The Scapegoat*. London, 3rd edn., 1925.

Geertz, C. *Islam Observed: Religious Development in Morocco and Indonesia*. New Haven and London: Yale U.P., 1968.

———. *The Religion of Java*. Glencoe: Free Press, 1960.

Grant, C. *Rural Life in Bengal*. London: Thacker & Co., 1860.

Ghosh, J. C. *Bengali Literature*. London: Curzon Press, reprint, 1976.

Gopinath-Rao, T. A. *Elements of Hindu Iconography*. N.Y.: Paragon reprint, 1968.

Gruenbaum, G. E. von. *Medieval Islam: A Study in Cultural Orientations*. Chicago: Chicago U.P., 1946.

———. *Modern Islam: The Search for Cultural Identity*. N.Y.: Vintage Books, 1964.

———. *Islam: Essays in the Nature and Growth of a Cultural Tradition*. London: Routledge and Kegan Paul, printed in U.S.A., 2nd edn., 1961.

Guha, B. S. *Racial Elements in the Population of India*. Oxford: Oxford Pamphlets on Indian Affairs, no. 22, 1944.

Haq, M. E. *Muslim Bengali Literature*. Karachi: Pakistan Publications, 1957.

———. *A History of Sufism in Bengal*. Dacca: Asiatic Society of Bangladesh, 1975.

——— (ed.). *Muhammad Shahidullah Felicitation Volume*. Dacca: Asiatic Society of Pakistan Publication, no. 17, 1966.

Haq, M. E. (ed.). *Abdul Karim Sahitya-Visarad Commemoration Volume*. Dacca: Asiatic Society of Bangladesh Publication, no. 25, 1972.

Hardy, P. *The Muslims of British India*. Cambridge: Cambridge U.P., 1972.

Harvey, G. E. *History of Burma*. London: Longmans Green, 1925.

History of Bengal, vol. I, Dacca. See Majumdar, R. C., *infra*, p. 283.

History of Bengal, vol. II, Dacca. See Sarkar, J. N., *infra*, p. 284.

Ikram, S. M. *Muslim Civilization in India*. Ed. by A. T. Embree. N.Y.: Columbia U.P., 1964.

Islam, M. N. *Bengali Muslim Public Opinion as Reflected in the Bengali Press 1901-1930*. Dacca: Bānglā Academy, 1973.

Kane, P. V. *History of Dharmaśāstra*. Poona: Bhandarkar Oriental Research Institute. 1958.

Karim, A. *Social History of the Muslims in Bengal (down to A.D. 1538)*. Dacca: Asiatic Society of Pakistan, 1959.

———. *Murshid Quli Khan and His Times*. Dacca: Asiatic Society of Pakistan, 1963.

Karim, A.K.N. *Changing Society in India and Pakistan*. Dacca: Oxford U.P., 1956.

———. "The Modern Muslim Political Elite in Bengal." Ph.D. thesis, London University, 1964.

Khan, M. A. *History of the Faraidi Movement in Bengal, 1818-1906*. Karachi, 1965.

Kopf, D. *British Orientalism and the Bengal Renaissance. The Dynamics of Indian Modernization, 1773-1835*. Berkeley and Los Angeles: California U.P., 1969.

——— (ed.). *Bengal Regional Identity*. Ann Arbor: Asian Studies Center, Michigan State Univ., Occasional Papers, South Asia Series, 1969.

Law, N. N. *Promotion of Learning in India During Muhammadan Rule, by Muhammadans*. London: Longmans & Co., 1916.

Learmonth, A.T.A. See Spate, O.H.K. and Learmonth, A.T.A., *infra*, p. 285.

Levi, S. and Przyluski, J. *Pre-Aryan and Pre-Dravidian in India*. English tr. by P. C. Bagchi. Calcutta: Calcutta U.P., 1929.

Levy, R. *An Introduction to the Sociology of Islam*. 2 vols. London: William and Norgate, 1931-1933.

———. *The Social Structure of Islam*. Cambridge: Cambridge U.P., 1957.

Maity, P. K. *Historical Studies in the Cult of the Goddess Manasā.* Calcutta: Punthi Pustak, 1966.

Majumdar, D. N. and Rao, C. R. *Race Elements in Bengal. A Quantitative Study.* Calcutta: Statistical Publishing Society, 1960.

Majumdar, R. C. (ed.). *History of Bengal.* Vol. I. Dacca: Dacca U.P., 1943.

Mallick, A. R. *British Policy and the Muslims in Bengal, 1757-1856.* Dacca: Asiatic Society of Pakistan, 1961.

Massé, H. *Persian Beliefs and Customs.* English tr. of the French original by C. A. Messner. New Haven: Human Relations Area Files, 1954.

Mia, A. "Influence of Urban Technological Development on Common Man's Islam in Pakistan." Ph.D. thesis, Case Western Reserve Univ., 1968.

Mitchell, M. *A Missionary's Wife Among the Wild Tribes of South Bengal.* London and Edinburgh: John Maclaren, 1871.

Mitra, R. C. *The Decline of Buddhism in India.* Viśva-bhārati, 1954.

Morrison, B. M. *Political Centers and Culture Regions in Early Bengal.* Tucson: Association for Asian Studies Monograph no. 25, Arizona U.P., 1970.

Muir, J. (ed.). *Original Sanskrit Texts on the Origin and History of the People in India.* 5 vols. London, 2nd edn., 1868-1884.

Mujeeb, M. *The Indian Muslims.* London: Allen & Unwin, 1967.

Mukerjee, R. K. *The Changing Face of Bengal—A Study in Riverine Economy.* Calcutta: Calcutta U.P., 1938.

Nasr, S. H. *An Introduction to Islamic Cosmological Doctrines.* Harvard: Harvard U.P., 1964.

Nicholson, R. A. *The Mystics of Islam.* London: G. Bell & Sons Ltd., 1914.

———. *Studies in Islamic Mysticism.* Cambridge: Cambridge U.P., 1921.

———. *The Idea of Personality in Sufism.* Cambridge: Cambridge U.P., 1923.

Oddie, G. A. (ed.). *Religion in South Asia. Religious Conversion and Revival Movements in South Asia in Medieval and Modern Times.* Delhi: Manohar, 1977.

O'Leary, D. E. *How Greek Science Passed to the Arabs.* London: Routledge and Kegan Paul, 1948.

O'Malley, L.S.S. *Bengal, Bihar and Orissa, Sikkim.* Calcutta, 1917.

Paul, P. L. *The Early History of Bengal: From the Earliest Times to the Muslim Conquest*. 2 vols. Calcutta: Indian Research Institute Publications, 1939-1940.

Pickett, J. W. *Christian Mass Movements in India*. N.Y.: Abingdon Press, 1933.

Pillai, J.M.S. (ed.). *Two Thousand Years of Tamil Literature (An Anthology)*. Annamalainagar: the author, 1959.

Qureshi, I. H. *The Muslim Community of the Indo-Pakistan Subcontinent*. N.Y.: Columbia University, Near and Middle East Institute, 1960.

Radhakrishnan, S. *Indian Philosophy*. 2 vols. London: Allen & Unwin, 1923-1927.

——— (ed.). *The Principal Upanisads*. London: Allen & Unwin, 1953.

——— and Moore, C. A. (eds.). *A Source Book in Indian Philosophy*. Princeton: Princeton U.P., 1957.

Rahim, M. A. *Social and Cultural History of Bengal*. 2 vols. Karachi: Pakistan Publishing House, 1963-1967.

Rao, C. R. See Majumdar, D. N. and Rao, C. R., *Supra*, p. 283.

Raychaudhuri, T. *Bengal Under Akbar and Jahangir*. Delhi: Munshiram, 2nd impression, 1969.

Rizvi, S.A.A. *Muslim Revivalist Movements in Northern India*. Agra: Agra U.P., 1965.

———. *Shāh Wali Allāh and His Times. A Study of Eighteenth Century Islam: Politics and Society in India*. Canberra: Marifat Publishing House, 1980.

———. *Shāh Abd al-Aziz. Puritanism, Sectarian Polemics, and Jihād*. Canberra: Marifat Publishing House, 1982.

Roy, A. "Islam in the Environment of Medieval Bengal." Ph.D. thesis, Canberra: Australian National University, 1970.

Sarkar, J. N. *History of Aurangzeb*. 5 vols. Calcutta: M. C. Sarkar & Sons, 1912-25.

———. *Studies in Aurangzeb's Reign*. Calcutta: M. C. Sarkar & Sons, 1933.

——— (ed.). *History of Bengal*. Vol. II. Dacca: Dacca U.P., 1948.

Sarton, G. *Introduction to the History of Science*. 3 vols. Washington: Carnegie Institution Publication, no. 376, 1927-1948.

Sastri, H. P. *Discovery of Living Buddhism in Bengal*. Calcutta: the author, 1897.

Sen, D. C. *History of Bengali Language and Literature*. Calcutta: Calcutta U.P., 1911.

———. *Eastern Bengal Ballads*. 4 vols. Calcutta: Calcutta U.P., 1923-1932.

———. *The Folk-Literature of Bengal*. Calcutta: Calcutta U.P., 1920.

———. *Behula. The Indian "Pilgrim's Progess."* English tr. by J. W. Petavel and K. C. Sen. Calcutta: R. Cambray & Co., 1923.

———. *Glimpses of Bengal Life*. Calcutta: Calcutta U.P., 1925.

Sen, S. *History of Bengali Literature*. New Delhi: Sahitya Academy, 1960.

Shils, E. *The Intellectual Between Tradition and Modernity: The Indian Situation*. The Hague: Mouton & Co. Publishers, 1961.

Simon, G. *The Progress and Arrest of Islam in Sumatra*. London: Marshall Bros., 1914.

Singer, M. *Introduction to the Civilization of India*. Chicago: Chicago U.P., 1957.

———. *When A Great Tradition Modernizes. An Anthropological Approach to Indian Civilization*. Delhi: Vikas, 1972.

——— (ed.). *Traditional India: Structure and Change*. Philadelphia: The American Folklore Society, 1959.

——— and Cohn, B. S. (eds.). *Structure and Change in Indian Society*. Chicago: Aldine Publishing Co., 1968.

Spate, O.H.K. and Learnonth, A.T.A. *India and Pakistan: A General and Regional Geography*. London: Methuen, 3rd edn., 1967.

Spear, P. *India, Pakistan and the West*. London: Oxford U.P., 1958.

Srinivas, M. N. *Religion and Society Among the Coorgs in South India*. London: Oxford U.P., 1952.

———. *Caste in Modern India and Other Essays*. Bombay: Asia Publishing House, 1962.

———. *Social Change in Modern India*. Berkeley and Los Angeles: California U.P., 1966.

Stewart, C. *History of Bengal (from the first Muhammadan invasion until the virtual conquest of that country by the English, 1757 A.D.)*. London: Black & Parry & Co., 1813.

Subbarao, B. *The Personality of India; pre- and proto-historic foundation of India and Pakistan*. Baroda: M.S.R. Univ., 2nd rev. edn., 1958.

Subhan, J. A. *Sufism; its Saints and Shrines: An Introduction to the Study of Sufism with special reference to India*. Lucknow: Lucknow Publishing House, 2nd rev. edn., 1960.

Tarachand. *Influence of Islam on Indian Culture*. Allahabad: The Indian Press Ltd., 1936.

Tarafdar, M. R. *Husain Shāhi Bengal, 1494-1538 A.D. A Socio-Political Study*. Dacca: Asiatic Society of Pakistan, 1965.

Thomas, F. W. *Mutual Influence of Muhammadans and Hindus in India*. Cambridge, 1892.

Titus, M. *Islam in India and Pakistan*. Calcutta: Y.M.C.A. Publishing House, rev. reprint, 1959.

Toynbee, A. *A Study of History*. 10 vols. New York: Oxford U.P., 1962.

Watt, W. M. *Muhammad at Mecca*. Oxford: Clarendon Press, 1953.

———. *Muhammad at Medina*. Oxford: Clarendon Press, 1956.

———. *Islam and the Integration of Society*. London: Routledge and Kegan Paul, 1961.

Wheeler, R.E.M. *Five Thousand Years of Pakistan: An Archaeological Outline*. London: Christopher Johnson, 1950.

Winternitz, M. *A History of Indian Literature*. English tr. by S. Ketkar. 2 vols. Calcutta: Calcutta U.P., 1927-1933.

Woodroffe, J. *The Serpent Power*. English tr. of *Ṣat-chakra Nirupana* and *Pādukā-Panchaka*. London: Luzac, 1919.

———. *Shakti and Shākta. Essays and Addresses on Shākta Tantraśāstra*. Madras and London: Ganesh & Co./Luzac & Co., 2nd and rev. edn., 1920.

Wylie, M. *Bengal as a Field of Missions*. London: W. H. Dalton, 1854.

Zaehner, R. C. *Hindu and Muslim Mysticism*. London: London U.P., 1960.

Zbavitel, D. *Bengali Folk-Ballads from Mymensingh and the Problem of Their Authenticity*. Calcutta: Calcutta U.P., 1963.

Zwemer, S. M. *Influence of Animism on Islam. An Account of Popular Superstitions*. London: S.P.C.K., 1920.

———. *Across the World of Islam. Studies in Aspects of the Mohammedan Faith*. N.Y.: F. H. Revell Co., 1929.

———. *Studies in Popular Islam*. London: Sheldon Press, 1939.

B. ARTICLES

Ahmad, N. "Some Aspects of Land Utilization and Settlements in East Bengal in Ancient and Medieval Times," *The Dacca University Studies*, VIII, 1956, pp. 29-35.

Ali, S. A. "Islamic Culture in India," *Islamic Culture* (Hyderabad), I, 1927, pp. 331-57.

Ansari, G. "Muslim Caste in India," *Eastern Anthropologist* (Lucknow), IX, 1955-1956, pp. 104-11.

Askari, S. H. "New Light on Rājāh Ganesh and Sultān Ibrāhim Sharqi of Jaunpur from Contemporary Correspondence of Two Muslim Saints," *Bengal Past and Present* (Calcutta), LXVII, 1948, pp. 32-39.

———. "The Correspondence of Two 14th Century Sufi Saints of Bihar with the Contemporary Sovereigns of Delhi and Bengal," *Journal of the Bihar Research Society* (Patna), XLII, no. 2, 1956, pp. 177-95.

Banerji, A. "Traces of Jainism in Bengal," *Journal of the U.P. Historical Society* (Calcutta), XXIII, nos. 1-2.

Beames, J. "The Saint Pir Badar," *JRAS*, July-Oct. 1894, pp. 838-40.

———. "Mahuan's Account of Bengal," *ibid.*, 1895, pp. 898-900.

Beveridge, H. "The Saint Pir Badar," *ibid.*, 1894, pp. 840-41.

———. "The Antiquities of Bagura," *JASB*, XLVII, no. 1, 1878, pp. 88-95.

———. "Rājāh Kans," *ibid.*, LXI, no. 1, pp. 117-23.

Bhattacharya, A. "The Cult of the Village Gods of West Bengal," *Man in India* (Ranchi) XXXV, no. 1, March 1955, pp. 19-30.

———. "The Tiger-Cult and Its Literature in Lower Bengal," *ibid.*, XXVII, no. 1, 1947, pp. 44-55.

———. "Munshi Abdul Karim Sāhitya Viśārad and Folk-Literature of East Pakistan," in *Abdul Karim Sāhitya-Viśārad Commemoration Volume*, pp. 267-75. See Haq, M. E., *supra*, pp. 282-83.

Blochmann, H. "The Firuzshahi Inscription in the Chota Dargah, A.H. 761," *JASB*, XLII, 1873, note no. 38.

Bonnerjea, B. "Some Notes on Magic and Taboo in Bengal," *Indian Antiquary* (Bombay), LVII, pp. 107-12.

———. "The Power of Magic in Bengal," *ibid.*, LVIII, 75-78, 81-84.

Brown, J. D. "The History of Islam in India," *The Muslim World*, XXXIX, 1949, pp. 11-25, 113-35, 179-94.

Brown, W. N. "Theories of Creation in the Rig-veda," *Journal of the American Oriental Society* (Boston), LXXXV, 1965.

Chakladar, H. C. "The Pre-Historic Culture of Bengal," *Man in India*, XXXI, 1951, pp. 129-63.

Chakravarti, C. H. "The Cult of Bāro Bhāiyā of Eastern Bengal," *JASB*, XXVI (N.S.), 1930, pp. 379-88.

Chakravarty, M. M. "Pre-Mughal Mosques of Bengal," *ibid.*, VI (N.S.), 1910, pp. 23-38.

Chakravarty, T. N. "A Few Literary Glimpses of Social and Religious Life in Medieval Bengal," *Indian Culture* (Calcutta), X, 1943-1944, pp. 91-102.

Chatterji, S. K. "Kirāta-jana-Kṛti. The Indo-Mongoloids: Their Contribution to the History and Culture of India," *ibid.*, Letters, XVI (N.S.), no. 2, 1950, pp. 143-235.

———. "Review of Hārāmani . . . by Muhammad Mansooruddin," *JASB*, XIV, 1948, pp. 149-51.

———. "Buddhist Survivals in Bengal," in *B.C. Law Commemoration Volume*, ed. by R. G. Bhandarkar *et al.* (Poona: Bhandarkar Oriental Research Institute, 1946), vol. I, pt. 1, pp. 75-87.

Chopra, R. "Sufi Poets of Bengal," *Indo-Iranica* (Calcutta), XII, no. 2, 1959, pp. 45-52.

Chowdhury, B. "Some Problems of the Peasantry in Bengal Before the Permanent Settlement," *Bengal Past and Present*, LXXV, 1956, pp. 134-51.

Clark, T. W. "Evolution of Hinduism in Medieval Bengali Literature: Śiva, Candi, Manasā," *Bulletin of the School of Oriental and African Studies* (London Univ.), XVII, pt. 3, 1955, pp. 503-18.

Colebrooke, H. T. "On the Origin & Peculiar Tenets of Certain Muhammadan Sects," *Asiatic Researches* (Calcutta), VII, 1801, pp. 338-44.

Damant, G. H. "Notes on Shāh Ismāil Ghāzi, etc.," *JASB*, XLIII, no. 1, 1874, pp. 215-39.

Dani, A. H. "The House of Rājā Ganeśa of Bengal," *ibid.*, Letters, XVIII, no. 2, (3rd Ser.), 1952, pp. 121-70.

———. "Early Muslim Contact with Bengal," *Proceedings of the All-Pakistan History Conference* (Karachi), I, 1951, pp. 184-202.

Datt, K. K. "Relations between the Hindus and the Muhammadans of Bengal in the Middle of the Eighteenth Century (1740-1765)," *Journal of Indian History* (Trivendrum), VIII, 1929, pp. 328-35.

De S. K. "The Theology and Philosophy of Bengal Vaiṣnavism," *Indian Culture*, II, no. 2, Oct. 1935, pp. 291-307.

De Tassy, G. "On Some Perculiarities of the Musulmans of India," *Asiatic Journal*, VI, 1931-1932.

Dimock, E. C., Jr. "Muslim Vaiṣnava Poets of Bengal," in *Bengal Regional Identity*, see Kopf, D., *supra*, p. 282.

———. "Hinduism and Islam in Medieval Bengal," in *Aspects of Bengali History and Society*, pp. 1-12. See Baumer, R. Van M., *supra*, p. 279.

———. "Goddess of Snakes in Medieval Bengali Literature," *History of Religions*, I, Winter, 1962, pp. 307-21; also Dimock and Ramanujan, A. K., for its part 2, III, no. 2, 1964, pp. 300-22.

Donaldson, D. "Islam in India," *The Muslim World*, XXXVIII, 1948, pp. 90-99.

Dutt, R. C. "The Aboriginal Element in the Population of Bengal," *Calcutta Review*, LXXV, pp. 233-51.

Ehrenfels, O. R. von. "The Pre-Aryan Cultures of India and the Theological Background of Islam," *Islamic Culture* (Hyderabad), XIII, April 1939, pp. 176-88.

———. "The Socio-Religious Role of Islam in the History of India," *ibid.*, XIV, Jan. 1940, pp. 45-62.

Forlong, J.G.R. "Bud, Bad-a-ar, and Badra," *JRAS*, 1895, pp. 203-10.

Forrester, D. B. "The Depressed Classes and Conversion to Christianity, 1860-1960," in *Religion in South Asia*, pp. 35-66. See Oddie, G. A., *supra*, p. 283.

Foster, G. M. "What is Folk-Culture?" *American Anthropologist*, LV, no. 3, pt. 2, 1953, pp. 159-73.

Garlington, W. "The Baha'i Faith in Malwa," in *Religion in South Asia*, pp. 101-17. See Oddie, G. A., *supra*, p. 283.

Gruenbaum, G. E. von. "The Concept of Cultural Classicism," in his *Modern Islam: The Search for Cultural Identity*, pp. 48-128. See *supra*, p. 281.

Habibullah, A.B.M. "Review" of *Social History of the Muslims in Bengal* by A. Karim, *JASP*, V, 1960, pp. 210-18.

Halim, A. "An Account of the Celebrities of Bengal of the Early Years of Shāh Jahān's Reign by Muhammad Sadiq," *Journal of the Pakistan Historical Society* (Karachi), I, no. 4, 1953.

Haq, M. E. "The Sufi Movement in India," *Indian Culture*, II, no. 2, July 1935, pp. 17-22.

———. "Sufi Movement in Bengal," *Indo-Iranica*, III, no. 1, July 1948, pp. 9-32; also III, no. 2, Oct. 1948, pp. 1-12.

Hardy, F. "Mādhavendra Puri: A Link between Bengal Vaiṣnavism and South Indian *Bhakti*," *JRAS*, no. 1, 1974, pp. 23-41.

Hasan, N. "The Problem of Nationalities in Medieval India," *Proceedings of the Seventh Indian History Congress*, 1944, pp. 370-76.

Husain, M. "The Hindus in Medieval India," *Proceedings of the Third Indian History Congress*, 1939, pp. 712-24.

Ikram, S. M. "An Unnoticed Account of Shaikh Jalāl of Sylhet," *JASP*, II, 1957.

Imamuddin, S. M. "Raja Ganesh of Bengal," *Proceedings and Transactions of the Thirteenth All-India Oriental Conference*, XIII, pt. 2, Oct. 1946, pp. 438-43.

Ishwardas, B. C. "Hindu-Moslem Relations in India," *The Muslim World*, XXII, 1932, pp. 291-95.

Jordens, J.T.F. "Reconversion to Hinduism, the Shuddhi of the Arya Samaj," in *Religion in South Asia*, pp. 145-61. See Oddie, G. A., *supra*, p. 283.

Kabir, H. "Indian Muslims," *Indo-Iranica*, VIII, no. 3, 1955, pp. 1-14.

———. "Indian Muslims," *Indo-Asian Culture*, IV, 1956, pp. 280-300.

Karim, A. "Aspects of Muslim Administration in Bengal Down to A.D. 1538," *JASP*, III, 1958, pp. 67-103.

———. "Early Muslim Rulers in Bengal and Their Non-Muslim Subjects (until A.D. 1538)," *ibid.*, IV, 1959, pp. 73-96.

———. "Did Ibn-Battutah Meet Sheikh Jalāl al-Ḍin Tabrizi in Kamrup?" *Journal of the Pakistan Historical Society*, VIII, 1960, pp. 290-96.

———. "Nur Qutb Alam's Letter on the Ascendancy of Ganeśa," in *Abdul Karim Sahitya-Visarad Commemoration Volume*, pp. 334-43. See Haq, M. E. (ed.), *supra*, pp. 282-83.

Khan, A. M. "Early Medieval History of Bengal—the Khaljis: A.D. 1204-1251," *Islamic Culture*, X, 1943, pp. 145-57.

Khan, M. A. "Research in the Islamic Revivalism of the Nineteenth Century and Its Effect on the Muslim Society of Bengal," in *Social Research*, pp. 38-65. See Bessaignet, p. (ed.), *supra*, 279.

———. "Taayyuni Opposition to the Faraidi Movement," *Journal of the Pakistan Historical Society*, April 1964, pp. 150-64.

Khan, M. S. "Badr Maqams or the Shrines of Badr al-Din Auliya," *JASP*, VII, no. 1, June 1962, pp. 17-46.

Khan, Y. H. "Sufism in India," *Islamic Culture*, XXX, July 1956, pp. 239-62.

Kopf, D. "Bibliographic Notes on Early, Medieval, and Modern Sufism, with Special References to Bengal," *Folklore*, III, no. 2, Feb. 1962, pp. 69-84, and III, no. 3, March 1962, pp. 113-22.

Mahalanobis, P. C. "Analysis of Race-Mixture in Bengal," *JASB*, XXIII (N.S.), no. 3, 1927, pp. 301-33.

Mandelbaum, D. G. "Hindu-Moslem Conflict in India," *The Middle East Journal*, I, no. 4, Oct. 1947, pp. 369-85.

Meyerhof, M. "On the Transmission of Greek and Indian Science to the Arabs," *Islamic Culture*, XI, no. 1, Jan. 1937, pp. 17-29.

Mitra, A. K. "Physical Anthropology of the Muslims of Bengal," *Bulletin of the Department of Anthropology* (Govt. of India), I, no. 2, 1952, pp. 79-103.

Mitra, D. "Some Jain Antiquities from Bankura, West Bengal," *JASB*, Letters, XXIV (3rd ser.), no. 2, 1958, pp. 131-34.

Mitra, S. C. "On a Muhammadan Folk-Tale of the Hero and the Deity Type," *Journal of the Bihar and Orissa Research Society*, IV, pt. 4, 1918, pp. 492-97.

———. "Curious Cults of Southern and Western Bengal," *Journal of the Anthropological Soc. of Bombay*, XI, 1919, pp. 438-54.

———. "The Worship of the Sylvan Goddess," *The Hindustan Review*, March 1917, pp. 178-89.

———. "On the Cult of the Tree-Goddess in Eastern Bengal," *Man in India*, II, no. 2, 1922, pp. 228-41.

———. "On the Cult of the Godlings of Disease in Eastern Bengal," *ibid.*, III, 1923, pp. 37-55.

———. "On the Cults of the Maritime Deities in Lower Bengal," *ibid.*, VIII, 1928, pp. 33-60.

———. "Indian Folklore Beliefs About the Tiger," *JASB*, LXV, pt. 3, no. 1, 1896, pp. 1-8.

Mukherjea, C. "Bratas in Bengal," *ibid.*, XXVI, no. 1, 1946, pp. 202-206.

Nicholas, R. W. "Vaiṣnavism and Islam in Rural Bengal," in *Bengal Regional Identity*, pp. 33-47. See Kopf, D., *supra*, p. 282.

———. "Ecology and Village Structure in Deltaic West Bengal," *Economic and Political Weekly*, XV, pp. 1185-96.

Nizami, K. A. "Some Aspects of Khānqah Life in Medieval India," *Studia Islamica*, VII, 1957, pp. 51-69.

Oddie, G. A. "Christian Conversion in Telegu Country, 1860-1900: A Case Study of One Protestant Movement in the Godavery-Krishna Delta," *Indian Social and Economic History Review* (Delhi), XII, no. 1, Jan-Mar. 1975, pp. 61-79.

———. "Christian Conversion among Non-Brahmans in Andhra Pradesh, with Special Reference to Anglican Missions and the Dornakal Diocese, c. 1900-1936," in *Religion in South Asia*, pp. 67-99. See Oddie, G. A., *supra*, p. 283.

Paterson, R. M. "Mohammedanism in India," *Glasgow University Oriental Society. Transactions from 1901-1907 with Historical Sketch*. Ed. by G. Anderson. Glasgow: J. MacLehouse & Sons, 1907, pp. 31-32.

Qanungo, K. R. "Dacca and Its Medieval History," *Bengal Past and Present*, LXVI, 1946, pp. 58-62.

———. "Impact of Islam on Orissa and Bengal Contrasted," *ibid.*, LXVIII, 1949, pp. 31-36.

———. "How Local Custom Modifies Scriptures," *ibid.*, LXX, 1951, pp. 23-33.

Qureshi, I. H. "Relations Between the Hindus and the Muslims in the Subcontinent of India and Pakistan," *Civilizations*, V, 1955, pp. 43-51.

Rahim, M. A. "The Saints in Bengal: Shaikh Jalāl al-Din Tabrizi and Shāh Jalāl," *Journal of the Pakistan Historical Society*, VIII, 1960, pp. 206-26.

Rāya, C. "On Tree-Cults in the District of Midnapur in South-western Bengal," *Man in India*, II, no. 2, Dec. 1922, pp. 242-64.

Ray, N. "Medieval Bengali Culture—a Socio-Historical Interpretation," *Viśva-bhārati Quarterly*, XI, May-July 1945-1946, pp. 45-55, 87-95.

Redfield, R. "The Social Organization of Tradition," *The Far Eastern Quarterly*, XV, no. 1, 1955, pp. 13-21.

Rehatsek, E. "Early Moslem Accounts of the Hindu Religion," *Journal of the Royal Asiatic Society of Bombay*, XIV, 1880, pp. 29-70.

Roy, A. "The Social Factors in the Making of Bengali Islam," *South Asia*, III, August 1973, pp. 23-35.

———. "The Pir-Tradition: A Case Study in Islamic Syncretism in Traditional Bengal," in *Images of Man*, pp. 112-41. See Clothey, F. W. (ed.), *supra*, p. 280.

Roy, N. B. "Glimpses into the History of Bengal, the 14th and the Early 15th Centuries," *Sardesai Commemoration Volume*, 1953.

———. "Hinduism and Islam," *Viśva-bhārati Quarterly*, XVI (N.S.), 1950-1951, pp. 204-16.

Roychoudhury M. L. "Hindu-Muslim Relation during the Mughal Period, A.D. 1526-1707," *Proceedings of the Ninth Indian History Congress*, 1946, pp. 282-96.

Schuman, H. "Social Change and the Validity of Regional Stereotypes in East Pakistan," *Sociometry*, XXIX, no. 4, Dec. 1966, pp. 428-40.

Sen, S. "Is the Cult of Dharma a Living Relic of Buddhism in Bengal?" in *B.C. Law Commemoration Volume*, Ed. by R. G. Bhandarkar *et al.* Poona: Bhardarkar Oriental Research Institute, 1946. Vol. 1, pt. 1, pp. 669-74.

———. "Folk-Loric Background of Old Bengali Literature," *Viśva-bhārati* Quarterly, XXV, nos. 3-4, 1960, pp. 215-24.

Sen, S. N. "Hinduism and Muhammadan Heretics during the Pathan Period," *Proceedings of the Third All-India Oriental Conference*, 1924, pp. 401-405.

Singer, M. "The Cultural Patterns of Indian Civilization," *The Far Eastern Quarterly*, XV, no. 1, 1955, pp. 23-36.

Sircar, D. C. "Spread of Aryanism in Bengal," *JASB*, Letters, XVIII (N.S.), no. 2, 1952, pp. 171-78.

———. "Decline of Buddhism in Bengal," *Bhāratiya Vidyā* (Bombay), XIII, no. 1, 1952, pp. 55-61.

St. John, R.F.S.A. "Correspondence," *JRAS*, 1894, pp. 149-54.

———. "A Burmese Saint," *ibid.*, pp. 566-67.

Sweetman, J. W. "Islam in India," *The Muslim World*, XXVII, 1937.

Temple, R. C. "Buddermokan," *Journal of the Burma Research Society*, XV, pt. 1, 1925.

Wali, M. A. "Hinduism According to Muslim Sufis," *JASB*, XIX (N.S.), 1923, pp. 237-52.

Wolf, E. R. "The Social Organization of Mecca and the Origins of Islam," *Southwestern Journal of Anthropology* (Albuquerque, Univ. of New Mexico), VII, no. 4, 1951, pp. 329-56.

Zwemer, S. M. "Islam in India," *The Muslim World*, XV, no. 2, April 1925, pp. 109-14.

———. "The Diversity of Islam in India," *ibid.*, XVIII, no. 2, April 1928, pp. 111-23.

III Others

Agrawālā, V. S. *Prāchina Bhāratiya Loka-dharma*. Varanasi: Indological House, 1964.

De Tassy, M. G. *Mémoire sur les Particularités de la Religion Musalmane dans l'Inde*. Paris, 1831.

Gardet, L. "La Mention du Nom Divin (Dhikr) dans la Mystique Musalmane," *Revue Thomiste* (Paris), LII-LIII, 1952-1953.

Glasse, R. "La Société Musalmane dans le Pakistan Rural de l'Est," *Études Rurales*, XXII-XXIV, 1968, pp. 188-205.

Index

Library of Congress Cataloging in Publication Data

Roy, Asim, 1937-
The Islamic syncretistic tradition in Bengal.
Bibliography: p.
Includes index.
1. Islam—India—Bengal—History. I. Title.
[DNLM: 1. Hospitals—History—New York. WX 28 AN7 S67s]
BP63.I42B426 1983 297'.0954'14 83-42574
ISBN 0-691-05387-1